Divisions of Labour

For the people of the
Isle of Sheppey

Divisions of Labour

R. E. PAHL

Basil Blackwell

First published 1984
Basil Blackwell Limited
108 Cowley Road, Oxford OX4 1JF, England

Basil Blackwell Inc, 432 Park Avenue South, Suite 1505,
New York, NY 10016

British Library Cataloguing in Publication Data
Pahl, R.E.
  Divisions of labour.
  1. Industrial sociology
  I. Title
  306'.36   HD6955
  ISBN 0-631-13273-2
  ISBN 0-631-13274-0 Pbk

Library of Congress Cataloging in Publication Data
Pahl, R. E. (Raymond Edward), 1935–
  Divisions of labour.

  Bibliography: p.
  Includes index.
  1. Labor and laboring classes.   2. Division of labor.
  3. Work.   I. Title.
  HD4901.P18   1984   306'.36   86-11092
  ISBN 0-631-13273-2
  ISBN 0-631-13274-0 Pbk

Typesetting by Katerprint Co. Ltd, Oxford.
Printed in Great Britain by T. J. Press Ltd, Padstow

The endpapers show women's informal work
in an industrial city *c*.1900.

Contents

Illustrations

Illustrations may be found between pages 54 and 55 and between pages 182 and 183.

The author and publisher are grateful to the following for permission to reproduce illustrations:

First plate section   Oxfordshire County Libraries for plate 2; Sheffield City Art Galleries for plate 3; The Institute of Agricultural History and Museum of English Rural Life, University of Reading, for plate 4; The Sutcliffe Gallery, Whitby, for plate 5; Hitchin Museum and Art Gallery, Waldren Swann Collection, for plate 6; Gordon Winter for plate 7, reproduced from *A Country Camera*; Lord Walston and the Trustees of the Artist's estate for plate 8.

Second plate section   J. Styles for plates 4, 6, 7, 8; Claire Wallace for plates 5 and 9.

Acknowledgements

When I think back over the last seven years I am overwhelmed by the number of people who have helped in some way in the production of this book. Without doubt, it would not have been possible to do the empirical research in ethnography, historical demography and quantitative survey analysis without supporting grants from the Nuffield Foundation and the Social Science Research Council (SSRC, now the Economic and Social Research Council). The latter provided me with three grants to do separate aspects of some of the work reported here. In addition, the University of Kent at Canterbury is a particularly generous institution in providing study leave to encourage research, although I recognize that, in practice, it is one's immediate colleagues who do the extra teaching when one is away. I am very conscious of such positive and practical support.

Over the years many people have been generous in ideas and help of various kinds. I have explored my ideas in such a variety of contexts, formal and informal, that it is impossible to give an accurate account of all those who have provided suggestions. However, I am glad to acknowledge particular instances of help from:

Hugh Cunningham, Frances Evans, Ruth Finegan, Duncan Gallie, William Gourley, A. H. Halsey, Michael Harloe, C. C. Harris, Anthony Heath, Krishan Kumar, Jennifer Mason, Enzo Mingione, Eric Pawson, Nanneke Redclift, Bryan Roberts, Ivan Szelenyi, Peter Taylor-Gooby, Clare Ungerson, Colin Ward and John Westergaard.

I recognize how invidious it is to name but a few among many and I know that not all those I mention will be pleased with the result. I would also like to acknowledge the help and stimulation I have received from those many contributors to discussions at seminars and conferences to which I have given papers over the past five years.

The actual research on the Isle of Sheppey was a collective enterprise: the study of the naval dockyard in the nineteenth century (funded by the SSRC) was largely carried out by Dr N. H. Buck; the sample survey of the Island's population was imaginatively and meticulously supervised by Gillian Courtenay of Social and Community Planning Research; and the computation of the results owes much to the assistance of Spyros Missiakoulis and Joan Dobby of the University of Kent. Spyros Missiakoulis is joint author of Chapter 10. J.I. Gershuny of the Science Policy Research Unit at the University of Sussex was an extremely amiable, helpful and provocative consultant to the project. His enthusiasm and intellectual support never flagged. The research team on the contemporary study of household work strategies in the Isle of Sheppey comprised Jane Dennett, Claire Wallace and myself. Jane Dennett was project administrator, computing assistant and total organizer and producer of this book, from helping me with my survey of employers in the first year of the project to providing the magnetic tape of the page proofs for the publisher. Her range of skills was particularly needed to complement the other activities of Claire Wallace and myself.

Claire Wallace has worked with me in the Isle of Sheppey for five years, and what is published here is but the tip of the iceberg of the knowledge and understanding we have gathered together. We have shared the business of a large project as equally as we could possibly manage. Some of our collaborative work is being published jointly elsewhere. While I was writing this book, Claire Wallace was developing her own distinctive study, which she is completing separately. I am glad to acknowledge how much I have benefited from her cheerful support and capacity for hard work. Doing empirical research in sociology involves more cold waits in the rain, and more cups of tea or coffee when one really wants a solid meal, than is perhaps recognized. I found it a very great help to have a colleague with whom I could share both the day-to-day burdens of fieldwork and the intellectual excitement of struggling to develop new social understanding. It is a great pleasure to acknowledge the courage, determination and imaginative insight of the staunchest colleague I could hope to have.

The actual writing of this book at great speed in the last few months was supported by many people in Kent and Tuscany. I am grateful to Pat Evans and the staff of Darwin College secretarial office, who have coped with my erratic demands, to Joan Denning and Pat Wilson, who have helped Jane Dennett in preparing the typescript, and to Sue Hughes for her imaginative and creative copyediting. I am grateful to Jim Styles of the University of Kent Photographic Unit for help in providing some of the illustrations. Lorino Marriotti ensured that I produced a mounting pile of manuscript at D'Autore, when I might have slept longer in the olive groves. John Davey has been both publisher and friend, since well before I had the slightest thought of this book: his interest, encouragement and suggestions have helped me at times when I most needed support.

I have dedicated this book to the people of the Isle of Sheppey. My claim that I was writing a book about the Island was sufficient justification for countless people to give unstintingly of their time and attention. I never took this for granted.

Books are greedy and demanding creatures to produce, and Jan Pahl knows this particularly to her cost. I am glad to recognize and to acknowledge all the domestic and intellectual support and encouragement that she has so generously given.

Introduction

This is a book about work. It is not simply about employment, although that is often what people mean when they talk about work. Focusing on a shifting target is always difficult, and it is surely incontrovertible that in the last years of the twentieth century we must approach the notion of work in new ways. No longer is the 'right to work' an unproblematic political goal; no longer can 'women's work' be referred to without some awareness of the wider implications of what is being assumed. In the late twentieth century, industrial societies have been thrown into confusion as patterns of work have changed in unexpected ways, owing to such elements as the fluctuations of economic expansion and recession, a new consciousness associated with the development of the women's movement and new developments in technology.

In an attempt to come to terms with these problems and confusions, a popular literature has arisen in which certain aspects of the contemporary situation are seized upon and then extrapolated to make unwarranted conclusions about the overall pattern of change. In a turbulent environment, soothsayers are not lacking in encouragement. These 'exagger-books', as they have been called,[1] frequently have counter-productive results: if all futures are possible and 'work' will never be the same again, yet everyday life is evidently not changing in any overly dramatic way, then perhaps we can all muddle through, with no great changes in our attitudes or behaviour. Fatalistic regard for the wider forces of change that some now detect may be one response to the cacophonous clamour of the conflicting cries. 'A plague on all your houses', says the member of the queue at the supermarket checkout and the local farmer at the stockbroker's dinner party.

Whatever is happening to work in these last decades of the century,

---

[1] In an article in the *Wall Street Journal* in the summer of 1983, Anthony Downs attacked authors such as Alvin Toffler whose books (e.g. *Future Shock* and *The Third Wave*) reach a very wide public. Downs argued that such exagger-authors have raised the art of pseudo-scientific hyperbole to new heights. Exagger-trends, Presumptive but Plausible Inter-relatedness, and Revelation by Relabelling are the ingredients of exagger-books, which, Downs claimed, 'continue to outsell carefully researched studies of the same subjects by stupendous ratios'.

there is widespread tacit acceptance that things were different in the past. Writers as diverse as Braverman, Illich and Seabrook postulate a 'Golden Age' of work which follows on a long, romantic tradition encouraged in their different ways by Marx and William Morris.[2] As with similar myths referring to past times, the precise period that is held up for approval is always some time before a given author is writing: for some, the Golden Age is the post-war era of 'full employment'; for others, some vague and unspecified medieval period provides the context for work as an ideal of integrated living. Furthermore, the past may provide clues for the future: if de-industrialization is, in some sense, the reverse of the process of industrialization, then by, as it were, running the film of history backwards, we may discover a guide to the future. There may be possible parallels between what happens in the 1980s and 1990s and what happened two hundred years earlier. Our notion of what is unusual must depend on our notion of what is usual or normal. And if our knowledge of the latter is confused, then so too will be our conception of the former. It is impossible to escape the grip of the real or imagined past upon the present; so also is it difficult to escape from seeing the present as a point on a piece of graph paper. There may be straight lines that rise or fall or there may be various more or less symmetrical waves, but invariably 'the present' can be given appropriate coordinates and a latent evolutionism is tacitly accepted. Typically, a situation is 'getting better' or 'getting worse' at the highest or lowest points of some cycle or other. It is hard to escape from such domain assumptions.

We can avoid the constraints of a benign or a malign historicism by adopting the kaleidoscope theory of social life. The coloured pieces can form a variety of patterns: the pieces are the same but the pattern can change dramatically depending on the severity of the knock. Alternatively, the kaleidoscope can shift imperceptibly, so that we do not notice that the pieces are shifting until the new pattern jumps into our view. This book arose out of a sense that I had in the early 1970s that the pattern was starting to shift and that a world I had got used to for twenty-five years would never be the same again.[3]

The final form of this book is substantially different from the plans and ideas that I began to formulate in the mid-1970s. Inevitably, the interaction between ideas and contexts is constantly changing. By the time the book is published, my ideas will quite likely have developed further — whether in some linear or curvilinear fashion or as the result of

---

[2] H. Braverman, *Labor and Monopoly Capital*, Monthly Review Press, New York, 1974; I. Illich, *The Right to Useful Unemployment and its Professional Enemies*, Marion Boyars, London, 1978; J. Seabrook, *Unemployment*, Quartet Books, London, 1982; B. Ollman, *Alienation*, Cambridge University Press, 1971; A. Clayre, *Work and Play*, Weidenfeld and Nicolson, 1974; William Morris, *The Collected Works*, Longmans Green, London, 1910-15; S. Wood (ed.), *The Degradation of Work?* Hutchinson, London, 1982.

[3] Perhaps I, too, am in danger of creating a 'Golden Age' for myself?

a shake of the kaleidoscope will be for others to judge. The interaction between ideas and contexts, theory and practice or contemplatives and activists is a never-ending dialectic. There is not a single set of uncontroversial facts 'out there' to which one fits the best theoretical explanation. Rather, there is an iterative process between ideas and actions that cannot be divorced from each other.[4] I hope I have no false illusions about the role and force of ideas, but nor do I subscribe to a nihilistic scepticism, which sees little point in the men and women of ideas concerning themselves with the practical problems of the society in which they live. Very often the recognition that certain kinds of information, hitherto disregarded, have a substantial bearing on the issue in question is considered innovation enough. Relating social statistics to social policy should be part of the research responsibility of the civil service.

It is hard to be sure how one arrives at a particular intellectual position, but since I think there is a pattern to my 'line' of thought, it may be helpful for me to make this explicit. In giving various talks and seminars over the past five years, I have been surprised by certain responses that have imputed to me points or ideas that I do not recognize as my own, but that I may have raised and put down in passing. My attempt to describe something of my intellectual trajectory is not, I trust, mere self-indulgence but does serve a purpose in putting this book into context. It also enables me to move on beyond it in good faith.

In the intellectual climate of 1975 and 1976, certain issues and questions had a salience that no longer existed seven or eight years later. In the early 1970s I became more and more uneasy about the disjunction between different forms of knowledge about ordinary working people, and, in particular, about the assumptions concerning the pervasive influence of male employment. The fashion of the times was for higher-level theorizing, and many of those best able to comment in general terms about working-class people and their work were more concerned to engage with the abstract theorizing of the French structuralist Marxist Louis Althusser than in doing empirical research.[5] In the period from the late 1960s to the mid-1970s, very little field research in Britain was done by sociologists and social anthropologists, yet this was a time in which

[4] It is possible, although I hope unlikely, that some of the ideas I discussed in the past, for example my concern with corporatism in 1974, affected in some very minor way the context some years later with which I had come to terms.

[5] I think that courses of action and trajectories of work are often triggered off by chance happenings that somehow stay fixed in the mind. I remember that, about this time, I was sitting in a pub chatting to a colleague about his lecture course and he was somewhat mockingly outlining the various 'debates' on the nature of industrial societies that he was expounding that year. He then broke off and, with a laugh and in a different tone of voice, went on to describe the informal work practices of his cleaning woman. That same disjunction came up in a variety of contexts where there was a marked difference between personal experience and anecdote and general formulations.

there was quite substantial discussion about working-class (male) images of society stimulated by a lecture given by David Lockwood in 1966.[6] The fruits of this discussion appeared in a book published in 1975,[7] and students in higher education read and wrote about the issue until the early 1980s.

This example is worth exploring in greater detail. In his 1966 paper, Lockwood was attempting to draw up a heuristic typology of the images of society held by ordinary working people, based on a few available studies of working-class life. In the case of what he described as 'the traditional worker' — of course, male — he referred to only two studies, one on Liverpool dockworkers and the other on Yorkshire miners.[8] Both of these studies were carried out in the early 1950s, and Lockwood draws from them an ideal-typical account which epitomizes the 'Golden Age' view of the traditional male worker:

workmates are normally leisure-time companions, often neighbours, and not infrequently kinsmen — the existence of such closely-knit cliques of friends, workmates, neighbours and relatives is the hall-mark of the traditional working class community. The values expressed through these social networks emphasize mutual aid in everyday life and the obligation to join in the gregarious pattern of leisure, which itself demands the expenditure of time, money and energy in a public and present-oriented conviviality and eschews individual striving 'to be different'. As a form of social life, this communal sociability has a ritualistic quality, creating a high moral density and reinforcing sentiments of belongingness to a work-dominated collectivity.[9]

Whether such a traditional community ever did truly exist continues to be a matter of debate. Even the evidence on which such a stereotype is based has been questioned. Dennis Warwick has returned to the Yorkshire village that was the subject of *Coal is our Life* and the source of so much working- class mythology, and has talked to some of the men who were informants some thirty years earlier. They claimed that many of the stereotypes in the book were brought to the mining village by the researchers themselves, who looked for support for their own preconceptions.[10] Certainly, the neglect of any serious consideration of the employment of women in working-class life for some twenty-five years now appears extraordinary, although the study in question was completed before the rapid growth of married women's employment.

[6] D. Lockwood, 'Sources of variation in working class images of society', *Sociological Review*, 14(3), 1966, pp. 249-67.
[7] M. Bulmer (1975), *Working Class Images of Society*, Routledge and Kegan Paul, London.
[8] These were: University of Liverpool Department of Social Science, *The Dock Worker*, Liverpool, 1954; and N. Dennis, F. Henriques and C. Slaughter, *Coal is Our Life*, Eyre and Spottiswoode, London, 1956.
[9] Lockwood, 'Sources of variation', p. 251.
[10] D. Warwick, *Talk of the Village, Introduction to a Contemporary Study of the Social and Cultural Organization of Featherstone*, University of Leeds, 1984.

Furthermore, even if the account had been more accurate, it was clearly a mistake to fossilize it for ever as it was in the early 1950s. Even if the pattern of male employment did colour all aspects of collective and private life for a period, the nature of the work was itself changing. The coal mining industry itself continues to change, so that the experience of one generation is not the same as that of the next. The way in which certain researchers appeared to project their own socio-political goals on to the working class has been noticed by John Goldthorpe, who referred to 'wishful rather than critical thinking' and 'a tendency to assert that what was desired was already historically in train'.[11]

Despite the fact that one of the most widely-quoted studies of the traditional working class was limited, partial and outdated, it was still assumed to be among the soundest evidence for linking male employment experience with behaviour in the traditional working-class community. Only very recently are sociologists making up for past lapses by reconstructing the life of other traditional working-class communities by means of oral history. Thus, it is now possible to contrast the stereotypical Yorkshire mining village with, for example, an East Anglian fishing community. Here, the work experience was individualistic for the men and notions of collective solidarity came from the women in the community. Women's social attitudes were more salient than the work experience of their husbands in generating distinctive community attitudes and behaviour.[12] This empirical evidence was not, of course, available in the mid-1970s. Very little field research was undertaken during the decade, and it was easy to echo Colin Bell and Howard Newby, who summarized some of their discipline's troubles and asked, 'should sociology's epistemological anomie be more accurately described as epistemological anarchy?'[13]

So, pity then the students. In the second half of the 1970s they were discussing the relationship between male employment and working-class attitudes and behaviour, based on an ideal-type drawn from few, and perhaps partial, studies carried out well before they were born. The disjunction between the students' personal experience, gained from the places where they lived or had worked during vacations, and what was said in their lectures must have been marked. Even some of those who were concerned about the lack of distinction between male employment and work were initially concerned more with the issue of whether women's domestic work was 'productive labour' than with doing field

[11] J. H. Goldthorpe, *Intellectuals and the Working Class in Modern Britain*, University of Essex, 1979, p. 28; H. Newby, *The State of Research into Stratification in Britain*, Social Science Research Council, London, 1982.

[12] P. Thompson with T. Wailey and T. Lummis, *Living the Fishing*, Routledge and Kegan Paul, London, 1983.

[13] C. Bell and H. Newby, *Doing Sociological Research*, Allen and Unwin, London, 1977; R. E. Pahl, 'Sociology's conflicting tradition', *New Society*, May 1974, pp. 504-7; reprinted in Paul Barker (ed.), *The Social Sciences Today*, Edward Arnold, London, 1975.

research on ordinary women's working lives inside and outside the home.[14]

Between 1968 and 1976 I had been persuaded to take various jobs that involved working inside government as an Adviser or Assessor.[15] I was obliged to immerse myself in official statistics rather than textbooks in sociological theory, and so my view of what was happening in British society was given a different colour. In 1969 I formulated an approach to the social structure that was substantially at variance with what was being taught in sociology courses. I distinguished between the senior salariat, the middle mass and the underclass; sensitive civil servants later persuaded me to re-name the underclass 'the less privileged'. My concern was mainly with London and the South East, and the data I worked with made me very sceptical of the optimism about the future that was then currently fashionable. In our report, published in 1971, we suggested that in the middle mass 'men may take on second jobs in order to maintain the high consumption style they feel impelled to achieve.'[16] We noted that in London the low-paid jobs appeared to be on the increase, and we concerned ourselves with the likely dangers of social polarization. 'Low pay, insecurity, unemployment and lack of skills characterize a large number of wage earners.'[17] My work on the South East of England in the late 1960s enabled me, perhaps, to get a clearer view of what was happening to most ordinary working people.

A few years later I returned to material that I had gathered for other purposes: in the winter of 1975-6 I looked ahead to the next fifteen years. As I said then,

the typical image of the factory worker attending meetings of his union at the workplace is increasingly outdated. Those living in many inner city areas are increasingly service workers, who do not conveniently gather in easily organizable production units. Rather, they are scattered in many varied locations, working shifts or unusual hours. Part of their wages may be earned in tips, they may have various 'dirty pound note' arrangements for earning extra by doing 'extra' and so on . . . the view from the kerb level is unlikely to get any better in the years ahead. There will be other economic matters to attend to rather than channelling new employment into declining urban areas.[18]

[14] Anna Pollert's excellent and vivid study of female workers in a Bristol tobacco factory was carried out in the early 1970s, but was not published until 1981: A. Pollert, *Girls, Wives, Factory Lives*, Macmillan, London, 1981.
[15] R. E. Pahl, 'Playing the rationality game: the sociologist as hired expert', in C. Bell and H. Newby (eds), *Doing Sociological Research*, Allen and Unwin, London, 1977.
[16] South East Joint Planning Team (1971), *Strategic Plan for the South East Studies*, vol. 2, Social and Environmental Aspects, HMSO, London, 1971, p. 16.
[17] Ibid., p. 19.
[18] R. E. Pahl, 'Patterns of urban life in the next fifteen years', *New Universities Quarterly*, 30(4), 1976, p. 414.

I concluded by pointing to:

the possible importance of the informal, the personal, the small scale and the slightly illegal as the basic ingredients of a new style in the next decade. People are becoming increasingly practised at getting work done by men 'out of work time' for straight cash. Income Tax and VAT officials could never possibly cover such activities 'done for friends' in 'spare time' and repaid with 'a gift'. With statutory wage controls, increasing state intervention and the proliferation of rules and procedures, the development of this subsidiary economy is likely to flourish. . . . It may not take long for a nation of shop-keepers to turn into a nation of hustlers. However, it is perhaps worth considering that a society based on *whom* you know rather than what you know, may be a more humane, pleasant and happy society in which to live.[19]

I was convinced that the nature and experience of work was changing, but I was unsure how to formulate an appropriate research project at that time.

In this attempt to reconstruct the context out of which the idea for this book emerged, I am fortunate in that I have published various articles that do much to remind me of past sets of ideas. One such piece, written with Jack Winkler, on 'The Coming Corporatism' aroused much interest and was republished in France, the United States and elsewhere.[20] I remember being asked what ordinary people thought about living in a corporatist state. Of course, I had no idea. Nor had I any idea of how ordinary people were coping with the then very high levels of inflation. I was readily lecturing about public issues without any knowledge of how, in practice, these created private troubles for ordinary people. I remember being something of an Ancient Mariner, stopping one in three at conferences and bemoaning the lack of detailed ethnography of ordinary people's lives.

In my main concern to focus on the connections between public issues and private troubles, I was very anxious to understand social processes and the dynamics of change and I was reluctant to fall back on the snapshot approach of the social survey. Fortunately, I was at a university in which sociologists and social anthropologists worked together, where I could be influenced by the style of research and assumptions of the latter. I remember that I was considering a new programme of research that would be sure to get me much closer to ordinary people's experiences than most sociologists had managed to do in the 1970s. In a memorandum written in the winter of 1976-7, I said:

---

[19] Ibid., pp. 416-17.
[20] R. E. Pahl and J. T. Winkler, 'The coming corporatism', *New Society*, October 1974, pp. 72-6.

In the interwar period, Mass Observation attempted to make contemporary documentation more systematic, and observers such as Orwell and Priestley made lasting contributions, with their own individualistic accounts of their journeys and experiences. In the postwar world, the more widespread use of the social survey and the development of sociology as an established university discipline have produced a new social knowledge of a different kind from that produced in the 1930s, but not necessarily any better. Indeed, it is unlikely that a future historian of the 1970s, writing in 2077, will make much use of the work of sociologists. The shift in fashion has directed many able minds away from the limited empirical studies of particular occupations, residential areas or work places to the higher levels of abstract theory or the niceties of day-to-day talk. As a result, many sociologists fall back in private on gossip and journalism to tell them what is 'really' happening in contemporary society. There seems to be a gap between the world as perceived by the media and the world of people round the corner.

I then went on to discuss the problems involved in doing good ethnography: how does the sociologist get an advantage over the good investigative journalist? Two books, published a year or so before I wrote, each included a substantial number of photographs:[21] should I attempt to follow their example? How much should I depend on a tape recorder? What is the most appropriate way of expressing the reality of ordinary people's lives? I was extremely puzzled about how to proceed and I felt that the tools of sociological investigation were coming between me and the people whose everyday lives I was trying to understand. I was still concerned with the question of public issues and private troubles, and my plan was to allow the public issues of a given year to determine my research agenda. I intended to write my own personal, sociologically informed account of a particular year based on press cuttings, official statistics and so on. I would then see how these national issues were reflected in the everyday lives of the families I had selected.[22] I spent considerable time in 1977 considering how many households I could manage, how they should be selected in terms of occupation and area of residence, and so on. The logistic problems were substantial, as, at the time, I was planning to base the study on East Kent, North London, Dorset and Prescot, Lancashire. The work would be costly and time-consuming. By the time I had decided what I was going to do, the period I had been given by the university to do it in was half over. I was also kindly but firmly told by the Assistant Director of the Nuffield

---

[21] J. Berger and J. Mohr, *A Seventh Man*, Pelican Books, Harmondsworth, 1975; D. Marsden and E. Duff, *Workless: Some Unemployed Men and their Families*, Pelican Books, Harmondsworth, 1975.

[22] In 1983, BBC TV broadcast a series of television programmes called *Voxpop* which did exactly what I had in mind. The producer and his team settled in the town of Darwen in Lancashire and reported each week, through a group of informants, how they individually and collectively coped with the public issues that impinged upon them. The series was excellent, and future historians will surely be grateful.

Foundation that it all seemed very expensive and I would do better to talk to the people at some convenient place in Kent. She also encouraged me to sharpen my focus on a more limited problem.

Thus it was that I found myself, in the autumn of 1977, talking to unemployed people in Rochester about their lives. I sat around in cafes and visited people in their homes. Many of the people I was introduced to were unemployed but were working illegally or were petty criminals. I said I wanted to see how people without jobs in the formal sense were getting by, since, at that time, I had a rather confused idea of a separate, underground economy. The people to whom I spoke were very varied and many had a spirited and aggressive view towards the world. Some of them ended up in gaol before I had learned much about them. (I felt particularly sorry for the one sent down by the judge whose house he had recently re-wired 'for cash'.) I felt I was sharing a Dickensian, rather colourful stage where the 'characters' lived in a world of second-hand cars and bikes and stalls at the market, and flitted from one semi-derelict house to another.

Talking to these individuals in Rochester was giving me plenty of variegated ethnography and I was in a good position to write a paper on 'The Urban Pirate — A Contemporary Style of Getting By', but I felt uneasy about so doing. First, I had no idea of the general context, the local labour market of the Medway towns, into which I could place my ethnography. Second, I was being accused by my colleagues that I was implying that it was fun to be unemployed and working illegally — as long as you didn't get caught. I paused to think.

I decided that I would concentrate my efforts not in the Medway towns, but on the Isle of Sheppey, for reasons that I outline in the Introduction to Part II. In January 1978 I submitted an application to the Nuffield Foundation to get some modest resources to do a pilot study on issues that I judged would be of increasing importance during the next decade. I wrote:

First, I see relatively high levels of unemployment continuing; second, I see a continued growth of the informal economy as a source of income; and, finally, I see changes occurring in how the work of sustaining the domestic unit gets done. I am interested to find out how people get by in a number of specific circumstances — such as being unemployed each winter or being involved regularly in undeclared work. I want to know how the ordinary routines of life and the sexual division of labour within the domestic unit may be changing, as a result of the growth of a wide range of economic activities outside the formal economy. . . .

I have become increasingly dissatisfied in recent years with a type of sociological analysis which discusses 'industrial society' or 'capitalism' in broad terms without specifying or demonstrating very precisely what the direct effects on ordinary people are likely to be. Two main tendencies, which it hardly needs sociological analysis to reveal, are the growing levels of unemployment —

connected with the restructuring of manufacturing industry and our changing position in world markets — and the increasing intervention of the state, in all its forms, to regiment and guide its citizens from the cradle to the grave.

Yet, paradoxically, it is also now possible for people to get by without necessarily engaging in formal employment. A man can own his own tools – power drills, chain saws, welding equipment; he can control much of his time, whether or not he is formally employed: and the state provides a long-stop to prevent starvation with its unemployment and social security benefits. Far from the immiseration of the workers which Marx predicted, welfare capitalism may have handed back to some the ownership of the means of production: there is a market demand for craft skills, and there are ways of avoiding paying taxes. I have done some preliminary interviews with 'unemployed' men which have led me to think that the incentives for some skilled workers to remain unemployed in a formal sense outweigh the advantages of a regular wage.

The idea that all normal domestic units should have one 'breadwinner' and one 'housewife' is hard to sustain when opportunities for male employment are low and domestic tasks are shared. With the growth of single-parent households, increased opportunities for female employment in some localities and a range of private and public services and facilities that can handle domestic tasks, the traditional ways of getting work done within the home may be changing. Certain tasks have to be done — cooking, cleaning, repairing — and over a year a certain amount of money is necessary. This money need not come in every week, nor need it be provided by the same person. Tying one person to a low-paid job for most hours of the day may be seen as one of the less satisfactory ways of getting money, particularly if a sizeable proportion of the money earned must be compulsorily donated to the government.

This book shows the limitations of my early assumptions. Happily, however, the Trustees of the Nuffield Foundation were persuaded, and I started my pilot research in March 1978. As I explain later in the book, I was introduced to a variety of working-class households and I opened the conversation simply by saying that I was interested in understanding how ordinary people were managing in these difficult times. I interviewed thirty people in depth, and most of the interviews were recorded and transcribed. One household's experiences are reported at length in Chapter 11 and two case studies that appeared in an article published in 1980 are reproduced in the Appendix. A number of other articles were published arising out of this pilot study.

Since there had been so very little detailed ethnography done in Britain in the 1970s, my little study on Sheppey, which I carried out in 1978 and 1979, received an embarrassing amount of attention. The 1980 article has been translated into German and Italian and has been reproduced in other collections. The other articles have also been widely noticed and reproduced.[23] In the winter of 1979-80, I was awarded a grant from the Social Science Research Council (SSRC) to convene a series of linked workshops on local labour markets and informal economies (see p. 115 below), and I was asked to give many seminars and public lectures in

Britain and elsewhere in Europe. The idea that 'the informal economy' was a positive alternative to an ailing capitalism was the kind of good news people wanted to hear.

By early 1980 I felt like a character in a Greek drama who has unlocked something he cannot control. As I wrote in my end-of-grant Report to the Nuffield Foundation in 1979, 'I cannot stop now.' What began as a modest exercise in working-class ethnography, exploring how people were managing during an economic recession, escalated very quickly into a large-scale, multi-faceted research project. In order to respond adequately to these and other questions, it was no longer possible to rely on the more qualitative and exploratory research style of the pilot project. Much more precise quantitative answers were required on the social and economic history of the Sheppey labour market. Employers' strategies had to be explored systematically, and details of the Island's land and labour markets precisely documented. Claire Wallace was appointed as a full-time research worker on the Sheppey project, and, later, three postgraduate students linked their research to the enterprise. A large-scale social survey was commissioned that provided precise documentation on all types of formal and informal work carried out by household members and their internal domestic division of labour. A Work Strategies Research Unit was established at the University of Kent, and premises were found on the Island. Informal qualitative work continued: at times four researchers were engaged in various activities on the Island at the same time.

This book is, in part, a product of three years' intensive research in the field and does much more than develop the pilot work. In large measure, we engaged with the earlier work and used that as a base from which to build a new set of ideas. Other work published in the late 1970s was also influential, particularly that of Stuart Henry, Jay Gershuny and Sandra Wallman, all of them friends who were generous with their ideas.[24] Probably the most influential study in terms of methodology was that by L. A. Ferman and his team on 'The Irregular Economy', published in 1978.[25] The development of a broader notion of work owes much to social anthropologists and historians, and I am glad that I was in an intellectual environment in which I could learn from Marshall Sahlins or

[23] The two most quoted and reproduced articles were J. I. Gershuny and R. E. Pahl, 'Work outside employment', *New Universities Quarterly*, 34(1), 1979, pp. 120-35; and R. E. Pahl, 'Employment, work and the domestic division of labour', *International Journal of Urban and Regional Research*, 4(1), 1980, pp. 1-20. As late as 1984 I received requests to republish the latter article. Even though this book is largely a refutation of the article, I rather fear that many people will prefer to believe the article.
[24] S. Henry, *The Hidden Economy*, Martin Robertson, Oxford, 1978; J.I. Gershuny, *After Industrial Society?* Macmillan, London, 1978; S. Wallman (ed.) Introduction, in *A Social Anthropology of Work*, Academic Press, London, 1979.
[25] L. A. Ferman, L. Berndt and E. Selo, *Analysis of the Irregular Economy: Cash Flow in the Informal Sector*, University of Michigan/Wayne State University, Chicago, 1978.

John Davis in the former field and E. P. Thompson or Krishan Kumar in the latter.[26] I am quite sure that if I had approached work in a more traditionally sociological way I would have had greater difficulty escaping from established categories.

I began the study of all forms of work on the Isle of Sheppey in 1981, having just completed a study with Dr N. H. Buck on the historical demography of the Admiralty dockyard at Sheerness in the mid-nineteenth century. Because we had access to the Census Enumerators' books, I knew more about some aspects of the Island's social structure in the past than I was likely to learn in the present. For this and other reasons, I was very conscious of the importance of placing my empirical study in historical context — not just in terms of the actual locale, but in terms of the way forms of work in general had changed and developed. There did seem, initially, to be a parallel between the forms of work more common in eighteenth-century households and the pattern found in certain Sheppey households. One must be careful not to push such apparent convergences too far, but I found that seeking such connections encouraged lateral thinking and helped me to see all forms of work in a better perspective.

Many who are happy to accept my emphasis on history and social anthropology may be less sure about the quantitative style in some of the later chapters of the book. Those who enjoy the case studies in Chapter 11 and Appendix 2 may wish there were more of such qualitative material elsewhere. I may even get attacked for distancing myself from my respondents and for losing the authentic voices of ordinary people. That would be truly ironic. I have spent many years interviewing people on the Isle of Sheppey, and so too has my colleague, Claire Wallace. However, in the light of the criticisms of some of my earlier work, I am very wary about attempting to convince my readers with anecdotes or memorable phrases. There are indeed some respondents whose household work strategies epitomize precisely certain of the themes and arguments I develop. Nevertheless, it is much more important to avoid the trap that researchers — including myself — sometimes fall into: that is, of finding what one expects to find. Many of the conclusions of this book are at variance with the conventional wisdom about the nature of the so-called 'informal economy'. Some of those who hold to conventional views — economists, geographers and social psychologists, as well as sociologists and perhaps civil servants — will not be convinced of the force of my arguments unless they are very solidly buttressed.

[26] M. Sahlins, *Stone Age Economics*, Tavistock Publications, London, 1972; J. Davis, 'Gifts and the UK economy', *Man*, 7(3), 1972, pp. 408-29; J. Davis, 'The particular theory of exchange', *European Journal of Sociology*, 1975, pp. 151-68; E. P. Thompson, 'Time, work discipline and industrial capitalism', *Past and Present*, 38, 1967, pp. 56-97; Krishan Kumar, 'Unemployment as a problem in the development of industrial societies', paper prepared for the EEC-FAST programme, Marseilles, 23-26 November 1981.

I am more confident now about presenting some material in the second half of the book in quantitative terms because it is based on years of informal and qualitative interviewing and observation. Claire Wallace lived on the Island for periods of several months at a time, and the more we learnt, the less sure we were, in one sense, about our capacity to distil understanding that we acquired in a relatively unsystematic way. I have become more suspicious of social research methods that purport to be able to generalize from unsystematic observation and interviewing: it is simply not possible to check on the validity of much of that kind of social reporting. Very few researchers who rely on a very few informants publish the field notes on which they base their generalizations and conclusions. Given the importance and urgency of the theme of this book, I did not want its conclusions to be open to criticism for being too subjectivist. The data set in the ESRC Survey Archive are available for analysis by others.

As I explain and discuss throughout this book, while my ideas in 1980 were, I was told, plausible, sociologically interesting and challenging. I have since had to modify them substantially. My earlier ideas were based on partial ethnography which served a very useful heuristic purpose at the time. Notwithstanding such modifications, I believe that the overall *focus* of the work was absolutely right, and so was the shift towards a more historical analysis in Part I. The household continues to be the basic social unit around which people conduct their lives, and my assumption that, as finding employment becomes more difficult, the household, with its distinctive set of work practices, becomes of greater salience still stands. We began in October 1980 with a more basic question than I had considered in the pilot work: namely, how do all forms of work get done? 'Whose work?' was the underlying question, and how is it changing? The focus shifted away from separate economies and towards all forms of work and the distinctive divisions of labour that are involved.

In the chapters that follow, I try to keep the focus consistently on work, and, since I am trying to develop new ideas about the subject, I have to use old words in new ways. This may create a potential confusion, since, although the words are familiar, the concepts to which they refer will be less so. This is an inevitable problem in social science. If we use familiar words in fresh ways, we are liable to be misunderstood; if we invent new words for new notions, we get scorned for our clumsy neologisms. I will keep to the old words wherever possible and I will endeavour to make clear what new nuances of meaning I wish to suggest.

The first part of the book is not specifically about Sheppey and reflects my growing interest in historical sociology. The second part is dependent on the first part — particularly Chapters 8 and 9, where the analysis is based on the distinctions made in Chapter 5. Finally, in Part III, I take up some of the implications of the Sheppey study for concerns of both theory and practice. Thus, Chapter 12 is not really a conclusion to the book but is an essay in its own right. However, for those who seek the nub of a book in two sentences, I can offer the following. Work has to be understood both historically and in context; it has changed in the past, it is changing now, and it will continue to change in the future; above all, work done by members of households is the central process around which society is structured. In different periods and contexts some work becomes of greater significance: women's waged work is of particular importance for ordinary middle-mass households in Britain in the 1980s.

Part I

Past and Present
Ways of Work

1

Households, Work and Ideology in Pre-industrial Times

Words take their meanings in social contexts: when a word loses its precise meaning it loses something of its currency. It is deeply significant that, as we come to the final years of the twentieth century, 'work', an apparently fundamental and unambiguous word, has come to lack precision. Part of the difficulty may be simply that the word is being asked to do too much. From voluntary work through doing the washing up to being a brain surgeon, a vast range of activities is encompassed in the term 'work'.[1] Whatever the reason, a society that falters when referring to something apparently so basic to human existence is likely to be changing in a fundamental way. The resounding confidence of the mid-century slogan in the United Nations Charter — 'the right to work' — should now, perhaps, be formulated more cautiously as the right to some minimum level of subsistence. Some societies are now recognizing that it is economically (if not socially) better sense to pay people a modest income directly, rather than to burden employers with workers they do not want to pay, simply because they are able to get higher profits without them. The situation in which one society — say an oil-rich Middle Eastern sheikdom — gets members of another society or other societies to do most of its work for it is no different in principle from what happened in the households of English gentlemen in the eighteenth century. Societies well-endowed with energy, technology and capital are unlikely to generate the same slogans as those more plentifully supplied with labour but rather short on the other factors of production. The workers of the world are manifestly not uniting.

The same word, 'work', generates equal confusion and often, indeed, conflict within the household. It is now less easy and less likely for men to return home from employment to a wife who is 'not working'. The woman's work may or may not be paid, but few would argue that the question of payment is the sole determining factor in deciding whether her activity can be appropriately described as work. Whether prompted

[1] An attempt to clarify these distinctive usages will be made in Chapter 5.

by the high levels of unemployment in the advanced industrial societies and the gloomy forecasts of most economists, or by the tensions generated by the uneven distribution of paid employment within and between households, the confusions surrounding the word 'work' are now widespread.

As with most things, these current confusions are not without historical precedents. M. Godelier has reminded us that the words 'work', 'to work' and 'worker' took on their meanings in our language at a certain period and it was not until the development of political science in the nineteenth century that the idea of work became a central concept:

According to Lucien Febvre, it was in the sixteenth century that the word 'to work' (*travailler*) entered the French vocabulary, replacing, in part, two earlier words, *labourer* (now meaning to plough) and *oeuvrer* (no longer in use as a verb; as a noun it means a work of art). *Travailler* (to work) came from the latin which meant torturing with a *tripalium*, an instrument made of three stakes. Before that in about 1120, *labeur* (now meaning toil), from the Latin *labor*, became common usage for agricultural activity; also in the 12th Century *ouvrier* (worker) made its first appearance, derived from the Latin *operarius* (man of pain or affliction), a term which itself went back to two words, *opus* (an action or piece of work) and *operae*, the tasks or obligations which had to be performed in respect of someone else, as for example, those of a liberated serf towards his old master, or those of the artisan in respect of the customer with whom he had a contract. But even before these words had appeared, *travailler* meant to torture an offender on a tripalium and *travailleur* in this case was not the victim but the torturer.[2]

We cannot, of course, understand what these distinctions of meaning implied for the contemporary experience of the people involved. Presumably, they implied some changes in social relations; but it is not possible to infer simply from etymological evidence the exact nature and timing of these. Godelier suggests that these new ideas and new meanings emerged at different and distinct historical periods: at the height of the feudal era in the twelfth and thirteenth centuries, when towns and domestic manufacture first emerged, and then, later, at the end of the fifteenth and beginning of the sixteenth century, with the rise of international trade, the colonial system, banking and state and private manufacture. The final period was at the end of the eighteenth century, when the contemporary meanings of worker and wage earner appeared. It may be that the last two decades of the twentieth century will see yet a further redefinition of work.

Much of the current debate about the future of work begins from

---

[2] M. Godelier, 'Work and its representations: A research proposal', *History Workshop Journal*, 10, 1980, p. 165.

assumptions that should initially be questioned. The fact that 'work' can apply to all kinds of activity, much of which is not paid, but that 'employment' refers more precisely to activity that is paid is evidently of crucial importance now. It is likely that the 'right to work' in the late 1940s then meant 'the right to employment for a reasonable wage, primarily for males in households with dependent women and children'. Yet by 1980 about a third of all households were married couples with dependent children and, of that third, half of the wives were in full or part-time employment.[3] So, in less than forty years, implicit meanings have substantially changed. Households with more than one adult supported by a single earner are now a special category, not the norm. Women now doing unwaged work in their dwellings are unlikely to claim that this is fulfilling their right to work.

A problem with many of the scholarly discussions of work, certainly since the time of Adam Smith and Karl Marx, is that too much emphasis has been given to that work narrowly perceived to be connected with a specific conception of production and too little to the other productive work connected with reproduction and consumption. A recent book entitled *The Ideology of Work*[4] is almost entirely about employment — that is, waged work for an employer. Self-employment and unwaged work are largely ignored. Implicitly, that was the common view of work that held sway until very recently. Antecedents of the conventional view have a long pedigree: God cursed Adam, according to the Judaic myth, in a very thorough-going way. First, He imposed a gender-based conflict ('enmity between thee and the woman'); second, biological reproduction was to be painful ('in sorrow shalt thou bring forth children'); third, patriarchal relations were to be formally established ('thy desire shall be to thy husband and he shall rule over thee'); and, finally, production, implicitly a male activity, was to be made difficult ('cursed is the ground . . . thorns also and thistles shall it bring forth') and tiring ('in the sweat of thy face shalt thou eat bread').[5] Thus were the social relations of a pastoral tribe confirmed and supported. Happily, conditions are not as tiring and painful now as that particular myth predicted. Some women may choose to bear children even when they are not economically necessary for the survival of the household; some men and women may also choose to engage in employment, seeing it as more liberating than constraining.

Until very recently, in European societies certainly, the notion that work was the prerogative of one gender more the other would not have been understood. Work was done by members of *households* for the

---

[3] *Social Trends*, 12, 1981, HMSO, Table 2.2; L. Rimmer and J. Popay, *Employment Trends and the Family*, Study Commission on the Family, London, 1982, Table 7.
[4] P. D. Anthony, *The Ideology of Work*, Tavistock, London, 1977.
[5] Genesis, 3.

collective well-being of household members. The analytical distinction that can arguably be made between work for production and work for reproduction could also have been made in the past, but was not very important. Individuals were largely obliged to be members of households, and they had to get a livelihood, had to get by, and would have seen little need to philosophize about whether or not the roof should be repaired or the cow milked. In practice, households in pre-industrial England, as elsewhere, had to be based on an economic partnership between men and women and other household members. A *household work strategy* developed which made the best use of resources for getting by under given social and economic conditions. It is one of the central concerns of this book to demonstrate that this emphasis on the household rather than the individual as the basic economic unit is a more fruitful way to approach the work of production, reproduction and consumption. This focus makes no *a priori* assumptions about either internal conflict or consensus within the household and none about the necessity for identifying putative household heads. Households are simply units for getting various kinds of work done. They were not, of course, isolated units: households were bound to each other in many complex ways and the boundaries between them were often very fluid, as members moved back and forth at different stages of the life cycle. Certainly, in the past the Church and more recently the State have imposed gender ideologies and hierarchies within the household — the former as a reflection of the development of hierarchy and organization with the Church[6] and the latter as a convenient way of gathering taxes. Even in Britain today, it is the Inland Revenue and the Office of Population Censuses and Surveys (OPCS) that are still most concerned about defining the 'head of household'.

Household Work Practices in Pre-industrial England

Reconstructing past household work strategies[7] is inevitably complex and difficult. Records are scanty and, in so far as they refer to specific types of work, they generally do so only selectively. It would be wrong therefore to infer, if a given task is not mentioned, either that it was done or that it was not done. Thus, we may learn that a given woman bears a child, but we cannot infer that she then has the task of caring for it, nor can we be sure that we know what the task of caring comprises; similarly, if a man

[6] Peggy Reeves Sanday, *Female Power and Male Dominance: On the Origins of Sexual Inequality*, Cambridge University Press, 1981, Part V.
[7] Household work practices or strategies are used interchangeably. The particular mix of practices is a strategy: households do not have to be self-conscious in the balance of work or sources of labour that they use — the fact that these balances and sources vary is the sole point at issue.

buys a cow at market, it certainly does not follow that he will milk it or look after the calves. However, if a child of the same name remains in the household or if later calves are sold at market, we know that *somebody* has looked after the child or cared for the cow. Yet even here there are pitfalls. The degree of co-operation and collectivity in the way work is done *between* households is also open to question and discussion.[8] The divisions of labour both within and between households can be revealed only after very careful analysis, and historians have only recently turned their attention to this.

One of the few attempts to grapple with the problem of understanding the detailed mechanisms by which households managed to get by in a precarious economic environment is provided by a painstaking study by R. M. Smith of a Suffolk village in the thirteenth century.[9] An analysis of the records of Redgrave's manor court from 1259 to 1293 provides an astonishing amount of detailed evidence on interpersonal relations in the village. Much of the data refer to pledging, and it was possible for Smith to identify a large proportion of those involved as tenants on an extent of the manor in 1289. On the basis of these data he divided his sample into three categories, depending on how much land each individual could farm. This was primarily an arable farming area, and Smith reports 'throughout the period of this study there existed a buoyant and at times volatile land market which, combined with the fragmentation of holdings caused by inheritance customs, had produced marked social differentiation among the landholders.'[10] A regular market at Botulesdale, about two miles from Redgrave, provided the incentive and the opportunity for other work to be done in order to produce goods for sale.

Those with the smallest amount of land, under two acres, were in no position to combine their holdings with neighbours to provide a common resource that could provide adequate subsistence. The amounts of land were simply too small: in Wallman's term, their 'resource options' were limited.[11] Those in this position were thus unable to be small-scale farmers, instead becoming day labourers on the demesne, working for their welthier neighbours or engaging in commerce. Thus,

[8] O. Harris, 'Households as natural units', in Kate Young et al. (eds) *Of Marriage and the Market*, CSE Books, London, 1981, pp. 49-67; M. Chaytor, 'Household and kinship: Ryton in the late sixteenth and early seventeenth centuries', *History Workshop Journal*, 10, 1980, pp. 25-60.
[9] R. M. Smith, 'Kin and neighbours in a thirteenth-century Suffolk community', *Journal of Family History*, 4(3), 1979, pp. 219-56. I recognize that I am open to criticism from historians for concentrating on case studies that those who disagree with my argument will claim are not typical. The second part of this book is also a case study, and methodological justification is developed there (pp. 146-7). Since so much is uncertain, it is better, perhaps, to make the best of what is known in detail: a few solid stones may make a better foundation than a greater spread of less substantial material — particularly when I cannot claim to be a trained historian well apprenticed in applying the mystique of historical cement.
[10] Smith, 'Kin and neighbours', p. 222.
[11] S. Wallman and associates, *Living in South London*, Gower Press/LSE, London, 1982.

Reginald Warenner, for instance, was a stallholder in Botulesdale market and held under an acre of land in one of the hamlets of Redgrave manor. He was, with his wife, an active brewer and baker and had little land to serve as the basis for his grain supply. We know from the relatively large number of debt cases involving him or his wife in the court proceedings that he was the purchaser of considerable quantities of brewing barley.[12]

Those in this category had, perforce, to limit their household size: there were more childless couples and more celibate males and females. They were obliged to adopt a household strategy of being small and relatively isolated nuclear families, little dependent on economic links with neighbouring households, except through the market for their labour or products.

In the second, middle, category — that is those with more than two but less than ten acres of land — co-operation and contact with kin and with neighbours produced mutual support and mutual animosity. Those in this category had enough land to encourage co-operation but not enough to provide for their own independence. Hence, Smith is able to demonstrate high network densities and frequencies of contact between individuals of similar standing, with sons generally being able to establish families before their fathers' deaths. Siblings would live in separate accommodation in the near vicinity and households would be bound to each other in common agricultural enterprise. However, as the records of the manorial court demonstrate, combination and collaboration in the work produced as much animosity as concord through interconnecting household work strategies. Unlike the owners of small amounts of land bound by market relations to kin and to neighbours, those in this middle group were bound by ties of responsibilities and reciprocities impossible to evaluate precisely. It is clear, however, that the social context in which the work was done would be crucial. The social relationships between households would be based not simply on the activities of one household member but on all household members severally and collectively.

In the third category — those households where an individual farmed more than ten acres of land — there was more opportunity to be

---

[12] Smith, 'Kin and neighbours', p. 245. Reginald Warenner puts one in mind of the similar account of *Piers Plowman* (Passus V, Everyman Edition, London, pp. 211-23):

> My wife was a webbe and wollen cloth made;
> She spak to spynnesteres to spynnen it oute
> The pound that she paied by peised a quatron moore
> Than myn owene auncer wh(an I) weyed truthe.
> I boughte hire barly – she brew it to selle
> Peny ale and puddyng ale she poured togideres;
> . . . Rose the Regrater was hir righte name;
> She hath holden hukkerye (this ellevene Wynter).

A Regrater was a retailer and Rose 'hath holden hukkerye', practised retail trade, as well as being a weaver.

self-reliant. There was less need for informal relations between households: their economic needs depended less on the balance of reciprocities and more on their capacity to use their greater wealth and power by hiring or extending credit to others. It is possible, although not certain, that a determination to maintain a family's social and economic position could have encouraged the stem family form, whereby brothers remained within the patrimonial household and only one of them inherited the family farm.

Smith's analysis certainly undermines the notion of a 'stable village community' which has such a hold on the popular imagination. One cannot, of course, take this single study as a guide to medieval household work strategies, but it is nevertheless striking that even in the middle category there is no question of viewing the agricultural household as a stable unit interacting with a socially homogeneous village society. In the lowest category of cottagers and farm labourers,

the household exerted a centripetal rather than a centrifugal force in social organization, members travelling daily from the house, which served primarily as a base of operations, to work as day labourers or for longer periods away from the household as servants. Those who worked in cottage industry may well have had a rather more integrated domestic unit, but it still remained apart from, rather than integrated with, the neighbourhood of the wider kin group.[13]

Inevitably, Smith's analysis is constrained, bound as he is by the limitations of his data, which relate to the frequency and type of interaction between kin and neighbours. He does, nevertheless, illustrate very nicely the relationship between distinct and diverse material conditions and distinctive households' economic behaviour. Inevitably, it is hard to get precise evidence on who did the work in medieval England. R. H. Hilton cites a case from the Ombersley court rolls for 1420 reporting a gang's attack on a family at work on its holding.

One of the gang attacked the tenant, Henry Pleydur, whilst he was cultivating his ground; meanwhile another assaulted his daughter Christina, and cut the halter of the horse which was pulling the harrow as Christina harrowed. It is evident that women were not confined to traditional (*sic*) womanly tasks such as looking after the poultry, milking the cows and winnowing the grain.[14]

He goes on to say:

on some Leicestershire estates around 1400, countrywomen were doing the same manual jobs as men, such as haymaking, weeding, mowing, carrying corn, driving

[13] Smith, 'Kin and neighbours', p. 248.
[14] R. H. Hilton, *The English Peasantry in the Later Middle Ages*, Clarendon Press, Oxford, 1975, pp. 101-2.

plough oxen, and breaking stones for road mending. Owing to the fact that accounts give total payments, it is not always easy to tell whether they were being paid at the same rate, but it is my impression that this was usually the case. Female reapers and binders at Minchinhampton, Gloucestershire, in 1380 certainly got the same rates, 4d a day, as the men. . . . But this fortunate situation certainly did not apply to all forms of hired labour.[15]

In order to understand household survival practices in more detail in the pre-industrial period, one is obliged to move forward in time, at least to the late sixteenth century. M. Chaytor examined a small number of households over a period of eighteen years in the Durham village of Ryton. Gathering her information from household listings in title books, she is able to document the size of each household and its wealth and domestic economy. She emphasizes that the households she describes were inevitably those prosperous and settled enough to appear in the records and that, given the economic marginality of the area, these were in a minority. She demonstrates very clearly that economic survival depended on the size and structure of the household:

For some parishioners (the old, the poor, the landless) the death of a spouse or a parent must have brought destitution; for those were the families that were permanently broken; the men and women forced to migrate, to seek work or service in another household or to take to the roads as vagrants. But for the others — for those with land — remarriage was a better strategy for survival. On the death of his wife, a young yeoman or husbandman sought a replacement as soon as possible; without a woman's domestic labour there was no-one to rear the children, tend the kitchen garden, the bees, cow or poultry, cook, spin or brew. Wives could be, and sometimes were, replaced with servants (and older widowers could turn to a daughter or daughter-in-law) but for the young, remarriage was preferable, and for the childless, it was essential. But remarriage ensured more than sons to work the land and daughters to give away in marriage; a wife could bring valuable resources to the household whether in land, a dowry of money or animals, or simply the goodwill of her original kin group. Such men or women, marrying for a second or third time, formed small but complex households, filled with step-children and foster children as well as the offspring of the current marriage.[16]

The important point, which Chaytor's study illustrates, is that work is not something that an already established household then organizes to

---

[15] Ibid., pp. 102-3. Again, it is worth quoting from Langland's *Piers Plowman* (Passus III, Everyman Edition, London, pp. 255-8):

That laborers and lewede (leodes) taken of hire maistres,
It is no mannere mede but a mesurable hire.
In marchaundise is no mede, I may it wel avowe
It is a permutacion apertly — a penyworth for another.

This is a remarkably early and astute commentary on the nature of wage labour.

[16] Chaytor, 'Household and kinship', p. 38.

survive, but, rather, that establishing an appropriate household structure is itself a kind of work. Certain patterns of work were simply not possible without the appropriate household structures. 'Households were the point where the kin groups, joined by marriage, shared and redistributed their resources.'[17] Chaytor shows how individuals were virtually obliged to remain in or to enlarge their households, and she demonstrates the degree to which households were interconnected by such matters as shared child care arrangements and the pooling and borrowing of money and other resources. Households were in a constantly changing dynamic situation which would be very misleadingly presented in a snapshot view. At any one time a household might include a man and a woman and some children, but one or other of the partners might be in their second or third marriage, with the consequent mixture of offspring. Broken marriages with the consequent stepchildren and foster children were common in Ryton, according to Chaytor, partly because of the frequency of famines and epidemics. Destitution was as likely through the death of a spouse as through crop failure or disease. Individuals as individuals could not survive on their own: they were obliged to leave the area or to become a servant in another household. The sharing of tasks and resources and the frequent fission and fusion of households produced a situation where, as it were, getting the appropriate clustering of people and resources in a household was an intrinsic part of the work.

In this dynamic situation, 'Marriage initiated a cycle in which people and property moved from one household to another, but it was a consequence of these loans and exchanges as much as a cause.'[18] Inevitably, therefore, marriages were to a degree arranged, but probably no more so than through recognizing that certain matches would be more economically and socially suitable than others. Chaytor does not believe that women were regarded purely as merchandise, seen largely in terms of their dowries or other economic resources. Any underlying rationality or exchange system had the willing collaboration of the women, even though a high incidence of apparently economically unnecessary marriages among propertied widows might suggest to some a male concern to limit economic and sexual independence. 'In a society where marriage ensured an ordered flow of goods and services within households and between them, male control over women's sexuality was essential: female chastity was essential to prevent property from passing to the wrong people.'[19]

Chaytor's detailed analysis of individual households suggests a striking diversity of arrangements in Ryton at this period, including extended family households. 'Parents lived with married sons and married

[17] Ibid., p. 39.
[18] Ibid., p. 41.
[19] Ibid., p. 44.

daughters, and a widow headed a household which included a couple who may have been only distantly related to her.'[20] Daughters were more useful than female servants because of their local knowledge and influence. Hence, although about one in four households had servants who were not kin, if daughters could be supported at home they would stay there. Chaytor concludes:

Households, while technically separate units of production, reproduction and consumption, were not fixed or isolated structures; the boundaries between them and the hierarchies within them were constantly broken and rearranged as marriages and death moved people between households, redefining their status and the relationships between them. . . . Social and economic divisions between the sexes must also have broken down barriers between households, for the men worked adjacent strips of land and grazed their cattle in the same pastures, while women spent time together, washing, brewing, spinning and gossiping.[21]

Such diversity is somewhat at variance with the stance of P. Laslett and others of the Cambridge Group of historical demographers. It is clear that their emphasis on the near-universality of nuclear family households in pre-industrial England was powerfully motivated by the need to refute assertions connecting the nuclear family with industrialization and so-called modernization. On this there can be no contention. However, Laslett's concern to emphasize the importance of the 'collectivity' over the family[22] may be over-insistent. There is a danger that the powerful forces of the Cambridge Group will tend to underplay the significance of Chaytor's work. Support for her position comes in a less well-known work by R. Machin on three Dorset villages.[23] His account of the way tenants transferred their land suggests that it was, in practice, virtually freehold and the tenants ran the manorial court as if it were their own:

The new tenant paid the lord a reasonable fine (assessed by the homage), gave a gallon of ale and a loaf of bread to the homage and two shillings to the steward: 'which is the customary hold and there never was any other writing within the manor saving Copies of Excepts'. The except was a statement made by the tenant when transferring his holding in which he said that he excepted from the transfer for his own use whatsoever he wished 'provided there be assigned sufficient to the tenant over and above the Except to pay the lord's Rent' and the entry fine. . . . It was in every tenants' interest to make an except since no reversions were allowed and if any tenant died without making an except the lord was able to grant the holding for one life at any time he wished.[24]

[20] Ibid., p. 47.
[21] Ibid., pp. 48-9.
[22] P. Laslett, 'The family and the collectivity', *Sociology and Social Research*, 63(3), 1979, pp. 432-42.
[23] R. Machin, *Probate Inventories and Manorial Excepts of Chetnole, Leigh and Yetminster*, University of Bristol, 1976.
[24] Ibid., p. 26.

Machin analyses the Upbury manor excepts and matches these with probate inventories in order to get some measure of the cycle of inheritance. His data suggest an average cycle of fourteen years, which leads him to some highly pertinent speculations. What seemed to be happening at Yetminster during the period 1568-1627 was this: the first fourteen years of his working life the farmer was a tenant to an exceptor; for the next seven years he was a tenant of the entire farm; then for another fourteen years he was exceptor to the new tenant. In this way the farmer spent the full thirty-five years of his working life running the farm. The family cycle was in three stages. In the first the heir apparent (i.e. the son) learnt from the father and had a share in the farm buildings and probably lived in the house. In the second phase he ran the entire holding himself before his son, in turn, took over the work and he excepted in his favour. In the third, handing-over, phase the farmer might be moving into semi-retirement. This is the classic stem-family pattern of peasant households and is a household work strategy not commonly held to apply in England. The Yetminster evidence is modest, to be sure, but, as Machin remarks:

Excepting was described in the custumal and recorded in detail in the court books because the Yetminster customary tenants ran the manor almost as if it were their own. In the majority of manors, customary law was the law of the tenants: it was oral and only written down if it affected the landlord's interests. Excepting was congenial to the peasant mind at Yetminster; might not customary tenants elsewhere follow similar practices — which were privy to the family and community and of little concern to the landlord?[25]

This is an exciting, if not provocative, line of thought. As Machin reasonably notes, the sharing of kitchens in the excepts does suggest that the incoming tenant headed his own family under his parents' roof. Two generations of the same family partly sharing and partly dividing one house and farmyard was probably, suggests Machin, 'a regular feature of the 16th Century family life-cycle in Yetminster, as it is today'.[26] I do not feel qualified to judge the wider significance of these suggestions but they seem, on the face of it, to be perfectly plausible.

Chaytor's research demonstrates the variety of household work strategies that developed to cope with distinctive circumstances of both economic and demographic insecurity. The households she describes appeared to be essentially pragmatic and *ad hoc* in the way they used the available resources: her emphasis on a variety of arrangements and strategies indicates the flexibility and adaptability of pre-industrial household practices. Also, her focus on the developmental cycle of the domestic group avoids the difficulties of the snapshot cross-sectional

[25] Ibid., pp. 27-8.
[26] Ibid., p. 28.

approach.[27] Living-in servants clearly affected the organization and division of all domestic tasks: bearing children need not necessarily imply full-time caring for them and domestic tasks might be shared among a number of people in the household. Since most young people left home to be servants in other households at 12 or 13,[28] it would not be unusual for someone aged 36 to have spent an equal period of his or her life in three different households — the natal home, the home of employment and the home of procreation. The domestic division of labour would inevitably, therefore, be substantially affected by the size and structure of the household.

Knowledge of who did what work in former times is, as already noted, extremely hard to discover. First of all there is the problem of whether tasks that are taken for granted in common understanding now were in fact done at all in the past, and whether, even if they were done, they could be classed as the same task. A good example of this problem is domestic cleaning. The rudimentary cottages of ordinary people had rough, insubstantial walls, earth floors covered with rushes and a smoking fire in the middle. This rude habitation was shared more or less regularly with poultry and livestock. Moving dirt from one place to another (which is one way of viewing cleaning) would seem a singularly unproductive exercise when there were so many more useful tasks to do. Even richer households had rush floors, and it seems likely that the bottom layers of these remained undisturbed for twenty years or more;[29] floor boarding, not introduced until the mid-seventeenth century, was largely restricted to parlours.[30] Certainly there is no mention of any cleaning equipment in probate inventories, even though there are detailed records of cooking utensils and farm implements.[31]

By and large, it seems fair to say that up until the eighteenth century

[27] As Harris remarks in an article that generally supports Chaytor's position, 'the presence of servants necessarily affects the degree of co-operation in different forms of labour between kin and neighbours. Where servants were engaged in domestic tasks, this will have affected the lives of all women household members, and also the degree to which women would rely on assistance from women in other households' (O. Harris, 'Households and their boundaries', *History Workshop Journal*, 14, 1982, p. 148). This is clumsily expressed, but I take it Harris is not claiming that servants affected the lives of only female household members. She appears to be making an unwarranted assumption about gender-linked tasks. However, in general her commentary is astute. One always has to watch that one does not impose one's knowledge of the more recent past on the more remote past, although sometimes the temptations are great.

[28] V. B. Eliott, 'Mobility and marriage in pre-industrial England', unpublished doctoral thesis, University of Cambridge, 1978; A. Macfarlane, *The Origins of English Individualism*, Basil Blackwell, Oxford, 1978; R. S. Schofield, 'Age-specific mobility in an eighteenth-century rural English parish', *Annales de Demographie Historique*, 1970, pp. 261-74.

[29] C. Goff, *A Woman of the Tudor Age*, John Murray, London, 1930, p. 266.

[30] See M. W. Barley, 'Rural housing in England', in J. Thirsk (ed.), *The Agrarian History of England and Wales*, vol. IV, *1500-1640*, Cambridge University Press, 1967.

[31] See the work by R. Machin in this context, discussed on pp. 26–7.

the only historical records of domestic cleaning are in the account books of the gentry: those show that the task was largely done by female employees paid on a daily basis. They did not seem to be living-in servants but more likely were the wives of men who were employed on the estate. The names in the account books showed that these women were hired to do specific unskilled tasks of which house cleaning was but one. It appeared to be an activity that took place on an annual basis and then lasted only for a few days. Goff reports that in 1562 one Katherine Willoughby paid a total of 12s for the annual cleaning of the house, whereas six months earlier she had paid 28s 6d for a pair of silk riding reins.[32] The rate of pay was low: Sarah Fell in the 1670s paid casual women an average of only 1d a day for cleaning, whereas a wheelwright was paid 6d.[33] Evidence from early domestic conduct books in the late sixteenth and early seventeenth centuries, while providing very detailed instructions on how to run a home, make very little reference to the need to clean or the need to supervise the standards of servants' cleaning.

The same pattern applies to the washing and cleaning of clothes. In the better-off houses, clothes were again washed by the wives of estate employees as wage labourers on a casual basis. This was apparently an infrequent event, causing substantial fuss and upheaval, taking place once or twice a year.[34] What was a rare occurrence for the rich probably hardly occurred at all for the poor.

The one point about cleaning which bears close relation to its twentieth century form is that it seems to have been a female task. Women ordered that it be done, and employed other women to do it. The gender concentration of the employees seems to have been caused by the casual nature of the work. Men were employed continuously in agricultural production on the estate, partly because these jobs required a superior physical strength.[35]

Not only did most people not have the clothes or the furniture to keep as possessions defining the possessor, but, more importantly, there was not the ideological reinforcement that this was necessary and essential women's work. The first point, therefore, is that the task may not have been done at all in the past or, if it was done, may have been done in a very different way. The second point has arisen in our discussion of the

---

[32] Goff, *A Woman of the Tudor Age*, pp. 266, 273.

[33] N. Penney (ed.), *The Household Account Book of Sarah Fell of Swarthmore*, Cambridge University Press, 1920, accounts for October 1674 and March 1675.

[34] See, for example, G. E. Fussell and K. R. Fussell, *The English Countrywoman: A Farmhouse Social History AD1500-1900*, Andrew Melrose, London, 1953; Penney, *Household Account Book of Sarah Fell*.

[35] I owe this remark and references on this topic to Ms Frances Evans, whose research has helped me to clarify my thoughts. See in particular her very stimulating paper, 'Absent from history? Constructing and deconstructing a history of domestic labour: The seventeenth century transition' (forthcoming).

first: what counts as evidence? Scattered references here and there, the few account books that are available and even the more comprehensive probate inventories provide, at best, a very patchy understanding. Diaries and personal accounts are virtually non-existent before the late seventeenth century and, where they do exist, provide partial and perhaps misleading information on the richer and literate social categories. One is obliged to accept that there is no alternative to making the best use of very limited sources and to recognizing the limitations of the generalizations that are made.[36]

In very simple terms, household work strategies are made up of the different kinds of work undertaken by members of a household and the use of other sources of labour on which they can draw. Workers need not necessarily be co-resident: sons or daughters who work elsewhere and send money home are, to that extent, working for the household. The discussion that follows is limited to certain broad categories of work: I simply differentiate between waged work and domestic work in the household and other non-waged work outside the household. Waged work may range from a few hours a week or, at certain busy times of the year, to being an overwhelming dominant activity, taking up 60 or more hours a week. Domestic work can include caring for children or repairing the roof, and other work may include gathering fuel in the woods or along the coast or raising poultry.

Typically, in most accounts of work, much attention is given to the regular waged employment undertaken by men. For that reason, little attention is given here to that kind of work. Rather, more attention is given to the *other* work that men do — the easements of their occupations, their by-employments, whether waged or unwaged, and the work they do within and for their domestic groups. Until very recently, substantial amounts of work in and around the household were done by servants. The distinction between indoor work and outdoor work was not always very clear, and by the eighteenth century many self-employed craftsmen often expected an apprentice to double up as a footboy, 'dividing his time between the shop and attendance on his mistress'.[37] Since it was common in pre-industrial English society for children at 12 or 13 to leave home and begin service in another household, it is

---

[36] It would obviously be a ludicrous enterprise to attempt a comprehensive historical survey of household work practices in what are to some extent simply introductory chapters. The only justification is that the notion of what is work is so limited and so narrowly defined that an attempt must be made, however partial, to shift the bias. This is what is attempted in the following pages. As Runciman has reminded us, there is obviously no limit in principle to the historian's or the sociologist's descriptive task. 'All descriptions are partial, just as all explanations are provisional' (W. G. Runciman, *A Treatise on Sociological Theory*, vol. 1, *The Methodology of Social Theory*, Cambridge University Press, 1983, p. 227).
[37] J. J. Hecht, *The Domestic Servant Class in Eighteenth Century England*, Routledge and Kegan Paul, London, 1956, p. 8.

unsurprising that servants — that is, other people's teenage sons and daughters — were regarded as members of the family.

Ralph Josselin remarks in his diary in the mid-seventeenth century that one of his maids was 'the first that married out of my family':[38]

'Trouble and greife' are the words Josselin used to describe a servantless household, and his frantic searchings for one, and calls on the Lord to help, indicate how very important servants were in the household economy. 'My mayde went away', he recorded on one occasion and after asking God's help in getting a replacement asked in desperation two days later, 'Many times I sought god for a servant, a mercy I prize'. A year later he was complaining of the 'trouble and greife it would bee to us to bee destitute [of a servant] but a few dayes', and his wife was described as 'tired and without a servant'. Although evidence from other diaries is needed before any conclusion can be reached, these few entries do suggest the urgent need for a servant in a seventeenth-century house of quite modest means.[39]

Pre-industrial Divisions of Labour within the Household

In very broad terms, therefore, we can distinguish between different forms of work and different categories of worker, which may be expressed diagrammatically in Figure 1.1. Because of the nature of the historical sources, it is not possible to reconstruct past household work practices for all members of given households.[40]

Evidently, household work strategies were heavily determined by social and material conditions in pre-industrial times. While, in theory, literate commentators might attempt to define what was woman's work and what was men's, in practice there was likely to be substantial variation. As M. Segalen laconically remarks, referring to peasant families in France, 'the household had to produce in order to live, and often lived in order to produce, production guaranteeing the perpetuation of the human grouping.'[41] She goes on to observe that there has been no systematic historical analysis of the distribution of tasks carried out by members of the household. She doubts whether the concept of 'domestic life' separate from the life of production is a meaningful concept in terms of the peasant household, where what has to be done is determined more by cycles of work connected with the seasons and the reproductive cycle. Reporting on accounts by French folklorists, Segalen shows how tasks are intermeshed on the farm.

There is no distinction in kind drawn between cultivation and cooking. Preparing

[38] A. Macfarlane, *The Family Life of Ralph Josselin, A Seventeenth Century Clergyman*, Cambridge University Press, 1970.
[39] Ibid., pp. 147-8.
[40] This poses problems enough for contemporary households, as the detailed material in Chapters 8 and 9 indicates.
[41] M. Segalen, *Love and Power in the Peasant Family*, Basil Blackwell, Oxford, 1983, p. 78.

	Waged work	By-employments	Occupational easements	Child care	Household self-provisioning	Accounting money-management
Senior woman						
Senior man						
Other female kin						
Other male kin						
Female children						
Male children						
Female servants						
Male servants						

Figure 1.1   Whose work in the household

a meal or giving the pigs their swill, all come under the household; men, women and children, servants and animals are all equal beneficiaries of this work. Thus, work in the kitchen should no more be considered part of a strictly defined category of housework than tilling the soil should be excluded from the category of 'production' insofar as it is an activity of preparing the soil.[42]

Tasks are divided, but they are also complementary: certain tasks connected with the hearth, home and garden were evidently largely reserved for women, although very often what is conventionally called 'housework' would more likely be done by servants or young girls. Certainly, in the order of priorities, housework came below working in the fields and caring for the children and animals. Much time would have to be spent in the garden digging, sowing, hoeing and harvesting. Yet Segalen notes that even the most gender-linked tasks are taken over by the other partner in certain regimes. In the case of bread-making — traditionally a female task — by breaking down the task into its constituent elements, she suggests that it is not always so clear who in practice does the task, since both men and women may share different aspects of the work. In one area women make the dough but men knead it; elsewhere men handle the process of heating up the oven or perhaps the whole baking process. This interchangeability of apparent gender-task linkages makes Segalen wonder whether the term 'domestic' has any precise meaning: 'Certain activities were carried out by either men or women, depending on the region. Everything to do with livestock was dealt with in this way. While sheep were rather regarded as being the men's province . . . cows could be the responsibility of either one or the other.'[43] Evidently, according to Segalen, any attempt to document precisely the gender-linked division of tasks in French peasant households as a basis for generalization is hardly a realistic enterprise. There would be a division of labour in any one household, to be sure, but the variations appear endless — 'the amount of feminine contribution to the work on the land depended on the composition of the household and the particular stage of its evolution, on its economic level, on the time of year, and finally perhaps on cultural models which are the most difficult of all to come to grips with.'[44] That generalization must be hard to refute: it is quite clear that women played an essential role in production and their labour was essential to the economic survival of the household unit.

Nevertheless, if the arguments of A. Macfarlane and others are to be followed — and they are extremely persuasive — the notion of a small farming, virtually self-sufficient, peasantry is not necessarily appropriate for England. We have already noticed the vigorous market in land in thirteenth-century Suffolk and villagers were engaged in wage labour

[42] Ibid., p. 81.
[43] Ibid., p. 97.
[44] Ibid., p. 106.

from at least that period. It is unnecessary to discuss in any detail here the reasons for this English individualism in contrast to the pattern found elsewhere, especially in southern Europe. However, the consequences for the division of labour by gender do need to be explored.

Ideological Determinants of a Gender-based Division of Labour

It is not unlikely that in England, up until the fourteenth or fifteenth centuries, there was perhaps a kind of rough justice between men and women[45] and that, as Dorothy Stenton has suggested, 'The nearer the household was to the land, the stronger the tie between man and wife, the more nearly they were on equal terms.'[46] However, the move away from the woman as a mate to the woman as a dependant cannot be attributed in a simple, monocausal way to the development of trade and industry. At least of equal, if not of greater, importance was the ideological enforcement of gender-linked role differentiation in the seventeenth century. Perhaps the neatest and certainly a highly persuasive account of these ideological shifts is provided by Margaret George in her important article, 'From "Goodwife" to "Mistress": The Transformation of the Female in Bourgeois Culture'. There she shows how the debate 'about the nature of women and the value and morality of marriage that had intermittently entertained and instructed the English reading public for more than half a century'[47] came to a head. During the seventeenth century, Margaret George argues, following C. B. Macpherson, C. H. George and others,[48] there was 'a concentrated effort to bring politics, law and religion into line with the economic power of private property. A shift, indeed a transformation, of human consciousness, perception and thought accompanied the "new class forming", the emergence of a bourgeois personality consonant with a "possessive market society".'[49] This culminated in the eighteenth-century glorification of 'Man' in which women's contribution to social and productive life drastically declined.

---

[45] Incidentally, 'women-baiting in the Middle Ages' is nicely illustrated by the medieval lyric — possibly a drinking song — in which the virtues of women are extolled in a series of verses each containing the last line 'Cuius contrarum verum est' — the joke being that none of the women present could understand Latin. This division of learning between the genders seems to be in contrast to pre-Conquest England where women were the repositories of learning in the household: Alfred, for example, learnt how to read when quite old (i.e. over 30) from his mother.

[46] D. M. Stenton, *The English Woman in History*, Schocken Books, New York, 1977, p. 98 (first published in 1957 by George Allen and Unwin, London).

[47] M. George, 'From "Goodwife" to "Mistress"': The transformation of the female in bourgeois culture', *Science and Society*, 37(2), 1973, p. 152.

[48] See, for example, C. B. Macpherson, *The Political Theory of Possessive Individualism*, Oxford University Press, 1962; and C. H. George, 'The making of the English bourgeoisie 1500-1750', *Science and Society*, Winter, 1971.

[49] M. George, 'From "goodwife" to "mistress"', p. 155.

Women suffered an absolute setback at the end of the seventeenth century from which, perhaps, they have still to recover. Alice Clark has argued that, until well into the seventeenth century, women played an active and productive part in various trades. A tradesman and his wife would work as a parternship, with neither being necessarily dependent on the other.[50] However, by the early eighteenth century Daniel Defoe complained that, even in those trades that were 'proper' for women to work in, and even if they were willing to do so, their husbands now prevented them: . . . 'our tradesmen, forsooth, think it an undervaluing of them and to their business, to have their wives seen in their shops, that is to say, that because other traders do not admit them, therefore they will not have their traders or shops thought less masculine or less considerable than others, and they will not have their wives be seen in their shops.'[51] So the 'lady' was put back to sit in the parlour while the purposeful husband 'strode out to make his mark' in the all-male 'real' world, vastly pleased that his all-male business could not be thought 'less masculine' and therefore 'less considerable' than others.[52]

A very large quantity of pamphlets, tracts and sermons were published in the seventeenth century describing and analysing with more exactness the specificities of gender roles and relations. 'More particularly,' writes George, 'they were asserting male dominance and superiority with an intellectual precision wholly alien to woman-baiting of the medieval past.'[53] The contrast between a struggle between rough equals, rather like the distinction between townsmen and countrymen, now shifted to a characterization of a new ideology of dominance based on the woman-as-dutiful-wife. The supporting justification and rationale behind this ideology were provided by the English Protestant preachers. Women were to be chaste, constant, understanding, decent and docile. For the preachers, the regeneration of men had to begin through the appropriate behaviour for males in marriage and family life: a seventeenth-century version of Old Testament patriarchy was developed, whereby authority came from God to the (male) heads of families. Domestic conduct books — published in great quantities — made it clear to women how they should fulfil their docile and subservient roles. 'The confinement of the female to domesticity and the home was crucial to the creation of the godly society for one primary reason — to prevent promiscuity.'[54] In Robert Cleaver's 'A Godly Form of Household Governement', published in London as early as 1598, and William Perkins's *Christian*

[50] A. Clark, *The Working Life of Women in the Seventeenth Century*, Frank Cass, London, 1968 (originally published in 1919).

[51] D. Defoe, *The Complete English Tradesman*, London, 1926; quoted in M. George, 'From "goodwife" to "mistress"', p. 158.

[52] M. George, 'From "goodwife" to "mistress"', p. 159.

[53] Ibid.

[54] Ibid., p. 166.

Oeconomie, or, A Short Survey of the Right Manner of Erecting and Ordering a Family, according to the Scriptures, published in London in 1609, a woman who was a 'gadder abroad' or who took the 'libertie of wandring, and straying abroad from her owne house, without the man's knowledge and consent' was vigorously reproved.

All these speeches, sermons and tracts, which were pumped out for a century or more, probably took a very long time to have much general effect. It is unlikely that women would be that easily subjugated, but certainly the pressure built up towards the end of the seventeenth and the beginning of the eighteenth centuries. As George concludes, bourgeois women were 'both pulled, by the given rules of social esteem, and pushed, by men exulting in a newly defined masculine superiority to the private — privatized — concerns for the nuclear family. There they would stay, shut out of a world exploding with individual opportunity by their lack of education and specialized training and by the self-fulfilling prophecy of their "natural" place and inferiority.'[55]

However badly things were developing for women's long-term social and economic status in the late seventeenth century, happily there was a long time to go before there would be much impact on ordinary working women in rural areas. Richard Gough, describing the daily life of Myddle in Shropshire, reflects a pattern probably fairly common throughout rural England when he comments on the regular and widespread drinking.[56] Between 1690 and 1750, there was little difference in the pattern of male and female participation in agricultural work: during that period 'gender differences appear to be almost a matter of indifference to employers.'[57]

By and large, male and female wages fluctuated at about the same rate around the period from 1740 to 1760. K.D.M. Snell does, however, show that the female index of money wages was above those of males in west and south-west England from 1790 to 1830, as specialization in pastoral farming in these areas enhanced the role of female farm servants. According to Snell, the marked differentiation of wage rates after 1750, particularly in eastern England, was due to the pressure of wider market forces and the development of technology. Rising grain prices encouraged tenant farmers to speed up the harvest in order to catch the highest prices. One way to do this was to rely on the heavier hand-scythe, supplanting the light sickle used by women. Those areas in the south and east that specialized in grain production introduced heavier tools from about 1750. The extension of the use of the scythe, which had been used for barley,

---

[55] Ibid., p. 170.

[56] Thomas Downton's wife 'went dayly to the alehouse. Her husband payd £10 at a time for alehouse scores.' William Crosse of Bilmarsh and his wife 'went dayly to the alehouse, and soone after the cows went thither alsoe' (D. G. Hey, *An English Rural Community*, Leicester University Press, 1974, p. 227).

[57] K. D. M. Snell, 'Agricultural seasonal unemployment, the standard of living and women's work in the South and East, 1690-1860', *Economic History Review*, 1980, p. 413.

oats, peas and beans, to the harvesting of wheat and rye had the effect of excluding women, since they had never used the scythe. By the end of the eighteenth century, a marked division of labour by gender had appeared in agriculture, particularly in south-east England. Snell argues that the squeezing of women out of agriculture and limiting them to certain lighter work, such as weeding corn and haymaking, 'cannot be held to have been primarily a product of Victorian morality and middle class assumptions regarding the role of women'.[58] There was a much greater continuity of female participation in agricultural employment. A different pattern of agriculture produced different practices in the division of labour by gender. These regional variations have deep roots and, as is shown below, these variations continue until well into the twentieth century.

While agriculture was the main occupation of working women in the mid-eighteenth century, by the mid-nineteenth century it was overwhelmingly domestic service. From 1830 to the end of the century, one in three of all girls in the urban working class spent part of her life in domestic service. Unlike the situation, say, in France, where women remained working in agriculture right through the nineteenth century, unmarried women in England had little choice but to become servants. This had the effect, as it were, of feminizing the servant class, since by 1850 about three-quarters of all servants were female. Furthermore, since the employers of these young women were increasingly members of the new middle class, this had the effect of partially acculturating the young women to middle-class norms and values. Thus, in the leading form of urban employment for women, a role model was provided that emphasized domesticity, privatization and a distinctive pattern of 'feminine' tasks and attributes.

We left the wife of the tradesman being pushed into gentility in the early eighteenth century: we now return to consider how the development of trade and industry affected women during the nineteenth century, and this is elaborated in Chapter 3. Inevitably the increasing scale of production and commerce in the late eighteenth century reinforced what has come to be termed 'the separation of spheres' — women in the home, men away from the home, 'at work'. But changing material conditions were not overwhelming. Religious, political and cultural factors also helped to determine the separation.[59] First, the heart of the productive enterprise was still the family unit enlarged by partnership, and, since legal and banking systems were still in their infancy, the development of trust was of crucial importance. Unfortunately, a woman who had been *de facto* her husband's partner in small

[58] Ibid., p. 429.
[59] L. Davidoff and C. Hall, 'The architecture of public and private life: English middle class society in a provincial town 1780-1850', in D. Fraser and A. Sutcliffe (eds), *The Pursuit of Urban History*, Edward Arnold, London, 1983, p. 328.

enterprises in the past could not enter into formal partnership since, legally, she could not control her own property, make contracts, sue or be sued: in a phrase, she was not a legal person. Hence partnerships were made with kin: Smith & Sons, Smith & Nephew or Smith Bros could grow and flourish, but there was no place for Mrs Smith except in the home, and that is all for which she and her daughters were prepared.

It was important for the new middle class men of business and industry to generate an impression of reliable and solid respectability. Their wives had to provide the gentility to demonstrate their husbands' creditworthiness. Customers and creditors would be more impressed by a domestic establishment with a dependent wife, servants and all the physical trappings symbolizing success. Since the town has connotations of dirt, disorder and struggle,

The 'unnatural' world of the market-place was counterposed to a nostalgic Arcadian ideal of home in a rural community. Women and children were thus seen as part of nature, associated with the countryside. One of the results of this potent symbolic association was that the middle class never came to terms with town life and constantly attempted to recreate their rural vision in their houses and neighbourhoods.[60]

In line with the Protestant preachers of the seventeenth century, Evangelicalism a hundred years later continued to stress the importance of a religious household in which the wife and mother provided the focus. The difference between moral virtue and managing the household was elided, so that the distinction between cleanliness and Godliness was slight: 'What had started as the creed of a small but extremely active group within both the Anglican and Non-Conformist churches had become the common sense of a class by mid century and was being widely propagated to those members of the working class who aspired to respectability.'[61]

What was defined as respectable became more demanding between the middle of the eighteenth to the middle of the nineteenth century. Standards of cleanliness and comfort were rising: clothes and household linen were rarely washed in the eighteenth century, even among the gentry, but this gradually became a more necessary task, especially after the introduction of cotton. In the kitchen, coal-burning iron ranges were introduced in the 1780s and had become standard equipment by the middle of the following century.

Gardens, like the internal parts of the house, came to carry symbolic meanings especially connected with gender. . . . Women, who in the past had been responsible for functional vegetables and herbs, were now becoming associated

[60] Ibid., p. 329.
[61] Ibid.

primarily with flowers, their brilliant colouring, fragility, fragrance and their existence for decorative purposes only. . . . Such symbolism had class as well as gender overtones. It was part of the natural refinement of ladies to appreciate flowers and to be able to arrange them artistically. These inborn qualities were assumed to be not only part of the middle class woman's innate femininity, the 'womanly touch' which makes a house a home, but also an essential indication of gentility.[62]

The desire for what Davidoff and Hall nicely refer to as 'the ordered naturalness of the home in a garden' was becoming hard to satisfy in the centre of the expanding towns of manufacture and commerce. From the early nineteenth century, the rising middle class began moving out to the suburbs where the women could remain isolated in their gentility and the men would 'go to work' in the towns each day. This move had the double advantage of providing space for display and also separating the new middle from the working class, spreading in the estates of terraced housing. This produced a sharp physical segregation, reinforcing the social segregation. Men moved about freely; they walked or rode on horseback, took part in public life and met in various places for conviviality and recreation. Women were increasingly constrained: 'for the prosperous middle and upper class woman, walking had become either a sign of poverty or eccentricity.'[63]

Of course, most women were not thus constrained. While those men aspiring to economic and social success cocooned their wives and daughters in gentility, ordinary working-class girls were spearheading the development of an industrial workforce.

The Household Work of Servants

Historians have spent more time arguing about the numbers of servants in Victorian England than considering in any detail precisely what work they did.[64] 'Consequently, the domestic economy of the nineteenth century household is *terra-incognita* for modern historians.'[65]Much material is anecdotal, and the reminiscences of servants and employers cannot be held to be representative of most Victorian households. 'To fall back on the evidence of manuals of domestic economy, as do practically all historians of the subject, is equivalent to using *Vogue* to reconstruct the life-style of the "typical" modern family. Such manuals reflected the

[62] Ibid., p. 335.
[63] Ibid., p. 343.
[64] T. McBride, *The Domestic Revolution*, Croom Helm, London, 1976; M. Ebery and B. Preston, *Domestic Service in Late Victorian and Edwardian England 1871-1914*, Department of Geography Paper No. 42, University of Reading, 1976.
[65] E. Higgs, 'Domestic servants and households in Victorian England', *Social History* 8(2), 1983, p. 200.

aspirations, if not the daydreams, of Victorians, rather than the detailed workings of their homes.'[66] The empirical work by E. Higgs on a sample of households in Rochdale and Oldham in the mid-nineteenth century taken from the Census Enumerators' Books provides some of the best data so far available, although evidently there is considerable scope for further work on this source. He shows that 16 per cent of his sample in Rochdale that had living-in servants were artisans, clerks or semi-skilled and unskilled workers, including joiners, 'overlookers', weavers and labourers. In Rutland, 13 per cent of the households with living-in servants were from that social category. This finding must cast doubt on the widely quoted phrase coined by J. A. Banks,[67] on the basis of household manuals, that servants were part of the 'paraphanalia of gentility' of the middle class. As Higgs categorically states, 'the number of servants employed by a family was not automatically determined by its income.'[68] He suggests that, in the term used in this book, it was more a question of the household work strategy of the household as a productive unit than social status alone that determined the pattern of living-in servants:

Factors affecting the choice of employing servants, and how many, must have included the family size, the number of potential household workers in the family, crises such as widowhood or childbirth, the amount of entertainment undertaken, the relative efficiency of the household plant, the availability of manufactured commodities such as polishes, starch, pickles, jams, and so on . . . only by shifting the emphasis from the home as a unit of conspicuous consumption (or gross underconsumption) to the home as a unit of production can we rescue this institution from the historians of social ideologies or 'superstructures'.[69]

Some historians have already adopted such a stance. For example, L. Davidoff[70] has emphasized the economic relations of landlady and lodger as an important aspect of household work practices. At least there is some comfort from knowing that more detailed analyses of nineteenth-century household work strategies are likely to be undertaken in the next decade.

[66] Ibid., p. 203.
[67] J. A. Banks, *Prosperity and Parenthood*, Routledge and Kegan Paul, London, 1954.
[68] Higgs, 'Domestic servants and households', p. 207.
[69] Ibid., pp. 208-9.
[70] L. Davidoff, 'The separation of home and work? Landladies and lodgers in nineteenth and twentieth-century England', in S. Burman (ed.) *Fit Work for Women*, Croom Helm, London, 1979.

2

Patterns of Work Before the Dominance of Wage Labour

Work as Wage Labour in the Past

The last decades of the twentieth century are clearly a period of falling demand by employers for waged workers in many industrial societies. Manual workers, both male and female, are a declining proportion of the working population and there is widespread discussion about the necessity for reducing hours of employment over the lifetime or on a weekly basis. Job-sharing and various part-time arrangements are being canvassed.

Mistakenly, this decline in the demand for wage labour, particularly in the manufacturing sector, is perceived to cast doubt on 'the future of work'.[1] It would be more useful and more accurate to recognize that people in the 1980s and 1990s are living through a period when the proportion of work done by individuals in the form of wage labour is changing. There are absolutely no signs of a 'collapse of work'. The notion that there should be, in general, one waged worker or 'breadwinner' in a household who, typically, should be male is, in historical terms, a very odd idea. The notion that people should actually want to be wage labourers, and should resent a situation in which wage labour is in decline, illustrates first an unprecedented cultural dependence on simply *one* form of work and, second, a failure to recognize the importance that *other* work has had in the past in confirming and creating social identity.

Some historical perspective is required for a proper understanding of the nature and meaning of work at the end of the twentieth century, yet curiously little is known about the true meaning of wage labour for the pre-industrial worker.[2] Waged labour is not even something discovered by the political economists writing from 1780 to 1880, the great century

---

[1] C. Jenkins and B. Sherman, *The Collapse of Work*, Eyre Methuen, London, 1979.
[2] This chapter will focus on men's work and the next chapter on women's. I would prefer not to have to divide my labours in this way, but I feel trapped by the secondary sources upon which I draw.

of British industrial supremacy. Macfarlane has reminded us that 'extensive evidence of a cash economy is contained in thirteenth century treatises on estate management and accounting', and he goes on to observe: 'It would seem that already this was a society interpenetrated at the very lowest levels by the market and cash, by contractual relationships of a kind familiar from later history. . . . Production was often for exchange, not for use.'[3] Even in the long-settled areas of Kent, where the records of Canterbury Cathedral Priory allow a most detailed account of the monastic finances, R. A. L. Smith concluded that 'by the year 1314 the economy of the Kentish estates of Christ Church rested almost entirely upon a money-rent and wage-labour basis.'[4]

There was, of course, substantial variation from one part of the country to another. There was a contrast between the better-off labourers working their holdings but also supplementing their income with seasonal wage work, and the poor husbandmen, more obliged to turn to wage labour to support their families. By 1524 the proportion of these assessed on wages, rather than land and goods, was as high as two-thirds in some Devon parishes, but only about a fifth of some Leicestershire parishes — and even in the latter county, in some places the proportion was as high as 90 per cent. By and large, rural tenants with holdings of less than five acres had to augment their income by working as wage labourers, and one estimate suggests that 'in the Tudor and early Stuart period the labouring population probably formed about one quarter or one third of the entire population of the countryside.'[5]

By the end of the seventeenth century, much of England was still a country of labourers, cottagers, and paupers. By that time there was a growing army of landless labourers *entirely* dependent on wage labour, although, of course, England was still a country of small family farms with wage labour generally being undertaken only at peak periods. The Tudor and Stuart periods were characterized by a gradual reduction of grazing rights in common pasture and the reduction of other common rights, largely because of the enclosure movement. While in the fourteenth century wage labour meant freedom in contrast to serfdom, by the seventeenth century the situation was reversed. It was assumed by then that wages were supplementary to an agricultural holding and this had the effect of keeping them low: thus, those completely dependent on wage labour became synonymous with the poor. 'In such circumstances men fought desperately to avoid the abyss of wage labour', as Christopher Hill has remarked.[6] It has even been suggested that 'the falling standard of

[3] A. Macfarlane, *The Origins of English Individualism*, Basil Blackwell, Oxford, 1978, p. 152.
[4] R. A. L. Smith, *Canterbury Cathedral Priory*, Cambridge University Press, 1943, p. 125.
[5] A. Everitt, 'Farm labourers', in J. Thirsk (ed.) *The Agrarian History of England*, vol. IV, *1500-1640*, Cambridge University Press, 1967, p. 398.
[6] C. Hill, 'Potage for free born Englishmen: Attitudes to wage labour in the sixteenth and

living of wage labourers in the sixteenth and early seventeenth centuries may have led to differences in physical appearance — a greater incidence of rickets among workers' children and an earlier loss of teeth in adults.'[7]

Wage labourers in industry or agriculture were members of an outcaste class, likely to be conscripted for overseas service in the army or navy. So bad was their situation that even the radical Levellers would have excluded them from the franchise, since they had ceased to be 'freeborn Englishmen': they had become economically dependent on others. The radicals of the Civil War were not struggling for landless labourers. Oliver Cromwell thought it 'was absurd that "men that have no interest but the interest of breathing" should have voices in elections'.[8] Yet by the end of the century wage labourers were probably a majority of the population. It is not surprising that men and women hated going into factories in the eighteenth century.

The early factories were, in fact, largely worked either by pauper children and women, or by Welshmen, Irishmen and Scots. . . . To accept a merely wage status in the factories was a surrender of one's birthright, a loss of independence, security, liberty. 'It takes centuries', observed Marx, ''ere the "free" labourer, thanks to the development of capitalist production, agrees, i.e. is compelled by social conditions, to sell the whole of his active life, his very capacity for work, for the price of the necessaries of life, his birthright for a mess of pottage.'[9]

Resistance to the Time Disciplines of Wage Labour

Edward Thompson, in his classic essay 'Time, work discipline and industrial capitalism',[10] notes that in the seventeenth and eighteenth centuries there was, typically, a considerable irregularity of labour patterns and even 'in the early development of manufacturing industry many mixed occupations survived: Cornish tinners who also took a hand in the pilchard fishing; Northern lead miners who were also smallholders; the village craftsmen who turned their hands to various jobs in building, carting, joining; the domestic workers who left their work for the harvest; the Pennine small farmer/weaver.'[11] According to Thompson, 'the work pattern was one of alternate bouts of intense labour and of idleness, wherever men were in control of their working lives',[12] and he

---

seventeenth centuries', in C. H. Fernstein (ed.), *Socialism, Capitalism and Economic Growth*, Cambridge University Press, 1967, p. 340.
[7] Ibid.
[8] Ibid., p. 343.
[9] Ibid., pp. 349-50.
[10] E. P. Thompson, 'Time, work discipline and industrial capitalism', *Past and Present*, 38, 1967, pp. 56-97.
[11] Ibid., p. 71.
[12] Ibid., p. 73.

goes on to wonder whether, since this is still the pattern for artists, writers and, perhaps, students, it might not be a 'natural' human work rhythm. Be that as it may, Thompson is able to document the imposition of a time discipline, both in school and factory, that 'filled the day' and, through the structuring of time, controlled children and workers alike.

William Temple, when advocating, in 1770, that poor children be sent at the age of four to work houses where they should be employed in manufacture and given two hours' schooling a day, was explicit about the socializing influence of the process: 'There is considerable use in their being, somehow or other, constantly employed at least twelve hours a day, whether they earn their living or not; for by these means we hope that the rising generation will be so habituated to constant employment that it would at length prove agreeable and entertaining to them . . . .'[13]

It does, indeed, seem a great irony that this attack upon the traditional working habits of the people, initially so vigorously resisted, should have become so widely accepted that disorientation and stress follow from the withdrawal from the time disciplines of wage labour. This appears to be the case even when payments from the state are greater in unemployment than had been previously earned in employment.[14] Not only has wage labour become time-disciplined, but the contractual relationship has also become largely depersonalized. Until relatively modern times, the relationship between servant and master imposed far wider responsibilities on both partners than those of merely providing or discharging employment. In the Middle Ages, the old tradition of work as a social responsibility still survived, and even as late as 1614 a rough waller, presumably self-employed, was nevertheless presented at the Quarter Sessions for going out of North Riding 'into other cuntryes to worke in sommer so as his neighboures cannot have his worke in hay-time and harvest'.[15] In general, it seems that labour services were extremely unpopular and that manorial overseers had to carry a stick; yet is also unclear whether the myth of the happy medieval craftsman has much substance: as K. Thomas remarks, 'There were strikes in thirteenth century France and bad industrial relations everywhere.'[16] The inhabitants of the village of Myddle in Shropshire, about whom we know a great deal in the late seventeenth century, seem remarkably like rural workers three hundred years later, except that perhaps the men and women of Myddle had a greater capacity for drinking strong ale.[17]

[13] Cited in Thompson, 'Time, work discipline and industrial capitalism', p. 84.
[14] One cannot help noticing that a slogan demanding 'the right to work', if that implies time-ruled wage labour, is also demanding at least to some degree the right to be dominated.
[15] K. Thomas, 'Work and leisure in pre-industrial society', *Past and Present*, 29, 1964.
[16] Ibid., p. 55.
[17] D. G. Hey, *An English Rural Community*, Leicester University Press, 1974.

Whether we are concerned with agricultural or industrial wage labour in early industrial England, it was certainly seen as a distinct activity, and people did less of it if they could. Douglas Reid's case study of attitudes to work in Birmingham from 1776 to 1876 provides some illuminating insights. The custom of Saint Monday epitomized the lack of work discipline which carried on into the middle of the nineteenth century in that area:

The prime supporters of Saint Monday were the better paid. High piece rates could provide good wages for skilled men, but they often elected to take a moderate wage and extensive leisure. Tuesdays, and even Wednesdays, were sometimes their holidays. For such 'playing away' followed not merely from weekend drinking but from deeply held traditional attitudes towards a potential surplus of wages: 'the men . . . [are] regulated by the expense of their families, and their necessities; it is very well known that they will not go further than necessity prompts them, many of them'. Even 'the lowest class' of workmen who received 'the second rate wages' would try to observe the custom.[18]

D. A. Reid describes the continuing battle in the early nineteenth century between the capitalist wanting the most efficient employment of his investment and the worker attempting to defend his way of life. Sometimes the Birmingham employers had to resort to lock-outs to kill Saint Monday. One company adopted a more contemporary tactic, as its manager confessed to the Children's Employment Commission in 1862: 'It is a pity that females should work in factories at all, as it interferes with their proper life, the domestic. They are, however, very useful. . . . Indeed, we have employed them on a branch of work which was formerly done by men because the latter were so much more difficult to keep steady at their work.'[19]

According to Reid, the decline of Saint Monday was more to do with the workers' raised aspirations for housing and travel than with the employers' demand for work discipline. The growth of consumption provided the most effective motor of change. It is unclear whether men and women were equally opposed to the expansion of the work discipline, or whether either or both readily accepted the mores of expanding personal consumption.

The question of the internalization of the work disciplines of industrial capitalism is highly contentious. Industrial conflict, which is said to relate to the length of tea breaks or the access to and availability of fringe facilities, may well reflect, at a deeper level, the tensions of resistance. The suggestion that young people do not now have the same commitment to the work ethic that may still be present in their parents may again indicate

[18] D. A. Reid, 'The decline of Saint Monday 1766-1876', *Past and Present*, 71, 1976, pp. 78–9.
[19] Ibid., p. 90.

how easily and quickly work disciplines may be lost if they are not both inculcated at an early age and regularly reinforced. If Reid is correct in claiming that personal consumption was the key element leading to a form of accommodation between capital and labour, then this provides an independent 'cultural' motor for social change. Critics would claim that this so-called independent motor was more a product of the manipulations of the capitalist market. Either way, there is an important issue to explore: if people can develop new cultural practices endogenously, then presumably they can do so again when the pattern of work is once more being restructured and renegotiated. If, on the other hand, they are easily manipulated by capitalist commercial interests, they may be equally easily manipulated by more progressive and altruistic interventions.

Less controversially, it is clear that the process of incorporation into the disciplines of industrial capitalism proceeded very unevenly. Some industries and some parts of the country were much less deeply affected. Pre-capitalist attitudes and practices continued. This is particularly well shown in the so-called secondary labour market: those engaged in seasonal employment, or who expect to move between jobs relatively frequently, are following the practices of pre-eighteenth-century wage labourers more closely than their contemporaries in traditional highly unionized manufacturing industries.

From By-employments to Occupational Easements

Ordinary English people have traditionally had all kinds of possibilities for acquiring extra resources to help them to get by more easily, given the uncertainties and irregularities of wage labour. Grazing rights on commons were, of course, widespread; but there were also privileges of access to woodland for timber, to provide the basic structure for their dwellings or to make fences and hurdles; other wood, and coal from certain mines, were available for cooking and heating. Rabbits, hares, fish, pigeons and a mass of wild nuts, berries and herbs were there to be caught or collected. Customary rights were regulated by village by-laws and manorial customs. In the sixteenth and seventeenth centuries, 'the labourers' rights of common formed part of a carefully integrated economy, whose balance could rarely be altered without serious consequences for the commoners themselves.'[20] According to A. Everitt, these common rights and privileges provided 'a sense of hope and independence' among the ordinary working people. They could build and repair their houses themselves using communal raw materials and household labour. Depending on the area, stone was available from certain quarries or loam and sand were available for bricks.

[20] Everitt, 'Farm labourers', p. 405.

Of equal, if not greater, significance during Tudor and Stuart times was the widespread incidence of secondary occupations or by-employments. Detailed studies of probate inventories show that many agricultural workers were engaged in some other industry or craft and, conversely, craftsmen were also engaged in agriculture. 'Of those labourers wealthy enough to leave an inventory, nearly two-thirds took up some kind of by-industry.'[21] These were mostly either woodland-based crafts or the spinning and weaving of flax, hemp or wool. Depending on the local opportunity structure, the proportion engaged in by-employments varied across the country. 'In Hertfordshire, where labourers often engaged in two or three employments at once, they were better off than in almost any other county.'[22] These extra employments provided the cash to pay the rent and provided a cushion against periodic unemployment. In an analysis of the probate inventories of carpenters between 1550 and 1650, it has been shown that nearly all had some form of by-employment; some had mills, one was a pawnbroker, others had shops or owned a boat. All of the sample of sixty rural carpenters in Lincolnshire and all but one of the twenty-two rural carpenters in the North West produced for the market, at least to some extent. Most craftsmen in the building industry would get part at least of their income from the garden or small plot of land that they cultivated.[23] As Everitt notes, 'the number and variety of local crafts, often highly specialized and recondite, was legion.'[24]

Up to the eighteenth century, therefore, work was carried out by *households* and was a combination of self-provisioning subsistence, wage labour and by-employment. Regular, full-time employment at a single job was exceptional in the eighteenth century, although in the Royal Dockyards like Chatham and Sheerness it was becoming more normal. Under these circumstances, it made little sense to focus on occupational categories, since people were typically engaged in a variety of tasks. 'It is better to speak of the work itself — farm labour, weaving, housewifery — and to try to understand how such work contributed to a family's living. Moreover, labour of any kind was rooted in a particular local economy and derived much of its character from the specific opportunities and limitations of the local environment; and in the eighteenth century there was an immense diversity of local economies.'[25]

The crucial point about work in England on the eve of the great expansion of industrialism was its *diversity*. All kinds of work were needed in order for the household to get by. As R. W. Malcolmson

[21] Ibid., p. 425.
[22] Ibid., p. 429.
[23] D. Woodward, 'Wage rates and living standards in pre-industrial England', *Past and Present*, 91, 1981, pp. 28-46.
[24] Everitt, 'Farm labourers', p. 427.
[25] R.W. Malcolmson, *Life and Labour in England 1700-1780*, Hutchinson, London, 1981, p. 23.

remarks in his excellent account of *Life and Labour in England 1700-1780*, 'the viability of the household economy was the crucial priority in life.'[26] Common rights, regular wage labour and domestic production or self-provisioning were all essential elements in a household work strategy. Even those who survived largely on wage labour would be engaged in it for only part of the time: most men were hired for less than 250 days in a year. Underemployment and low wages in agriculture provided the essential encouragement for the putting-out system.

Typically, there was an *economy of dual occupations* throughout much of rural England. Metal workers in south Yorkshire and the West Midlands in the early eighteenth century were also part-time farmers, and in rural south Lancashire families frequently combined small-scale farming with textile work. Indeed, the term 'yeoman' in the latter area often indicated 'a landholder who divided his time between farming and weaving'.[27] In the clay and heath regions of Dorset, small farmers might be occupied in making ropes or nets, tanning, glove-making or the quarrying of stone. In Cornwall, miners worked in the pilchard fishery during the peak autumn season. In Kent the farm labourers of Thanet spent the intervals between the autumn and spring sowings and the summer harvests in their boats.

These by-employments strengthened the position of working people: landowners wanted a docile and dependent workforce and resented any interference or competition from alternative employment. However, occupations that were directed mainly towards women and children presented less of a threat, and merchant manufacturers were able to recruit underemployed women more readily. In parts of southern Bedfordshire and north Hertfordshire, the workforce in the straw-plaiting industry was made up almost entirely of women and children.

Diversity, therefore, was the norm — diversity in occupations, in opportunities for by-employment, in access to common grazing, wild game or fishing and in the particular mix of activities in specific households. Self-sufficiency reduced the need for reliance on waged labour, and most families were able to get a modest living outside the economic arena of contractual wage payments. Certainly, the 'family economy was not normally centred around a single breadwinner: rather, it was assumed that the family's sustenance would depend on the productive contributions of all its members, each of whom helped to sustain the whole. A wife was always a working woman.'[28]

A common complaint of employers in the eighteenth century was that employees persistently embezzled materials. However, since the idea of an exclusive money wage as the main household resource was developing

[26] Ibid., p. 23.
[27] Ibid., p. 39.
[28] Ibid., p. 57.

only very slowly in the eighteenth century, much of what was called embezzlement was a product of a process of change from a time when money formed simply a part, albeit a substantial part, of the payment, to a situation where the sole payment was in money.[29]

As J. Rule remarks, the use of these specific colloquialisms in such practices, instead of some general term such as 'pinching' or 'nicking', suggests a different view of legitimacy. All occupations have traditionally had their easements: those taking part would no more think of themselves as criminals than would a civil servant using a departmental envelope to send a personal letter or the police superintendent calling his wife on the office phone.

Underemployment and Getting By

'Full employment' is not a simple notion to define. It would be especially difficult if it involved the provision of suitable work to match the skills and capacities of all the men and women who seek it. Such a situation has never existed in Britain. The only time that British society has come fairly close to a period of full employment was for a brief two decades in the middle of the twentieth century: historically, to be unemployed for a period was the normal experience of working people. In the mid-nineteenth century, Mayhew estimated that only about a third of the labouring people in the country were fully employed, another third were partially employed, and the remaining third totally unemployed. Unemployment was very often simply the result of bad weather. 'Wet days deprived thousands of bricklayers, painters, agricultural labourers and street sellers of their means of livelihood. An easterly wind prevailing for a few days spelled no work for 20,000 dock labourers in the Port of London.'[30] There were busy seasons and slack seasons in most trades — owing partly to the weather and also to fashion. Most of those engaged in the clothing trade or in the manufacture of boots and shoes had a seasonal pattern to their work.

The very idea of unemployment as a social and economic problem did not emerge until the 1890s, as J. A. Garraty has shown:

[29] In one analysis of this process it was remarked: 'Bugging to the hatter, cabbage to the tailor, blue pigeon flying to plumbers and glaziers, chippings to shipwrights, sweepings to porters, red sailyard docking to navy yard workers, fints and thrums to weavers, vails to servants, privileges to west country clothiers, bontages to Scottish agricultural workers, scrappings and naxers to coopers, wastages to framework knitters, in all these the eighteenth century labourer appropriated part of his product or a part of the materials of his labour' (quoted in J. Rule, *The Experience of Labour in the Eighteenth Century*, Croom Helm, London, 1981, p. 125). See also Jason Ditton, 'Perks, pilferage and the fiddle: The historical structure of invisible wages', *Theory and Society*, 4, 1977, pp. 1-38.
[30] J. F. C. Harrison, *The Early Victorians 1832-1851*, Weidenfeld and Nicolson, London, 1971, p. 49.

In 1894 an English civil servant, Geoffrey Drage, prefaced his study of *The Unemployed* with the sentence: 'As far as I am aware, no attempt has yet been made in any country to deal comprehensively with the question of the unemployed.' [Then,] . . . Suddenly unemployment had become a burning issue; books and articles and the reports of government legislation began to come out in ever-larger numbers.[31]

As E. J. Hobsbawm has remarked, it was 'underemployment rather than cessation of work' that was the problem for most trades.[32] It has been suggested, too, that 'there is substantial evidence to indicate that, until about the end of the century, conditions of work and subsistence persisted which mitigated the bare fact of unemployment and modified its significance in the lives of the workers.'[33] This may or may not be so: it is very hard to come to a balanced assessment. Thomas Wright's account of the Isle of Dogs in the 1860s presents, perhaps, a more widely applicable set of circumstances. When there was what was known as 'a slap of dull trade' in the shipbuilding business, there came a time when:

it becomes evident even to the most hopeful that things will be worse before they are better, the unemployed islanders naturally lose heart and begin to look anxious and careworn. Their little savings, however carefully handled, are soon expended, and small shopkeepers, however long-suffering, cannot go on giving credit for ever. The time inevitably comes when a little ready money *must* be raised; and then spare clothing and articles of furniture are parted with; next, necessary clothing, bedding and furniture have to go, and want and misery sit down in the once comfortable home. When reduced to this strait, those who have friends able and willing to give them shelter, go to those friends. Many of the Clyde men return to Scotland, and numbers of the Lancashire and Staffordshire operatives tramp down home, where — if, as is generally the case with the iron trade mechanics of those counties, they can turn their hand to general work — they often find employment. But for the islanders who have not these resources, there is nothing left but to 'hang on'. They manage to live, as they say to themselves, 'God knows how'.[34]

This acute precariousness of existence described by Wright, which followed from complete dependence on wage labour for a family's livelihood, related to well-established craftsmen in an established industry. Most workers, as Mayhew recognized, were much more 'casualized'; this was especially the case for women.

[31] Quoted in J. A. Garraty, *Unemployment in History*, Harper and Row, New York and London, 1978, p. 121.

[32] E. J. Hobsbawm, 'The British standard of living 1790-1850', in E. J. Hobsbawm (ed.), *Labouring Men*, Weidenfeld and Nicolson, London, pp. 72-82.

[33] K. Kumar, 'Unemployment as a problem'.

[34] T. Wright (alias A journeyman engineer), *Some Habits and Customs of the Working Classes*, Tinsley Brothers, London, 1867, pp. 258-9.

Most women were casual workers in the sense that their employment was irregular, or seasonal, or both, . . . so much women's work tended to be the sort that was easy to pick up or put down — washing or mangling for instance, cleaning, folding, packing, stitching and sewing. It was for similar reasons that married women sought employment near their husband's work. The location of the man's trade determined the family home.[35]

Our knowledge of life and labour is much greater for the period from the end of the nineteenth century, which can be tapped by oral history. It is clear that in some parts of the country people developed survival strategies, which enabled them to cope with periods in which there was very little wage labour available. One such area was Headington Quarry near Oxford, which is the subject of a particularly fine study by Raphael Samuel. He sees it as one of the 'dark corners of the Kingdom', that was not fully colonized by the expanding capitalism. For people in such villages — and also, as we shall see, in parts of some cities — employment was characteristically irregular. Yet, despite this marginal situation, 'subsistence never gave out, however severe the season, nor was charity ever called upon to take its place.'[36] Samuel describes in detail the various coping strategies adopted by the Quarry people, who used kinship ties extensively as support networks: people kept a few chickens or a couple of pigs, horses grazed by the roadside, and many men got extra money by using a horse and cart for road haulage. Trading activity in the village was diffused and nearly everyone had second or third jobs:

Businesses in Quarry — like other forms of livelihood — were usually made up of a mix of different activities. Harry Coleman, the blacksmith, for instance, kept a pigyard for speculative breeding, and a bacon shop (later turned into a café) for the sale of hogs' puddings; he was also 'a bit of a saddlemaker'. The Corby brothers, wheelwrights, also made coffins, kept cows and sold milk at their house; they added another string to their bow by acting as undertakers at village funerals; and yet another by shoeing horses. Retail businesses were usually run in tandem with other activities rather than as a single-minded pursuit. William Coppock, the grocer, for instance, was also a fruit grower with a well-protected orchard behind his home, grazed his cow on Haines's Field, and had a cowshed and a little dairy by his shop. . . .[37]

Samuel's account is extensive and it would be possible to quote at much greater length. Overwhelmingly, he documents the importance of being self-employed — at all social levels and in all categories of skills. But

[35] S. Alexander, 'Women's work in nineteenth-century London: A study of the years 1820-1850', in J. Mitchell and A. Oakley (eds) *The Rights and Wrongs of Women*, Penguin Books, Harmondsworth, 1976, p. 97.
[36] R. Samuel, ' "Quarry roughs": life and labour in Headington Quarry, 1860–1920. An essay in oral history', in R. Samuel (ed.), *Village Life and Labour*, Routledge and Kegan Paul, London, 1975, p. 227.
[37] Ibid., p. 232.

being self-employed was rarely a full-time occupation in a particular trade. Many would also work for wages but would, as they put it, make a 'bit of a livelihood' on their own. The ordinary working man was not tied to a particular master or to a particular trade: 'his employments were often short-lived, and his prospects, from month to month, precarious. But he enjoyed an element of real personal freedom in his work.'[38]

Typically, in this period before the First World War, men would engage in a variety of jobs during any one year, often doing more than one job at a time. Such men would work reasonably regularly but it would be in a variety of contexts. They would, as it were, fit in a bit of work for themselves with work for various employers. Farm work would be done when there was a short-term need for extra labour — as at mowing or harvest time — when men would 'get an extra bob or two'. In the building industry, despite the demands from Oxford colleges, permanent jobs simply did not exist — even with the larger firms. When a given job was finished, that was it: regular unemployment was the norm — what the building industry workforce referred to as 'being a gentleman' for a spell. Seasonal work was accepted as an inevitable part of life: frost nipped off the painters and bricklayers, who were habitually on the look-out for work. Men got accustomed to travelling some distance in order to find employment: when they were some distance away they would stay during the week, returning to the Quarry at the weekend. In the Oxford building trade, Samuel notes, a man 'wasn't a tradesman until he had been to London'.[39]

The pattern changed radically after the First World War. Men left, as they did from every town and village in the country, and very often did not return. The self-provisioning for food and fuel declined in favour of formal purchasing from shopkeepers and dealers: the balance between 'traditional' kinds of work and 'modern' kinds of work was fundamentally changed. Regular employment became available at the Cowley motor works; regular buses enabled school leavers to find employment in Oxford; the local brickyards and stone pits closed as machine-made bricks were introduced. The waste land and allotment ground was lost to speculative house building — a real loss of an important resource in the work of getting by — and gardens and sheds no longer housed laundries and pigs. So, in the 1920s, capitalism closed in: men clocked in in the mornings and took home their weekly wages. 'Women no longer worked together in family-based gangs, and instead of having to produce their subsistence, they could buy it in the shops.'[40]

It would be easy to dismiss Samuel's account as a rural oddity out of phase with the general development of capitalist penetration, although

[38] Ibid., p. 236.
[39] Ibid., p. 240.
[40] Ibid., p. 243.

this same style of work has continued up to the present in the Isle of Sheppey and probably in many other places as well. However, before coming to the last twenty years, it is useful to consider one further account, which is of Campbell Road in Finsbury Park in the 1930s, so vividly recreated by Jerry White, largely through interviewing people who were living there at the time. He describes a 'rough' population existing outside regular employment — and, indeed, outside wage labour of any kind. 'Their families had lived for generations by working at odd jobs here and there, and clawing out a living by economic enterprise which counted its profits in halfpennies and farthings.'[41]

People spent their lives in casual and irregular employment; their links with the labour demands of a capitalist economy were, White remarks, fragile. An example of such a style was a man born in 1902, who left school when he was 14 to help push out barrel organs and to be a totter. He always came back 'to working with a barrow and living on his wits when he was bored or laid off. . . . He worked as a trench-digger, shop boy, machine-minder in a battery factory, horse van driver, tar block cleaner, hod carrier, brush hand, and general business labourer. When he left the army after the last war he stayed at a Salvation Army hostel for a time, hired a barrow again and collected cardboard from shops.'[42]

White describes a very unstable and rumbustious community resulting largely from the inhabitants' loose relationships to the disciplines of wage labour. Some of the people there had no links at all with the world of wage labour. White refers to 'an older, freer tradition in the space between town and country' inhabited by gypsies and other travellers. Such people consciously developed a life style free from the domination of the time disciplines of industrial capitalism. The actual employment available to them would always be the most physically demanding and mind-numbing. Alternative ways of getting by, however illegitimate and unreliable, appeared more attractive. So such people learned to live off their wits, 'scratching out a living in the gaps left by capital'.[43] White describes the economy of Campbell Road in graphic detail: there always seemed to be ways of eking out a few coppers, even in the depths of the inter-war depression. Totters and rag-and-bone men and women in the street spread their economic influence over surrounding streets and to a degree helped to develop a safety net for those not in employment. A large number of the houses were owned or managed by people living in the street who employed others as casual labourers to keep these properties maintained. The shops on the street gave credit as, too, did the street's moneylenders. These landlords, shopkeepers and moneylenders

---

[41] J. White, 'Campbell Bunk: A lumpen community in London between the wars', *History Workshop Journal*, 8, 1979, p. 14.
[42] Ibid., p. 15.
[43] Ibid., p. 18.

3 (Above) The Labourer's Welcome
by Joseph Clarke. A late nineteenth century
middle-class woman as an object in the
home. *4 (Right)* A woman worker in the
turnip fields, Herefordshire. Photograph by
Sir George Clausen, *c.*1880. To see the
working-class woman as being in any way
'liberated' would be simplistic.

5 Women gathering driftwood on Whitby beach: it is not known whether
this by-employment was specifically a woman's task. Photograph by Frank
Meadow Sutcliffe, 1853–1941.

6 *(Above)*   The world of Lucy Luck (see page 70): child plaiters at Titmore Green near Stevenage.

7 *(Below)*   Kit and Betty Metcalfe knitting stockings outside their cottage at Gayle in the North Riding of Yorkshire, around 1900. They specialized in stockings for cyclists, Kit knitting the fancy tops while his wife did the rest.

8 Stanley Spencer's celebration of washing up – one of a series of domestic
scenes which he painted in 1935.

As wage labour grew over that period of two hundred years, so other forms of customary work declined, with one important exception: women's work inside the home expanded. Much of women's self-provisioning work done outside the home, such as rearing poultry and growing herbs and vegetables, either did not get done or was left to men who had allotments. This shift of the women into the home, doubly dependent on the wages of a male chief earner and the local shops and public services, took place at different rates among different social categories and in different parts of the country. In some towns women continued to keep hens and geese well into the twentieth century; in some rural areas the pattern has barely changed.

It is quite possible to describe households in the 1980s where the mix of work is broadly the same as it was in the thirteenth century. The man may hold some form of employment and so, too, may his wife and this may be seasonal and highly irregular. In East Kent, women pick fruit or vegetables in the summer and autumn to get more money in preparation for the winter, much as they have done for centuries. Now, instead of buying cloth or leather, they may buy their children's school uniform or some extra toys at Christmas. People still keep hens, have allotments and poach rabbits and pheasants. They still go to the local markets with honey from their hives or cherries from their trees that they have picked themselves. In the case studies in Appendix 2, a pattern is described that has a long historical pedigree. People work to get money to get by without necessarily having regular employment. There are anecdotes everywhere of people getting money in unrecorded ways: rarely are such anecdotes put into the context of a complete household work strategy. The rural household where the man is unemployed or 'early retired' but spends his time doing odd jobs for neighbours, supplying the household with vegetables and the occasional rabbit, may also include his wife earning regularly as a domestic cleaner, his son doing various labouring jobs from time to time and also, perhaps, doing a paper round or helping in a local garage. His daughter may also be a cleaner — possibly in the local pub — and in addition may help out in a shop at holiday periods and other busy times. 'Earning an extra bob or two' is still a current phrase. No member of the household is permanently bound by the rigid disciplines of wage labour, but some money has to be earned on a more or less regular basis.

No one would pretend that this casualized labour force is particularly privileged. It still flourishes particularly in holiday areas, where services and goods can be sold to people with money to spend, who want 'bed and breakfast', home-made jam, a row in a boat, fresh strawberries, seafood in the street and, of course, endless cups of tea. The man at a Kent seaside town who bought a ton and a half of misshapen boiled sweets — the product of a firm's misplaced confidence in youngsters taken on under a government-sponsored training scheme — will have a stall every week at the Sunday market throughout the summer, making a profit of £50 a day. All this is little different from the street traders of eighteen or even fourteenth-century London.

Contemporary Incapacitation:
The Result of Over-dependence on Wage Labour

What is unusual, exceptional and probably now in lasting decline is a situation where households in many towns are entirely dependent for regular wage labour on one or two large employers. The industrial town of the Midlands or North of England, divided like a model town plan into the shopping centre, the factory zone at one side and the residential areas at the other, is a fossil marking a particular stage in the development of industrial capitalism. Opportunities for by-employment or occupational easements may be strictly limited. The only public land is likely to be parks with rules and open space near high-rise housing on which no ball games are allowed and certainly no goats, chickens or geese. Since most of the houses may still belong to the local authority, there is little scope for home improvement, and even keeping rabbits in the back garden may be either forbidden or too risky, given the importance of maintaining good relations with neighbours.

Again, because it has been mainly an industrial town, there is likely to be very little alternative employment in the service sector. Washing is done in washing machines or at the laundrette and not by local laundresses; there is negligible scope for living off private rented accommodation. Private taxis are expensive, as is the infrequent bus service connecting the housing estates to the town centre. People are caught in a number of traps. After 6 p.m. only the pubs, a few take-away food or hamburger bars and the off-licence are open. It is probably unsafe to cycle round the town as new roads to speed the circulation of traffic do just that. In such an environment, men and women have had their capacity to do other forms of work whittled down so far that even repairing a car in the street is a cause for comment.

In retrospect, the years when it was said they never had it so good, in the period of recovery after the Second World War, were the years of incapacitation. The messy back streets with their potential premises for small workshops were knocked down as part of slum clearance. The factories were rebuilt and rationalized. The unions got stronger and led their members to believe that collective solidaristic action would lead to a permanent position in the rising escalator of incomes. Men were pulled out of their households and, as it were, put in the block votes with other men in an all-male fraternity. It was held to be a victory when overtime was 'won', keeping the men away from home when their wives were at their busiest feeding the children and putting them to bed. Those in these expanding and flourishing unions and factories were the affluent workers. They were also those most likely to want to own their own homes — so when the factory closed or laid them off, they had little to fall back on and still had a large mortgage to pay. The physical and social infrastructure of the post-war period was developed on an assumption of smooth and continuing growth. Households with a limited and narrow view of work as factory employment were exactly as employers in the 1950s and 1960s most liked them to be. Completely socialized to the time and work disciplines of industrial capitalism, they had, perhaps for the first time in English history, lost the means of getting by with a household work strategy.

Happily, this account is overdrawn and does not apply generally across the British Isles: various alternative ways of getting by still exist, and the period of incapacitation was not, perhaps, long enough to do as much damage as it might have done. Nevertheless, many of the politicians, social scientists and journalists writing in the 1980s and 1990s grew up in this atypical period, providing them with misleading personal experience. Getting back to the way it was in the 1950s and 1960s would be as irrelevant as putting all women back to the equally atypical pattern of the 1920s and 1930s. It cannot be sufficiently stressed that a full understanding of the nature of work within a society requires a longer historical perspective than a mere thirty years.

Men's Work inside the Household

The attempt to provide a more all-embracing view of work is frustrated both by conventional attitudes and scarcity of data — the former sometimes being the cause of the latter. The evidence is exceptionally sparse on the domestic work of men.[47] How far, for example, did ordinary working men in pre-industrial England concern themselves with caring for children? When Sir Thomas More wrote Latin verses for his children in 1517, when they were still young, he prefaced his work with some remarks which suggest a fond and doting father:

It is not so strange that I love you with my whole heart, for being a father is not the tie which can be ignored. Nature in her wisdom has attached the parent to the

---

[47] A very interesting study, published too late to be taken into account in this chapter, is that by Linda A. Pollock, *Forgotten Children: Parent Child Relations from 1500-1900*, Cambridge University Press, 1983. However, even in this study, the heavy reliance on diaries skews the analysis towards the more literate and self-conscious. Nevertheless, Pollock has provided a formidable critique of the argument of Philippe Aries, *Centuries of Childhood*, Jonathon Cape, London, 1962.

child and bound them together with a Herculean knot . . . this tie is the reason why I regularly fed you cake and gave you ripe apples and pears. This tie is the reason why I used to dress you in silken garments and why I never could endure to hear you cry.[48]

However, the emphasis in this book is less on the wealthy, powerful and propertied and more on the ordinary men and women who comprise the majority of the population. There is a popular misconception that childhood was 'discovered' some two hundred years ago, fostered by such popular accounts as E. Shorter's *The Making of the Modern Family*. This argues, largely from material relating to France, that the nuclear family, based on affection, depended on the breakdown of traditional forms consequent upon the development of market capitalism around the year 1800. The evidence of Ralph Josselin's diary in the seventeenth century casts doubt on this view. As has been mentioned, Josselin was not a particularly wealthy person, and there is no reason to suppose that this seventeenth-century clergyman was exceptional. Macfarlane suggests that Josselin and his wife shared much of the work in and around the house. Certainly, they helped one another in the farm work. For example, in August 1644 Josselin described how '"when my wife and I pulling down a tree with a rope with our pulling, all fell together, but no hurt God be praised". In a situation where kinsfolk lived at a distance, and children left home at puberty, husband and wife were the effective economic producers and depended on one another's labours.'[49] Macfarlane suggests that all important decisions were jointly taken and 'Husband and wife seem to have shared, to a considerable extent, the task of rearing the children; their father's interests in them and in their progress is evident all through the Diary.'[50] Josselin took considerable interest in the health of his wife and children as they were born, and difficulties with breastfeeding, the ages at which they were weaned and the ages at which their first teeth were cut are all recorded. He complains about the disturbed nights when they are young as a result of their 'sudden cryings out in the forepart of the night', although it is not clear how often, if at all, it was Ralph Josselin who got up to quieten them. However, it does seem very unlikely that someone taking such a keen interest in the details of his wife's labour and delivery and the early physical development of his children would take no hand in their practical day-to-day care.

Clearly, it would be wrong to take one diary as sufficient evidence for fathers' involvement in child rearing in the seventeenth century; nevertheless, it is unlikely that the attitudes of a Puritan clergyman were less authoritarian and patriarchal than others, presumably not so strongly

---

[48] Quoted in C. Tomalin, *Parents and Children*, Oxford University Press, 1981.
[49] A. Macfarlane, *The Family Life of Ralph Josselin, A Seventeenth Century Clergyman*, Cambridge University Press, 1970, p. 109.
[50] Ibid.

influenced by Puritan ideology. Be that as it may, clearer evidence of men's involvement in child rearing and domestic work does not become available until a century or so later. It is very frustrating that one possible source — the 142 working-class autobiographies from 1790-1850 analysed by D. Vincent — should yield so little. Vincent does not consider that this reticence implies a lack of affection for the diarists' children. Rather, these working-class men, struggling to make sense of their own biographies, did not feel that the way they related to their children, or the work that they did around the home, was of much interest to their class or in understanding their own life history. There is a general tendency to sentimentalize their family life but also an understanding that for many people the sheer struggle to get by dominated their writing. Vincent quotes a cabinet maker, Henry Price: 'The Bread Winner has to be up and off early, and home late and too tired to be merry. His little ones are fast asleep. He gets a peep at them. God Bless them is his silent prayer. A look at the wife a painful one. What is the matter dear oh nothing. Poor Dear she has been hard at work too. Trying to earn a bit to keep them decent.'[51]

Such, clearly, was the conventional view of the 'little ones' and 'the wife'. However, by the end of the nineteenth century, in areas where well-paid employment for men was scarce, women took over as 'breadwinners'. As the factory inspectresses notes, 'it is no uncommon sight to find a man cleaning and sweeping, caring for the children and even putting them to bed on the evening when the women were engaged in the family washing.'[52] This attitude was said to be common in the northern textile towns like Preston or Dundee. Stella Davies describes her father, born in 1857, who left school when he was 12 and married when he was 20 and helped to bring up fifteen children of which ten survived to adulthood. He educated himself and became a committed Methodist. Mrs Davies remarks: 'My mother had not the intellectual capacity of my father nor his strength of character. . . . She was an affectionate wife and mother but was ill-equipped to deal with the problems presented by so large a family. My father "carried" the household, controlled the family purse and did a great deal of the shopping.'[53] The family had a very unstable career, as her father resigned from being the manager of a co-operative store, set himself up as a shopkeeper on his own account and rented a variety of premises in the Midlands. Inevitably, he had to spend much of his time in the shop: 'It was about this time that we acquired Fat Ellen, a maid-of-all-work who stayed with us for many years.'[54]

[51] D. Vincent, *Bread, Knowledge and Freedom*, Europa Publications, London, 1981, p. 55.
[52] Quoted in M. Hewitt, *Wives and Mothers in Victorian Industry*, Rockliff, London, 1958, p. 193.
[53] C. S. Davies (1963) *North Country Bred: A Working Class Family Chronicle*, Routledge and Kegan Paul, London, 1963, p. 53.
[54] Ibid., p. 56.

It is very unsatisfactory to have to rely on such scattered memories for an understanding of who did the work within the dwelling. It is conventionally assumed that the majority of ordinary working-class men in regular employment did virtually no domestic work when they were out for a long day. However, there is other evidence that should be considered. M. E. Loane, a district nurse, wrote an account of working-class life in 1908 which presented a very different view of the male breadwinner. She could not understand why 'the prejudice against him is so strong that all evidence in his favour is unread or misread', and goes on to argue very positively that 'there are really no bounds as to what a mere ordinary father will do — or do without — for the sake of his young children. To spend his half-holiday at the wash-tub, or to finish up his day's work with the hardest part of the house cleaning, is by no means unusual.'[55] On the other hand, there is no shortage of information about boorish and tyrannical behaviour by pig-headed and dominant men. Sons and daughters remember but excuse it by arguing that 'he had a lot to put up with.' Being the chief breadwinner and only earner, the father expected to be waited on; indeed, as one of the respondents in Paul Thompson's work on Edwardian oral history put it, 'It was illegal for a man even to use needle and cotton in those days. . . . A boy wasn't supposed to bake, he wasn't supposed to wash up, he wasn't supposed to make beds.'[56]

However, as Thompson goes on to point out, 'the truth is that in the privacy of their homes many working class husbands ignored the conventional prohibitions imposed by a male-dominated society. For probably a quarter marriage could be described as partnership.'[57] Even the traditional view of the miner getting his back scrubbed by his wife, or a neighbour if his wife or daughter wasn't there, and throwing his meal down to express his displeasure was almost certainly an overdrawn stereotype. Paul Thompson's respondents can again provide a very different picture:

One Longton wife who had been a cup sponger was married to a miner, but he would help with both house and children:

> I've seen him bath 'em. Seen him bath 'em, oh aye, when they were new. . . . He'd do the cooking perhaps — well he'd help with the cooking any road. Aye, and then he always used to make the beds. . . . Aye, and make the fires. Oh he wasn't a bad old stick!

In the countryside, where it had been normal for women as well as men to work as agricultural labourers until the late nineteenth century, there were also many

---

[55] M.E. Loane, *From Their Point of View*, Edward Arnold, London, 1908, pp. 147-8.
[56] P. Thompson, *The Edwardians*, Paladin Books, London, 1977, p. 85.
[57] Ibid.

adaptable husbands. A Wiltshire baker's assistant, for example, would 'do the dusting, polishing floors, do all that, do all the garden' although his wife did not work and had no children.[58]

This is important evidence, and Thompson suggests that the withdrawal of men from housework, like the exclusion of many women from paid employment, was a relatively recent tradition of the previous seventy or eighty years. Hence he concludes that 'the home-centred working class husband is certainly not a new phenomenon of the more affluent late twentieth century.'[59] Those men who ill-treated or attacked their wives received more public attention: the quiet and more gentle men kept their privacy and reserve and did not boast about their domestic work. Their wives would doubtless be aware that, in the conventions of the time, it was not considered manly to be seen working and cleaning and so said little to neighbours. Thomson's estimate that perhaps a quarter of all husbands were doing substantial domestic work before the First World War is probably the most precise statement than can be made.

By the middle of the twentieth century, G. Gorer claimed that 'there has been a marked change in the expectations of the help which a husband should properly give in a household, with the dividing line among those who were born in the first decade of this century or earlier.'[60] Gorer's data, based on a sample of 5,000 readers of *The People* newspaper, suggested that there was more dissatisfaction among middle-class wives that their husbands wouldn't help in the house than in the upper and lower sections of the working class.[61] These figures must be treated with extreme care, since levels of expectations would also vary between classes so Gorer was not truly comparing like with like. Nevertheless, it is certainly arguable that by the 1950s more universal expectations of joint conjugal role relations were spreading throughout the social hierarchy. In a discussion of the variations in conjugal normative behaviour, Elizabeth Bott, in a much-quoted study, remarked: 'One couple carried the idea of joint sharing of tasks to a point that almost denied the basic (*sic*!) division of labour between husband and wife.'[62]

Perhaps social scientists were more trapped in conventional thinking than they recognized. Certainly, J. Klein's review of the studies of family life between 1945 and 1965 relied almost entirely on an extended quotation from Richard Hoggart's *The Uses of Literacy* to support her statement that the older tradition was for men not to participate in

[58] Ibid., pp. 87-8.
[59] Ibid.
[60] G. Gorer, *Exploring English Character*, Cresset Press, London, 1955, p. 131.
[61] Ibid., Table 56.
[62] E. Bott, *Family and Social Network*, Tavistock, London, 1957, p. 198.

domestic duties.[63] This uncritical acceptance of what was 'normal' in the past now seems curiously unscholarly. The same approach was adopted by M. Young and P. Willmott in their study of the family in Bethnal Green;[64] hence they contrasted the more progressive 'younger husband of today' with a universal stereotype, no doubt widely shared, of men generally not doing domestic work or, if they did, seeing it as an exceptional favour. The work of oral historians makes us substantially doubt that stereotype.

[63] J. Klein, *Samples from English Cultures*, vol. I, Routledge and Kegan Paul, London, 1965, pp. 165-8.
[64] M. Young and P. Willmott, *Family and Kinship in East London*, Penguin, Harmondsworth, 1957.

3

Women, Work and Social Change

Patterns of women's work outside the home were given very little scholarly attention until about twenty-five years ago. The pioneering work of A. Clark and I. Pinchbeck encouraged only a few scholars to follow their lead. More recently, of course, there has been a rather breathless rush to catch up.[1] It is the historical divisions of academic labour that have led to the necessity for a separation between the last chapter and this as much as any intrinsic difference in the subject matter. But there are, of course, differences. An historical account of the changing patterns of female employment must consider different themes and issues from those that were raised in Chapter 2.

I do not intend to be comprehensive but rather to pick out certain themes on women's work practices. Although I recognize that this must be a partial view, I think it is important to emphasize the role of ideology in constraining the work practices and divisions of labour of women, both inside and outside the household. If the divisions of labour are changing, it is no bad thing to recognize that such change has been the normal pattern of things for the last two hundred years. It is unlikely that change in the pattern of work between men and women will cease or that some utopian steady-state situation will ever emerge. The complexity of the dialectic is too full of contradictions.[2] The directions of change can, however, be observed, and the chapter concludes with an attempt to assess the future prospects of ordinary working women in employment.

[1] See the valuable survey of this literature in M. Evans and D. Morgan, *Work on Women*, Tavistock, London, 1979.
[2] One of the irritating aspects of some recent writing on women's work and employment is that the gender of the author is made strongly intrusive. Thus, a male reader of a book written by a female in this style is made to feel excluded and somehow at fault. This assumption by some writers that all their readers will be of the same gender is a divisive aspect in scholarship which cannot be welcomed. There are, of course, appropriate outlets for political or polemical writing. Not that there is anything wrong in being conscious of one's biases or assumptions: some of the most distinguished Marxist historians, for example, make no secret of their allegiance. But they don't habitually address their readers with the comradely 'we', recognizing, wisely enough, that all their readers need not be Marxists — but admire them and pay attention to what they say none the less vigorously for that.

It will be assumed that readers wanting more detailed historical accounts of women's work will be able to use the sources cited: in some ways the literature on the ideology of women's work is richer and more theoretically structured than that available for a similar approach to the work of men.[3] However, the theme of this book is focused on the household with its forms of work and divisions of labour.

Women in Employment in the Nineteenth Century

It is not always recognized that women are more likely to be employed as factory workers in the mid-1980s than at any time in the past. Although it is true that, in the textile areas, women were employed in factories in the early nineteenth century, too much should not be made of this. The 1841 Census shows that, out of 1,382,000 factory workers, a mere 8,789 were women. Employment for women was strictly limited: most women operatives in Lancashire cotton mills in 1833 were between 16 and 21. Only 25 per cent of female cotton workers were married in 1841. The absolute number of women in textile manufacturing — wool, cotton, linen and silk — amounted to 184,709, indicating that most women involved in this industry were not employed in factories. Domestic servants, on the other hand, outnumbered factory workers by four to one. Again, these servants were almost entirely unmarried. As J. W. Scott and L. A. Tilly noted,[4] while by 1911 69 per cent of all single women were in employment, only 9.6 per cent of married women were thus engaged. As industrialization developed through the nineteenth century, fewer married women were in formal employment.

Perhaps the best way to view women's employment in the nineteenth century is as the employment of *daughters* but not mothers. Two-thirds of all domestic servants in England were daughters of rural labourers. The normal pattern in pre-industrial England was for daughters to contribute to their natal household in a positive and productive way, either in their own family of origin or from another household. Throughout much of the nineteenth century, therefore, Scott and Tilly argue that women's employment was in direct continuity with previous patterns: change in material conditions did not immediately lead to changes in values and behaviour. Rather, it was pre-industrial values that justified and supported the employment of young women in the nineteenth century: there was nothing new in terms of cultural patterns. Traditionally families had always sent their daughters out to take advantage of new opportunities.

[3] See, for example, J. A. Mathaei, *An Economic History of Women in America: Women's Work, the Sexual Division of Labour, and the Development of Capitalism*, Harvester Press, Brighton, 1982.
[4] J. W. Scott and L. A. Tilly, 'Women's work and the family in nineteenth century Europe', *Comparative Studies in Society and History*, 17(1), 1975, pp. 36-64.

The household work strategies of ordinary working people in the nineteenth century were, inevitably, very varied. In one recent attempt to give precision to the concept, J. C. Holley has documented two contrasting strategies in the manufacturing towns of the Scottish Borders in the mid-nineteenth century. Holley selected his sample from a paper mill and a woollen mill and matched the wagebooks with the household census. From this material he described contrasting and polarized household work strategies. The respectable family economy of the skilled workers was at one pole, with good rates of pay and a consequent higher standard of living. Holley estimated the total family income by adding up the earnings of individual family members, and then he divided this by a conventional rating of all individuals in the family. He showed that the head's income provided 57 per cent of all family income of skilled woollen workers, and 44 per cent among skilled paper workers. By contrast, the unskilled heads provided only about 30 per cent of their families' incomes.

Among the skilled workers no special strategy to survive was adopted when only the head provided income for the household. The families of the skilled workers could survive well enough on the 'family wage', and economic calculations could be made with reference to one person and his career prospects and opportunities. Skilled workers were likely to gain most by staying with the same firm and moving up its opportunity structure. 'While between 55 and 60 per cent of skilled workers had ten years or more service with the same employer, under a third of labourers worked as long.'[5] The poorer workers, on the other hand, were obliged to move to other areas to get through the poverty stage of their life cycle. These poorer labourers were porters and assistants to the skilled workers and they did the heavy manual work of loading and moving. Holley shows that about a half of labourers' families suffered from poverty before their children were 13 and old enough to work in the mills. Labourers' households, with their lower income from the 'chief earner', were more heavily dependent on married women working. However, the two main employers, the Cowans of Penicuit and the Ballantynes of Walkerburn, were strongly paternalistic and had a clear policy that excluded married women from work and confined them to the home to take care of children. The Manager of the Cowan Mill reported to the Children's Employment Commissioners in 1865: 'With a view to prevent the neglect of children in the home, we do not employ mothers of young children in our works, unless in the case of widows or women deserted by their husbands, or having husbands unable to earn a living.'[6]

So the household multiple earner strategy, essential for the low paid,

[5] J. C. Holley, 'The two family economies of industrialism: Factory workers in Victorian Scotland', *Journal of Family History*, 6(1), 1981, p. 60.
[6] Cited in ibid., p. 64.

was simply not possible in these small factory towns, and such households were obliged to migrate at a certain stage in their domestic cycle. These poorer families developed what Holley describes as an 'unrespectable life course' involving a more calculative and bargaining style of domestic strategy.

They changed employers and moved house more often than the higher paid: they probably sent their children to work while young, and expected the wife and mother of the family to work; and they shed their children as the economics of unemployment dictated. All this shows not that such families were heartless, or that they were immoral; on the contrary, it seems that they were following a well-understood alternative pattern, namely, the multiple earning family economy of the labouring poor.[7]

This so-called unrespectable pattern (as perceived by the respectable skilled workers) was evidently directly related to the proto-industrial family economy based on domestic outwork. The many-earners strategy was not a Victorian innovation; rather, as Holley suggests, industrial society *re*created the 'unrespectable family form'. Similar variations in family strategies have been reported for France in the nineteenth century.[8]

The fact that so few married women were in employment in the nineteenth century does not imply that they did not earn money and engage in productive activity in a variety of ways. S. Alexander[9] has documented the importance of such activities as taking in laundry and lodgers. As one of the great documenters of household work practices in the mid-nineteenth century, Frederic le Play, noted:

Like their rural counterparts, urban working-class women contributed to the family economy by tending vegetable gardens and raising animals — usually some pigs and hens — and marketing the surplus. Some women set up cafes in their homes, others sold the food and beverages they had prepared outside. A Sheffield knifemaker's wife prepared a fermented drink called 'pop' which she bottled and sold in summer to the inhabitants of the city.[10]

Le Play thought that women worked harder and in a more sustained fashion that men and he argued that they were better at running the family than men. Where the domestic sphere is important for the economic and

---

[7] Ibid., p. 66.
[8] L. A. Tilly, 'Individual lives and family strategies', *Journal of Family History*, Summer, 1979, pp. 137-52.
[9] S. Alexander, 'Women's work in nineteenth-century London: A study of the years 1820-1850', in J. Mitchell and A. Oakley (eds), *The Rights and Wrongs of Women*, Penguin Books, Harmondsworth, 1976.
[10] Quoted in Scott and Tilly, 'Women's work and the family'. This description seems to match very closely that relating to Rose in *Piers Plowman* (see note 12, Chapter 1).

social life of the family, wives' power will be greater. They were more likely to keep the household's accounts; they controlled the purse strings and were the chief buyer for the household. It was not until the 1890s in England that single working girls living at home kept some of the money they earned; generally they handed it all over to the family fund. 'Whether they worked outside the home or not, married women defined their role within the framework of the family economy. Married working-class women, in fact, seem almost an internal backwater of pre-industrial values within the working-class family.'[11] This can be illustrated very clearly in women's involvement in domestic industry: dressmakers, mostly working at home, outnumbered textile workers in England by nearly two to one as late as 1870. Women broadened the range of domestic manufacturing, leaving the formal labour force when they got married. Whether by taking in work or lodgers, or perhaps by selling formally through a shop or informally — in the way Le Play described above — women's work for money continued, even though they were not in formal employment.

In the nineteenth century the attitudes of ordinary working women to-wards employment were different from those of men: employment was seen as essentially temporary. Before marriage, as has been mentioned, women were most likely to be employed as domestic servants. This short time horizon — they knew they would not be doing similar employment after they got married — led to a lack of industrial activism and a strong preference for home or shop industry, where familial or friendly contacts could be maintained. This does much to explain the preference for servanthood over factory work. Between 1871 and 1891, women employed in factories grew by 20 per cent, whereas those in domestic service grew by 106 per cent.[12] Women appeared to be concerned more about the quality of the relationships they experienced at work than about the pay and working conditions. Despite generally bad conditions of service, women more often complained about their mistresses' behaviour: the most frequent reason for changing jobs was to get a better mistress. Even in factory work, the most common complaint by women at the turn of the century was not the working conditions but the ungraciousness of the foreman or forewoman. The continuation of this emphasis well into the twentieth century is seen by Patricia Branca as evidence that women saw employment as temporary in a way not possible for men.

Women's employment as factory workers forming a significant part of the workforce should be dated realistically from about 1870: they have a history of just over 100 years as full-time factory workers.

---

[11] Scott and Tilly, 'Women's work and the family', p. 148.
[12] P. Branca, 'A new perspective on women's work: A comparative typology', *Journal of Social History*, 9(2), 1975, p. 141.

Apart from domestic service, textiles, stitching and washing, there was little else open to women of any class before the final decades of the century. . . . The real origins of the 'emancipation of women' (in the modern sense of economic opportunity and independence) must be sought in the shifting balance of the occupational framework which began to emerge in the last quarter of the nineteenth century.[13]

Between 1891 and 1911, the female labour force in metal manufacturing expanded by 4 per cent per year, but overall there was hardly any change. In 1891 women comprised 21.5 per cent of the manufacturing labour force and in 1911, 23 per cent. From 1870 there was a rapid increase in women as service workers: by 1914 there were half a million female shop assistants and the growth of female clerical workers from 1871 to 1911 was 116 per cent. Branca claims that women were a more flexible and adaptable workforce, less resistant to the introduction of new technology because they had not committed themselves to a specific way of working. According to this position, working-class women, as a category, at no time made employment a primary means of identification in their lives. For women, domestic work was their first responsibility, and employment had to fit in with that: for men the reverse was the case. So women 'rejected it when it conflicted with family-centred goals and welcomed it when it could supplement not only earnings but also the diversity of personal experience. This may mean that their adaptation to industrialization was cleverer than that of men, for they minimized their psychological risks.'[14]

Branca's view has been challenged by Peter Stearns. In his exemplary study of working-class women in Britain from 1890 to 1914, he suggests that the psychological welfare of those involved in the factory labour force probably deteriorated at that time. 'The evidence is impressionistic and comes largely from male sources, but it suggests that there was at the turn of the century a surprisingly unhappy transition period for working-class women.'[15] One detailed account of the period is provided by Lady Bell in her study of the ironworkers of Middlesbrough, published in 1907. Here there was very little opportunity for women to engage in waged work and the struggle to get by was more than most women could manage.[16] 'The purpose of life was to endure, and there was no room for hope.'[17]

Employment outside the home, usually in factories, became the norm for working-class women in their late teens and early twenties, as we have

[13] E. Richards, 'Women in the British economy since about 1700: An interpretation', *History*, 59, 1974, pp. 349, 351.
[14] Branca, 'A new perspective'.
[15] P. N. Stearns, 'Working class women in Britain', in M. Vicinus (ed.), *Suffer and Be Still*, Bloomington, Indiana University Press, 1972, p. 103.
[16] H. Bell, *At The Works*, Thomas Nelson and Sons, London, 1907.
[17] Stearns, 'Working class women in Britain', p. 106.

seen, but the *total* number of women employed rose far less dramatically, more or less in line with the growth of population. This produced what Stearns describes as a 'virtual revolution' in the life style of working-class women *before* marriage. After marriage there was little change.[18] The working class were said to have absorbed much of the middle-class pedestal image of women, despite its evident inappropriateness.

Of particular importance, as far as women's position in the household economy is concerned, was the change in the system of the allocation of the family budget. Around 1900 there is a strong indication that, as wages advanced, men ceased to follow the traditional pattern of handing over their wage packet to their wives for family use. Instead, they put their wives on to a fixed allowance system and kept most of the increase for themselves. The economic role of the women in the household declined and they were more confined to the home. 'Small wonder that many wives slept late and let themselves go to seed.'[19] The period of inflation in the early years of this century impoverished poor households, particularly the women and children, more than might have been the case, because of the system of money allocation within the household. For those not in employment, betting was the only significant new interest.

Clearly, information about the economic activity and earnings of all household members is not very readily available for this period and, where it is, it needs to be interpreted in the context of local labour markets. James Treble has argued that, in the case of female casual employment, it is important to relate it to its male equivalent. If a woman's husband was paid below-subsistence wages, then she, too, would be compelled to take poorly paid employment in unskilled occupations, very often at home. Treble provides evidence from a number of distinct labour markets that home work was an essential element in a household survival strategy. In West Ham, for example, 'male workers are often dependent on the earnings of their wives and daughters at home to eke out their own irregular earnings.'[20] In Cambridge in the early 1900s, many families were kept going more by the earnings of wives, 'which are small but comparatively regular, than by the odd shillings brought in by the husband'.[21] And in Scotland in the same period, casually employed women moved readily from one occupation to

[18] 'The working class wife was not supposed to work, at least outside the home. To do so would offend her husband's manhood, for it would demonstrate his inability to provide for her. It was firmly established in working class culture that only the sick or the depraved sent their wives out to work, and indeed outside of the textile towns only women whose husbands were ill or injured or drunkards or otherwise unemployable normally worked' (Stearns, 'Working class women in Britain', p. 113).

[19] Ibid., p. 118.

quoted in J. H. Treble (ed.), *Urban Poverty in Britain 1830-1914*, Batsford/Academic Press, London, 1979, p. 70.

[21] H. Bosanquet (ed.), *Social Conditions in Provincial Towns* (publisher not known), 1912, p. 25; quoted in Treble, *Urban Poverty*, p. 71.

another: 'charwomen do fruit picking, fur-pullers go to "the herrings" and the "potatoes", ironers to the seaside, according to the season.'[22] In Cambridge, too, female college servants went fruit picking in the long vacation, and those who lost their jobs in mineral water bottling plants in the autumn transferred to jobs such as washerwomen, charwomen or workers in a pickle factory.[23] However, I should not over-emphasize this point since, as Treble acknowledges, most female home workers had few sources of alternative employment when they were seasonally unemployed. They had few skills and were often tied to their homes by age or family responsibilities. Of course, not all wives of men in casual employment were obliged to take employment themselves.

For self-supporting single women, a small element saw part-time prostitution as the only way of providing food. As a contemporary writing in 1897 put it, 'in the West of London at least, milliners, and dressmakers and tailoresses, are frequently driven upon the streets in the slack season, returning to their shops with the advent of the new season's trade. In other words, *morals fluctuate with trade.*'[24]

Understanding of patterns of women's work in the nineteenth century must inevitably be patchy. Despite the admirable work by Professor Burnett and David Vincent in gathering together a very large number of working-class autobiographies, very few of these are by women.[25] One gleans certain information from official statistics and from reports of the factory inspectors and various commissions. However, once women got married, little of what they did got recorded apart from giving birth to children and eventually dying. One may be forgiven for seeing Victorian women in the polarized way common in children's history books: they are either crawling along a tunnel hauling a coal cart or sitting demure and corsetted in a room stuffed with Victoriana.

The few case studies that are available do give some insights into the lives of ordinary working women. Burnett provides an account of Lucy Luck, a straw plait weaver, born in 1848 at Tring in Hertfordshire, and, he suggests, there is no reason to doubt its accuracy. Like all such working-class autobiographies, it is rather sentimental and novelette-ish, but that is only to be expected, given the material that such a person would be reading. Lucy was not yet 9 years old when she started work in a silk mill at Tring where she took lodgings. By the age of 11 in 1859 she was working all day at the mill from 6 a.m. to 6 p.m. Later, she was taken away to work as a servant in a pub at St Albans. 'There I was, cast upon

[22] C. Williams and T. Jones, *Royal Commission on the Poor Laws Report*, HMSO, London, 1909, p. 240; quoted in Treble, *Urban Poverty*, p. 71.
[23] Treble, *Urban Poverty*, p. 77.
[24] A. Sherwell, *Life in West London* (publisher not known), 1897, p. 146; quoted in Treble, *Urban Poverty*, p. 80.
[25] SSRC Work Histories Symposium, 26-27 September 1983, University of Surrey.

the wide world when I was only 13 years old, without a friend to say yea or nay to me.' Lucy provides some details of her life as a servant in a prosperous town. She worked in

a shop and beer-house combined. Mr and Mrs H-, who kept it, were elderly people and had only been there one month themselves. They kept something of a general shop on one side of the doorway and a taproom the other. I know they had a cow, and a donkey, and I used to make butter and sausages, and sometimes serve in the taproom, and sometimes go out with milk. I know I was not much of a servant, for I had never been taught to do it. Mrs H- always had a charwoman in once a week, and this woman often told me her 'wipes' were better than my 'scrubbing', and I don't doubt it.[26]

At that time, Lucy received 1s 6d a week, but that was all spent on necessary clothes. Her mistress was good to her, she says, but they could not manage to keep on the business and Lucy was unemployed again. When she was 15 her mother died and she was still working in service. The couple for whom she worked were always quarrelling and the man made sexual advances to her which she resisted.

By now I had begun to bitterly hate service, and a fatherly old man who used the public house where I had been, told of a place in Luton where they wanted a girl to learn the straw work and help in housework. Although this was another public house, I thought it was a chance to learn a trade so I went there . . . but they did not keep to their promise. They would not pay me more than 2s a week, but said they would teach me the straw work. You may think it strange, straw business going on in a public house, but it was so, and I think the reason was, part of the business belonged to a sister and daughter.[27] I sometimes did housework, sometimes served in the bar, and other times did the finishing of straw hats. They never attempted to teach me the making of them, but I was determined to learn, and would get a piece of straw and sit up half the night trying to do it.[28]

So Lucy left again and got a six-month apprenticeship with a woman to make straw hats. She liked the work but was set too much to do and so eventually, in despair, she was virtually obliged to leave. 'The season was over, and I was homeless, penniless, and with only the clothes I walked in.'[29] However, she did find another job and reasonable lodgings for a while, although work was hard to find. She describes her moves from one lodging to another, often helped by another friendly girl in better circumstances. She eventually finds herself in a small farm three miles outside Luton where she meets a local ploughboy, Will, who later asks her to marry him. On an occasion just after a row with her mistress she

[26] J. Burnett, *Useful Toil*, Allen Lane, London, 1974, p. 71.
[27] It would have been nice to know more about this particular household work strategy!
[28] Burnett, *Useful Toil*, p. 72.
[29] Ibid.

agrees. Will's master rents them a cottage at 2s a week and Lucy writes, 'I could not have thought more of it if it had been a palace.' At the age of 18½ she is married. 'My husband's money was only 12s a week, and at that time bread was 8d a quartern loaf; also meat, tea and sugar and other things were very dear. He had to be up every morning soon after three o'clock, as he had to walk two miles to work. I worked on as hard myself as ever I had done, so we got on very well, adding a little more to our home whenever we could.'[30] Lucy's first child was born two years after they were married and she had two others — all girls; the third, however, died at the age of 8 months. Lucy and Will then moved to a neighbouring farm where she had another child and they lived in a tied cottage until they were evicted for asking for a rise which other farmers in the area were paying. There was no alternative accommodation locally so they decided to go to London. She took her three children to her brother-in-law and Will looked up an acquaintance who had been a groom at the same farm and was now working near the Edgware Road. Three days after arriving in London, Will got a job as a horse keeper for a railway company and Lucy came to live with him in lodgings near Paddington Green.

Lucy continued to work at straw plaiting at home, sending it up to Luton once a week and receiving the raw materials in return. On one occasion, when the thread did not arrive, she had to find a local supply. In doing this she discovered she could earn more by working directly for a woman in Westbourne Grove. She adopted a system whereby she spent part of the time working in the workshop and part of the time at home. She continued in this way for thirteen years with her eldest daughter helping her for ten of these.[31] Then the lease of the premises expired and the new owners were engaged in different work. Lucy then shifted to another job in the West End, where she 'worked for one gentlemen for twenty years'. As she remarked, her skill as a straw plaiter 'has been a little fortune to me'.

I have been at work for 47 years, and have never missed one season, although I have a large family. I have had seven together not earning a penny piece. In my busy seasons I have worked almost night and day. I don't like to talk of what I have done, but I generally bought up what I could at sales, and made up my children's clothes in my dull season, and I don't think I have paid away 30s for any kind of needlework. . . . The straw work is very bad, as a rule, from July up to about Christmas. During that time I have been out charring or washing and I have looked after a gentleman's house a few times, and I have taken in needlework. This was before any of my children were old enough to work. I have done my best to bring them up respectable.[32]

---

[30] Ibid., p. 75

[31] This mother-daughter partnership in earning income is not well documented as a general pattern but I suspect it was not an unusual work pattern.

[32] Burnett, *Useful Toil*, pp. 76-7.

The story of Lucy Luck is vivid and her comments on her own feelings and attitudes provide valuable and important insights. One is struck by the mobility and unstable nature of the early part of her work history and by the tremendous determination she had to find employment right through her life. Because during most of her time in London she was working from home, it is quite likely that she would appear in the Census as unemployed. Unfortunately, we get no clue as to how Lucy and Will work out their collective strategy: he disappears from the story once they reach London. What is clear, however, is that Lucy seems to take complete responsibility for her children and prides herself on always having the money to get by with dignity. It is a story of a life totally dominated by work and of a woman who must have had considerable drive and energy. None of her children, she says, ever brought her any sorrow or disgrace. She must have died in the early years of this century. As Burnett remarks in the Introduction to the book from which Lucy's story is taken, the workers whose lives we know something about in detail 'did not, if their writings are to be trusted, either think very much about their work or derive a sense of fulfilment from it. Work was a means to an end, and the end was survival in a hostile world which often seemed to deny even this modest ambition.'[33]

Women's Work in the Twentieth Century: The First Forty Years

The pattern of women's work changed dramatically in the early years of this century.[34] Most women spent some years in employment before marriage, and while service was still the largest occupational category at the beginning of the period, there was a steady trend in non-manual, especially clerical, occupations and less skilled work in the so-called new industries.[35] While in the upper middle class there might still be status in daughters not engaging in employment, for the majority of the population respectability was attained through the type of occupation pursued by members of this unmarried workforce.

Once they had married, however, it was exceptional for women of *any* class to be in employment. The inter-war period was the high water mark of the privatized little domestic unit: in the period previous to that, as the

[33] Ibid., p. 15.
[34] Stearns, 'Working class women in Britain', p. 110.
[35] 'The growth of the clerical sector was an urban phenomenon, and was particularly marked in the Greater London area; similarly, the expansion of job opportunities for women as unskilled workers in light industry was concentrated in the South-East. The decline of domestic service was also concentrated in the major conurbations. Further, the tendency was for more single, and fewer married, women to work; the percentage of all women working in 1901 was 29.1 per cent; in 1931, 29.7 per cent, while the percentage of married women working was 6.3 per cent in 1901 and 4.8 per cent in 1931' (D. Gittins, *Fair Sex: Family Size and Structure 1900-1939*, Hutchinson, London, 1982, p. 45).

story of Lucy Luck illustrates, ordinary working women did a whole variety of paid work in and around the home to make ends meet. In the 1920s and 1930s, for large sections of the middle and working class, it was considered shameful for married women to go out to work, particularly in the south-east of England.

The reasons for this inter-war home-centredness are complex and have been discussed elsewhere.[36] Perhaps of primary importance was the much greater involvement of central government in matters of everyday life and including the introduction of the Marriage Bar, which, for example, prevented women civil servants who married colleagues remaining in the same employment. The development of new, cheap forms of transport, coupled with the growth of new estates of council or privately built estates at the edge of the major towns and cities, intensified the physical separation of homes (for women) and work (for men): women worked at home in housing estates and suburbs; men were employed elsewhere.

No doubt for very worthy reasons initially, there was at the same time a growing public concern about the health and welfare of children.[37] The First World War had emphasized the point, already established by the Boer War, that the nation depended on the health of ordinary people, whether as soldiers or factory workers. Many new policies in public health, housing and social welfare were established and implemented. A very thorough documentation of the growth of institutions concerned with motherhood has been provided by J. Lewis, who shows that their main purpose 'was to pass onto the mother information about, a sense of responsibility towards, and pride in home and family'.[38] This clearly had the effect of tying mothers in particular places to particular tasks; the new notion that 'the community as a whole' was responsible for the welfare of children referred implicitly to them.

There is no doubt that infant mortality was high at the beginning of the century, but it did not follow that the solution necessarily had to be individualized in the way that it was. The infant welfare movement quite properly emphasized cleanliness and personal hygiene, but instead of supporting the provision of public facilities, emphasized the importance

---

[36] See, for example, J. Lewis, *The Politics of Motherhood*, Croom Helm, London, 1980; J. Lewis, 'The social history of social policy: Infant welfare in Edwardian England', *Journal of Social Policy*, 9(4), 1980, pp. 463-86; C. L. Mowat, *Britain Between the Wars*, Methuen, London, 1963; Gittins, *Fair Sex*.

[37] As McCleary noted in his review of the subject published in 1933, 'During the nineteenth century, some hundred Acts of Parliament were passed for this purpose. Child labour in factories, mines and theatres, and in chimney sweeping was either abolished or subjected to increasingly stringent regulations. Free elementary education was provided, and with the Prevention of Cruelty to Children Act 1889, a new code of child protection was introduced. When the century ended the principle had been established that the community as a whole had become responsible for the welfare of its children' (quoted in Gittins, *Fair Sex*, pp. 48-9).

[38] Lewis, *Politics of Motherhood*, p. 97.

of 'educating' women to be 'good' mothers. 'Pioneers in health visiting not only gave instructions on cleanliness and hygiene, but also on thrift, temperance and religion.'[39] Pregnancy, childbirth and child care were rapidly professionalized during this period. Child welfare clinics more than doubled in eighteen years to 4,585 in 1938. Women who had previously relied on mutual aid and support from female kin and neighbours became more dependent on their husbands and state agencies: 'over and over both the government and the medical profession emphasized the importance of women *as mothers* and their "natural" duty to their children; married women working was discouraged, often prohibited, as a danger to the health and welfare of their children.'[40]

The 1920s and 1930s, therefore, comprised a period which emphasized small-scale domesticity centred around young children. Houses were built equipped with gas, water and electricity, enabling people to buy cookers and vacuum cleaners to make their domestic life easier. Mass-produced clothing and furniture, tinned food and a better educated population helped to produce a warmer, more comfortable and better fed population. As many commentators have observed, married women became more useful to the economy as consumers carefully constructing cosy nests than as producers. Women increasingly read women's magazines regularly and many new monthly and weekly magazines were established.[41] The founding of the BBC soon led to the widespread activity of 'listening to the wireless'. The image of Chamberlain 'addressing the nation' is a photograph of a couple and one or two children 'listening in' by their own fireside.

For these new 'good' mothers, life in their new, clean homes was not a life of leisure, but nor was it a life of misery and toil. Housework expanded to fill the time available and, as Hartman and Vanek have shown in separate studies for the more affluent Americans of this period, new technology created more work, not less.[42]

---

[39] Gittins, *Fair Sex*, p. 49.
[40] Ibid., p. 51.
[41] *Good Housekeeping* was established in 1922, *Women and Home* 1926, *Life and Home* 1929; weeklies were also established in the 1930s: *Women's Own* in 1932, *Woman's Illustrated* in 1936 and *Woman* in 1937.
[42] H. I. Hartman, 'Capitalism and women's work in the home', unpublished PhD thesis, Yale University, 1974; J. Vanek, 'Keeping busy: Time spent in housework, United States 1920-1970', unpublished PhD thesis, University of Michigan, 1973. But extrapolations from the United States must be undertaken with caution. Another of Gittins's respondents, who had been a shop assistant before she married a male nurse, recalls her early married life, indicating that *new* child-centred activites were expanding at the expense, certainly for some, of the earlier drudgery of housework:

> A: Before the children went to school we used to take them out on picnics and all that sort of thing, long walks and all that . . . and then when they got a bit older they could have bicycles . . . we all had bicycles . . . and we used to go off . . . to Mersea and Clacton and Walton and all that sort of thing and we thoroughly enjoyed our-selves. That was our pleasure and we used to have a real good time.

There is certainly evidence that for many middle and lower middle-class women their home life was relatively happy. The fact that that did not fit the mores of later generations does not undermine its importance and significance for those concerned at the time. There were, of course, enormous regional variations, and the women reported in the study by D. Gittins were very different from those who talked to J. White about Campbell Road, Islington, in the 1930s[43] or even those who talked to Elizabeth Roberts about their working lives in three Lancashire towns before 1940.[44] Certainly, Roberts's oral evidence shows that most women in her area were obliged to work in order that their families could be adequately clothed, fed and housed. Among the poorest households, all the wives worked unless there was some alternative way of getting money. Income could be made up by selling the produce from an allotment, or by the wages of children who started part-time work at the age of 9 (as delivery boys). 'In Lancaster, three labourers' families had mothers who did not earn wages. In two of them the allotment was responsible for providing an important part of the family's diet, in the other the father and children were skilled in "living off the land", collecting a variety of foods both to eat and to sell.'[45] Put bluntly, in the area Roberts studied married women did not choose to take employment; they were obliged to do so.

While Gittins gives many examples of men preventing their wives from being employed when they wanted to be, the reverse seems to be the case for Roberts's sample: 'women who worked full-time were certainly *not* regarded as emancipated by their contemporaries, rather as drudges. Women whose husbands earned sufficient money to clothe, feed and house the family preferred to have a reduced work load rather than extra income.'[46] Roberts takes issue with sociologists and feminists who have argued that women between the wars were economically and socially penalized by their lack of employment once they were married. On the contrary, argues Roberts, 'pre-war working class women in so far as they

---

Q: What would you do in the evenings?

A: Play games, play cards, anything the children wanted.

Q: Did you ever go to the cinema?

A: We couldn't afford it . . . we just didn't think about it . . . You know, we were quite happy in our home life and looking after the children and taking them out and all that sort of thing. As I say, amusing them in the house and all that (Gittins, *Fair Sex*, p. 135).

[43] Ibid. and J. White, 'Campbell Bunk: A lumpen community in London between the wars', *History Workshop Journal*, 8, 1979, pp. 1-49.
[44] E. Roberts, 'Working wives and their families', in T. Barker and M. Drake (eds), *Population and Society in Britain 1850-1980*, Batsford, London, 1982.
[45] Ibid., p. 145.
[46] Ibid., p. 147.

consciously thought about the question at all, perceived their emancipation as a movement away from outside paid employment and towards domesticity.'[47] Indeed, Roberts goes on to claim that even the availability of employment was a less important factor than the simple economic need of households for more income. 'Part-time work . . . seems to have been available as and when it was required.'[48] However, it is also quite likely that wages in the area were depressed on the assumption that several members of a household would be in employment.[49] Roberts provides a nice example of women's economic activity in Lancaster.

Mrs Manning, born in 1914, grew up in one of the poorest streets in Lancaster. Her own mother took in washing and she was able to remember the money-earning activities of many of her neighbours in the 1920s:

> Mrs A had this lodging house, and then Mrs H had the pub. Mrs H used to brew pop and sell it. Next door to us Mrs P, she used to make apple-pies and jam pies, and charge a penny a piece. She used to roast potatoes and make a living like that. There was a shop just a bit lower down. . . . Mrs R, a halfpenny of milk, a halfpenny biscuit, and a halfpenny packet of cocoa and have it for school. . . . There was Mrs H, she used to cut up firewood and sell it in bundles, 3d or 6d a bundle.[50]

Sometimes these part-time shops developed into proper 'house shops'; 'others disappeared as and when the financial need which created them disappeared. In Barrow, Mrs Morris's mother opened a parlour shop to make enough money to send all her children to the Higher Grade school.'[51] Roberts further contests Gittins's claim that whether the wife worked or not would affect the power relationship within marriage. She claims that some of the most powerful women in the three towns she studied — who were very often the dominant partner in the marriage — worked part-time or not at all.

The best that can be said on the evidence of the oral history that has so far been published is that there was considerable diversity in women's employment practices, work patterns and domestic ideologies. These were as much regional as class-based.[52]

---

[47] Ibid., p. 148.

[48] Ibid., p. 150.

[49] 'The wages in most of the Lancashire cotton towns assume the double earnings of man and wife' (Pilgrim Trust, *Men Without Work*, Cambridge University Press, 1938, p. 235).

[50] E. Roberts, *A Woman's Place*, Basil Blackwell, Oxford, 1984, p.142.

[51] Ibid.

[52] There was considerable continuity in some parts of the country with nineteenth-century work patterns. One of Roberts's respondents, born in 1913, summarizes one position: 'My mother, their life, well they had no life. It must have been a terrible life. It was all work. It was real drudgery. But they enjoyed it. It was their family and they lived for their families. It wasn't drudgery to them' (Roberts, *Working Wives*, p. 162).

Women's Employment 1940-1990

The employment of married women remained very stable at around 10 per cent of all married women until the start of the Second World War. By 1945 the number of married women employed was over 2.5 million, that is, more than five times the number in paid work before the war. This is probably a substantial underestimate of the number of married women workers, many of whom would have engaged in essential work on a voluntary basis. For example, there were 2,000 British Restaurants, and some of these were run by voluntary committees and some married women worked in them without pay, although these were a minority. As we have seen, many married women in employment before the war were (certainly in south-east England) 'deviants' — shaming their husbands, who felt that this demonstrated that they were not looking after them properly. However, during the war public opinion changed radically. As Gertrude Williams remarked at the time: 'War necessity has swung public opinion so far the other way that the woman who does *not* add to her household duties feels guilty and apologetic, and there is no doubt that if, after the war, society looked upon it as normal to combine home and work the majority of women should do what was expected of them.'[53]

If women were to follow all Williams's prescriptions they would stay at home with their children (which it was their natural duty to have) until they had 'launched' them — at whatever mature age that would be. Then they would look for jobs that could be undertaken 'with only the scantiest previous experience'.[54] Restaurants and personal service were two of the areas that Williams thought were likely to provide suitable employment for women, whose lives were set to a different pattern from those of men.

These assumptions were firmly built into the post-war period of reconstruction managed by the Labour Party. Perhaps the clearest embodiment of these principles can be seen in the way New Towns were planned. Neighbourhood units were laid out some distance from the main shopping and recreational facilities in the town centre, with just a few shops within walking distance for daily needs. Men went to the industrial estates, segregated some distance from the main living areas, so

---

[53] G. Williams, *Women and Work*, Nicholson and Watson, London, 1945, p. 124. Mrs Williams made no secret of what her values were, despite being a lecturer in economics herself: 'The way to express our sense of the most important work that women do in society is not to pay them to do less important work; it is to recognize the unique contribution that wives and mothers make to the community and to give them the opportunity to do it properly. . . . One of the happiest innovations proposed in the Beveridge Report is the emergence of the housewife as a separate and honoured category of the population' (pp. 125-6).

[54] Ibid., p. 127.

that earning and consuming were kept physically separated. There was no expectation that women would would want to have employment near to their homes or that opportunities for part-time work might encourage women to combine the care of small children with paid employment.

There was no absolute reduction in the number of married women working in the period immediately following the Second World War, but the female labour force as a whole did decline in the late 1940s as single women married and started their families. By the early 1950s, the proportion of married women in employment (one in four) returned to the level it had been in 1851: the rigours of married women's domestic imprisonment seemed to be abating. Despite the ideological bias in the social policies and programmes of the immediate post-war period, married women in employment began to increase both proportionately and absolutely. Numbers employed rose from 2.85 million in 1950 to 3.77 million in 1957, the latter figure being about half of the total of all female workers. Inevitably, however, conventional attitudes were maintained, even by Viola Klein, the author of a sociological survey of *Britain's Married Women Workers* published in 1965:

It is not suggested here that it is — or is likely to become so in the near future — the general practice for married women to accept employment away from their homes. Housewives without jobs, after all, still outnumber those in employment by 2 to 1; and as something like half of them have one or more children under the age of 16, the size of the reserve that can be drawn on will probably always remain limited to a minority of married women.[55]

Despite recognizing that the trends towards the greater employment of married woman would continue, Klein completely misread the situation: the middle 1960s were the beginning of an unprecedented increase in the proportion of married women in employment. By the early 1980s there were about 10.5 million women in the labour force, representing two-thirds of all women between 16 and 60. Over 60 per cent of the wives of employed men were in employment but only 32 per cent of the wives of the unemployed. While 40 per cent of the British labour force are females, 40 per cent of all female employees are part-time workers, compared with only 5 per cent of male employees. The growth in women's activity rates is related to the growth of services in the economy: service industries account for 60 per cent of all employment, but 54 per cent of all service employees are women.[56] This brief summary must now be elaborated.

The decade 1966-1977 was a period of unprecedented change in the labour force. A. R. Thatcher wrote in 1978 that the change was 'almost

[55] V. Klein, *Britain's Married Women Workers*, Routledge and Kegan Paul, London, 1965, p. 28.
[56] Lloyds Bank, *Economic Bulletin*, 42, June 1982.

entirely due to the tremendous increase in the proportion of married women working, particularly the proportion who return to work after having their families. The participation rates for married women in Britain are amongst the highest in the countries of the industrial West, and so far have confounded each successive forecast by rising more than expected.'[57] Between 1951 and 1976 the number of men in the labour force remained stable at around 15.9 million; married women, on the other hand, increased from 2.7 to 6.7 million. From 1966 to 1976, in very broad terms, those employed in the 'index of production' industries declined by just under 2 million in rough proportions of three men to one woman. In the public sector, however, there was a substantial increase of 1.4 million workers, over two-thirds of whom were women. There was, therefore, a clear scissors effect: men moved out of traditional manufacturing industries and women moved into service industries, particularly in the public sector.

In 1979 the Department of Employment drew up labour force projections to 1991 in which it forecast a continuing increase in married women's activity rates from 26 per cent of the labour force in 1976 to 27.6 per cent by 1991.[58] However, it later became clear that the post-war trend of increasing female activity rates had peaked, as the overall activity rate of married women remained about 50 per cent from 1977 to 1981, in sharp contrast to the rapidly increasing rates of the preceding years. Table 3.1 gives the age-specific activity rates for selected

Table 3.1   Activity rates of married women, 1971–1981

Age groups	Percentages employed		
	1971	*1977*	*1981*
16–19	42.4	54.7	48.9
20–24	46.7	59.0	56.8
25–34	38.4	52.2	51.3
35–44	54.5	67.4	66.6
45–54	57.0	65.1	66.8
55–59	45.5	54.9	51.9
60–64	25.2	24.6	23.3
65+	6.5	5.0	4.7
All	42.3	50.4	49.5
Estimated totals (thousands)	5,816	6,922	6,714

Source: Department of Employment Gazette, February 1983.

[57] A. R. Thatcher, 'Labour supply and employment trends', in F. Blackaby (ed.), *De-industrialization*, Heinemann Educational Books, London, 1979, p. 27.
[58] Department of Employment, 'Changing composition of the labour force, 1976-1991', *Employment Gazette*, 1979, p. 548.

years. This levelling out in married women's activity rates is explained partly by increases in fertility rates between 1977 and 1981.

From the late 1960s onwards there was a substantial shift towards part-time work. By 1981 90 per cent of part-time workers were women: nearly 45 per cent of working women were in part-time employment and nearly 75 per cent of female part-time workers were aged between 25 and 55. Eighty per cent of the femal part-time wokers in 1981 were married, suggesting that the pattern of women's employment is related to their pattern of other work and responsibilities. The proportion of employed women who were employed part-time increased with the appearance of dependent children, from about one-third employed part-time with no children, through one-half employed part-time with one child, to two-thirds employed part-time with two children. The existence of a third dependent child did not increase the tendency to take part-time employment, while the presence of four or more dependent children somewhat reduced the tendency to be employed part-time if in employment. Nearly 90 per cent of young women without dependent children were in full-time employment, but within this group married women work shorter hours than non-married women. Indeed, the proportion of non-married young women in full-time employment is much the same as for males.[59] Older women, even without dependent children, are still more likely to be in part-time employment than younger women, indicating, perhaps, the continuing responsibilities of parenthood even after the children are grown up. A large proportion, 40 per cent, of females in part-time employment are in personal service occupations (catering, cleaning, hairdressing and other personal services), compared with 10 per cent for full-time workers.[60]

Full-time employment consistently plays a less important part in women's work patterns: around 55 per cent of employed women were in full-time employment in 1981 and even among the non-marrieds the proportion of full-time employed women — about 75 per cent — was less than the rate for men. Women employed full-time had a median of 39 hours a week: women full-timers worked shorter hours than men within all industries and occupations, apart from managerial occupations where the proportion was much the same. This suggests that for women employment is evidently only one form of work. 'Traditionally we[61] have thought in terms of people being employed or unemployed. The position is, however, more complex; choices are made between work, non-market

---

[59] It is interesting to note that employment statistics differentiate only women according to marital status. Men are not so divided, yet unmarried men in employment could, arguably, be expected to behave in qualitatively different ways from married men. Discussion of male docility or militancy rarely mentions their marital status and whether they live with their mothers or on their own.

[60] Department of Employment, 'Changing composition', p. 481.

[61] The 'we' here is taken to be economists analysing labour force statistics.

work and leisure: households make joint decisions with respect to the hours of work of husband and wife.'[62] How households make these decisions is, of course, not so obviously apparent: in practice, it appears that very few households have full-time employed wives with their husbands working part-time in order to take over some of their parental responsibilities.

In broad terms, therefore, women are employed part-time and in service industries. Typically, women's jobs are classified as less skilled than men's, even though they cover a wide range of skills: their employment is undervalued.[63] However, it is important to note that part-time employment has stood up well during the current recession, the unemployment rate for those seeking part-time employment remaining consistently below that for those seeking full-time employment. This may, of course, simply be a function of married women 'adjusting to a lower demand for labour', as economists put it. That is, the women perceive there are no jobs in their locality so they see little point in registering as seeking work. Evidently, married women at present unemployed could dramatically change the unemployment rate if they registered in large numbers.

Before leaving this particular issue of women's employment to up 1990, some consideration should be given to the effect of micro-electronics. What, in particular, is likely to be the impact of micro-electronics on the 1.25 million women employed as operatives in manufacturing? Clearly, the pattern will vary between industries. In the textile industry electronic innovations have primarily affected craft skills — that is men's jobs — in the past, but in the future women's jobs are likely to be more at risk.[64] In a study of the paper, printing and publishing industries in America, micro-electronic applications increased women's job opportunities at the expense of men's. But this may not be the pattern in Britain. 'In the present climate of change, combined with redundancies, there are some indications that men, and the trade unions representing them, may be anxious to retain their traditional areas of work and may resist new technology and women workers where they can.'[65] As the authors of a recent review of the impact of micro-electronics on women's work

---

[62] Thatcher, 'Labour supply', p. 54.

[63] Department of Employment, 'A changing labour force: Constants and variables', *Employment Gazette*, 91(2), 1983, pp. 49-54.

[64] In a survey on *New Technology and Women's Employment* focusing on West Yorkshire by the Leeds Trade Union and Community Resource and Information Centre (published by the Equal Opportunities Commission in 1982), it was concluded that 'where new technology is introduced into mixed workplaces, women's jobs are much more likely to be affected than men's jobs. In the TUC RIC Survey, 60 per cent of workplaces employed more men than women, but in only 17 per cent of cases were more men's jobs than women's affected by automation' (p. 105).

[65] E. Arnold et al., 'Microelectronics and women's employment', *Employment Gazette*, September 1982, p. 380.

conclude, 'women are vulnerable because they are clustered in unskilled and semi-skilled assembly work or routine white collar jobs and are failing to acquire the technical education and training necessary for the new jobs.'[66]

Paradoxically, it seems that the only way women can keep their hold on employment is through the downgrading of their work as semi-skilled and by employers preferring to have more flexible part-time employees rather than full-time male workers. In a recent detailed study of the semi-conductor industry, it has been claimed that there is a 'feminization' of the workforce as a disproportionte number of the routine jobs are taken by women. 'Thus in the assisted areas 74 per cent of all manual production workers were women, while in the non-assisted areas female production workers were 48 per cent of the total.'[67] It has been shown that there are strong grounds for thinking that many employers prefer part-time workers, since employees working less than eight hours a week, and those working up to sixteen hours if they have worked for less than five years with the same employers, are not eligible for redundancy compensation, minimum period of notice, guarantee payments during periods of short-time working, maternity leave, maternity pay or appeal against unfair dismissal. It has been estimated that a million part-time workers are excluded from the main provisions of employment legislation.[68] An analysis of New Earnings Survey data has demonstrated that the proportion of part-time workers falling in the unprotected categories increased between 1975 and 1979 from 20 to 30 per cent for women in manual occupations and from 18 to 23 per cent for women in non-manual occupations.[69] However, it would be premature to jump to the conclusion that part-time work is growing at the expense of full-time work; rather, it should be seen in the context of a switch in employment from manufacturing to services.

Conclusions

It is a truism to note that most of the world's work is done by women, and yet it still may cause some surprise to be reminded that the admonition urging the workers of the world to unite is logically addressed to a largely female audience. Unhappily for women, they have more to lose than their chains of servitude to employers: they also have other chains, binding them to husbands and dependent relatives. Most

[66] Ibid., p. 384.
[67] P. Cooke et al., 'New technology and regional development in austerity Britain: The case of the semiconductor industry'. Paper prepared for SSRC Conference on Urban Change and Conflict, Department of Town Planning, UWIST, 1983 (mimeo), p. 13.
[68] C. Leicester, 'Towards a fully part-time Britain', *Personnel Management*, June 1982.
[69] J. Hurstfield, 'Part-time pittance', *Low Pay Review*, no. 1, 1980.

women's conception of work, until quite recently, has been very close to what I suggest in this book, namely a necessary and pragmatic activity essential to getting by. They have shifted between work for an employer and work on their own account. Sometimes they have worked more for the household, sometimes more for themselves; yet typically work in and around the household is always, inevitably, an essential element in their overall work-load.

Women have earned money for as long as the history of wage labour, and they have contributed this money to their families and households. Before marriage young women either handed most of their earned income to their mothers or, if they were lodging elsewhere, sent home all but a small subsistence income. Alternatively, they busily saved for their own marriages and the new homes and families that that would entail. After marriage their pattern of work was structured by the exigencies of child rearing, and their level of economic activity as employees was frequently constrained by real or imposed limitations attributable to their roles as wives and mothers. If it has become conventional to refer to the married man as the 'chief earner', it should be equally conventional to refer to his wife as the 'chief worker'.

The one-sided emphasis on employment, with the implication that this is the only significant form of work, tends also to emphasize the individual earner rather than the household as the basic economic unit. Women are perhaps more likely to perceive the household as the basic economic unit and to arrange their balance of work in terms of the needs of the household as a whole. Furthermore, in general women are more likely to manage the non-waged work of all members of the household: if anyone is to take final responsibility for the order and amount of domestic and child rearing work, it is most likely to be the woman. Women in upper-class households are in the most atypical position, and are in many ways more dependent than ordinary working women since, paradoxically, their relative economic importance in the household is less.

Evidently, it is a serious error to underestimate the importance of women's waged work as an essential element in most household work strategies. For eight hundred years women have made an essential contribution of money into the family budget. From the very early days of the industrial revolution, households needed the money that women earned before they were married in order to set them up and very often after they were married to maintain them. The notion that ordinary households can be maintained adequately with the earnings of one (male) worker is a dangerous fallacy. Some households in the labour aristocracy and in the middle classes can, of course, be adequately supported in this way. But to infer from that that most households of the ordinary working people do not need, and have not always needed, the wages of other earners is quite unwarranted. There are strong indications that such households will similarly need multiple earners in the years up to the end of the twentieth century.

The employment of married women is sometimes perceived as a novelty — a product of the growth of the service sector in the 1960s and 1970s. This too, as we have seen, is a fallacy. Women's waged work has not always been counted or, more often, has passed notice simply as women's 'money-earning activities', in Roberts's phrase quoted above. Such dilatory accounting is no good reason to make women's economic activity socially invisible. What *is* new is the large-scale employment of married women from all social classes for most of their married lives on a full-time basis. There certainly is not a historical precedent for that. But it would be unfortunate if women's waged work were perceived in too narrow and limited a way. Historically, women have been the most flexible in engaging in all forms of work: the likelihood is that that, too, will be the pattern for the future.

4

Work Outside Employment

In this chapter, the focus is on work outside employment mainly between 1973 and 1984. Britain was then seen to be in the midst of the most serious recession for half a century: aspects of work, employment and unemployment were perceived as matters of considerable public interest. There were hopes that some new conceptualization of all forms of work might have more practical, as opposed to simply theoretical, value.[1]

The Over-emphasis on Male Workers and Formal Employment from the 1780s to the 1980s

At a very simple level there was some recognition, in the early 1980s, that if substantial gains in productivity could be realized without commensurate increases in employment — the phenomenon known as 'jobless growth' — then British society as a whole could get richer, even though the numbers and proportions of those employed might decline. If this happened, then the period from 1980 to 2000 would be a transitional phase, as significant, perhaps, as a similar period of transition two hundred years earlier. There was a shift, in this first period, from a world where wage labour was only one among a variety of forms of work necessary to get by, to a world where *it was perceived* that only one form of work was significant, that is employment.

This elision of the distinction between employment and work in the nineteenth century was due partly to the growth of the study of political economy and economics. Marx's preoccupation with manual labour, for example, was understandable in the context of his time: when all that the landless proletariat had was their labour power, the struggle over the level of wages paid to the 'breadwinner' gained an inevitable centrality. 'The need for money is, therefore, the real need created by the modern

---

[1] A good example was provided by the *Report of the House of Lords Select Committee on Unemployment*, HMSO, London, 1982.

economic system and the only need which it creates.'[2] The experience of the labour process was, according to Marx, supposed to provoke some deeper consciousness of an extra-systemic goal towards which the proletariat should strive, which would transcend the existing economic system to achieve the unalienated condition of 'socialized man, the associated producers, rationally regulating their exchange with Nature, bringing it under their common control, instead of being ruled by it as by the blind forces of Nature; and achieving this with the least expenditure of energy and under the conditions most favourable to, and worthy of their human nature'.[3] The connection between systemic goals (the struggle over the level of wages) and the extra-systemic goal (the struggle over the 'wages system' itself) was to be made partly by the capitalists in their unending demands for capital accumulation and increasing the amount of surplus value extracted from labour power, and partly by the proletariat, who would acquire revolutionary consciousness and thus exploit the self-destructing mechanism set in process by the capitalists. Lockwood described it as follows:

The fusion of immediate and fundamental interests comes about, so it is argued, through the process of revolutionary practice in which the proletariat's unfolding power of reason plays a crucial role. As it stands, however, the famous formula that the changing of people goes hand in hand with the changing of their circumstances possesses no more cogency than an incantation. To grasp its concrete meaning requires a specification of the nature of the people and circumstances in question.[4]

Lockwood's exposure of the great weaknesses of Marx's political sociology on both empirical and logical grounds is important for the present argument, which emphasizes all forms and sources of labour. It has taken much thought and a hundred years of history to isolate what Lockwood aptly terms the 'weakest link in the chain', namely the inadequacy of Marx's theory of action. In particular, 'Marxism lacks a clear conception of the interrelationship between class and status structures. This is because the analysis of the institutionalization of status has no place in its theory of social integration. The entire problem of status is lost sight of in highly general and essentially functionalist conceptions of ideological domination.'[5] It is not necessary to rehearse here all the arguments that lead Lockwood to state that the only Marxism that remains from much recent rigorous sociological analysis is 'a form of Marxism that begins where Weber left off'.[6]

[2] K. Marx, *Early Writings*, translated and edited by T. B. Bottomore, Penguin Books, Harmondsworth, 1964, p. 168.
[3] K. Marx, *Capital*, Volume III, Lawrence and Wishart, London 1972, p. 820.
[4] D. Lockwood, 'The weakest link in the chain: Some comments on the Marxist theory of action', *Research in the Sociology of Work*, 1, 1981, p. 440.
[5] Ibid., p. 448.
[6] Ibid., p. 475.

Others have commented on the misperceptions of those writing about the 'working class' in the nineteenth century.[7] Marx and the other political economists focused on only *some* of the work of *some* of the workers. Marx's research was heavily biased towards the empirical results provided by the Reports of the Factory Inspectors, and he himself did not do any empirical research of a more anthropological style, such as that by his contemporaries Frederick le Play or Henry Mayhew. His colleague F. Engels did, certainly, do more fieldwork in preparing *The Condition of the Working-Class in England*.[8] Undoubtedly this was a brilliant and precocious work, and it exposed the inhumanity of early capitalism with unparalleled polemical vigour. His account of role reversal does, however, reflect his own bourgeois preconceptions.

In many cases the family is not wholly dissolved by the employment of the wife but is turned upside down. The wife supports the family, the husband sits at home, tends the children, sweeps the room and cooks. This happens very frequently; in Manchester alone, many hundred such men could be cited, condemned to domestic occupations. It is easy to imagine the wrath aroused among the working-men by this reversal of all relations within the family, while the other social conditions remain unchanged.[9]

As the nineteenth century progressed, other values and forms of consciousness developed within the working class, and the documentation of its fragmentation and diversity of values has been effectively presented by historians in the last twenty years.[10] Writing of the second half of the nineteenth century, M. J. Daunton summarizes some of the arguments:

'Privatization' and 'encapsulation' involved a wide range of social and economic factors. One was the spur of profit in response to increased incomes. Specialization is limited by the extent of the market: increased purchasing power generated change in shopping habits and leisure pursuits; it also led to the wider

[7] K. Kumar, 'Can the workers be revolutionary?' *European Journal of Political Research*, 6, 1978, pp. 357-379; K. Kumar, 'Class and political action in nineteenth century England', *European Journal of Sociology*, 24, 1983, pp. 3-43; C. Calhoun, *The Question of Class Struggle*, Basil Blackwell, Oxford, 1982. The crucial point is that workers were not simply male wage labourers, nor was their consciousness solely determined by the labour process in certain traditional workplaces.
[8] First issued in Germany in 1845, when, as Engels acknowledges, the author 'was young, twenty-four years of age, and his production bears the stamp of his youth with its good and its faulty features' (K. Marx and F. Engels, *On Britain*, Lawrence and Wishart, London, 1962, p. 17).
[9] Ibid., pp. 177-8.
[10] See particularly G. J. Crossick, *The Artisan Elite in Victorian Society: Kentish London 1840-1880*, Croom Helm, London, 1978; R. Gray, *The Labour Aristocracy in Victorian Edinburgh*, Oxford University Press, 1976; and G. Stedman Jones, *Outcast London: A Study in the Relationship between Classes in Victorian Society*, Oxford University Press, 1971.

adoption of factory production with its attendant work discipline. Of course, this links with the development of housing, for the home was where the goods were consumed. On the most general level, there was a reorientation of working-class culture from being work-centred to home-centred. Of course, this was not a uniform trend; it applied less to mining towns, for example, than to large industrial towns where work-place and residence were distant. But generally, shorter working hours and increased real wages eroded work-centred culture and increased the role of the home as a centre of life. G. J. Crossick has indicated how artisans in Kentish London were absorbing 'privatized and family-centred values'. This was not merely the filtering down of ideas from above, for he suggests a specifically working-class justification, the residential form being part of the artisan's claim to respectability. This was impossible if he were forced to live cheek by jowl with those lacking respectability, and there was an often articulated desire to escape from promiscuous mixing and sharing. The working-class acceptance of privatized and family-centred values had both a negative and positive dimension. In a negative sense, the stress upon the home as the crucial element in life was in part a defensive retreat from the loss of control over work, a compensation in the home for an increased sense of dependence in the work place. In a positive sense, many working-class families in the last quarter of the nineteenth century had increased real wages, and could direct the budgets toward improved standards of accommodation and home-based consumption.[11]

The Decline in Formal Employment

If status-consciousness has always been more important than class-consciousness, it would be well to remember the importance of all forms of work in influencing the way members of households perceive their social situations. Returning now to the attempt to get some general indication of all forms of work undertaken in Britain in 1981 or as close to that date as data are available, it is relatively easy to show that formal employment is in decline. Other forms of work may or may not follow a similar pattern.

First, it is irrefutable that the pattern of work in the formal economy is changing: full-time employment, particularly for men in manufacturing industry, is declining, and this has been offset only partly by an increase in part-time employment, mainly for women in the service sector. The overall pattern is given in Table 4.1. It will be seen that, while men outnumber women as full-time employees by more than two to one overall, for both full-time and part-time employees, the differential is narrowing as the number of women employees declines less rapidly than that of male employees.

Of course, it is important to remember that statistics relating to

---

[11] M. J. Daunton, 'Public place and private space: The Victorian city and the working-class household', in D. Fraser and A. Sutcliffe (eds), *The Pursuit of Urban History*, Edward Arnold, London, 1983, p. 224.

Table 4.1   Employees in employment in Britain, by sex and full-time/part-time status (thousands)

	June 1978		September 1981		Change	
	N	%	N	%	N	%
Men						
Full-time	12,396	55.6	11,426	54.0	−970	−7.8
Part-time	704	3.2	709	5.3	+5	+0.7
All	13,101	58.8	12,135	57.3	−965	−7.4
Women						
Full-time	5,486	24.6	5,254	24.8	−232	−4.2
Part-time	3,688	16.5	3,759	17.7	+71	+1.9
All	9,173	41.1	9,013	42.3	+161	+1.7
All persons						
Full-time	17,882	80.3	16,680	78.9	−1202	−6.7
Part-time	4,392	19.7	4,468	21.1	+76	+1.7
All	22,273	100.0	21,148	100.0	−1126	−5.0

Source: Manpower Services Commission, Labour Market Quarterly Report, February 1983.

employees cannot reveal how those employees are distributed within households. An increasing proportion of families are reliant on two earners, which varies according to the age and number of children in the family. Data from the 1980 *General Household Survey* (GHS) relating to married couples with spouses of working age show that a half of one-child families had two earners as against 38 per cent of four-children families. In those families without children two-thirds have two incomes, and where the wife in such couples is aged 16-29 this increases to 84 per cent. Only 29 per cent of families with a pre-school child have two earners, whereas the proportion is 68 per cent where the youngest child is over 10. Broadly speaking, therefore, where husbands are employed and are in the economically active age range, of those with children, 60 per cent of their wives are in employment and of those without children 80 per cent are in employment.[12] Not surprisingly, perhaps, married women work for financial incentives.[13]

[12] L. Rimmer and J. Popay, *Employment trends and the family*, Study Commission on the Family, London, 1982, p. 63.
[13] Multiple regression analysis on GHS data 'suggests that a rise of 1 per cent in the wife's wage will increase the proportion of women working by 22 percentage points. But an increase of 1 per cent in the husband's wage will lower the proportion of women working by 11 percentage points. These two facts help to explain the growth in women's labour force participation over the post-war period. Between the war and 1973, women's and men's real wages roughly doubled. These changes would predict an increase in participation of about 10 percentage points — compared with the increase of 30 points which actually occurred for women under 60. Between April 1973 and April 1977, women's gross real wages increased

Indeed, it is absolutely clear that 'whether a wife works is a crucial determinant of whether a family is financially speaking poor. Even when the husband has very low earnings, only 18 per cent of families have incomes below 140 per cent of supplementary benefit if she works, compared with 76 per cent if she does not.'[14] There has to be a household work strategy involving more than one earner if most households are going to get by.

Information about labour force participation is easily available and quite frequently updated, using regular government surveys published in the Department of Employment's *Employment Gazette*, the Manpower Services Commission's *Labour Market Quarterly Report* and from other university centres specializing in labour market studies and labour economics. Debate is vigorous and readily accessible to a wider audience through academic journals and the media. Nevertheless, employment is only *one* form of work. Much work is done that is not recorded in official statistics and has, until recently, been disregarded by economists and sociologists alike. However, in the last decade attention has been directed to the by-employments, domestic labour, occupational easements and a range of other activities that have been grouped together and have been referred to as one, two or more separate economies with different and sometimes colourful names. Black, white, red, green and mauve economies have been detected with varying degrees of seriousness, and the notion of a separate 'informal' economy was put forward by various commentators to serve different purposes at different times. As I argue in the next chapter, there was little or no analytical rigour behind the deployment of such terms, but the idea of another economy did serve to encourage some economists, politicians and research foundations to view work in a wider frame.

How Big is the 'Informal Economy'?[15]

During the 1970s it became increasingly apparent that substantial amounts of work that were being done by men and women were not recorded — at least in any obvious and direct way — in the official statistics. Work in this sphere generally, but not always, involves cash transactions, and one approach to measuring the size of this so-called economy has been to use the number of high-denomination bank notes in

by about 10 per cent while men's real wages fell by nearly as much. This of itself would predict an increase of over 3 percentage points compared with an actual increase of 5 percentage points' (R. Layard et al., 'The causes of poverty', Background paper no. 5 to Report no. 6, *Royal Commission on the Distribution of Income and Wealth*, HMSO, London, 1978, p. 64).
[14] Ibid., p. 129.
[15] This term is accepted uncritically here: there is further discussion in the next chapter.

circulation as an appropriate indicator.[16] Yet very often cash is not exchanged, even though services are given and exchanged. The man who supplies 'cheap' (i.e. stolen) goods to his friends and neighbours but receives in return 'gifts' and 'favours', like virtually unlimited credit at his local pub, is certainly part of the world most people are thinking of when they refer to the 'secret', 'black', 'irregular' or 'hidden' economy. Another man who works with his own tools, in his own time, to do a job for a friend to get 'a bob or two' for himself is also in the uncounted sphere, if he does not declare his earnings to the Inland Revenue. Every occupation has its easements, and, as we have seen, by-employments and easements have been part of the pattern of work for at least the last eight hundred years. Attention to the topic may have increased, but it does not follow that this is matched by a growth in the work itself.

Interest in the unenumerated sphere of work was not so much in terms of its novelty, even though it appeared to many to be a discovery, but to its apparently increasing importance. This importance was measured either in money — amount of tax lost to the Inland Revenue — or in time — hours spent in activity that was seen by the person concerned as work rather than leisure. Hence, two lines of inquiry were established. The first was concerned with problems of accountancy — how to measure the imputed tax loss.[17] The second approach was to carry out detailed analyses of time budgets to show the increase in work outside employment over the last twenty years.[18] This focus on people's use of time was related to a whole host of policy and scholarly issues such as the relationship between technological innovations and time spent in housework, the relationship between hours spent in formal employment and hours spent in domestic work in and around the home, the substitution of DIY activities for formally provided goods and services, the relative balance between male and female 'formal' work and other kinds of work, the degree to which poor people engaged in other kinds of

[16] P. M. Gutmann, 'The subterranean economy', *Financial Analysts' Journal*, November-December 1977; R. D. Porter and S. S. Thurman, *Currency Ratio and the Subterranean Economy: Additional Comments*, Federal Reserve Board, Washington DC, 1979.
[17] A. Dilnot and C. N. Morris, 'What do we know about the black economy?' *Fiscal Studies*, 2(1), 1981, pp. 58-73; L. Feige, *The Theory and Measurement of the Unobserved Sector of the US Economy* (publisher not known) Leiden, 1981; Gutmann, 'Subterranean economy'; P. M. Gutmann, 'Statistical illusions, mistaken policies', *Challenge*, November-December 1979, pp. 14-17; K. Macafee, 'A glimpse of the hidden economy in the national accounts', *Economic Trends*, February, 1980, pp. 81-87; M. O'Higgins, *Measuring the Hidden Economy: A Review of Evidence and Methodologies*, Outer Circle Policy Unit, London, 1980; R. D. Porter, *Some Notes on Estimating the Underground Economy*, Federal Reserve Board, Washington DC, 1979; A. Smith, 'The informal economy', *Lloyds Bank Review*, 141, 1981, pp. 45-61.
[18] J. I. Gershuny and G. S. Thomas, *Changing Patterns of Time Use*, Occasional Paper Series no. 13, Science Policy Research Unit, University of Sussex, 1980; G. S. Thomas and C. Z. Shannon, 'Technology and household labour: Are the times a-changing?' Paper presented at British Sociological Association Conference, Manchester, 1982.

work to cope with the current recession, the growth of a so-called 'domestic economy' based on self-provisioning and so on.

J. I. Gershuny, in particular, focused on the informal economy as a way of exploring the changing pattern in the provision of services. Briefly, he argued that people were using manufactured goods like cars, washing machines, deep-freezes, electric drills and so on to provide goods and services for themselves. He showed that, with differential rates of productivity increases as between goods and services, it would be more expensive to pay for the labour in formally acquired services. Hence, in effect, we would end up serving ourself or doing it ourselves. Gershuny initially developed this argument in terms of three 'economies'.[19] He distinguishes between the formal, the informal and the household or communal economy. However, he also refers to the informal and household economies as 'sectors', and it seems clear that he is making analytical distinctions simply as a way of getting more precise measurement and in stimulating debate, as I show in the next chapter.

The So-Called 'Hidden Economy' in Decline?

For accountants and statisticians 'the hidden economy is defined for national accounts purposes as being the economic activity generating factor incomes which cannot be estimated from the regular statistical sources used to compile the income measure of gross domestic product.'[20] Since tax losses have been variously estimated as between 1 and 10 per cent of gross domestic product (GDP), even if a modest estimate is taken, the loss of revenue can be substantial. Research using the *Family Expenditure Survey* compared reported income with reported expenditure and produced a figure of less than 3 per cent of GDP. This would still imply a loss of revenue of around £5,000 million in 1981.[21] Since, as Smith argues, figures of such orders of magnitude come to about a third of the British government's public sector borrowing requirements,[22] it is perhaps no surprise that public interest in the informal sector should be growing at a time when for a variety of reasons this sector may well be in decline.

First, it is generally agreed that income from self-employment is probably the largest element of undeclared legal income; the General Secretary of the Inland Revenue Staff Federation remarked in 1976, 'The low incomes to which the self-employed admit defy belief. Only 70,000 of them declare the average wage of £60 or more. Only 250,000 of them

---

[19] J. I. Gershuny, 'The informal economy: Its role in industrial society', *Futures*, February, 1979, pp. 3-15.
[20] Macafee, 'A glimpse of the hidden economy', p. 81.
[21] Dilnot and Morris, 'What do we know about the black economy?'
[22] Smith, 'The informal economy'.

admit to more than £30 a week.'[23] But the numbers of self-employed declined in the 1970s. In 1975 there were 1,875,000 self-employed people in Britain; by mid-1979 the total had fallen by 80,000.[24] Furthermore, many self-employed people do earn low incomes. Since a high proportion of the self-employed are in construction and small-scale retailing, including dealers in secondhand goods and antiques, which have declined since 1979 and show few signs of recovery, it seems likely that this trend will continue; the same pattern has been documented for the United States, where self-employed professionals and businessmen — those best positioned to under-report income — declined from 20 per cent of the labour force in 1947 to less than 10 per cent in the early 1980s. This led one economist to suggest that 'the underground share of GNP has probably declined by one-third or one-half over the past generation . . . the only thing about the underground that is growing is the amount of attention it receives.'[25]

The second reason for considering that the unrecorded sector may be in decline is that, with the dramatic increase in unemployment and the collapse in manufacturing industry, there are fewer opportunities for using the workplace as a place of trade or source for information in the informal sector.[26]

Those who wrote about fiddling, pilferage and various types of cheats at work[27] were referring almost entirely to the period between the late 1960s and the early 1970s when that kind of activity may well have flourished. A group convened by the Outer Circle Policy Unit in 1976 reported in 1979, at what may well have been the high watermark of the informal sector, that estimated pilferage and allied crimes contributed to the equivalent of 1.8 per cent of the visible economy in 1974.[28] However, between September 1979 and September 1982 there was a reduction of 2.2 million employees in employment in Britain, mostly in manufacturing, where 21 per cent of all jobs were lost in those three years. Unemploy-

[23] Quoted in O'Higgins, *Measuring the Hidden Economy*, p. 23.
[24] Department of Employment, 'Numbers of self-employed people 1971-1979', *Employment Gazette*, 90(1), 1982, pp. 15-18.
[25] In a letter to the *New York Times*, 19 April 1981, from David A. Levine, economist with Sanford C. Bernstein and Co.
[26] One graphic description from a rigorous SSRC-sponsored research project in the early 1970s illustrates the importance of the place of employment: 'The plant itself is a society in miniature. It provides a variety of facilities and activities which are not task based. . . . We estimate that there are over twenty bookies' runners on the shop floor and there are regular snooker, dominoes, football and crib games. From the workers themselves it is possible to buy food, cigarettes, fresh fish (at highly competitive prices), meat, shoes and clothing, and car spares (including resprays), and to lay bets and get your hair cut. We even heard references to the "supermarket"' (E. Batstone et al., *Shop Stewards in Action*, Basil Blackwell, Oxford, 1977, p. 127).
[27] J. Ditton, *Part-Time Crimes: An Ethnography of Fiddling and Pilferage*, Macmillan, London, 1977; S. Henry, *The Hidden Economy*, Martin Robertson, London, 1978; G. Mars, *Cheats at Work*, George Allen and Unwin, London, 1983.
[28] Outer Circle Policy Unit, *Policing the Hidden Economy*, London, OCPU, 1979.

ment rose by about the same amount, and by January 1983 over 1 million people, 34 per cent of the unemployed, had been out of work for more than a year.[29]

Increases in productivity achieved by the substitution of capital for labour have forced less competitive companies to close and have forced redundancies in others. Fewer workers, more rigorously controlled, while reducing the 'over-manning' that was seen by some commentators as being part of the reason for Britain's poor economic performance, were likely to have fewer opportunities to use their employment as a way of making extra money or obtaining cheaper goods and services.[30]

Related to the preceding point is, third, the fact that the unemployed, who in the late 1970s were perhaps in a strong position to engage in informal work, had by the early 1980s become a larger, poorer element under increasing surveillance from neighbours who, for a variety of reasons, were ready to 'shop' real or putative offenders to the local social security office. A variety of reasons could be adduced for this: the new ideological stance of the radical right, introduced by Mrs Thatcher in 1979, appeared to encourage a more punitive approach to scroungers, and low paid manual workers were certainly not discouraged from displaying aggressive envy to those unemployed people with larger families who sometimes appeared to be 'doing better on the dole'.

However, it is necessary to be very cautious about imputing the readiness to 'shop' as evidence of a recent corruption of working-class solidarity not evident in previous periods of adversity. For example, in a number of books and articles J. Seabrook has claimed that there is something unprecedented in current local antagonisms. 'As the traditional associations that grew up around the workplace and the streets have been discarded, people are set increasingly against one another. . . . There is a competitive vigilance about who is getting more benefits than he should, who have given up work for easy dole money and a bit of undeclared on the side.'[31] Such assertions about working-class life in the past by popular authors like Seabrook have a pleasing nostalgia, but they are probably not true. It seems likely that the golden age of solidarity was always a generation earlier than the period in which the author was writing. Thus, in the 1930s a widely quoted and respected study refers to just the same circumstances in Rhondda, presumably an ideal-typical working-class area, that Seabrook finds in Sunderland half a century later. It is, perhaps, worth quoting the earlier account at length:

The most striking evidence comes from one of the most isolated of the Rhondda

[29] Manpower Services Commission, *Labour Market Quarterly Report*, February, 1983.
[30] In my own employment as a university professor, I am obliged to sign a book whenever I need some ball-point pens or envelopes. This is symptomatic of an attitude that has spread widely very quickly.
[31] J. Seabrook, *Unemployment*, Quartet Books, London, 1982, p. 32.

villages, a village which used to be famous for its working class solidarity. One of the men interviewed was discussing the possibility of earning a little extra to supplement 'the dole'. 'The neighbours are on to you at once', he said, 'if they hear of you earning. No-one wants to see a shilling or two more going into other people's houses than goes into their own'. He was thinking of the anonymous 'informers' through which the Unemployment Assistance Board sometimes may get information of illicit earnings, and he maintained that such things would have been unthinkable a generation ago. There was at least one instance in the sample where a man had given up a perfectly legitimate spare time occupation owing to a neighbour's threat to make trouble for him with the Board, and others where such trouble was mentioned. If practices of this kind became widespread the effect on the morale of the community would be deplorable. On the whole it seems unlikely that this particular trouble has gone very far.[32]

Another, more scholarly, contemporary study of the same area about which Seabrook writes suggests that work on the side, which Seabrook sees as an emerging phenomenon, is actually a practice that is dying out in the North East:

For generations, in regions of high unemployment, work 'on the side' has been a vital means of defending self-respect, maintaining basic income and preserving existing skills. . . . The jobs vary from tasks undertaken for family or neighbours (painting, putting in fireplaces, babysitting) to more organized work (window cleaning, tiling, delivering newspapers). But on council estates where a large percentage of the residents are receiving State benefits, there may not be enough income around to finance such jobs. If your neighbours are all on social security, few of them can afford to have their windows cleaned.[33]

The authors go on to claim that those in employment as regular window cleaners would ensure that others did not encroach on their patch and that the community was being split by an informer 'shopping' those doing informal work to the Department of Health and Social Security. 'There are also the periodic purges by the "super snoopers" as the special DHSS inspectors are called. The result is that whole communities and not just individuals feel under attack in their struggle to survive.'[34] Such examples could be readily multiplied. Substantial evidence in the early 1980s suggests that unemployed people are too poor to work informally: they cannot afford to go to pubs in order to make essential contacts, and they cannot afford the tools and equipment to do such jobs as decorating or car repairs. Again, there is little to suggest that redundancy payments cushion the effects of financial hardship.[35] For most unemployed people,

[32] Pilgrim Trust Report, *Men Without Work*, Cambridge University Press, 1938, p. 279.
[33] F. Coffield et al., 'How young people try to survive being unemployed', *New Society*, 2 June 1983, pp. 332-4.
[34] Ibid., p. 334.
[35] One sample survey showed that, of those reporting as unemployed in May 1980, 63 per cent had not been made redundant and a further 19 per cent had been made redundant but

who are overwhelmingly unskilled manual workers, 'the opportunities to receive undeclared payments are limited to less well paid jobs, such as window cleaning or gardening, the rewards for which are unlikely to be sufficiently attractive to encourage systematic fraud.'[36]

A fourth reason why the amount of uncounted work may be in decline is that Her Majesty's Inspectors of Taxes are getting more efficient. In a paper prepared in 1981 by the Civil Service Unions representing the staff employed by the Board of Inland Revenue, it was shown that the special offices set up to investigate the 'black economy' had been very effective. Extra revenue increased from £6.4 million in 1977 to £20 million in 1980 as the number of special offices were increased to a total of six. It was claimed in this document that only 0.25 per cent of company accounts and 2.5 per cent of non-company accounts were investigated by inspectors in 1979, and yet 82 per cent of the businesses examined were found to have underestimated their profits.[37] When the same source reported that examination of PAYE practices in Fleet Street provided an additional tax yield of £2 million a year, it perhaps puts the undeclared payments for scrubbing the floors of pubs into better perspective.

The concern with the modest by-employments of the poor at the expense of the substantial tax evasion of the rich at the end of the 1970s and early 1980s must be understood in terms of the distinct ideological currents of the times.[38] The 'moral panic' about people on supplementary benefit earning more than £4 a week without declaring it was out of all proportion to the amount of extra revenue lost. The suggestion that tax inspectors should spend time 'following up advertisements in shop windows' is perhaps more a sign of a willingness to engage in social control. 'The taxation of directors provides particular problems for the Inland Revenue because they are so closely involved in the running of their companies. It is not always easy to detect payments and other benefits drawn from company funds until long after the period concerned, by which time the company may have ceased to exist.'[39] As a financial journalist caustically remarked, 'evasion is still basically the working man's illegal version of the professional's legal tax avoidance or perks.'[40] The need to control the black economy, accepted to be in recession, was seen to be necessary to confirm the rule of law and respect

---

did not qualify for redundancy payments, since they were under 20 or had been with the firm for less than two years. A further survey by the Institute of Manpower Studies in May 1981 suggested that 35 per cent of those made redundant received nothing, 15 per cent received less than £500 and only 4 per cent received over £5,000 (Manpower Services Commission, *MSC Manpower Review*, London, MSC, 1982).

[36] Ibid., p. 21.
[37] Report in *The Times*, 2 March 1981.
[38] P. Golding and S. Middleton, 'Why is the press so obsessed with welfare scroungers?' *New Society*, 26 October 1978.
[39] Quoted in *The Times*, 2 March 1981.
[40] Graham Seargeant, *The Sunday Times*, 15 August 1982.

for the law for the workers who are well-behaved or who do not have the opportunity to get money on the side. This political aspect is understood by all shades of political opinion. In the words of a Conservative Party researcher,

Social security abuse is generally regarded as more blame-worthy than tax evasion and avoidance. Taking benefit money without entitlement seems tantamount to stealing, whereas tax avoision (*sic*) is more like not paying the government's bill. This attitude explains the disproportionate emphasis placed by governments on anti-abuse work by the DHSS as compared with the Inland Revenue. In 1981-82, 2250 DHSS officers were engaged in fraud investigations alone, at a total cost to the taxpayer of £33.4 million. Fully trained DHSS staff are sent out with binoculars, 'claimant spotting' in the potato fields, or sitting in their cars watching for signs of 'cohabitation' by lone mothers. The Inland Revenue employs only 1,870 detectives in the tax underground.[41]

Turning now to a fifth reason for the likely decline in what is still imprecisely termed the black economy, the growth in self-provisioning, do-it-yourself activities by household members for their own use and satisfaction in the household can be documented. All housework, DIY, gardening, charity work, lift sharing and so forth is quite explicitly *excluded* from assessments of the size of the so-called hidden economy. K. Macafee of the Central Statistical Office firmly states: 'This is outside the boundary of production. It is termed here the household economy.'[42] Yet it is *this* work that has been growing substantially in recent years and that provides much of the focus of Part II. While the attention directed to the imputed growth of the hidden economy may be misconceived, the neglect of the growth of self-provisioning work in the household has more fundamental implications and will, accordingly, be given greater emphasis here.

Domestic Self-provisioning in the Late Twentieth-century

In so far as it is possible to refer to any one form of work as 'traditional', the work done by household members for other members of the same household must be so classified. Growing vegetables, repairing the roof if the rain comes in, putting up or repairing fences — these and a multitude of other tasks are essential for most households to get by. Households that became almost completely dependent on employment in urban factories and workshops in the nineteenth century may still have managed to keep poultry or even a pig while living in towns. Those who were still

---

[41] H. Parker, 'Social security foments the black economy', *Journal of Economic Affairs*, 3(1), 1982, p. 33.
[42] Macafee, 'A glimpse of the hidden economy', p. 83.

able to live in villages and commute into the towns to work could do this self-provisioning work more readily. For example, men working in the Great Western Railway workshops at Swindon just before the First World War have been well described in a classic autobiographical account.

Very often the village resident will work for an hour in his garden or attend to his pigs and domestic animals before leaving for the railway shed. If the neighbouring farmer is busy, or happens to be a man short, he may help him milk his cows or do a little mowing with the scythe and still be fresh for his work in the factory. I have known those who, during the summer months, went regularly to fishing in the big brook, or practised a little amateur poaching with the ferrets, and never missed going to gather mushrooms in the early mornings during autumn.[43]

Again, it is unfortunate that we have very little idea how widespread this self-provisioning activity was. The likelihood is that outside the main conurbations and large estates of municipal housing, such activities have continued right through to the present.

However, it is possible that during the short-lived heyday of full employment in the 1950s and 1960s, this kind of self-provisioning declined. It is hard to get precise evidence, although it is clear that very substantial quantities of food were produced from gardens and allotments during the Second World War, so that by 1944 it was officially estimated that the produce from gardens, allotments and similar plots of land represented 10 per cent of all food produced in Britain;[44] but the indications are that by the late 1960s vegetable growing for household consumption was in decline. The Thorpe Report on allotments in 1969 showed that 62 per cent of allotment holders were aged 40 or over and over 50 per cent of allotment holders had held them since 1945. The typical allotment holder was shown to be more likely an elderly or retired manual worker whose children had left home. The Report's survey indicated that the typical allotment holder generally did not return from his employment until 7 p.m. which would reduce the time available for further work but there was an evens chance that he would go to his allotment also on Saturday. The allotment holders claimed that the main reasons for having them were to help the family budget and to get better quality and fresher produce than they could buy. They also valued gardening as a hobby. The indications were, however, that the popularity of allotments was in decline and that there was not a new generation taking over from their fathers.[45]

Self-provisioning from 1955 to 1969 for many ordinary working-class

[43] A. Williams, *Life in a Railway Factory*, Duckworth, London, 1915, p. 123.
[44] G. P. Wibberley, *Agriculture and Urban Growth*, Michael Joseph, London, 1959, p. 119.
[45] H. Thorpe, *Departmental Committee of Inquiry into Allotments*, Cmnd 4166, HMSO, London, 1969.

households was largely a matter of providing the domestic unit with
manufactured goods such as refrigerators, enabling them to store
packaged 'fresh' food, or with cars, enabling them to drive to the rapidly
growing farm-gate outlets for fresh fruit, vegetables, eggs and other
products. From 1955 to 1969, average weekly earnings, including
overtime, increased by 130 per cent. 'While prices of food and other
necessities were steadily rising, the price of small cars, in relation to
earning power, were falling, and the many products of the new
technology, such as television sets and washing machines were, despite
inflation, actually costing less.'[46] In 1956 only about 8 per cent of
households had refrigerators; this rose to 33 per cent in 1962 and 69 per
cent by 1971. Few households had television sets in the early 1950s, but
by 1961 75 per cent of families had one and this proportion rose to 91 per
cent by 1971. By that year, 64 per cent of families had washing machines.
As married women entered employment in increasing numbers, expenditure on convenience foods increased from a fifth of expenditure on food
in 1960 to a quarter in 1970.[47] Fish fingers became a staple of children's
diets and were readily stored in refrigerators. Similarly, the ownership of
cars and vans increased from 2.3 million in 1950 to 5.65 million in 1960,
9.13 million in 1965 and 11.8 million in 1970. By 1981, 62 per cent of all
households had at least one car or van, 81 per cent had washing machines
and the proportions having refrigerators and television sets were 96 and
97 per cent respectively. Three-quarters of all households had a telephone
and 61 per cent had central heating (full or partial).[48]

In 1950, out of a total stock of 13.9 million dwellings, 4.1 million or 29
per cent were owner-occupied and 6.2 million or 45 per cent were rented
from private owners. By 1977 the stock of dwellings had increased to 20.9
million but, by then, 11.1 million, or 53 per cent of the total stock, were
owner-occupied and only 14 per cent of all dwellings were rented from
private owners. The remainder in each period were rented from public
authorities.[49]

Clearly, in order to equip households with all these goods and
properties, there was a strong incentive to work long hours to earn the
maximum amount of money in employment. In the second half of the
1950s, male manual workers spent, on average, more than 48 hours a
week in employment. However, thereafter the number of hours in
employment steadily declined until, by 1973, only a third of all manual
workers spent more than 48 hours a week in employment.[50] How these
long hours in employment affected men's capacity to engage in other

[46] A. Marwick, *British Society Since 1945*, Allen Lane, London, 1982, p. 118.
[47] Ibid., p. 121.
[48] *Family Expenditure Survey*, HMSO, London, 1982.
[49] *Social Trends*, nos 1 and 9, Central Statistical Office, London 1970 and 1978.
[50] *Social Trends*, nos 2 and 5, Central Statistical Office, London 1971 and 1974.

forms of work is not entirely clear, as the interest of researchers in the full-employment heyday was not deflected from what seemed to be the only work that men do. Time budget studies, already referred to, give some clues, but there is a need for a new wave of oral history to explore all forms of work in the 1950s and 1960s.

There are indications that from around 1973 there was a substantial increase in certain forms of self-provisioning among British households. A substantial amount of production once again took place in the home by household members, which earlier in the century might have been done by employing another individual or firm. Table 4.2 provides an assessment of the growth of self-provisioning based on trade figures.[51]

Table 4.2 Indicators of the growth of various forms of self-provisioning 1974–1980 (trade in £ million)

	1974	1976	1978	1979	1980*
DIY repairs and improvements	96	142	205	256	325
Tools etc. and wood products	232	351	571	703	890
Home decorating	483	608	775	866	1,035
Total	811	1,101	1,551	1,825	2,250
Gardening equipment	235	289	399	460	600
Car maintenance	374	490	670	820	950
All of above	1,420	1,880	2,620	3,105	3,800
Deflator (1975 = 100), all consumer prices	80.9	115.6	145.0	163.4	189.5
All self-provisioning expenditure at 1975 prices	1,755	1,626	1,807	1,900	2,004

* Estimates
Source: Euromonitor Publications published in *Report on DIY/Home Improvement,* Earnshaw Hayes & Sons, privately printed 1980, p. 6. The deflator was kindly worked out by Dr J. I. Gershuny.
Overall expenditure shows a 14 per cent growth 1974–80 whereas final expenditure and GDP grew by 8 per cent over that period. DIY, tools and home decorating shows a 19 per cent growth over the period. The deflator is for all consumer prices. The particular items on the table probably had a slower than average growth so the estimates are likely to underestimate the growth in consumption of these categories.

A number of reasons were adduced for this substantial increase in domestic work. First, the sale of local authority houses and the encouragement of owner-occupation by the Conservative government, which came into office in 1979, helped to maintain demand; second, middle-class home owners found that the combination of lower disposable incomes and higher labour costs squeezed them into doing

[51] In the assessment of the DIY trade at the end of the 1970s, it was seen to be 'one of the most profitable in the retail sector'. The research organization Euromonitor suggested that the market would amount to £4,500 million in retail price terms by 1981.

more work for themselves; third, both manual and non-manual workers were reducing their hours in employment, thus giving them more time for other activities.[52]

By the late 1970s, DIY had become the fastest growing sector of the building industry. In 1976, repair and maintenance of dwellings accounted for 33 per cent of construction work; in 1979, for 40 per cent.[53] There seems also to have been a shift in scale and style of DIY activity from the 1960s to the 1970s. Many of the DIY magazines were founded in the earlier decade,[54] and it seems clear that the nature of the market changed in the years that followed. *Practical Householder*, founded in 1955, had a circulation of 250,000 in the 1960s, but changes in fashion and the arrival of competitors reduced it to 82,000 by 1982. Increasingly, information was provided free by the manufacturers and the DIY superstores, and skills came to be more widely spread and understood. By the late 1970s there were clear signs of a more sophisticated market for aids in self-provisioning.[55] There were also clear signs of more aggressive competition between the largest capitalist interests in the industry.

The growth in this particular area of self-provisioning is obviously related to a number of factors not all operating together. To begin with, new tools and cheap, readily available materials encouraged experimentation in providing domestic comforts and improvements, such as draught exclusion and the like. Later, as inflation rapidly grew in the early 1970s, people saw the advantage of improving what was their strongest hedge against inflation; and, since the cost of labour for building and services was also escalating, it seemed good sense for people to paint their own houses and even to attempt more ambitious work. The political impetus to increased home ownership has already been noted, and many local authorities began to encourage tenants to maintain their own homes after 1979 as they reduced their direct labour operations. Finally, the growth of

[52] As the authors of the Report cited in Table 4.2 suggest, 'many in the trade believe that the home improvement, as opposed to DIY, boom is only now beginning in this country' (Earnshaw, Hayes and Sons, *Report on DIY/Home Improvement*, Eurometer Publications, London, 1980, p. 5).

[53] From 1978 to 1979, the maintenance and repair sector of the building industry grew by 16.5 per cent compared with 4.5 per cent for the industry as a whole (*The Economist*, 9 February 1980). The money committed by building societies for home improvement rose from £40 million in 1977 to £120 million in 1978, or 17.4 per cent of all building society commitments (*The Economist*, 13 January 1979). Over £400 million was made available in house renovation grants by local authorities in 1979.

[54] *Do-It-Yourself Retailing* (1961), *DIY Annual* (1959), *DIY Trade* (1961), *Practical Woodworking* (1966), *DIY* (1970). However, new magazines continued to be founded up to the early 1980s; for example, *Popular DIY* (1980), *Restore-It-Yourself* (1981) and *Home Improvement Guides* (1981).

[55] The trade adopted 'a more up market, life style, interior design strategy' (Earnshaw, Hayes, *Report on DIY*, p. 6). It was increasingly recognized that manufacturers 'were beginning to design, supply and promote products exclusively for the amateur, rather than merely redesign existing "trade" products and hope that their frequently over-engineered and hence expensive quality will win market shares' (p. 7).

unemployment and perhaps an increasing awareness that *whom* you know was coming to matter more than what you know contributed to a tendency for people to move houses less frequently: whatever the reason, between 1980 and 1981 there was a reduction of 7 per cent in households moving from one area of the country to another.[56]

Furthermore, according to market research data, women were said to be increasing their share of such work.[57] It was suggested that married women working part-time in the service sector, often in pleasant, well-decorated surroundings, would adopt a more critical approach to their own domestic environment. In a September 1980 survey of women aged between 16 and 45 who were first-time home owners, who had been living in their first home for less than five years and who had undertaken at least one DIY task in the past twelve months, 77 per cent claimed that they would consider doing home improvement jobs themselves before seeking professional help; 84 per cent said that they enjoyed working on home improvements and felt quite capable of tackling wallpapering and painting; the same proportion claimed that they were involved in planning DIY work, no doubt largely owing to the need to agree on style and colour schemes; and 80 per cent said that they were planning further improvements despite having already done substantial amounts. It is interesting that much of this DIY work is done by the man and wife jointly. This applies particularly to painting and papering, but about a fifth of the wives also claimed to be able to do plastering. The division of labour in domestic improvement work by region is given in Table 4.3.

When the women were asked (not as rigorously as one would have liked) about their attitudes to this work, 64 per cent agreed that they liked to share the work as much as possible but the same proportion also said

Table 4.3 Division of labour in domestic improvement work, by region (percentages)

Home improvement work done by:	North	Midlands	South	All*
Husband only	2	1	9	4
Husband mainly	26	34	43	34
Husband and wife together	60	45	39	49
Wife mainly	11	16	8	11
Wife only	1	4	1	2
				100

*N = 481
Source: Taylor Nelson and Associates Ltd, *Survey for Polycell,* September 1980.

[56] *OPCS Monitor*, MN 82/3, Office of Population Censuses and Surveys, London, 1982.
[57] 'IPC found that in 69 per cent of cases, women were the main decision makers in both selection and purchase. Only 25 per cent of husbands claimed to be the predominant influence ... in general product lines it is estimated that within five years the number of women doing DIY jobs around the house will have risen to 48 per cent' (Earnshaw, Hayes *Report on DIY,* p. 9).

that they had to prod their husbands before they would do DIY work around the house. Interestingly, 59 per cent of the women felt that they could do jobs themselves just as well as their husbands and only 21 per cent said they would rather get someone professional in to do the job.[58]

It is evidently extremely difficult to get a precise measure of this form of self-provisioning, and even within the trade estimates differ substantially.[59] However, it does seem clear that the work is becoming more specialized. Thus, the DIY market for wood board and laminates in 1980 was estimated at £240 million at retail prices and the growth of DIY timber has compensated for the decline in demand from the building industry. Ordinary householders are attempting more than putting up simple shelving, and the demand for moulded wood is growing. Similarly, in double glazing, 40 per cent of secondary installations are done by DIY.[60]

There seems little doubt that from the middle 1950s to the early 1980s there has been a substantial increase of work done by household members on the maintenance and improvement of their dwellings, stimulated and encouraged by the development of new products[61] and the spread of power tools (almost 60 per cent of households owned a power drill in 1981). This expansion must have been limited by the fact that only since the late 1970s have more than half the households owned their own dwellings, an increasing proportion of which have relatively modest incomes. While all the data provided by the DIY industry should be viewed with caution, if not scepticism, Table 4.4 suggests that a truly remarkable amount of work goes on in the dwelling.

It is important to recognize that the sale of DIY equipment and materials obviously appears in the national accounts, so there is no question of including this in any other hidden or informal 'economy'. What is not formally assessed in the national accounts is the unpaid labour of household members, except in so far as that is reflected in the increased capital value of the domestic property in which their labour is invested. Clearly, it would be misguided to assume that this self-provisioning was anything more subtle than substituting unpaid for paid labour. Documentation of the growth of garden centres and of the domestic maintenance of cars and other equipment would show the same trend towards more household work.

This activity may enable households to live more comfortably than they might otherwise be able to do, and it is hard to sustain a view that all this work is a form of 'sweat equity' imposed on those who would be

---

[58] Polycell, *The Polycell Report on the DIY Market*, Paragon Communications, London, 1981.
[59] Ibid., pp. 12-13.
[60] Ibid., pp. 14-15.
[61] Polyfilla was introduced in 1956.

Table 4.4   DIY jobs done in Britain over a twelve-month period

Task	% of adults aged 25 and over
Painted interior woodwork	84
Filled cracks and holes	72
Hung wallpaper	70
Painted internal walls	68
Painted exterior woodwork	45
Put up shelves	40
Put up tiles on walls	37
Regrouted tiles	30
Plastered	28
Painted exterior walls	21
Put up ceiling tiles	16
Installed some form of heat installation	13

Source: Gordon Simmons Research Ltd, reported in *The 1981 Polycell Report on the DIY Market*. From the context it would appear that the information in this table relates to 1980.

unable to afford to maintain their own dwellings if they were dependent on the wage labour of others. Certainly, some self-provisioning is a coping response for those with insufficient financial resources to hire labour in the market; but it also provides aesthetic satisfactions, pride in workmanship and a sense of domestic solidarity. It is also expensive and a product of affluence, not poverty. Indeed, work in and on the domestic dwellings by men and women may do as much to develop their broader political consciousness as their experience of employment.

Everyday Household Tasks

Much work has to be done to get through the everyday business of life — cooking, shopping, tidying, cleaning, collecting, caring and a host of other activities. There seems no clear way of determining how much of this is 'necessary', since practices vary between households. One household may consider that sheets *have* to be ironed and another than jam *has* to be made after the fruit *has* to be picked. But other households may not be bound by such normative constraints. Meals may be formal, family occasions involving substantial preparation and work, or they may involve little more than defrosting and warming up some factory-prepared meal. Some children may have considerable attention lavished upon them, with much of their time filled with diverting and edifying activity, while others are left 'to bring themselves up'. Perhaps the only adequate way of discovering whether more or less of this everyday activity takes place is by measuring the amount of time people devote to it. The assumption must be that, if more time is spent on one activity than another, then that activity ranks as more important or essential.[62]

What is held to be important varies both regionally and across the social structure. The sociology of consumption is not well developed, but one attempt to draw together market research data in the 1960s provides some indication of regional variations. While the picture may be slightly overdrawn, it is worth quoting one example to make the point. Apparently an unpublished consumer survey on home cooking and baking to which Elliston Allen refers indicated the importance of cooking in Yorkshire:

It is as a cook, as a supreme virtuoso of the oven, that the Yorkshire wife expects to excel — and to be recognized and praised for that excellence. As the native conservatism precludes much variety, the conspicuous energies poured into cooking have to be expended instead on stakhanovite achievements in volume and quantity. Yorkshire cuisine is geared, accordingly, to the turning out of batches; it eschews the 'one off' run of the elite-servicing specialist. Its high-spot, inevitably, is baking: a test of keeping to a time-honoured, regular and almost ritual process, which puts an absolute discount on inventiveness. Yorkshire wives still bake their own bread far more than wives in other regions — and far more of them, too, continue to do this daily. Cakes and scones, as well, are still made at home by a majority. This, of course, saves much money and allows the consumption of cakes and buns to remain as high as ever, unaffected by rising prices in the shops. Home-baked food in itself, moreover, tends to be devoured in greater volume, not merely on account of its normally greater tastiness, but in order to do honour to the labours of the cook. The wife can take comfort from the threefold thought: that she has saved the family money, that she has persuaded it to eat more and, above all, that she has provided it with more certainly wholesome sustenance.[63]

These assertions about the Yorkshire wives' cooking behaviour appear to be well documented. An insistence on what are seen to be the 'best' ingredients implies the rejection of synthetic substitutes.[64] Again, for the same reason, packet cake mixes have met with exceptionally stiff

---

[62] I recognize, of course, that people's 'needs', consumption styles and activity patterns are substantially determined by the capitalist system's demand to create ever new wants and desires by encouraging people that new and ever-changing products will make them happier. People are both aware and unaware of this tension in the creation of their social consciousness: the joke of having an eye-level grill so that the hot fat can go straight in your eye epitomizes the contradiction. This development of *consumption* as a form of work is, perhaps, the dominant new element that capitalism has imposed on household work strategies.

[63] D. Elliston Allen, *British Tastes*, Panther Books, London, 1969, pp. 148-9.

[64] During the Second World War, home baking declined in the North East, as is illustrated by the consumption of flour following the ending of 'white' flour by government order in 1942: the figure for flour consumption in the North East was reduced from 120 per cent above the national average in 1943 to only 50 per cent above in 1949 (Ministry of Agriculture, Fisheries and Food, *Studies in Urban Household Diets 1944-49*, HMSO, London, 1956, p. 87, quoted in Elliston Allen, *British Tastes*, p. 149).

resistance in Yorkshire.[65] Apparently, the meals in Yorkshire tend to be more numerous and more sizeable on average than for other parts of Britain. Elliston Allen describes them as follows:

As the day wears on, the eating steadily increases both in volume and duration. High tea, the climax, is eaten later on average than in either Lancashire or Scotland ... and is normally a repast so overwhelming in its size as commonly to defeat anyone not bred to it. Yet for many Yorkshire people even that is not enough. Later in the evening, in many cases even as late as 10 p.m., no less than one family in five sits down to a further hot meal — and a proper meal, be it noted, not a snack.[66]

All this is in contrast to Kent, Surrey and Sussex, where 'consumption of all starchy food is strikingly low: few potatoes or suet puddings are eaten and little rice or bread. Salads, in contrast, enjoy the highest popularity.'[67] This is obviously a theme that could be documented extensively, as manufacturers pay substantial sums on market research which shows that regional and class variations in cooking and eating persist. These, in turn, imply substantial variations in the amount of work involved.

Similar variations can be documented for child care. Very detailed longitudinal studies by the Newsons reported on a random sample of 709 Nottingham mothers who had babies in the early 1960s. A striking diversity of practices and attitudes was documented: in particular, the Newsons emphasized the contrast between social classes. 'Many working class women find the role of Mam highly satisfying in and of itself ... babies are for being picked up, petted and made a fuss of. They are to show off with to the neighbours, to be dressed up in their finery and pushed out in opulent and immaculate perambulators for all the world to see and admire.' Middle-class mothers, on the other hand, are more likely 'to see the period of infancy in particular, not as a time of fulfilment, but as an abnormal and in many ways deplorable interlude in an otherwise sane and well-ordered life: or at least, this is the impression which again, it seems conventional to put forward ... her aim is to get the babyhood stage over as soon as possible, in order to return to the civilized state she fondly thinks of as normal.'[68] Just over half of all fathers are described as having 'high' participation in child care, 40 per cent 'fair' participation and 9 per cent little or none. Middle-class husbands were likely to participate more.[69]

---

[65] Even self-raising flour sells less well, 'being still considered, we must suppose, a somewhat dubious intruder into this most fiercely ritualized domain' (ibid., p. 149).
[66] Ibid., p. 150.
[67] Ibid., p. 66.
[68] J. Newson and E. Newson, *Patterns of Infant Care in an Urban Community*, Penguin Books, Harmondsworth, 1965, pp. 222-4.
[69] J. Newson and E. Newson, *Four Years Old in an Urban Community*, Allen and Unwin, London, 1968, p. 514.

The same substantial variations could be documented for the 'house-work' of tidying and cleaning. Some tasks are considered obligatory, almost to the point of being fetishistic for some social categories in some parts of the country, whereas other categories in other areas either ignore the tasks or do them only very rarely. Studies of working-class life for the last century or more have emphasized the various signs of respectability that the more aspiring households display to mark them off from the rough and unrespectable others. The same applies *a fortiori* to the more marginal lower middle class, whose anxieties approach what has been termed a 'status panic'.

Concerns of respectability and gentility stretch back in English social life to Chaucer's Canterbury pilgrims and doubtless earlier. There have always been some social categories more concerned with social prestige and honour than others, and, as contemporary studies of Mediterranean societies illuminate so convincingly, the niceties of social ranking are observed with rigorous concern in small-scale peasant villages.[70] Certain categories make a convention of flouting convention — the rough working class with its rituals of exclusion, or the liberal intelligentsia with its self-conscious adoption of ethnic or proletarian dress and distinctive accent and mannerisms.

Certainly, the reorientation of working-class life to being more home-centred from the mid-nineteenth century pushed the burden of maintaining the household's social status in the community on to women. Hence, women became conscious of what, in their social world, other women would notice. Standards of cooking, cleaning and child care were determined by other women. Men, however well-meaning, remained very often bemused bystanders, not knowing the precise way in which neighbours are both kept friendly and held at a distance, not knowing the niceties of how 'shaming' given attributes or behaviour might be. This control by women of the social standing of the household has its parallels in many pre-industrial or peasant societies. In the British working class, the 'proper' way to behave was handed down from mother to daughter, often being reflections of styles taught when mother or grandmother was in service with a 'real lady'.

For a variety of reasons, therefore, cooking, cleaning and child care came to be seen as women's work by the women themselves in the nineteenth century. As a result, men found themselves always in the role of 'helper', frequently mocked for foolish male clumsiness, or for completely misunderstanding instructions. The good working-class husband appreciates his wife, is understanding and takes his boots off in the house. As Gorer remarked, 'The only specifically female complaint against husbands which increases appreciably after marriage is untidiness.'[71] The indications are that thoughtless men provoked their

[70] J. Davis, *People of the Mediterranean*, Routledge and Kegan Paul, London, 1977.
[71] G. Gorer, *Exploring English Character*, Cresset Press, London, 1955, pp. 129-30.

wives to what was frequently referred to as constant nagging. This may be a way of correcting male normative infractions. There are, unfortunately, very few autobiographies of working-class women to illustrate the taming of boorish men.[72]

According to Stearns, who draws on a wide range of historical sources, the domestic centredness of women 'created greater gender differences than had characterized the lower classes previously and obviously could lead to a female traditionalism opposed to a male adaptive mentality'.[73] This thesis of the *development* of traditional patterns of working-class culture over a short period in the nineteenth century is in accord with Paul Thompson's view (p. 61 above). The pattern is complex (see Chapter 3): ordinary working women left employment on marriage and remained out of it, largely for demographic reasons in the late nineteenth century, when they were trapped for much of their lives by the exigencies of child-rearing, and for economic and status reasons in the 1920s and 1930s. The social construction of motherhood and homeliness in the working class took place in a relatively short space of time. During that period a *variety* of normative styles of domestic work developed. Housework, despite what some may argue, is not a universally self-evident normative pattern of work. It means different things in different social strata, among different age cohorts and in different parts of the country. Men 'help' or 'share' in it to a greater or lesser degree, but everywhere it is overwhelmingly 'women's work'.

The best guide to the amount of housework done by different categories and by men and women is provided by time budget data. Studies by Hartman and Vanek in the United States have shown that the time devoted to housework remained remarkably constant up until the 1960s. Tasks may have changed, to be sure, as a result of technological innovation: less time may have been spent on washing clothes and more on taking children to school and other activities. In Britain, the research by Dr Gershuny and his colleagues in re-analysing BBC Audience Research Department Surveys in 1961 and 1974-5 shows a clear picture of the amount of housework that is done, who does it and how it is changing. On an 'average day' — that is, the total week divided by seven — the population as a whole did 3 hours 28 minutes of domestic work each in 1961; this had declined by 12 per cent to 3 hours and 3 minutes by 1975. The equivalent figures for paid work declined from 4 hours 22

---

[72] In the biography of Joseph Ashby, we are told that, when Joseph's grandfather, 'who refused to earn wages from a single employer for long at a time', came in one day with two fine cock pheasants he had poached, his daughter was very angry. 'She ordered her father to "take those things away", and when he did not obey she took the suet pudding of bacon and late mushrooms she had just lifted from the pot and threw it at him. Wouldn't he learn? Cook those? She would never cook for him again! The poaching ended' (M. K. Ashby, *Joseph Ashby of Tysoe*, Cambridge University Press, 1961, p. 4).
[73] P. N. Stearns, 'The effort of continuity in working class culture', *Journal of Modern History*, 52, 1980, p. 641.

minutes per day in 1961 to 4 hours 6 minutes in 1975, a decline of just over 6 per cent. However, such generalized data are of only limited interest. As Thomas and Shannon report:

When we look at differences between the sexes, we find that in 1961 women on average did 5 hours and 15 minutes domestic work per day, or 36 hours 45 minutes per week, which though probably an underestimation . . . is nevertheless a large amount when compared with the men's figure of 1 hour 37 minutes per day, equivalent to 11 hours 19 minutes per week. By 1975 this had declined by 14 per cent to 4 hours 30 minutes a day for women, whereas the man's figure had declined by only 3 minutes.[74]

Evidently the inequality is large: women overwhelmingly do domestic work, even though the difference is decreasing. The obvious reason for the difference is that women are spending more time in paid employment. When the domestic work done by women is compared with men, taking into account different employment status, it can be shown that in the cases of full-time employed women and full-time employed men, both were doing less domestic work absolutely in 1975, but the men's amount had dropped relatively further than the women's. Thomas and Shannon tentatively suggest that there may be a level of domestic work that is, as it were, the absolute minimum that women in full-time employment can do without a major contribution to domestic work being made by other members of the household.

More detailed analysis of the BBC's 1975 survey enables comparisons to be made *within* households. This showed that, while it is indeed true that in households where women are in full-time employment they spend less time on routine household tasks, they do not reduce housework enough to compensate for the time they spend in employment. The total work done in the household increases when the wife is in employment, but the bulk of this increase is made up by a lengthening of the wife's working day. Men with wives in full-time employment do spend more time in cooking, washing up and shopping than men whose wives are not in full-time employment, but not to any great or dramatic extent. Thus, when both partners are in full-time employment men spend an hour a day doing non-routine domestic work, against their partner's half-hour, but this is substantially offset by women doing nearly three hours of routine domestic work against their partner's 40 minutes.[75]

The evidence from time budgets up to the mid-1970s is, therefore, totally consistent and irrefutable. Domestic work may, overall, be declining somewhat, but, where women are in full-time employment, the reduction is not enough to prevent them having an overall increased length of the working day. In the United States there appears to be a more

[74] Thomas and Shannon, 'Technology and household labour', p. 12.
[75] Ibid.

marked convergence of the use of time between women and men. Married women in employment in America have reduced their time in such employment from 294 to 242 minutes per day from 1965 to 1975 and their time spent on housework from 181 to 143 minutes per day over the same period. Married men have reduced the amount of time they spend on their main job but have increased the amount of time they spend on housework only marginally.[76] The same conclusions came from a time budget survey in Vancouver in 1971.[77]

It is likely that, while men are doing more non-routine work in terms of domestic maintenance and improvement, their contribution to the routine domestic tasks is still in the order of 'helping' rather than any substantial shift to true role reversal.

Political and Theoretical Aspects of Domestic Work and Self-provisioning

In the early 1970s, while there was a growth of interest in what was generally referred to as housework or domestic labour, little interest was shown in the domestic self-provisioning done by men. Rather, it was held by many commentators that 'housework is an activity performed by housewives within their own homes.'[78] Much of the debate was based on slender empirical evidence and certainly did not take into account substantial regional and generational differences, particularly as demonstrated by oral history.[79] All this housework was perceived as a kind of hidden subsidy to capitalism's extraction of surplus value. It was held that women reproduced labour power (i.e. future generations of workers) and fed and maintained existing workers more cheaply than would be the case if the male workers bought these services in the market.

This astonishingly humourless argument was part of the so-called domestic labour debate that exercized the minds of many in the 1970s. The issue revolved around whether 'capitalism' or 'patriarchy' or some combination of the two was most responsible for women's oppression. Since it later transpired that 'the family' was also a candidate as a source of oppression,[80] this allowed men to join women, on the grounds that there was a debate about the extent to which 'capitalism' and 'the family' oppressed *them*. Men may be seen to be incapacitated by their mothers —

[76] F. P. Stafford, 'Women's use of time converging with men', *Monthly Labour Review*, 104(2), 1980, pp. 57-9, Table 2.

[77] M. Meissner et al., 'No exit for wives: Sexual division of labour and the cumulation of household demands', *Canadian Review of Sociology and Anthropology*, 12(4), 1977, pp. 424-39.

[78] A. Oakley, *Housewife*, Allen Lane, London, 1974, p. 7.

[79] For example, E. Roberts, 'Working-class women in the North West', *Oral History*, 5(2), 1977, pp. 7-30.

[80] M. Barrett and M. McIntosh, *The Anti-Social Family*, Verso Books, London, 1982.

or at least by the suffocating relations of the nuclear family — and so what they then do to women thereafter is really the fault of the family that socialized them.

The domestic labour debate has been adequately summarized elsewhere. Nevertheless, some aspects of it are relevant to the conclusions that can be drawn from the discussion in this chapter.[81] It is clear that there is substantial variation in what constitutes domestic labour and that much of this is determined by the expectations of other women. The fact that women are the most skilled guardians and gatekeepers of social status hierarchies cannot be blamed directly on either patriarchy or capitalism. Men show little enthusiasm for the inhibiting consequences of fetishized cleanliness — certainly in the working class — and social hierarchies antedate capitalism. The growth of what is termed 'traditional housewifely values' probably developed as a result of the increase in working-class fertility in the nineteenth century which kept women tied to the domestic dwelling. As Stearns points out, traditionalism developed *within* the working class and was not imposed from above.[82]

The care of children should not be considered part of the oppression of forced domestic labour. Many women now positively decide whether or not to have children and it seems clear that motherhood provides considerable satisfactions which would not necessarily be enhanced under socialism or some other alternative to capitalism.[83] Presumably reproduction would have to take place in all possible social formations, and, while it is clear that the public provision of day nurseries and other facilities is woefully inadequate, the provision of public facilities is a matter that divides both men and women equally in political debate. Furthermore, the most rapidly growing household type is single-parent families, which are, in terms of the arguments in the domestic labour debate, counterproductive to both capitalism and patriarchy.

The domestic labour debate cannot take account of the fact that there is substantial regiaonal and social variation in the nature and range of the tasks done and who actually does them. If women in the North cook and bake far more than in the South, it cannot be assumed that such women are more under the domination of capitalism or patriarchy or both. There

---

[81] N. J. Sokoloff, *Between Money and Love*, Praeger, New York, 1980.

[82] Stearns, 'The effort of continuity'.

[83] It is unlikely that ordinary working-class women in Britain would accept very enthusiastically the suggestion made by Barrett and McIntosh: 'a socialist society might wish to control its population growth or size. At its best this could involve collective decision-making by local groups of women as has been claimed for the anti-natalist policies of Maoist China' (Barrett and McIntosh, *The Anti-Social Family*, p. 136). Such collective control over what the women would surely consider to be a personal matter might well produce the female radicalism the authors in general wish to encourage. Elsewhere the authors remark: 'socialists putting forward the "the radical critique of the family" have found themselves increasingly isolated. The working class in its organized form has expressed considerable support for the family, has fought to protect it and improve its standard of living' (ibid., p. 132). Precisely.

are variations in values independent of these forces. Furthermore, technology *has* changed the nature of domestic self-provisioning. Cooking may take much less time with convenience foods, but ironing may take more time as women in employment, say, want to have freshly pressed clothes for each day. Women may spend an equal amount of time doing housework, but it may be on different tasks, more of which are 'for themselves'.

Housework cannot be defined as 'the work that women do' or that would have the effect of defining men's domestic work as *not* housework. Unquestionably, how households allocate their collective effort to getting all the work done that they define has, or they feel needs, to be done is a complex matter. This is what is termed here a household work strategy.

In this chapter the so-called 'informal economy', domestic self-provisioning, everyday household tasks and domestic labour have been discussed. Before the mid-eighteenth century this would all have been simply the work households had to do to get by. The development of capitalism and the market economy has made things less simple. An attempt to unravel some of this complexity will be made in the next chapter.

5

New Ways of Looking at Work

The Notion of 'Informal' Work

Interest in what came to be referred to as 'informal' work developed among sociologists, social anthropologists and economists in the 1970s largely through the study of marginal urban workers in Third World cities. In one early formulation, it was claimed that 'the distinction between formal and informal income opportunities is based essentially on that between wage-earning and self employment.'[1]

As it stands, that clearly helps little in contemporary British society, since the distinction may be found within both the counted and the less well counted or 'hidden' economic spheres. However, for a variety of reasons, not always connected with academic concerns,[2] the question of the informal sector gave rise to substantial debate, many of the issues of which were usefully brought together in the symposium on *Casual Work and Poverty in Third World Cities* published in 1979.[3] As one of the contributors to that collection observed: 'The abstract conception of the informal sector has no particular substance until placed in a historical context. It is impossible to lay down universally applicable concrete characteristics of informal trades and activities, since these characteristics will vary from economy to economy, depending on the nature of the social formation.'[4]

Despite such evident good sense, scholars persisted in attempting to generalize about *the* informal economy: bibliographies were compiled and seminars and workshops were convened — some, indeed, by the

[1] K. Hart, 'Informal income opportunities and urban employment in Ghana', *Journal of Modern African Studies*, 11, 1973, p. 68.
[2] P. Connolly, 'A critique of the "informal sector" as an applied concept', in N. Redclift and E. Mingione (eds), *Beyond Employment*, Basil Blackwell, Oxford, 1984.
[3] R. Bromley and C. Gerry (eds), *Casual Work and Poverty in Third World Cities*, Wiley, Chichester and New York, 1979.
[4] R. Davies, 'Informal sector or subordinate mode of production? A model', in Bromley and Gerry, *Casual Work and Poverty*, p. 89.

author of this book — in bland disregard of the non-comparability of the material presented.[5] Attempts to make generalizations based on knowledge of informal work in Nairobi, Naples, Norwich and Novosibirsk were doomed to create intellectual confusion.

Nevertheless, it was necessary for social scientists to put their minds to informal work, if only to prevent the idea being abused and misused by those who, on the one hand, saw it 'as an alternative to capitalism'[6] and perhaps a way of surviving better in the face of global capital accumulation[7] and, on the other, saw it as a dangerous element, perhaps undermining the basis for the social control of subordinate classes — hence the moral panic about 'scroungers' in Britain.[8] Others saw it as the reverse: if people were busy 'earning a dishonest penny', they would not be so free to engage in fomenting revolution.

It is, arguably, possible to recognize two distinct economies under state socialism. This was nicely illustrated in a rather unexpected way in the Hearings of the Subcommittee on Program and Budget Authorization of the Permanent Select Committee on Intelligence in the United States House of Representatives. Noting what seemed to be a growing wave of discontent among the general Soviet population, the subcommittee took the unprecedented step of holding hearings in public in January 1980. Professor Lipson, a very distinguished lawyer from Yale, was asked to give evidence in order to help the Committee 'to understand why decent people find it so difficult to live under a Communist regime'. The answer to this disingenuous question was not perhaps what the members expected. The second economy in the Soviet Union, according to Professor Lipson, 'serves the function of lubrication of the joints of a creaking system. It conduces to social stability by means of reciprocal latent blackmail . . . . I believe the second economy is an indispensable auxiliary to the first.' Elsewhere he stated: 'Every indication tells us that the second economy in the Soviet Union is not only a frequent event, but

[5] SSRC-linked workshops on Local Labour Markets and the Informal Economy, March and September 1980 (these workshops were initiated by R. E. Pahl, who commissioned detailed bibliographic studies from the participants); Centre National de la Recherche Scientifique Programme of Seminars and Workshops 1979-81, organized by Action Thematique Programmee, Observation du Changement Social et Culturel (Seminar on the Informal Economy, June 1980), Paris; Consiglio Italiano per le Scienze Sociale (ISS), The Informal Economy, Social Conflicts and the Future of Industrial Societies, International Conference at Villa Tuscolana, Frascati (Rome), November 1982; International Sociological Association World Congress at Mexico City, August 1982: specially commissioned symposium on Informal and Peripheral Economies in Sociological Theory convened by R. E. Pahl; Connolly, 'A critique'.
[6] I. Szelenyi, 'Structural changes of and alternatives to capitalist development in the contemporary urban and regional system', *International Journal of Urban and Regional Research*, 5(1), 1981, pp. 1-14.
[7] R. E. Pahl, 'Employment, work and the domestic division of labour', *International Journal of Urban and Regional Research*, 4(1), 1980, pp. 1-20.
[8] S. MacGregor, *The Politics of Poverty*, Longman, London, 1981, pp. 156-60.

pervasive; not only pervasive but routine; not only routine but planned for by the regime; not only planned for by the regime but planned by the regime'.[9] These conclusions are supported by other sources. For example, it has been claimed that 'the parallel market is a huge economic structure, simultaneously independent from and a part of the official Soviet economy. This private sector penetrates every segment of Soviet society.'[10]

In this case it does seem at least plausible to consider a distinct *economy*, since presumably there is a clear distinction between the official planned economic system and the other market-oriented system. The two systems are based on different economic principles. However, what keeps the people placid in the capitalist world might give them dangerous thoughts in a different context.

While it may be possible to recognize two distinct economies under state socialism, however, it is less easy to postulate a separate economy under market capitalism, since any quasi-peasant or family-scale economic activity would be closely geared to the price-setting mechanisms and the banking and credit systems of the formal economy. There is, of course, the possibility of a quasi-autonomous self-sufficient peasant sector, in which, once fairly modest needs have been met, there is no attempt to expand and to accumulate; this is illustrated by the backward-sloping labour supply curve of the economists. Certain small-scale activity in countries like Italy might fall into that category, where the principles of production and exchange differ from the quasi-monopolistic sector of international capitalism.[11] Such distinctions are undoubtedly useful but, again, are not transferable to other contexts without great care.

There may be certain benefits to employers in Britain to 'informalize' the conditions of employment of some of their employees. The growth of various forms of employment protection legislation, compulsory pension payments, union restrictions and various other measures may encourage some employers to avoid giving full accountability of their employment practices. Such unrecorded employment is more likely in countries like Italy, with a flourishing sector of family capitalism, and perhaps less likely in Britain, where the concentration of capital has proceeded further than in any other Western capitalist state. Highly self-exploiting family businesses are declining rather than growing in Britain.

It would be a peculiarly perverse kind of social anthropology that linked the small-scale sweatshop enterprises of Naples with the services in

---

[9] US Select Committee, *Soviet Internal Developments*, US Government Printing Office, Washington DC, 24 January 1980

[10] D. K. Simes, 'The Soviet parallel market', *Survey*, 21(3), 1975, p. 52.

[11] E. Mingione, 'Informalization and survival strategies in Southern Italy', in N. Redclift and E. Mingione (eds), *Beyond Employment*, Basil Blackwell, Oxford, 1984.

small enterprises by the upper middle class of Belgravia or Fulham.[12] However, over-enthusiastic supporters of a resurgent small industry sector might make just such an error. There are some more general statements that can be said about 'informal work practices' on a world scale, since in one sense or another they are all responses to overall processes of capital accumulation.[13]

The Issue of the Provision of Services Under Late Capitalism

As was mentioned in Chapter 4, discussion about an informal economy in Britain by Gershuny,[14] and then elaborated by Gershuny and Pahl,[15] used the term in a very limited way in order to emphasize different patterns of service provision. Indeed, it might have saved much subsequent confusion if different terminology had been used and if both of us had referred consistently to spheres of service provision. Gershuny's intention was to argue against a conventional view of economic development which postulated a unilinear development from primary production through manufacturing to services, which, he claimed, was 'wholly misleading'.[16] Rather, he claimed 'that technical innovations, changes in capital endowments and modifications in legal institutions, combined to produce a rather less tidy pattern of development'. He suggested that there were six possible transitions of production between the three 'economies' he formulated, and he expressed this diagrammatically as in Figure 5.1.

Gershuny used this highly simplified model to demonstrate that, at *specific* times and under *specific* circumstances — of technology, labour

---

[12] See, for example, F. Bechhofer and B. Elliott (eds), *The Petite Bourgeoisie*, Macmillan, London, 1981; R. Scase and R. Goffee, *The Entrepreneurial Middle Class*, Croom Helm, London, 1982. Perhaps one should acknowledge in passing that one group of perceptive journalists, who specialize in the ethnography of those in the upper middle class from public schools, claim to see a growth of small businesses in an unexpected quarter. 'The new thing in the upper middle class is butchering, fishmongering, carpentry, building, dressmaking, furniture moving, sandwich delivery (they love instant delivery), house painting . . . and hotel owning . . . they reckon that the present government is a good one for people with money in the background . . . . And if they have their own businesses, they work for cash wherever possible. . . . In fact, it's striking how easily the public school values of self-sufficiency and modest perfectionism can be adapted to the world of specialized, small-scale trade' (A. Barr et al., 'The incredible sloane hulk', *Harpers and Queens*, October 1982, pp. 232-5).

[13] A judicious assessment is provided by Redclift and Mingione's Introduction to *Beyond Employment*, which complements the argument of this book.

[14] J. I. Gershuny, 'The informal economy: Its role in industrial society', *Futures*, February 1979, pp. 3-15.

[15] J. I. Gershuny and R. E. Pahl, 'Work outside employment: Some preliminary speculations', *New Universities Quarterly*, 34(1), 1979, pp. 120-35; J. I. Gershuny and R. E. Pahl, 'Britain in the decade of the three economies', *New Society*, 3 January 1980, pp. 7-9.

[16] J. I. Gershuny, 'The informal economy', p. 9.

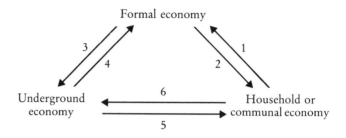

Figure 5.1   The six transformations

Source: J. I. Gershuny, 'The informal economy: its role in industrial society', *Futures*, February 1979.

supply and public regulation and organization — which pertain to the production of any commodity, certain sorts of transformations will develop. Overall, of course, household/communal production has been in decline as activities and functions have been taken over by the market or the state welfare system, but there is no *a priori* reason why such a decline should necessarily continue. He was also careful to say that the growth of household production of services was merely *inferred* from the growth of household ownership of domestic capital goods. People might own power tools, but, at that stage, Gershuny was not in a position to demonstrate that they actually used them.

Gershuny's later work on time budgets allowed him to argue the point with greater confidence. Work on time budgets is obviously less likely to provide information on the question of the informal provision of goods and services, and it was evident that Gershuny had considerable problems in moving from his aggregated analysis of consumer behaviour to the more specific analysis of households differentially placed in the social structure. He argued, at a general level, that substantial productive activity was taking place outside the formal economy and, hence, was unmeasured. Perhaps, he suggested, the unmeasured was growing in a way that would offset the manifest decline of the measured. It was an appealing prospect, which shifted the focus from the macro concerns of the economist to the more locally grounded work of sociologists, social anthropologists and the more empirically minded students of local labour markets.

In 1979, Gershuny and Pahl extended the notion of transformations between the three spheres as ways of showing shifts in the manner of the provision of *services*, to ways of getting *work* done. They argued that it was necessary 'to enlarge our notion of work to embrace a much wider set of activities than are usually considered in this context'.[17]

This focus on the notion of work rather than mode of service provision

[17] Gershuny and Pahl, 'Work outside employment', p. 128.

was a radical departure from the line of thinking that Gershuny had been developing. Gershuny and Pahl emphasized that work took place in spheres other than simply the formal economy:

Evidently the permutations between the three spheres for different members of a household over time can get very complex. But it is this very complexity that has to be explored and in which new mixes or choices have to be created. Job-sharing, seen in this light, means much more than just shorter hours in the formal economy; *which* work in *which* economy for *which* member of the household for *how long* are basically the questions at issue.[18]

The authors concluded that: 'We cannot segregate work in the different spheres to different categories of people.' Concerned with these other forms of work, Pahl suggested that 'a man with his own tools, his own time and a long-stop income in the form of unemployment pay may not be in such a vulnerable position' in the 1980s as his unemployed counterpart might have been fifty years earlier. Somewhat rashly, he went on to suggest that 'his *work* identity can still be maintained even if his employment identity is in abeyance.'[19] Two case studies elaborated in that contribution seemed to confirm the notion that there were a variety of ways of getting by and that what in one case was clearly a coping strategy of the poor could, in another case, be a voluntary choice, allowing a greater flexibility in the use of time and labour and a greater feeling of satisfaction through the greater personal control of the labour process.[20]

Attempts at a more macro-level to measure the 'hidden economy' have indicated that it has passed its peak, its size being associated with the amount of cash available for redistribution.[21] Gershuny has argued that he is not presenting a unilinear or evolutionary model, but is concerned with the consequences of the interaction of processes at given conjunctures, although there is perhaps an unintended evolutionary tone to his work. He was certainly right to emphasize the privatization of consumption, and this was an important point of departure for further work, but there were unstated assumptions in his model that should perhaps be made explicit. In particular, much of his analysis is in a highly aggregated form, hiding important differences.

Gershuny also avoids specifying any *essential* motor of change, although one infers that technological innovation is more important than distributions of capital and politico-legal arrangements in producing distinctive forms of service provision. There tends to be an implicit

---

[18] Ibid., p. 134.
[19] Pahl, 'Employment, work' p. 5.
[20] These case studies of the Parsons and the Simpsons are reproduced in Appendix 2.
[21] M. O'Higgins, *Measuring the Hidden Economy: A Review of Evidence and Methodologies*, Outer Circle Policy Unit, London, 1980.

optimism in his work, which assumes a benign state and limitless economic growth and expansion. It is important to disaggregate technological innovation: the domestic washing machine is equated as just another piece of domestic technology — to be seen in the same way as an electric drill or a gadget to allow blip games to be played on the TV screen. There is surely an analytical distinction of some value between a piece of technology that enables what has to be done to be done more efficiently or even more cheaply, and a piece of technology that occupies the mind while one's wits go woolgathering in front of a TV screen. It is surely necessary to know who buys and who uses the domestic gadgetry and the distributional consequences of whatever benefits they may produce.

Burns[22] and Gershuny, in their detailed documentation of work done in the household or 'domestic economy', unwittingly, perhaps, suggest that a common set of processes produces similar results – the mass consumers, as Gershuny describes them. This is too generalized: privatized consumption can be created by both increasing affluence *and* increasing poverty: richer people may be spending more time in the domestic environment with their electronic gadgetry, but poorer people may be privatized for opposite reasons. They cannot afford to buy services from the formal economy should they wish to do so. A conflation of processes of both choice and constraint is confusing and suggests an implausible consensus on goals and values. The motor of change in the way services are provided might well depend on class relations and on values as much as on the factors Gershuny adduces. While it may be more economical, for example, to buy meat in bulk and fruit and vegetables in season to put in a deep-freeze, this implies not just the resources to acquire capital equipment, but also the flexible cash flow required to run it effectively. The logic of higher productivity in the service sector may lead to self-service stores with lower prices rather than corner shops, which allow credit and provide social supports and sanctions for saving through Christmas clubs and similar schemes.

It is commonplace to note that innovations and more profitable ways of doing things are not universally progressive in their effects. The distributional effects of the self-service economy, postulated by Gershuny, need to be worked through very carefully. There are alternative ways of providing services or getting work done, and people may be just as 'rationalistic' or 'economistic' in their diverse courses of action. The differences are based on their distinctive value systems, and it cannot be claimed without argument that one is equivocally better than another. This point is not made in a purely negative sense, since different values and conceptions about status can have, as mentioned at the beginning of Chapter 4, important implications for economic behaviour.

[22] S. Burns, *The Household Economy*, Beacon Press, Boston, 1977.

It seems not unfair to characterize the work of Burns, Gershuny and others during the 1970s and early 1980s as more narrowly economistic than now seems reasonable to accept. It did, however, serve the valuable function of prompting others to ask questions about the different values of different social groups and about the patterns and consequences of distinctive household work strategies. There was a real danger, evident in my own paper of 1980, that unemployment would be misperceived as liberating people from employment in order to trap them in their homes. This was because the focus there was on the detailed and the precise mechanisms of how a distinctive category of the population was coping, or getting by, under difficult economic circumstances.

In discussing the 'informal economy' it was suggested that the same concept has been stretched to serve a variety of purposes — as a justification for more Inland Revenue staff, as an issue in the social control of the poor, as another way of understanding changing patterns of service provision and, finally, as 'evidence of self-employment which reduces the actual level of unemployment'.[23] It has become a kind of catch-all for all except the most conventionally accounted employment and self-employment. Because little attention has been given to the social relations within which various forms of work are embedded, there has been substantial confusion, certainly in public discussion and also in academic debate.

Exploring the Social Relations of Employment

Employment is the form of work that appears the easiest to understand: in very simple terms, a worker brings his or her skills and strength to an employer and in return receives a wage or salary for the time spent or the task achieved. However, it is not always quite as simple as that, since it would be wrong to see all workers as equally well-placed. Some have conditions of service agreements which give them almost complete security of tenure (such as dockworkers); others, such as contract research workers in universities and elsewhere, have no security and are obliged to waive their redundancy rights. Some employees work for large multi-national corporations, whose policy is to provide security and substantial fringe benefits; others work for companies with very uncertain futures, whose concern is to get the maximum return from labour at the minimum cost. Some employees are full-time, some part-time; some have facilities provided at formal workplaces — factories and offices — whereas others are employed on a piecework basis in their own homes.

[23] *Report of the House of Lords Select Committee on Unemployment*, HMSO, London, 1982, para. 2.8.

The state intervenes to a greater or lesser degree to regulate the employer-employee relationship: health and safety regulations, obligatory national insurance contributions, statutory paid maternity leave and so forth. However, there is a wide diversity of practice across the range of employment situations; employers may legally or illegally change the conditions of employment for their own or their employees' benefit. In the case of the former, they may shift from employing male full-time skilled workers to employing part-time semi-skilled married women workers. This strategy may produce a more docile, flexible and cheaper workforce, putting second incomes into some households and reducing some households to having no earners at all. Certain formal employment protection legislation, devised by the state for the protection of the assumed 'normal' male full-time worker, may be avoided. This must be seen as the 'informalization' of formal contractual systems. Whether the employee is male or female will substantially determine levels of pay and conditions of service, irrespective of skill or capacity. This is particularly likely when formalized grading systems are not in operation. In a study of a wide range of companies and industries designed to understand the determinants of women's pay and employment position, the authors concluded:

> Most of the small firms in the survey used relatively informal systems, either *ad hoc* individual systems or mainly flat-rate payment systems with little reward for skill, experience or differences in job content. The *ad hoc* systems were often described as merit-based systems, but in practice pay levels more often reflected the wage at which workers were recruited than an assessment of their current worth.[24]

The desire for informal employment practices is well illustrated in Scase and Goffee's study of small firms in the building industry, where there appears to be a constant battle to avoid the government's regulatory legislation.[25]

Sometimes employers will informalize the relations between them and their workers to the advantage of the employees. Thus, a minimally low 'declared' wage is provided and the remainder is paid in cash, thereby providing the employee with a tax-free bonus up to the level of the informally agreed wage. The employer also gains, since he pays less, but it

[24] C. Craig et al., 'Women's pay in informal payment systems', *Employment Gazette*, 91(4), 1983, p. 146.

[25] As one respondent in their study put it, 'Subcontracting has a distinct advantage in that you are working to a fixed price, whereas if you've got direct labour you've got to put a hell of a lot more work into getting them to work to a target . . . then there are more of the administrative problems that go along with direct labour . . . all the extra work and money that goes into things like holiday pay . . . . It's too much "aggro" to get involved with . . . . Plus there's a possibility that sooner or later you're going to get some bugger who's going to take you to unfair dismissal' (Scase and Goffee, *Entrepreneurial Middle Class*, p. 143).

depends on his having cash off the books. Some employers can, as it were, employ no one. All their wages are paid in cash: they can even do this legally if their payments are small enough. Many employers prefer to employ pensioners on a part-time basis for this reason.

There is no need to elaborate the point that the same kind of work — employment for a wage — can range from the stable, protected employment in a large organization to the unstable, informal employment practices of small organizations. Clearly, the social conditions of employment vary substantially, but so long as there is an employer and employee the social relations remain the same. However, the social relations of the self-employed are different.

According to Scase and Goffee, many of those starting an independent business do so as an explicit *rejection* of the capitalist ethic. It 'enables a person to escape from the constraints of authority, the wage-profit relationship and other features of being an employee'.[26] Some can, of course, combine wage labour with self-employment, and this is particularly likely in the building and allied trades. It should be recognized that under certain circumstances informal ties of mutual trust and obligation can bind an employer to an employee far more effectively than formal statutory legislation. However, there is generally a price to be paid in informal sanctions, which of course can work both ways, and the shift from status to contract, from *Gemeinschaft* to *Gesellschaft*, is generally held to be a progressive one.

There is, of course, a range of work where the social relations of the market and of capital do not apply so directly, where transactions take place partly or wholly on the basis of other imperatives such as the need to maintain social solidarity and to confirm the norm of reciprocity. There are many other kinds of work than simply selling labour power to an employer. It is these other kinds of work that were placed in an historical context in Chapters 1 and 2.

The Social Relations of Work outside Employment

Let us, by way of illustration, take some relatively simple task — a woman ironing a garment in a domestic dwelling. Viewing that activity on its own, without knowing the social relations in which it is embedded and which to a degree create it, is an inadequate basis for determining the precise nature of the work involved. The various possibilities will be systematically reviewed, providing an alternative typology of work.

The woman could be completing a task for which she is employed as an outworker for a garment manufacturer. This work would be unequivo-

[26] R. Scase and R. Goffee, *The Real World of the Small Business Owner*, Croom Helm, London, 1980, p. 35.

cally *wage labour*. If, on the other hand, the woman was proposing to sell the garment she has just made in her own boutique or market stall, she would be engaged in *petty commodity production* as a self-employed worker, since she would be producing for herself and not for her employer. Both of these forms of work could be undertaken without informing the controlling agencies of the state, which may be referred to then as *shadow wage labour* or *shadow petty commodity production*: the social relations might remain the same, but the system of national accounting would certainly be affected.

The woman could, on the other hand, be ironing a garment for which she received no direct monetary reward. If she is ironing her own blouse in preparation for her next day's wage labour, then she could be said to be engaged in *individual reproduction*. All wage labourers have to be, as it were, reproduced from day to day. Some have much of this activity done for them by others: young wage labourers get the support of their parents; men frequently get the support of their unpaid wives. This work, called *social reproduction*, is to do with the maintenance of existing workers or the reproduction of new ones and is typically done by women: it may be said to be structured by the social relations based on patriarchy, as wage labour is structured by the social relations of capitalism. In both cases, patterns of domination and subordination structure the social relations of the work. However, in the case of social reproduction, while the ironing of the shirt may be described as patriarchically structured social reproduction work, it could also be shared wage labour (the wife is preparing herself for business entertaining on behalf of her husband, for which she gets paid) or shared social reproductive work (tomorrow the husband does the ironing) or undominated subsistence work (the tasks have been equitably divided between all members of the household, none of whom is a wage labourer or self-employed worker, and the woman has agreed to do the ironing as part of her overall contribution).

It would be wrong to assume that all women ironing a garment for another person are constrained to do so by patriarchal values. If the woman were ironing the garment for colleagues in a local dramatic society, it would make a difference if the way the work had been allocated involved a degree of 'friendly coercion' or had been given without question because she was a woman. If, on the contrary, she had *offered* to do this work for her colleagues in the society, or for a neighbour who was sick, then she would be doing what may be described as *social solidarity work*. Such work, based on generalized or specific reciprocity, reflects the social constraints of sharing the same dwelling or locality and is essential if people are to live together reasonably amicably. This is distinct from *voluntary work*, which may be done anonymously and is not based on the constraints of interpersonal interaction or related to any reciprocal recompense.

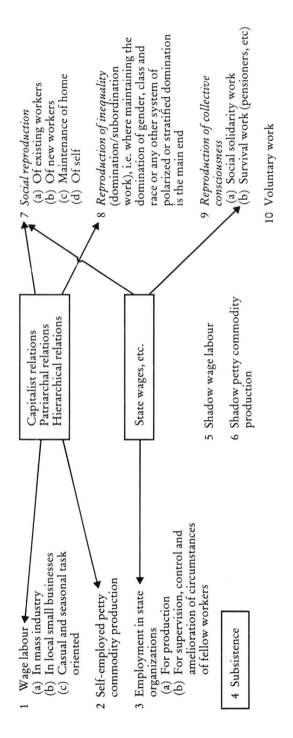

PRODUCTION

1 Wage labour
   (a) In mass industry
   (b) In local small businesses
   (c) Casual and seasonal task
       oriented

2 Self-employed petty
   commodity production

3 Employment in state
   organizations
   (a) For production
   (b) For supervision, control and
       amelioration of circumstances
       of fellow workers

4 Subsistence

5 Shadow wage labour

6 Shadow petty commodity
   production

Capitalist relations
Patriarchal relations
Hierarchical relations

State wages, etc.

REPRODUCTION

7 *Social reproduction*
   (a) Of existing workers
   (b) Of new workers
   (c) Maintenance of home
   (d) Of self

8 *Reproduction of inequality*
   (domination/subordination
   work), i.e. where maintaining the
   domination of gender, class and
   race or any other system of
   polarized or stratified domination
   is the main end

9 *Reproduction of collective*
   consciousness
   (a) Social solidarity work
   (b) Survival work (pensioners, etc)

10 Voluntary work

Figure 5.2   A Preliminary typology of work

In all these descriptions of a given task being done, the type of work may be understood by exposing the pattern of social relations in which it is embedded. It is these social relations of work that produce exploitation. The circumstances under which the ironing was agreed to be done and the relative balance of power between the woman doing the ironing and her significant others would need to be known and understood before the particular work task could be appropriately categorized. Such might be an advance in sociological conceptualization, but this intellectual exercise is not self-evidently of any more general significance.

Is All Social Activity or Social Behaviour 'Work'?

The attempt to set out systematically a preliminary typology of work (see Figure 5.2) shows that most types of work can be illustrated through the example of ironing, but this possibly supports the position rather too neatly. Some tasks cannot be so easily manipulated in and out of different categories of social relations, yet there are, perhaps, many more tasks in industrial society that could shift out of one category into another. Nevertheless, a valid criticism is that the typology, by attempting to be comprehensive, weakens the distinctive meaning of the word 'work' so that it becomes synonymous with 'activity', or 'task', or simply 'social behaviour'. Since, it may be argued, we live in a capitalist social formation, *all* activities are concerned with the production and reproduction of that system. According to such an extreme position, productive work[27] is seen as central and all other activities as secondary and subservient to it. Thus, people's leisure, free time or play can be seen as

---

[27] The notion of productive work is a notorious concept for generating confusion, paralleled only by the notion of reproduction. Sociologists and social anthropologists cannot seem to escape from being haunted by Marx's ghost. For present purposes I am content to adopt a fundamentalist materialist position, which probably relates to my early training in historical geography, and it goes something like this. People have to work to get by, to keep the rain out, to make tools and so forth. They are caught up in an endless cycle of 'birth and copulation and death', in Eliot's phrase, and the relationship between the domestic cycle (and the social arrangements connected with it) and the material conditions of life are mediated by cultural practices, values and the constraints imposed by given social formations. The unit for getting by is the *household*, whose members can use their own labour in distinctive ways (various forms of work or resource options) and can draw on distinctive sources of labour from outside. *These are the basic divisions of labour.* People spend a lot of time messing about with cultural artefacts on which they put value — cowrie shells, diamonds, hi-fi equipment, outboard motors, dresses, cars, bicycles, handbags and canoes, to name but a few. Some of these objects have high exchange value (cowrie shells) but little use value, others high use value (a much-loved tool) but little exchange value. Some social formations encourage the production of many objects and things which, in turn, implies substantial consumption. Since without this consumption the *raison d'être* of production would be undermined, consumption is essential for production and is a necessary form of work in such societies. However, such a logic is ultimately self-defeating, as we are currently able to observe.

recreating the energy and momentum to return to productive work, and, somewhat humourlessly, *re*productive work is seen as serving the function of reproducing the labour power and social relations of the social formation.

Again, those who are in receipt of state benefits because they are physically or mentally disabled or are over the official age of retirement are paid to survive — not because a capitalist social formation gets material benefit from dispensing such minimal largesse, but because the alternative would disrupt social stability. To make the point rather sharply, if those who, for whatever reason, are incapable of doing productive work (and here we include reproductive work as productive work) were obliged to take a painless death, the nakedness of the system of expropriation would be apparent and hence the system would be unsustainable. Paying out state benefits to people whose main work then becomes largely one of survival is, in this bleak perspective, a way of maintaining social stability and cohesion. From this point of view, neighbourly exchanges which promote social solidarity can also be seen as helping to create social cohesion and so may be functional for the stability of a capitalist social formation. Even the social relations based upon patriarchy can be seen as functional for the maintenance of capitalism, but they apparently seem to be functional for all other social formations as well.[28]

Such an obsessive and misguided radical functionalism is able to describe most of the processes and practices of social life as necessary to the maintenance of the present system. It is also necessary and in the interests of capital to mystify the workings of this self-sustaining exploitative system. All work — including even revolutionary sabotage — then becomes one kind of work: that necessary to perpetuate the system. (The saboteurs provoke a 'defensive' response which can then be legitimated by the state as necessary for the maintenance of peace and the control of violence. This response may be in the form of a secret police, an armed police, the armed forces used for civilian control and so on.) True subsistence work, which appears in the typology, is not therefore possible in capitalist society according to this perspective, except in very isolated and special circumstances. Certainly, it is difficult to escape from the exigencies of the money economy completely, although with determination and some privation a modest degree of self-sufficiency is possible, even in highly developed capitalist societies.

How then can one escape from this intellectual impasse? A number of points need to be made. First, it is clear that domination/subordination-determined social relations occurred in pre-capitalist societies; and, while it may be argued that patriarchal attitudes have been incorporated and

[28] P. R. Sanday, *Female Power and Male Dominance: On the Origins of Sexual Inequality*, Cambridge University Press, 1981.

'used' by capitalism, this does not deny that the social relations of, for example, domestic labour or social reproduction pre-date capitalism and are qualitatively different from the class domination associated with capitalist relations of production. Second, all societies require work to maintain the collective conscience, in a Durkheimian sense, and social solidarity has universal significance and importance in a way that canot be reduced, perhaps over-simply, to another of the 'needs of capitalism'. Third, and perhaps most important, people themselves recognize that work can be qualitatively different and that 'work' for a neighbour, 'work' for oneself or one's spouse and 'work' for an employer are different activities, even though, as shown in the example of ironing, they may involve the same task. Those who wish to reduce the types of work available to a person to simple dichotomies, as being either productive or non-productive, money-generating or non-money-generating, producing either exchange value or use value, do violence to people's experience and make the unwarranted assumption that the social relations of capitalism have become dominatingly all-pervasive. According to this view, principles of social reciprocity have become corrupted by ideas based on market principles, so that the metaphors of exchange infiltrate into personal relationships, with careful calculations of the costs and benefits of various courses of action.[29]

We are now in a better position to answer the question of whether all social activity is 'work'. Quite evidently it is not. But, equally, work cannot be narrowly defined by constraining definitions, which limit it either to employment, or as a result of abstract philosophizing on the nature of 'productive' labour. Work can be understood only in relation to the specific social relations in which it is embedded. Specific people in specific circumstances in specific sets of social relations and social relationships can be described precisely in terms of whether they are engaged in work or play. The word 'work' cannot be defined out of context: that, indeed, is the conclusion and answer to the question.

Given this sociological understanding of the nature of work, it is clear that attempts to quantify 'amounts of work' are fraught with difficulty. Neither the *Family Expenditure Survey* nor the various time budget studies nor any set of national statistics can do more than give very crude indications of who does what work, when and where. In terms of quantity of work, it seems not unreasonable to guess that in 1984 more hours of work are being done in about half the households in Britain than at any time in the century. This is because such households, with two or

---

[29] Sociologists may have fallen into this error in so far as they believe that 'exchange theory' is more than a metaphor. See G. C. Homans, *Social Behaviour: Its Elementary Forms*, 2nd edn, Harcourt Brace Jovanovich, New York, 1974, and P. M. Blau, *Exchange and Power in Social Life*, John Wiley, Chichester, 1974, together with the astringent critique by A. Heath, *Rational Choice and Social Exchange*, Cambridge University Press, 1976.

more earners, are increasing the total hours in employment, are doing more self-provisioning, and yet are not reducing substantially the amount of domestic work that is done. However, in the households of the unemployed, the elderly and retired and certain other single-person households, overall less work is being done.

This is an issue that the empirical case study in Part II is designed to illuminate. The quantification of work in terms of the social relations in which it is embedded cannot be divorced from localities with their distinctive patterns of social relationships. Similarly, the various forms of work are inextricably intertwined, and analytic disentanglement poses formidable difficulties.

The Provision of Services, the Domestic Cycle and Sources of Labour: The Making of Household Work Strategies

In the discussion so far, an attempt has been made to structure the elements involved in an understanding of the social relations of work. This led to a focus on the employer and the employee in particular and on the way the relationship between the two is more or less mediated by the state. This line of thinking led to a rejection of the notion of a separate 'informal economy', since that phrase covered too many disparate elements to be analytically useful. It is nevertheless recognized that Gershuny and others are perfectly correct in arguing that *the mode of the provision of services* is changing, and not necessarily in a unlinear direction, since the movement between modes may be, as it were, moving in different directions at the same time, depending on the nature of the service. Also, of course, tasks are not endowed with some kind of ontological status, independent of time, place and social formation: to a degree, social relations determine tasks; the social relations are a product of the social formation, therefore tasks are in that way related to the nature of the social formation.

It is the conflation of modes of service provision, separately labelled 'economies' and spheres of work and characterized by distinctive patterns of social relations, that is at the heart of the confusion in much contemporary discussion. If these are kept analytically distinct, then the likelihood of some advance in understanding is substantially increased.

As I have shown above, changes in the modes of service provision are a product of a variety of factors, including the government legislation of the time, the availability of and access to tools, technology and skills and the values of the actors concerned. Thus, for example, it is not now illegal to brew a certain amount of beer for home consumption; there is ready availability of equipment and knowledge, and many people get satisfaction from producing their own, possibly superior, product for home consumption. Such arguments have now been widely rehearsed, especially emphasizing the value of home-based production of a variety of goods and services.[30]

Gershuny has shown that the private ownership of cars and television sets has led to a decline of public transport and public entertainment, but he recognizes that the movement is certainly not always in the same direction.[31] The movement from cooking meals at home to getting them from take-away centres is an example of a transformation in a different direction. In addition to the English staple of fish and chips, it is common for Indian, American and Chinese food, and often Turkish or Greek and a variety of others as well, to be available on a take-away basis in working-class areas. Gershuny shows how the growth of self-service and, in the term used in this book, self-provisioning has repercussions in the manufacturing sector: in the same way that the invention of the internal combustion engine and the cathode ray tube led ultimately to changes in life style and service provision, so will developments in the new information technology lead to more such changes. More recently Gershuny has modified what appeared to be a more deterministic stance in his earlier formulations:

It can be extremely misleading to talk of '*the* information society'. The scope for policy choice, the range of different applications for IT, and the different ways that a given application may be embodied, mean that a wide range of alternative information societies are possible. Different balances between the level of application in different spheres would produce very different types of society, not least in conditioning the choice between goods and services by households. Furthermore, the consequences of such applications for ways of life are by no means determined by technology pure and simple. Even with industrial process applications, informatics have very different implications for work and organization structures.[32]

The issue of mode of service provision and the debates surrounding it relate to the theme of this book by affecting the *range* of work or tasks that a household does or is potentially capable of doing. Household work practices provide, as it were, a tracer of wider technological, political and economic changes and tendencies. There is, of course, a danger that households will be misperceived as passive social entities, responding like so many barometers to the pressures passing over them. Such a stance is dehumanizing and alienating and does not acknowledge the creative force of social values and practices.

---

[30] Burns, *Household Economy*.

[31] J. I. Gershuny, *After Industrial Society?* Macmillan, London, 1978.

[32] J. I. Gershuny and I. D. Miles, *The New Service Economy: The Transformation of Employment in Industrial Societies*, Frances Pinter, London, 1983, p. 232.

Households are not simply so many corks bobbing about in the currents of history. An equally powerful image can be adduced of households facing broadly the same problem — how to get by — despite endless change and variation in material conditions. The domestic cycle follows the same basic pattern, but, as the conditions of the social formations change, so households mobilize distinctive resource options. Under some circumstances households have organized collectively and worked with other households, as in Redgrave in the thirteenth century, Ryton in the sixteenth century and, to a degree, Sheppey in the twentieth century. On other occasions, in different material circumstances, individuals maximize their resource options by fragmenting household solidarity. Thus, youngsters may prefer to leave their natal home earlier or husbands and wives may split up when the economic benefits of staying together are less obvious. Anderson's study of family relationships in a Lancashire cotton town in the early nineteenth century demonstrates an individualized response to hardship.[33] Kinship obligations were recognized when it was materially rewarding to do so, but if the reward was greater elsewhere, then the individual would leave. Similarly, members of families who in better circumstances might share their resources — passing on discarded clothing and the like when it was needed — might, under economically more difficult circumstances, charge for the goods or services in relation to more universalistic market criteria. Studies of how American families faced the Depression of the 1930s showed how some families came together more strongly under adversity, whereas others cracked under the strain. Individual chief earners, apparently inexplicably, left their homes and families, some returning, if at all, after a number of years.[34] Rules relating to the social security payments to the unemployed in contemporary Britain reduce people's resource options: they are virtually obliged to stay in their dwellings, as they have no money for social life, are unable to earn any extra and are meant to be permanently available to be hired as wage labourers.

As an essential precursor to the style of analysis that is to follow in Part II, it is now necessary to unpack and to elaborate the notion of a household work strategy, beginning with an *ideal-type*[35] structured round the domestic cycle. This model is influenced to some degree by the empirical results that follow but is, of course, an abstraction.

---

[33] M. Anderson, *Family Structure in Nineteenth-Century Lancashire*, Cambridge University Press, 1971.

[34] R. C. Angell, *The Family Encounters the Depression*, Scrivenor, New York, 1936; M. Komarovsky, *The Unemployed Man and his Family*, Institute of Social and Religious Research, New York, 1940; reprinted by Octagon Books, New York, 1971.

[35] As subsequent discussion of the data gathered on the Isle of Sheppey shows, some of the assumptions in this model are mistaken. It is just as well that empirical research provides some counter-intuitive results.

1   Two adult earners, male and female, decide to share accommoda-
     tion permanently and thus to establish a household. Both are in
     full-time employment and come to an equitable bargain on how the
     various domestic tasks are to be distributed. Since they have not yet
     accumulated much capital and are involved in furnishing and
     refurbishing their dwelling, they are less likely to pay for much
     work to be done by outside contractors, apart from large jobs
     beyond their range of skills, and they will try to get these done as
     cheaply as possible — perhaps paying a friend. The allocation of the
     work outside employment that they do themselves may be largely
     pragmatic, depending on their respective length of journey to work,
     cycle of work pressure, range of skills and accomplishments and
     personal responsibilities. Since they are both away from the
     dwelling at their place of employment for much of the time, they are
     unlikely to be in the position to draw on the resources of others in
     the immediate locality, although there can be many circumstances
     when this is not the case. Informal contacts at work will, however,
     be important in finding sources of labour.

2   A new stage in the domestic cycle is established when children are
     added to the basic household dyad. This both adds to the amount of
     everyday tasks and self-provisioning that necessarily must be
     accomplished in the dwelling, and reduces the time and energy
     available for income-generating employment to one or both
     partners. Circumstances vary, but certainly the common pattern is
     still for the woman to take on a greater burden of domestic work
     and the man to maximize his earning potential in employment. At
     this stage, the woman, more visibly tied to her locality, is likely to
     engage in a variety of exchange relationships: child care may be
     modestly collectivized; clothes may be exchanged; social and
     psychological support may be reciprocally provided — in a phrase,
     women have to work hard at their social relationships within
     distinctive class-cultural styles. Children bring households together.
     Later, men also may form mutually interdependent relationships by
     exchanging tools and helping with heavier or mechanical tasks.
     Women's informal support networks can be exploited by commer-
     cial interests selling cosmetics or plastic containers.[36] Men's local
     social worlds in the home neighbourhood seem to be less permeable
     or less profitable.

3   Typically, when the youngest child reaches school age, the
     mother may then attempt to re-enter the labour market, initially,
     perhaps, on a part-time basis. This re-entry poses substantial
     problems for women who have lost the supportive relationships of

[36] R. Taylor, 'Marilyn's friends and Rita's customers: A study of party-selling as play and
work', *Sociological Review*, 26(3), new series, 1978, pp. 573-94.

previous employment and who, if the household has shifted to a
larger, possibly more isolated, dwelling to accommodate its growth,
may suffer serious geographical or logistic disadvantages in combining different forms of work. Unlike men, women consider their
family responsibilities first and then seek employmeng; men tend to
do the reverse. Most women find employment through their social
networks, and most experience a downward shift in occupational
status at this time of re-entry.[37] Most households cope with the
complexities of child care, other domestic work and different
employment demands from within their own resources, rather than
getting much support from the state, friends or relatives. This is not
to say that they would prefer to do otherwise: many households
may become conscious at this stage that they are operating a
collective strategy.

4   As children get older, they begin to take on domestic work
previously undertaken entirely by their parents. Even buying and
caring for their own clothes or making meals for themselves helps to
take away some of the burden of responsibility for collective
getting-by. Decorating, gardening and child care may be undertaken by offspring in their late teens, and those in employment or
receiving unemployment benefits may contribute usefully to the
family budget. Women's work load in the dwelling may be reduced
at this stage in the cycle, but there may be a shift to full-time
employment. If offspring stay as young unmarried adults in the
household and the mother moves into full-time employment, the
household may have three or more full-time earners contributing to
the household income. This creates substantial consumer resources;
and this is the most likely stage when the household will draw on
the market to provide added domestic comforts, such as double
glazing, an extension to the dwelling or formally organized
holidays. At this stage, members will not necessarily perceive that
their work strategy has changed, whereas in the next stage they will
be more sharply alerted to the consequences of changes in their
material circumstances.

5   The time when offspring finally marry, leave home and establish
their own household in a separate dwelling causes a renegotiation in
the domestic division of labour in their natal homes. The original
couple, now both, perhaps, in full-time employment, are alone in
the dwelling but have responsibilities both for their offsprings'
developing households and also, possibly, for their own elderly
parents. There is something in common with stage 1, but now there
are more resources to draw on — both formal market provision and

[37] J. Chaney, *Social Networks and Job Information: The Situation of Women who Return to Work*, Equal Opportunities Commission, SSRC/EOC, Manchester, 1981.

informal communal reciprocities. There are also likely to be more skills and experience to cope with substantially more self-provisioning and refurbishing: the couple may have acquired skills in painting and decorating, car maintenance, dressmaking, vegetable growing and a variety of other activities which they did not have when they were first married. More choices, more opportunities and more responsibilities are likely to make this a particularly busy period doing all forms of work.

6   There may be a further household work strategy before the final stage of retirement from formal employment. This may come about through early retirement or involuntary redundancy, movement to a new area and a smaller house or the result of serious illness or bereavement. Households may break up through death or divorce and unemployment may produce tensions caused as much by role reversal as by shortage of money. This is a complex stage which barely existed as a problem for ordinary working people before the twentieth century.

7   The final stage, of retirement, might be expected to be one where the household received more work from other sources of labour than it contributed itself. However, older people may become more active as the grandparent role provides new opportunities and the old age pension allows more work to be done, legally, for cash than is possible when receiving supplementary benefits. The domestic division of labour may be more equitable at this stage than at any other period.

In this schematic and fragmented account of the relationship between the domestic cycle, sources of labour and household work strategies, there are a number of assumptions that are not necessarily valid. First, it is by no means clear that formal employment will ever again be so readily available to fit the demands of different household members at different stages of the cycle. Second, the notion that 'the wife' will become 'mother' with two or more children, relinquishing her paid employment to do so, is questionable. Single-parent families are now the fastest growing family type.[38] Women in certain areas are in a stronger labour market position than men, and divorce encourages the development of more complex household structures. The model does, however, suggest connections between employment, work and the domestic division of labour, despite aspects of the model being empirically invalid, as the Sheppey case study material demonstrates.

There is, then, only one economy, and it is becoming increasingly pervasive, dominant and destructive of alternative ways of getting by: the need for a more ruthless, more greedy, more competitive and more

---

[38] J. Popay et al., *One Parent Families*, Study Commission on the Family, London, 1983.

single-minded commitment to capital accumulation is being forced on more and more of the world by the global processes of capitalist expansion. The nation's survival is said to be dependent on doing somebody else out of a job, whether through the protectionist strategies of the Left, reducing sales of goods from abroad, or by the 'jobless growth' of the Right, increasing productivity through shifts in the organic composition of capital. Those who emphasize the informal, undeclared aspects of this economy are turning their back on the fire to watch the flickering shadows on the wall.

However, not all work is done within the confines of the dominant mode of production. Domestic work by members of households for their own use and satisfaction has always been part of the essence of getting by, no matter what the dominant mode of production has been. Informal, communal work for friends and neighbours, whether or not it is paid, has also existed in all times and in all cultures. So, rather than limit the focus on the social relations of work, illustrated in Figure 5.2, it may be helpful now to consider the sources of labour in service provision as a more concrete and empirically measurable way of viewing the question of how work is changing.

The social relations of employment may be seen as the social relations of the producer, the consumer and the employer. However, services may be provided for the consumer by the consumer — what is called self-provisioning; it may be provided by a friend, a relative or someone not operating according to conventional market rules and regulations, or it might be provided by an agent of a capitalist enterprise. There are a variety of sources of labour. The consumer who pays for a new roof to be put on the house has one set of social relations with the owner of the building firm who formally submits the estimate, pays the employees and pays the VAT. The actual men who come to do the job have social relationships with the customer — they may chat and have cups of tea — but their work is fundamentally structured by their relations as wage labourers working for an employer. So, too, may the consumer's relations be structured when in formal employment. To summarize, the roof could be fixed in one of the following ways:

1   The owner of the dwelling could do the work with the help of other members of the household. The materials would generally have to be bought from an enterprise producing tiles and so forth, but they could be bought from a friend or neighbour who had saved some from an older building now collapsed. The money to pay for the materials would have to come from waged employment or petty commodity production.

2   The owner could get a friend or neighbour to do the work for him, either wholly or partly as a favour or with variable mixes of cash and kind payments. The owner would not contribute labour

but would be responsible for rewarding the labour of others and for providing the materials.

3   The owner could simply hire a contractor to do the work.

4   The dwelling may not be owner-occupied, in which case it is the responsibility of the landlord to do the work, and if he is a private individual he may adopt one of the above three strategies. If, on the other hand, the state or local authority owns the dwelling, then that body will have its own employees specifically engaged to do repair and maintenance work of this nature.

The first three ways of fixing the roof have probably not changed very much over the centuries: the job is done either by the household on its own or with the help of neighbouring households or by skilled workmen within the terms and conditions of their occupational craft. The last-mentioned category has, of course, changed as a result of the way the building industry has been developed and modified by capitalist expansion. Hence the home owner may have a choice of whether to employ a large organization, which may also be building office blocks in cities in Britain or abroad, or a small jobbing builder, which may in practice be little more than a man and his van — what the middle classes patronizingly call their 'little man'.

These three sources of labour for service provision are so important to the argument of this book that I want to be absolutely explicit about the nature of the distinctions I am making. It may be necessary, sometimes, under certain circumstances, to engage in convoluted abstract theorizing about the nature of domestic labour, the niceties of the distinctions between production and reproduction or use values and exchange values. There is a place for these arguments, but at this stage I feel that a more earthy, indeed materialist, approach is more useful. No one would deny the importance of keeping the weather out of the domestic dwelling; the need to keep the rain out is a basic need in most climatic regions of the world. Certainly, in Britain fixing the roof has been a concern of households since the establishment of fixed settlements. Wattle and daub dwellings obviously had a limited life, and if the roof fell in it was probably better to start again.[39] One should keep this task of fixing the roof firmly in mind: that is the task to be accomplished. If the distinctions between the social relations and social relationships and sources of labour involved in getting that work done are understood, we can advance in an understanding of all forms of work. There are three sources of labour; I now discuss each source of labour in turn.

1 *The roof is fixed by a member of the household.* In this case the worker is both producer and consumer. There is no set of social relations with an

---

[39] However, there are some houses still standing that were built by town dwellers in the thirteenth century, and even the odd examples from the twelfth century (C. Platt, *The English Medieval Town*, Secker and Warburg, London, 1976, pp. 62-91).

employer or an employee. The materials, if they are purchased, will have involved the buyer in other social relations of work, perhaps selling labour power to an employer, simply to get the money. But the actual work involves the social relationships of household members — such matters as the workers getting tired or cross. As a result of the work the household has a better dwelling to live in and, most importantly, the dwelling's *capital value* has been maintained or even increased. This would apply in all cases of domestic maintenance and improvement among owner occupiers.

The *values* that the workers bring to this domestic self-provisioning can vary. A person may fix the roof at considerable risk and personal discomfort, simply because he has no resources to get anyone else to do the work for him. Poor material circumstances generate such values. Second, at the other extreme, the home owner could have the resources to pay a contractor to do the work but prefer to do it himself, adding to his feelings of pride, satisfaction and, possibly, to a particular gender-stereotyped male identity. Third, the worker may not particularly want to do the task but calculates that, with the range of resources available to him, this seems a sensible strategy. Such a person would say 'It paid me to take an extra week's holiday from work to fix the roof.' He may be making complex calculations about the money he earns, the money he would have to pay to a contractor to meet wages, overheads and profit, the leisure time he forgoes and many other matters: his motivation is not known. It is possible to make comparisons to see if he has a similar household income to other households that get the task done by a contractor and simply assume that a relatively unconstrained choice has been made. But that does not provide certainty. Whatever the value orientations of the workers concerned, this source of labour is described as as *domestic self-provisioning*. This also includes cooking, cleaning, child care, car maintenance, vegetable growing and so on by members of the household for other members of the household.

2 *The roof could be fixed by friends, neighbours or relatives.* Here the consumer is not the producer: someone else does the work and may or may not get paid for it. The essence of such work is that the social relations are based on *informal ties* between the producer and the consumer which are not the same as between an employer and an employee. The cash nexus is not the sole and central feature: the norms of reciprocity and a complexity of social relationships surround the transaction. Payment may be deferred for many years if the task is done by a relative, and the account is unlikely to be settled by straight market principles: it is often safer to repay effort — work — with effort. Some measure of time and trouble has to be assessed and recompensed. The whole idea is not to make a profit out of the other but to break even. It is hard to break even by paying cash. It is far safer to do things — services, favours, whatever — for other people and to be repaid in kind. Here not

only is the skill of the worker engaged, but an intervention is made into a whole set of complex social relationships.

These *informal or communal sources of labour* exist not in a separate economy but as a distinctive sphere of work. Its rules, roles and relationships differ from those in the formal accounted economy: the morality of interpersonal relationships may supercede the cash nexus, but not to the extent that it could be referred to as a separate economy.

3 *The roof could be fixed by a firm of builders.* Little needs to be said about this source of labour. The consumer interacts with a workman hired by the employer whom the customer pays. Whether the employer declares all his income to the Inland Revenue, exploits his workers, is a large corporation or has simply his wife as an employee and sub-contracted workers for the rest is, in a sense, relevant to the consumer only as this is reflected in the price and the quality of the work. In much of the analysis that follows, focusing on the *mode of provision* of services, this source of labour is referred to as 'the formal provision of services' or sometimes simply 'the formal economy'.

These three sources of labour — domestic self-provisioning, informal/communal and formal — will be the basis for the detailed discussion of work on Sheppey in Chapters 8 and 9. Households differ both in the pattern of their participation in employment in the formal economy related to the structure of the local labour market and in the sources of labour they use in the provision of services. Household members may engage in informal work for others and domestic self-provisioning for themselves, but have no involvement in the formal economy (being unemployed or retired). Figure 5.3 illustrates the various possibilities.

SOURCES OF LABOUR

	Household	Informal		Firm
		Paid	Unpaid	
Household				
FORMS OF WORK				
Individual				

Figure 5.3   Forms of work and sources of labour

The Forms of Work are domestic self-provisioning, employment and various forms of informal work.
The Sources of Labour are the household itself, the formal provision of services and various sources of informal work.

It is obvious that the notion of a household work strategy is extremely complicated, involving different household members in different spheres of work using different sources of labour in a particular milieu as they move through the domestic cycle.

Conclusions

In this chapter I have been developing new ways of looking at work, consistently emphasizing that work cannot be defined out of context. I have explored the social relations of work in and outside employment and I have introduced the distinctions between forms of work and sources of labour. In general, throughout the first part of this book I have struggled to make connections between divisions of labour that are themselves fragmented by an academic division of labour. Thus, for example, industrial sociologists concerned with employment and labour market behaviour have rarely considered in any detail the domestic work of the household. Men and women are often plucked out of the complete context in which they do the various forms of work needed to get by, and considered in separate working roles — such as that of mother or employee. There has been some attempt in recent years to understand women's 'two roles' as employee and as 'housewife'. However, while this may be some improvement, unless the focus is on all forms of work of all members of the household, the advance in the understanding of the nature and meaning of work in contemporary society may be relatively modest.

In my attempt to bring together all forms of work by all members of households, I have explored who did the work in pre-industrial times — before the dominance of wage labour so heavily coloured our conception of work. I have also recognized that, as I said in the conclusions to Chapter 3, the chief worker in most households is a woman. The systematic neglect of women's work is inexcusable, given the overwhelming historical evidence. This neglect may be explained partially by the emphasis on the individual wage earner, rather than the household, as the basic economic unit.

This emphasis on the household is a major theme of the book: before large-scale industrialization and the development of the factory system, the importance of the household as an economic unit could hardly be questioned. In many respects its importance continued throughout the nineteenth century, but, in a flurry of male-dominated individualistic ideology, it began to get obscured. Reasons for this shift towards the male 'breadwinner' have been the focus of much scholarly attention in recent years, and I have referred to some of this work in earlier chapters.[40] The

---

[40] Some of the most interesting work in this area has been published by Jane Humphries. See

relative importance of ideological and materialistic elements in coming to an understanding of this shift will continue to be the subject of debate. Whichever way the blame is distributed between Protestantism, capitalism, patriarchy and their interaction in specific historical conjunctures, the results are irrefutable. Our taxation system and much of the way the welfare state operates is based on the assumptions of a male head of household who is responsible for one or more dependants.

Such a situation makes it more difficult to understand the nature of work and puts us in a poor position for better understanding the changing contemporary world. However, as I have shown, it is one thing to recognize and to make some attempt to document all forms of work by all members of households, and it is another matter to advance some general understanding to match that which has developed about the nature of one form of work — employment. Focusing on the divisions of labour seems a useful way forward. Each form of work and source of labour has to be, as it were, unpacked for the purpose of analysis, but if they are left like that it will not be possible to see how they interconnect and interact. My argument is that all forms of work must be explored in specific arenas. Up to now I have been focusing on the household; in Part II I will extend the analysis to a particular community. Finally, in Part III of this book I make some comments on wider social and political implications of this discussion of the divisions of labour between all forms of work.

her articles: 'Class struggle and the persistence of the working class family', *Cambridge Journal of Economics*, 1, 1977, pp. 241-58; 'The working-class family, women's liberation, and class struggle: The case of nineteenth century British history', *Review of Radical Political Economics*, 9(3), 1977, pp. 25-41; 'Protective legislation, the capitalist state and working class men: The case of the 1842 Mines Regulation Act', *Feminist Review*, 7, 1981, pp. 1-32. See also G. Sen, 'The sexual division of labour and the working-class family: Towards a conceptual synthesis of class relations and the subordination of women', *Review of Radical Political Economics*, 12(2), 1980, pp. 76-86.

Part II

Household Divisions of Labour

Introduction

The Isle of Sheppey

In Part I I emphasized the importance of households as working units and described their patterns of work and how these have changed over the centuries. This was inevitably highly generalized, and the evidence I adduced came from a variety of sources, some of which, by their nature, were unfortunately not very substantial. In this part of the book I provide much more detailed and solidly based empirical evidence about all forms of work in the Isle of Sheppey in 1981.

Inevitably, households and individuals who adopt different practices and strategies for getting by must do so in a specific context. The way in which all work is done is substantially determined by the opportunities available in a relatively restricted milieu which, in the case of formal employment, is generally assumed to be a local labour market. How local it is and whether the term 'market' has any empirical significance are matters of continuing academic debate.[1] It is generally accepted that labour markets are segmented to some extent so that certain jobs are almost entirely filled by men, whereas others, particularly certain forms of part-time employment, are almost invariably held by women. The particular mix of employment opportunities will obviously vary from one part of the country to another and so, too, will the opportunities for doing other work outside employment.

At present there are no good surrogates for measuring the opportunity structures for work outside employment in particular milieux. Probably the strongest candidate would be housing tenure: in areas of local authority and rented housing, particularly if it is high-rise, there are far fewer opportunities for self-provisioning than in areas of owner-occupation. However, there are probably more subtle indicators that have yet to be developed. No doubt Sheppey will be able to take its place

---

[1] R. M. Blackburn and M. Mann, *The Working Class in the Labour Market*, Macmillan, London, 1979.

on a continuum of 'getting-by potential' yet to be devised. Certainly, in order to put all forms of work in context, I felt that it was necessary to do more than simply provide a conventional account of the demand and supply of labour on the Island.

In order to explore the interconnection between these different forms of work, I focused my research on the Isle of Sheppey in Kent for a period of nearly six years from January 1978. It is reasonable to ask why I chose that area as the locale for this case study.[2] From the very beginning there was absolutely no attempt to justify working on the Isle of Sheppey in terms of its typicality. However, there were a number of features relating to the Island that initially made it appear very suitable. First, it was more self-contained than many alternatives: it is connected to the mainland by only one bridge, which can be raised and lowered to allow ships to pass up the Swale to docks on the mainland side. When the bridge is up, the Island is truly cut off, and if the lifting mechanism fails then nothing can be done, short of an airlift by helicopter, to get across to the mainland. This has the advantage that people are evidently aware of their distinctiveness of being Islanders and recognize that there are common problems and opportunities. This distinctiveness may be more apparent than real, but, in terms of the sociological truism, 'where people define situations as real, they are real in their consequences.' One of the first things I was told about Sheppey was that there were some people still living there who had never been off the Island. It is not, of course, a completely self-contained labour market — between 25 and 30 per cent commute off the Island each day, and there is a reverse flow of about 14 per cent, mainly managerial and professional workers.[3] There are some from Warden Bay at the far eastern end of the Island who commute as far as London, leaving at 6 in the morning and returning at 8 at night. In so far, therefore, as being self-contained in terms of employment provided some kind of unity, it made it easier to perceive the interconnections between the different forms of work which were the focus of this study.

Second, it was common gossip among those I talked to in the mainland towns that the Island was a seething heap of informal work. Long-established and traditional links with London's East End had perhaps encouraged a kind of notoriety, and it is true that murderers and kidnappers are flushed out from time to time after they have taken cover in the chalet land of Leysdown. The Island had the totally undeserved image of being unruly and somewhat violent. With 120 licensed premises for a population of 33,000[4] and with a reputation for petty crime and deviance, I was made to feel that I was entering dangerous territory when

---

[2] A note on 'The Case Study as a Method' appears on pp. 146–7.
[3] These figures are approximate and derive from Kent County Council Survey data relating to 1976-7, the time when the Island was first being considered as a site for research.
[4] There are thirty-five pubs and clubs in Sheerness High Street alone.

I went there. In the early days I remember checking each time I came back to my car that someone had not taken the wheels off while I was away.[5] The docks at Sheerness were said then to be the source of many 'cheap goods' circulating in the area and, given my interest in the hidden economy at the time, I was assured that I would have no difficulty in gathering information. The inference, which later turned out to be false, was that most of the work on the Island was done 'for cash'.

This notoriety, based on external labelling, encouraged me on to the Island in the belief that I would find what I was looking for: with hindsight, I recognize that I was well directed; if informal work is not flourishing in Sheppey it is unlikely to be flourishing anywhere, and by choosing what appeared to be a seething centre of fiddles, I had provided myself with a test case. Almost by definition, one could be directed to centres of informal work only through hearsay, gossip and informal sources of information: in the mid-1970s these all pointed to the Isle of Sheppey.

The third main factor that drew me to the Island was its pattern of unemployment. As an Admiralty dockyard from the late seventeenth century and also a military garrison, Sheerness had almost three hundred years of industrial history which might have produced a mature working-class culture. The dockyard had closed twenty years before the fieldwork began, but it was in the front of the minds of all those who had been living on the Island at the time. There were other traditional industries, such as glass and pottery manufacture, and more modern plants making pharmaceuticals and electrical components. A very wide range of manufacturing industry made the Island a more attractive area in which to explore the implications of de-industrialization than any other alternative town within reasonable radius of my home university. Furthermore, its level of unemployment was between 10 and 14 per cent in the early stages of the project, rising above 20 per cent in the autumn of 1983. In so far as other forms of work could serve as a compensation for the decline in employment, Sheppey seemed an appropriate choice to explore such a pattern.

In addition to its discreteness, isolation, relative self-containment, distinctive history of employment and apparent potential for deviance, Sheppey was also a marginal area, as was mentioned above, not well served with public facilities: many of the roads are unadopted and unmade-up, many of the industries are dirty and polluting, and much of

[5] I needn't have worried. Data kindly made available for Sheppey from the Chief Constable of Kent and for Kent as a whole from the Chief Constable's Report for Kent, 1982, Appendix I, enable a comparison to be made between Sheppey and Kent as a whole. The results show that Sheppey is *safer* than the rest of Kent. The rate per 100,000 population for thefts from vehicles was 474 in Sheppey and 656 for Kent as a whole. Similarly, for the theft or unauthorized taking of motor vehicles, the ratios were 542 for Sheppey and 564 for Kent as a whole.

the Island seems to have escaped planning control and regulation. Glibly referred to by one of the senior local government officers of the district as 'that sceptic Isle', it was perceived by the various 'agencies' — the police, the probation service, the educational service and the health and social services — as a 'problem' place.[6]

A Note on the Case Study as a Method

It is perhaps useful to draw attention to the methodological distinctiveness of the case study approach, seen as 'a way of organizing social data so as to preserve the *unitary character of the social object being studied*'.[7] Clearly, case studies can serve a variety of purposes which may be more or less theoretical in intent. First, they may serve as a simple descriptive device, showing how various elements in a situation interrelate. The emphasis here is likely to be on the *unique* nature of the event or circumstances. Second, such studies, although evidently unique or ideographic, are nevertheless interpreted in terms of general patterns, and it is these generalities that are emphasized and underlined. Third, a case study may be chosen in order to develop theory. Generalizable relations are deliberately sought out, giving such studies a clear heuristic purpose. Then, fourth, case studies may be seen as what have been referred to as 'plausibility probes' — rather like a pilot study before another stage of empirical research is launched.

Finally, there are crucial case studies which allow the investigator to disconfirm some hypothesis or argument or perhaps to support it when circumstances may appear to be loaded against it. This is rather like the crucial experiment in the natural sciences. However, as J. C. Mitchell concludes in his discussion of this issue,

In reality no case study can be presented in isolation from the corpus of empirical information and theoretical postulates against which it is has significance. . . . The single case becomes significant only when set against the accumulated experience and knowledge that the analyst brings to it. In other words the extent to which generalization may be made from case studies depends upon the adequacy of the underlying theory and the whole corpus of related knowledge of which the case is analyzed rather than on the particular instance itself.[8]

[6] In October 1982 an Inter Agency Conference focusing on Sheppey was held at Broadstairs, organized by Kent County Council, bringing together representatives from the police, the probation service, the social services and education. It was assumed that the Island had 'special problems' and there was a need for more inter-agency co-operation and more facilities on the Island. It was agreed that the Island should serve as the locale for an experiment in new ways of working together.
[7] W. J. Goode and P. K. Hatt, *Methods in Social Research*, McGraw Hill, New York, 1952, p. 331.
[8] J. C. Mitchell, 'Case and situation analysis', *Sociological Review*, 31(2), 1982, new series, p. 203.

Given such considerations, it becomes clear that there is abolutely no advantage in going to a great deal of trouble to find a 'typical' case: 'concern with this issue reflects a confusion of enumerative and analytic modes of induction.'[9] Obviously, all case studies are related to a specific context, and some account of this context is crucial to enable readers to judge how far the generalizations that are drawn from case studies, qualified with a *ceteris paribus* condition, can be accepted as such. Evidently, it is up to the investigator to help the reader see how far particular circumstances or events obscure, reflect, reinforce or reduce the general processes being considered. As one of the great pioneers of humanistic sociology put it, 'it is not the exception that matters, but our attitude toward it.'[10] The point is reinforced by Mitchell, who claims that the case study 'provides the optimum conditions in which the general principles may be shown to manifest themselves even when obscured by confounding side effects'.[11] That is, as long as the observer knows a great deal about the circumstances and conditions surrounding given events.

It is important, therefore, not to draw false parallels between two very different inferential processes. First, in the case of sample surveys, it is possible to make a statistical inference that what may be observed for the sample relates also to the population from which the sample is drawn. A second process claims that the logical connections perceived among the features observed in the sample relate to the parent universe. For case studies, the first process is clearly not relevant; rather, the inferential process turns on the theoretically necessary linkages in the case study. Here the validity of the extrapolation rests on the cogency of the theoretical reasoning. 'The rich detail which emerges from the intimate knowledge the analyst must acquire in a case study if it is well conducted provides the optimum conditions for the acquisition of those illuminating insights which make formerly opaque connections suddenly pellucid.'[12]

Outline of Part II

A more systematic portrait of the Island is presented in Chapter 6 and the results of the 1981 social survey are presented in Chapters 8-11. Chapter 8 explores the overall balance of work between the formal, informal and domestic spheres and focuses first on the relative importance of the material conditions of households, as determined by the occupation of the chief earner or the numbers of earners, and second on the demographic and life-cycle characteristics of households. Chapter 9 explores in more detail the divisions of labour of households and Chapter 10 the division of labour within households.

[9] Ibid., p. 204.
[10] F. Znaniecki, *The Method of Sociology*, Rinehart, New York, 1934, p. 306.
[11] Mitchell, 'Case and situation analysis', p. 206.
[12] Ibid., p. 207.

The two kinds of division of labour are based on an important distinction. Divisions of labour *of* households refers to the specific sources of labour that are drawn on to get work done. The division of labour *within* households relates to the question of which of the partners, in households with couples, does a range of tasks. Precise information on these matters involves formidable problems of measurement, and Chapters 8-10 are intended to provide a more accurate account of the divisions of labour than has hitherto been available.

When I was planning the research in the late 1970s, conceptions of what the 'informal economy' comprised were necessarily rather vague and tended to include under one heading a variety of distinct forms of work, which have been described in this book as self-provisioning, shadow wage labour, occupational easements and so on. In the early years of my research, I focused on a relatively small number of households and built up a picture in each case of all the forms of work in which members of those households were engaged. This was, inevitably, very time-consuming and involved establishing considerable trust among respondents. One family that I interviewed regularly over the full period of research is reported on in detail in Chapter 11.

However, I well understood, as reports on the earlier, more informal and impressionistic research were published,[13] that, however revealing and insightful such work might be, its credibility was severely limited. Critics could quite reasonably claim that respondents were untypical, that they were simply misleading me, or that I was being highly selective in the material I chose to report. Furthermore, with so few cases I could not make connections between the distinctive work practices of households and their other social and political characteristics.

A number of interesting questions relate to the sociological significance of work outside employment. How far, for example, does work outside employment serve as an alternative source of identity and a practical means of getting by? While one or two unemployed households were shown to be getting by successfully by — almost literally — hunting, shooting and fishing, I needed to know how *widespread* that pattern might be. Similarly, very little was known systematically about the interconnections between divisions of labour: was there any relationship between the way household members allocated their efforts between different forms of labour outside the household and how the work inside the household was distributed? Was there a division of labour by gender in the informal work done outside the household and, if there was, how did this affect the internal division of labour in the sphere of self-provisioning? Do households who are better placed in getting income

[13] R. E. Pahl, 'Employment, work and the domestic division of labour', *International Journal of Urban and Regional Research*, 4(1), 1980, pp. 1-20.

from the formal economy, either by a highly paid single wage earner or through multiple earners, do less work in other spheres? There has been some interest in how far women's employment affects their involvement in domestic tasks, but very little attention has been given to how far that involvement in formal employment affects their involvement in other informal work, or to how involvement in informal work affects levels of domestic self-provisioning. If, for the sake of simplicity, three spheres of work are described as A, B and C and partners in a household are referred to as M and F, there would, on these limited assumptions alone, be 49 different potential household work strategies (see figure). Since M's involvement in one sphere of work, employment, is itself structured into a hierarchy of positions through the occupational structure, the possible range of relationships between household work practices and various divisons of labour becomes quite unmanageably huge. Evidently the 49 combinations of the matrix refer to the different pattern of involvement of two household members in three spheres of work: it does not say anything about the sources of labour that the household uses and the relative balance between these. It may be helpful if I now list the distinctive elements that are to be analysed in Part II.

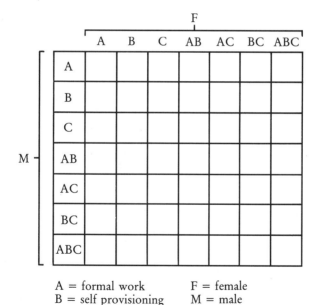

A = formal work   F = female
B = self provisioning M = male
C = informal work

1   The involvement of household members in particular *forms of labour* inside and outside the dwelling. This is the work they do for others such as employers or relatives. There are two divisions in this

work: (a) that based on how households and distinctive categories
of households distribute their labour between distinctive spheres of
work; (b) that based on how individual members of a household
distribute their labour within and outside the household.

2   The *sources of labour* that a household draws on to get a whole
range of tasks done. Households may use their own labour, they
may pay others or they may receive labour which has to be
reciprocated in more subtle ways. Households will have distinctive
balances or mixes of sources of labour on which they draw. There
are also two divisions in sources of labour: (a) that based on the
sources of forms of labour that a household uses; (b) that which
reflects the different pattern of labour used by different household
members.

3   It is evident that the divisions under the heading 1 relate to the
household as a producer, as a working unit, and under heading 2 the
divisions relate to the household as a unit of consumption. But
members of the household do work for themselves and hence
appear in one sphere under both headings. This work done by
household members for themselves provides the basis, in households with more than one member, for the household division of
labour.

There will clearly be distinctive mixes between the household's division
of labour as producer and consumer. In the last phase of empirical
research reported in this book, which began in 1980, I focused specifically
on how household work strategies — that is 1 and 2 above — related to
the domestic division of labour (3) and other social and political attitudes
and behaviour. My assumption was that social consciousness was shaped
largely by a household's economic circumstances but that these were
infinitely more complex than appeared to be generally understood. The
occupational characteristics of the male chief earner was simply one
element in determining a household's economic position: it was not
necessarily the most important.

People living in distinctive milieux have, as it were, inside knowledge
which colours their conception of the options and opportunities that are
available to them. Before exploring households' work practices in detail,
therefore, I put considerable effort in an attempt to get to a position
where the respondents already were. They knew, or they thought they
knew, much about the context in which they lived. They knew where
there were jobs, what it was like to do them; they also were highly
sensitive to how they were treated by employers, state officials, friends
and neighbours. Options are defined in a context that is explored in
Chapters 6 and 7. Three years of preliminary fieldwork showed that
housing location and tenure were crucial elements in the development of
distinctive household work strategies. This informed our understanding

when constructing the formal research instrument.[14] Similarly, it was important for us to know that geographical factors made it virtually impossible for women in certain parts of the Island to engage in formal employment and also to maintain their family responsibilities at the same time.

Chapters 6-11, therefore, explore the divisions of labour on the Isle of Sheppey from a number of perspectives. Chapter 6 is historical and necessarily so, for the sharp contrast in the periods before and after the closing of the dockyard provide the key to various homespun theories that exist in the area which are used to explain contemporary material and social circumstances. These theories are discussed in Chapter 7. The resource options of the Isle of Sheppey were as much socially as geographically or historically constructed. While the portrait that follows is unique, the processes that produced the distinctive pattern have wider significance. This is a theme to which I return in the final chapter, although the account of the process of de-industrialization on the Isle of Sheppey will surely prompt the reader to consider whether what the smaller Island faces in the 1980s its larger neighbour will face, in increasingly acute form, towards the year 2000.

[14] In discussing the results of the field survey in Chapters 8 and 9, I use the first person plural on occasions; this part of the research project was very much a collaborative effort with Gill Courtenay of SCPR and with Claire Wallace, the Research Fellow on the project.

6

Portrait of an Industrial Island

Introduction

The next six chapters are based on material gathered in the Isle of Sheppey in Kent. Inevitably, readers will want to have some idea of what the Island is like; however, as is shown below, to provide such an account is not entirely a straightforward exercise.[1] To understand the present situation it is necessary to know something of how that situation has developed, yet all historical accounts have to be partial and selective. The position adopted here is to acknowledge that the basic problems of getting by, of forming households and of caring for the young and the old have remained remarkably similar for centuries. Most people experience life as a struggle: they compare their own life with that of their mothers or fathers and perhaps gain some comfort that their life is better, but they might equally feel that things are getting worse. In the case of the Isle of Sheppey, those with long memories will almost certainly perceive the present as a sad and ugly decline from a better-ordered and more attractive past. Some attempt must be made to match 'scholarly' history with 'folk' history, recognizing that the latter may have more salience for contemporary attitudes and behaviour than the former.

Visually the Island has undoubtedly declined. When William Hogarth visited Sheppey in 1732, he and his friends walked through pleasant countryside to Minster, a little village on the highest part of the Island on which Minster Abbey stands, said to be founded in the seventh century by the wife of Ercombert, King of Kent. Old prints and drawings and even postcards dating from as recently as the early years of this century show a wooded countryside more reminiscent of villages in the more fashionable parts of the county today. Queenborough was a flourishing little borough in the seventeenth century, and Sheerness developed in the nineteenth century as garrison, Admiralty dockyard and seaside resort. So much was built between 1850 and 1900 that people's memories of a

[1] A map of the Island may be found on p. 342.

much cleaner town are likely to be substantially true. It is understandable that many islanders cannot see the present except in terms of its decline from the past.

Certainly, a contemporary visitor to the Isle of Sheppey is likely to be dismayed by its lack of visual character.[2] The road to the Island may well be clogged with huge lorries weighted down with containers, Japanese cars or steel rods from the mill. On one side, acres of marshland appear to be sinking under the weight of thousands of Toyotas and Mazdas; ahead, there is a pall of black smoke over the Sheerness Steel Mill with the Isle of Grain oil refinery towering in the background and appearing to be on the Island itself. On the other side, treeless marshes and sheep pasture stretch away for ten miles or so. The village of Minster in the middle of the Island is now overwhelmed by private housing development, put up in a seemingly chaotic way in the 1960s and 1970s. Much of the earlier development along unmade roads makes one forget that any Town and Country Planning Acts have been passed. Queenborough High Street has many of its period houses boarded up in bad repair, and turning off down Rushenden Road, past the industrial estate, the impression is of a northern industrial town. Heavy traffic has pitted the roads; factories making fertilizer, lavatory pans or glass bottles make little attempt to look presentable to visitors. Railway tracks cross the road; huge metal objects lie outside the rolling mill and iron foundry, and the horizon is again dominated by the endless sea of Japanese cars. Eventually, at the very end of the marshes where the Swale does a loop back before entering the Medway, there is the Rushenden Road Estate, an all too obvious machine for workers to reproduce themselves in. Remote from shops, privately built housing and such amenities as the cinema and swimming pool at Sheerness, visiting state officials or university researchers are viewed here with suspicion. Some of the houses look smart, with new front doors and obvious double glazing, indicating clearly that they have been bought from the council; others have the characteristic scuffed door and concrete path, with a scattering of broken toys and odd bits of wood that may or may not be rubbish in what was once a front garden.

The High Street of Sheerness, the town that houses about a third of the Island's population of 33,000, is the standard mixture of discount carpet stores, Tesco's, Boots and tawdry boutiques, interspersed with pubs and indeterminate shops selling sweets, greetings cards, cigarettes and newspapers. It could be transferred to New Cross, Kilburn or Wood Green in London and no one would notice the difference. Behind the shops, in the areas known as Marine Town and Mile Town, another

---

[2] In 1983 Swale District Council launched an 'Economic Programme', much of which was concerned with 'environmental improvements' on the Island. A new concern with the image of the area was based on the assumption that new investment would be clean and that industrialists would be attracted by physical appearances.

pattern of owner-occupied working class housing can be seen. Here, terraces built in the mid-nineteenth century front straight on to the street. Corner shops and pubs punctuate the scene and little alleyways criss-cross the areas, full of running children at 3.30 as they come home from school. Mothers and married daughters go shopping together. In summer elderly women put wooden chairs on the pavement to sit and chat and a group of lads strip a motorbike on the pavement. 'For Sale' signs appear permanently in all the streets and every front door is painted a different colour. One little terrace house with green interlocking tiles, pink pebbledash and a frosted glass front door adjoins another looking much as it did a hundred years ago. The roads are lined with elderly Fords and chromey Datsuns. Women cross the street in carpet slippers. A large Ford van with a 'J' registration, painted entirely black, has the words 'Funeral Service' on the side, but further information has been covered in with more black paint.[3]

Following the coast road from Marine Town to Minster, views of the sea are hidden by the huge new concrete sea wall, recently built to avoid flooding. The road has to turn inland at Minster Cliffs, which are gradually sliding into the sea, although a contractor is struggling hard to shore it all up. The clifftop land from Minster to Warden is a jumble of unmade roads, riding stables, little smallholdings and caravan sites. A determined driver with little regard for his car can zigzag his way over potholes, past home-made bungalows with goats grazing in the front garden and the odd run-down farmhouse.[4] One can emerge at Warden Bay into a new estate of houses, being a mixture of neo-Georgian and south-coast Spanish. Then more holiday camps, overblown pubs offering live entertainment (male strippers on hens' evenings), before one reaches Leysdown-on-Sea. Bingo halls, a disco, amusement arcades and gift shops are the focus for acres of holiday chalets, caravan sites and holiday camps. In winter it is hard to find anywhere to get a cup of tea; in summer the place is awash with the highest priced beer in Kent. Returning by the main road along the spine of the Island, one passes through the agricultural village of Eastchurch with nothing but Eastchurch Open Prison and a few farms on the pastures sloping away to the Swale. At Minster there is a hospital and the comprehensive school. Some larger houses in the best positions on the high land have paddocks for ponies, power boats on trailers and two or more cars in the drive. A small elite of red-faced men with large stomachs, large Fords and tinselly wives with long fingernails patronize the Playa Club on Minster Cliffs and drink many gins before their steak or scampi and chips.

---

[3] See plate 8. This is perhaps truly the black economy on wheels. I am grateful to Jim Styles of the University of Kent Photographic Unit for the sympathetic way he helped in providing this and other vivid documentation.
[4] On one safari trip with Colin Ward, I slipped a disc heaving my car out of the mud. Anthropologists in far-away places are not the only ones with hazards to face.

A perceptive observer visiting the Island would see and understand much by travelling about — the pub where the managers who live off the Island congregate for lunch, another pub (not always the same one) the centre for drugs and prostitutes, the fisherboats on Queenborough Creek, the light aircraft bringing in one of the farm owners from over the estuary in Essex, the Regency terraces, once the homes of officers in the dockyard and much the same as they were when first built, the apparently uncountable chapels and working men's clubs, the fish and chip shops, the markets on Tuesdays and Sundays, the truant teenagers in the coffee bars. Having spent six years visiting and doing fieldwork on the Island and spending time in particular factories, streets and communities, I feel daunted at times by the overwhelming wealth of information.

Nevertheless, it is important to try to make sense of the context: people's real or imagined knowledge of the past colours, to a degree, their present attitudes and pattern of behaviour. Newcomers to the Island have different traditions, to be sure, but Sheppey is a distinct milieu with its own distinctive traditions, experiences, possibilities and constraints. People have to grapple with the material circumstances of their existence, and because the Island is so relatively small and insular, in more than one sense, people can readily have a consciousness of its distinctiveness. Working-class culture is not an ahistorical response to existential circumstances — rather, it is an intensely conservative and traditional set of household practices for grappling with difficult material circumstances. In order to understand more of the complexity of the material context, it seemed necessary to gather a substantial amount of data on the historical development of the dockyard, the pattern of employment from 1960 to 1980 and a detailed analysis of housing development in the twentieth century.[5]

The Historical Development of the Sheerness Naval Dockyard[6]

Contemporary studies of local labour markets need to be seen in context, since present expectations and strategies may depend significantly on the experience that members of the family may have had in the past.

---

[5] Each of these themes provided the basis for separate reports, only the main points of which are referred to here. See N. Buck, *An Admiralty Dockyard in the Mid-Nineteenth Century: Aspects of the Social and Economic History of Sheerness*, Final Report to the SSRC on a research project funded by grant no. HR6939/1, 1981; R. E. Pahl with J. H. Dennett, *Industry and Employment on the Isle of Sheppey*, University of Kent at Canterbury, part of the Final Report to the SSRC of project no. G00230036, 1981; and C. Wallace with R. E. Pahl and J. H. Dennett, *Housing and Residential Areas on the Isle of Sheppey*, University of Kent at Canterbury, part of the Final Report to the SSRC of project no. G00230036, 1981.

[6] This account is based on the report to the SSRC by Dr N. H. Buck on the project directed by me. The research was carried out almost entirely by Dr Buck, assisted by Ms Theresa Sliney.

Particular styles of behaviour may be built up gradually over generations, and these expectations and strategies may become, as it were, fossilized, so that a given labour market may come to have distinctive attributes. This seemed a very relevant consideration in the case of Sheerness, since dockyard workers were said to be a special category of worker. This suggested one source of distinctive consciousness. Another possible consideration was simply the very isolation of the Island: being so self-contained and dominated by one employer for so long, there might have been grounds for making some connection between past circumstances and contemporary behaviour.

The isolation and self-containment of Sheerness provided a methodological advantage, making it a good context for the intensive use of mid-nineteenth-century nominal records, particularly the Census Enumerators' Books. This enabled very complete information on the dockyard workforce to be collected, and an intensive analysis of its characteristics and changes over time was carried out by linking households between censuses in order to illustrate recruitment and turnover.

On 18 August 1665, Samuel Pepys, secretary of the Board of the Admiralty, wrote in his diary: 'To Sheernesse, where we walked up and down, laying out the ground to be taken in for a yard to lay provisions for cleaning and repairing of ships, and a most proper place it is for the purpose.'[7] Pepys was right: the Medway Port Authority, which now runs Sheerness Docks, boasts that it has the deepest harbour between the North of Scotland and Wales. Clearly, Sheerness's position at the confluence of the Thames and the Medway, on the sea approaches to both Chatham and London, gave it immense strategic importance for the Navy: it was an inevitable site for a garrison and battery. Unfortunately, only two years after Pepys's visit, the Dutch fleet bombarded the fort and Sheerness and destroyed much of what was there, landing and capturing it on 11 June 1667. The following day the Dutch took Queenborough, the mayor having raised the white flag on the Town Hall '— the only Town Hall in England, which, since the Norman Conquest, has ever had the flag of a foreign invader floating over it. The Isle of Sheppey, thus humiliated, was wholly at the mercy of the invaders, who held possession of it for a period of eleven days, plundering the inhabitants, looting for stores and provisions, and carrying away thousands of head of sheep and cattle unmolested.'[8]

These events had a number of important consequences. First, the memory lived on that Sheppey had been conquered by a foreign power

---

[7] *The Diary of Samuel Pepys*, Vol. VI, transcribed and edited by R. Latham and W. Mathews, G. Bell and Sons, London, 1972 edn, p. 194.
[8] A. A. Daly, *History of the Isle of Sheppey*, Simpkin, Marshall, Hamilton, Kent and Co. Ltd., London, 1904, p. 224.

and the enemy had withdrawn, rather than being driven out by forces from the mainland. The local historian of the Island, writing at the turn of the century, claimed that 'even the lapse of two centuries scarcely effaced the recollection of it on either side.'[9] Today, with a regular twice-daily service from Sheerness to Vlissingen operated by the Olau Line, and a substantial flow of Dutch tourists through the town, one still senses a certain resentment, sometimes expressed in the reasonableness of 'ripping off the Cloggies'.[10] The second consequence was that landed families felt that their lives and properties were not safe on the Island, so they left to become absentee landlords and the houses of substance, such as they were, declined. This must have had social consequences for those who worked the land for the next 250 years. This truncation of the social hierarchy at the end of the seventeenth century doubtless contributed to the sense of apartness felt by Islanders and mainlanders alike. It has also been suggested that the area was severely afflicted by malaria in the seventeenth century.[11]

The third consequence of the conquest was the rapid expansion and strengthening of the fortification directly encouraged by Charles II who inspected the completed works in 1669. The development of the Admiralty dockyard in the last years of the seventeenth century was hindered by the unfavourable marshy hinterland: expensive foundations were necessary before building, water was a problem in the early days, and its exposed position meant that it was often threatened with inundation. As a protection against floods, old hulks were used as a form of breakwater, and these were also used to house the dockyard workers. This may have been the source of the myth of the Islanders being escaped convicts.[12] But it is true that other heavy labouring work *was* done by convicts held in other hulks in the Medway and, by the early nineteenth century, conditions in some of the hulks were very bad.

Throughout the eighteenth century, the numbers employed in the dockyard development varied between 300 and 600 and the period was

[9] Ibid., p. 228.

[10] However, the economic recession that began in 1979 has encouraged the forging of more friendly links between the Netherlands and Sheppey in the hope of developing trade and commerce. A party of fifteen 'leading citizens' of The Hague visited the Island in October 1983, partly arranged by the Olau Line, and further economic and social developments are likely. The Island is twinned with Brielle and regular exchanges take place.

[11] P. Macdougal, 'Malaria: Its influence on a North Kent community', *Archaeologia Cantiana*, 95, 1979, pp. 255-64.

[12] Given the damaging nature of such current misconceptions, it is perhaps worth quoting the impressions of John Wesley, who visited Sheerness in 1767 and recorded in his Journal for 16 December: 'Such a town as many of these living in is scarce to be found again in England. In the dock adjoining to the fort there are six old men of war. These are divided into small tenements, forty, fifty, sixty in a ship with little chimneys and windows, and each of these contains a family. In one of them, where we called, a man and his wife and six little children lived. And yet all the ship was sweet and tolerably clean; sweeter than most sailing ships I have been in.'

marked by corruption, inefficient organization and a system of recruitment based directly on dockyard families. The dockyard officers were old
and inept and accounts were sometimes five years in arrears. There was
substantial corruption in the supply of materials and pilfering from the
yards.[13] This led to a long-running conflict over the issue of men taking
'chips', off-cuts of wood up to 12 feet in length, which was a traditional
occupational easement. These were being used to construct houses in the
area immediately adjoining the dockyard known as Blue Town —
so-called, apparently, on account of the Admiralty paint used to decorate
the wooden houses.[14] The dockyard authorities attempted to prevent the
'chips' from getting too large and in 1753 a regulation specified that no
more could be taken than could be carried untied under one arm. This
provoked a riot at Chatham.

   This early militancy and solidaristic power of dockyard workers could
be strengthened during threats or periods of war, but by the nineteenth
century the Admiralty had all but tamed the workforce, having taken
steps to increase its control over them. For example, dockyard officers
had considerable discretion in awarding apprenticeships and pensions;
and the pay of apprentices was made entirely to their instructor, which in
practice meant that the instructor was invariably the father.[15]

Sheerness in the Nineteenth Century

The dockyard was reconstructed between 1815 and 1826, and Sheerness
expanded as an independent town. In 1854 a steam engine factory was
opened and building activity, associated with the Crimean Wars,
increased. New skills were required and metalworkers, particularly
engine fitters, engine smiths and boilermakers, came into the town, many
of whom had served apprenticeships in private shipbuilding firms or
railway workshops. In the 1860s, the development of the iron ship

[13] M. Oppenheim, 'Maritime history' and 'The Royal dockyards', in W. Page (ed.), *The
Victoria County History of Kent*, St Catherine Press, London, 1926, pp. 243-388.
[14] It is certainly still possible to see the dockyard timbers inside some of the few older
properties still remaining. Thus was established the tradition of the Islanders building their
own homes with their own materials and their own labour. Some of the work I have seen
looks decidedly rough, but the materials were good and the dwellings lasted well enough.
[15] In her companion study of the Chatham Dockyard, M. Waters remarks that
'apprenticeship appears as an important part of a system of reward and control and also as a
means of providing support for the old and widows' (M. Waters, 'The social history of the
Chatham dockyard workforce 1860-1906', unpublished PhD thesis, University of Essex,
1979, p. 5). Oppenheim similarly notes that up to 1764 many infirm and incapable
dockworkers were kept on the establishment because they had no other means of support
(Oppenheim, 'Royal dockyards', p. 376). A superannuation fund was set up in that year but
this relationship between father and son continued and, in general, families and the
dockyard officers were highly interdependent. Households were bound together and bound
in by the dockyard.

brought in more metalworkers. However, some shipwrights trained in woodbuilding were retrained and ended up doing the work of boilermakers and riveters in private yards.

This expansion of metalworkers and shipwrights in the mid-nineteenth century was based on substantial immigration, significantly from other dockyard towns. The proportion of shipwrights born in Sheppey declined from 40 per cent in 1851 to 34 per cent in 1861 and to 31 per cent in 1871. About three-quarters of the labourers were born on the Island or in the rest of Kent throughout the period. Detailed analysis of the birthplaces of dockyard workers at the three Census dates shows that a high proportion of those workers who moved long distances came originally from towns that had occupational links with Sheerness or industries containing similar types of workers. Up until 1834, much of the heavy labour in the yard was carried out by convicts — up to about 300; however, between 1851 and 1861 ordinary hired labourers increased from 307, or 22 per cent of the dockyard workforce, to 653, or 25 per cent.[16]

Table 6.1 shows in detail how recruits to the yard — that is, workers not recorded at the previous Census — came from well beyond the local community. Even in the decade 1861-71, when the dockyard declined slightly, 67 per cent of recruits came from off the Island. This meant that 970 dockyard workers, or about 40 per cent of the total workforce, had migrated to Sheppey in the decade 1861-71.

Table 6.2 shows the population distribution of the Island in the nineteenth and twentieth centuries. Sheerness grew rapidly at the very beginning of the nineteenth century; there followed a period of stagnation until it grew again between 1851 and 1861. The population was then relatively stable to 1891 and then grew until 1911 as the town gained popularity as a holiday resort. Queenborough developed as a small industrial centre in the early years of this century.[17]

For Sheerness, the dockyard dominated the employment structure.[18] In

---

[16] It is difficult to judge whether, in the middle of the nineteenth century, a turnover in employment in an isolated dockyard of 55 per cent over ten years and 70 per cent over twenty years should be regarded as a sign of stability or change. The fact that the dockyard was relatively stable as a unit of employment did not necessarily imply that the population of the town of Sheerness was stable, given that there were no other employment opportunities for those who did leave the dockyard.

[17] The Sheppy Glue and Chemical Works, established in 1883, still exists as Sheppy Fertilizers; a cement works opened in 1882 but was abandoned in 1916; and in 1910 Johnsons opened a pottery introducing sanitary ware in plaster of Paris moulds to Britain. The Queenborough site was found by Mr Johnson when travelling on the Queenborough-Flushing steamboat service between his factories at Stoke on Trent and Wesel in the Rhineland; 'a considerable number of skilled operatives came . . . from Wesel and Stoke to the newly erected plants' (K. R. Macdonald, 'The Isle of Sheppey and the Swale', MA thesis, Kings College, London, 1949, p. 81). In 1905 a glass bottle works was established and a sheet glass works was started in 1928.

[18] See plate 7, which shows relics of the old dockyard in today's docks.

Table 6.1 Birthplace of dockyard recruits

	Sheppey %	Rest of Kent %	London %	Rest of South East %	South West %	Dockyard towns* %	Other %	Total N
1861 recruits								
All	27.9	14.3	10.2	11.4	9.4	17.7	23.1	1999
Shipwrights	28.0	5.0	4.8	7.1	16.3	29.7	22.9	336
Metalworkers	8.2	9.1	26.4	10.2	10.5	16.2	34.6	352
Labourers	36.1	27.4	7.0	15.0	3.0	8.4	11.3	559
1871 recruits								
All	32.7	16.2	14.2	8.9	10.2	21.5	14.7	1445
Shipwrights	23.2	8.1	12.2	11.1	15.1	31.4	21.4	271
Metalworkers	27.2	11.7	31.8	10.0	8.8	25.5	19.7	239
Labourers	46.2	22.2	6.4	7.6	4.9	8.4	12.3	405

* Dockyard origins include Chatham, Deptford and Woolwich, Portsmouth, Devonport and Pembroke. The figures in this column are also included within the appropriate regional figures in the preceding columns.
Source: Census Enumerators' Books 1861 and 1871.

Table 6.2 Population distribution for the Isle of Sheppey and Sheerness, 1801–1971

	Isle of Sheppey	Sheerness Census	Sheerness Resident	Ships and Barracks	Blue Town	Mile Town	Marine Town	Minster	Queenborough	Remainder
1801	6,639							5,561*	545	533
1811	8,392							7,003*	805	584
1821	10,221							8,414*	881	926
1831	9,934							7,983*	786	1,165
1841	10,858		7,046		2,829	4,217		8,341*	634	1,540
1851	13,385	9,776	7,888	1,873	2,814	5,074		1,306	772	1,531
1861	18,494	14,552	12,015	2,537	3,386	6,236	2,468	1,412	973	1,557
1871	18,595	14,641	12,519	2,122	2,971	6,368	3,180	1,323	820	1,635
1881	18,204	14,286	12,197	1,759				1,372	982	1,564
1891	18,607	14,492	12,549	1,943				1,619	1,050	1,445
1901	22,275	18,179	14,317	3,862				1,306	1,544	1,246
1911	24,382	17,487	15,460	2,027				3,207	2,468	1,220
1921	26,344	18,673							3,081	
1931	25,464	16,833						3,687	2,941	2,003
1951	28,384	15,796						7,338	3,137	2,113
1961	27,211	13,691						7,860	3,044	2,616
1971	31,590	13,139						12,328†	3,102†	2,815†

* Whole parish, including Sheerness
† Estimates, owing to boundary revisions
Source: published censuses for the years given.

1861, two-thirds of male employees were in either the dockyard or HM Forces, and there was very little employment for women — nearly four-fifths of whom were classified as 'unoccupied'. By 1931 60 per cent of employed males were still employed in the dockyard or in the Forces. There was no alternative manufacturing employment.

The main outlines of the town of Sheerness were determined in the nineteenth century. Blue Town was mainly eighteenth-century, but Mile Town, built on the landward side of the fortifications, was largely completed by 1841. Marine Town was built during the period of expansion from 1850 to 1870 and the intervening land was developed from 1870 to 1890, with larger, three-storied houses to cope with the holiday trade. The houses in Marine Town were of a considerably better quality than in Blue Town or Mile Town and attracted the better paid dockyard workers. Shipwrights and metalworkers in particular were concentrated in Mile Town. Segregation by social status existed at a very local level.[19]

Impact of Cuts in Public Expenditure

After the expansion of the dockyard in the late 1850s, associated with the Crimean War, there were calls for economy in the later 1860s. Sheerness was thus faced with cuts in expenditure in the dockyard from 1867 and also with the threat of its complete closure. In 1868 an editorial in one of the Sheerness newspapers complained:

The inhabitants of Sheerness have recently seen that utterances of opinion respecting the dockyard have been heard in the House of Commons which threaten as it were its existence. . . . The Liberal MP for Pontefract, has filled up the measure of condemnation by declaring that a more extravagant yard in a more wretched place could not be conceived.[20]

---

[19] Different streets of Marine Town had greater concentrations of distinctive types of workers: thus, in 1871, while there were on average 22 per cent of shipwrights distributed around the town, James Street in Marine Town contained as many as 40 per cent. For labourers, on the other hand, while the average for the town was 23 per cent, the same street had only 11 per cent, whereas parts of Blue Town had well over 40 per cent and one area had 64 per cent. Clearly, Blue Town was in decline from early in the nineteenth century. Analysis of residential mobility in the town from 1851 to 1871 showed that the new residents of Marine Town who came from other parts of Sheerness came disproportionately from Mile Town. There did not seem to be much mobility to other parts of the town from Blue Town: residents of that low status area were more likely to move in and out of the town as a whole.

[20] *Sheerness Times and General Advertiser*, 18 April 1868. These and other quotations from the 1860s and 1870s are taken from reports prepared by Gary Harding and Tessa Ovenden as part of an undergraduate course in local history taught by Dr John Whyman of Rutherford College, University of Kent at Canterbury. Their research on the back numbers of newspapers was very time-consuming and I am glad to acknowledge their efforts.

A week later, 204 discharges at Sheerness were announced. There was a suggestion that all men over the age of 55 should be retired and the cuts caused a dramatic variation in the number of apprentices taken on. The other Sheerness paper responded to the cuts in much the same way as its equivalent contemporary would today. 'The value of prosperity in the locality is tangibly depreciated, business credit and general commercial confidence is unsettled.'[21]

Unemployment meant that the men had to leave. In August 1870 there is a reference to a farewell meeting of between 70 and 80 discharged smiths 'preparatory to their leaving Sheerness'.[22] Two troopships left for Canada carrying discharged dockers and their families from the four Kentish yards. In the winters of 1869/70 and 1870/71, soup kitchens were opened in the town. At about this time the suggestion was put about that Sheerness should be developed as a seaside resort. In tones echoing almost precisely those of editorials in the early 1980s, one written in July 1871 urged the people of Sheerness out of their apathy:

Surely the time will come when Sheerness people will be cured of this listlessness and go in for helping themselves. With a fine healthy locality and a beach second to none in Kent, a judicious effort of public spirit might make the future of Sheerness and rescue the place from being a mere government 'hanger on'.[23]

At about the same period there were suggestions for attracting other employers to take advantage of the surplus of unemployed women and young people. Certainly, efforts to attract more people to the Island as a holiday resort and to the growing industries at Queenborough were moderately successful.[24] By 1904 the Sheppey Light Railway was running from Queenborough across the middle of the Island to Leysdown and electric trams ran to make a connection from Sheerness to Minster East. Picture postcards provide glimpses of a modestly flourishing Edwardian seaside town.[25] Reports in local newspapers in 1871 provide substantial evidence of the wide range of voluntary organizations and social activities in Sheerness in that year. Musical entertainments were particularly popular. Attendances at meetings and concerts were often quite large. A literary institute reading in February 1871 was 'as thinly attended on Tuesday evening as any we should think during the season there not

---

[21] *Sheerness Guardian and East Kent Advertiser*, 13 February 1869.
[22] *Sheerness Times and General Advertiser*, 6 August 1870.
[23] *Sheerness Times and General Advertiser*, 29 July 1871.
[24] In 1874, for example, Macdonald has suggested that steamers landed 115,000 persons at Sheerness pier (Macdonald, 'The Isle of Sheppey') and various guides and brochures were produced encouraging visitors and housing development. The regular service from Queenborough to Flushing has already been mentioned, and a branch of the Chatham and South Eastern Railway with a spur up to the pier provided 'easy access to the mainland and the metropolis'. For a time this was, indeed, one of the fastest routes to the continent.
[25] See Michael Thomas, *A Picture Book of Old Sheppey*, Meresborough Books, Rainham, 1983.

being more than 350-400 persons present'.[26] Later meetings recorded 600 and 700 present. Musical entertainments brought out the larger numbers.

According to one informant, whose memories go back to the First World War, the Island generated its own social life since there was a toll of a penny to leave it. After the first bridge was built in 1860, 'you had to pay to go off the Island and you had to pay to come back.' Mr Sears came to Sheerness to train in the First World War and married a local girl. He then got a job in the dockyard as an upholsterer. He has taken a great interest in the community and has a collection of old photographs and other memorabilia.

The town was, er, one of the most marvellous towns in the whole country. In so far that you had a cooperative society — the oldest one in the country founded in 1816 — you had a medical society — you had a penny a week for the head of the household, I think it was an 'alfpenny for the children, and then a free doctor. You had a building society — one of the oldest in the country — you had a working man's club, you had a Conservative Club — Conservative working men's club if you like. You had what was known as the Ivy Leaf Club, which was the old Social and Literary Club. Not much literary about those clubs today, but there was years and years ago when it started. And you had your — the Services Club, that's still running, but it's just a club — no Services. . . . And so the whole town was a community on its own. Their whole world was Sheerness — or the Isle of Sheppey. They'd go off perhaps once a year. Mind you, they had no week's holiday in the old days. . . . We only ever had four days a year. . . . People were so poor that they couldn't go anywhere you see.[27]

In the period before the First World War there was little employment for women on the Island. As Mr Sears again confirmed:

Very few women worked in Sheerness before World War I. They just stayed at home and almost every other house in these streets would have 'Bed and Breakfast' in the window in the summer time. Earn a little extra money that way. Oh yes, that's quite right, women didn't go out to work then and it wasn't the thing for women anywhere really. Up in the north they did it in the mills, and in London they would go working, but in a place like Sheerness it was frowned on for a woman to work if she was a married woman. Single women would be in the shops, but a married woman — her place was in the home and that's where she — you'd find her.

However, Mrs Unwin remembers a deviant pattern in Queenborough before the First World War. Her memories of everyday life were unusually vivid and she could describe events in great detail. The Sheppy Glue and Chemicals Works, known as 'the chemicals', was well known for creating a disgusting smell and for its dirty and unpleasant work.

---

[26] *Sheerness Times and General Advertiser*, 11 February 1871.
[27] From the transcript of an interview with Mr Alfred Sears, one of the dockyard workers.

Local people would not work there and it is remarkable that women had to come in from as far away as Sittingbourne to do this, as it were, low-caste work. Mrs Unwin recalls coming back from a music lesson:

I know I should't'a done it . . . I'd never *seen* a woman in trousers and she'd got them tied round 'ere, you see. 'Cos they used to get rats and goodness knows what over there — it used to be terrible — and of course being young and silly, I turned round to look, you know, and I thought 'Oh, doesn't she smell 'orrible' — and she *swore* at me for looking at her.[28]

This confrontation with the outcaste women of the glue works clearly frightened the respectable young girl, whose grandmother had come to the Island as a school teacher from Wales. There are still plenty of rough, tough working women on the Island today, but in 1913 Mrs Unwin, perhaps mistakenly, thought them exceptional: she was at pains to emphasize how clean everyone kept their homes in those days.

The Decline and Closure of the Dockyard

Some general conclusions can be drawn about the impact of the dockyard on Sheerness. Perhaps the best starting point is to consider the needs of the Admiralty. There was a need for a reliable and highly skilled workforce, since the quality of the product was of considerable importance. The Admiralty had to produce ships at a price competitive with private shipbuilders, who formed a powerful lobby against the dockyards in Parliament. Second, they needed to be able to maintain their workforce cheaply at times of slack demand, and expand it rapidly when the need arose. These needs were met by two strategies. First, the workforce was isolated from the rest of the labour market to reduce competition from other employers paying higher wages. In Sheerness there was virtually no other source of employment, apart from services, until the 1960s. This had very serious implications for women's employment possibilities. Furthermore, by keeping the shipwrights as the general constructors of the ships — a group with no parallel in private industry — they helped to reduce the potential for unionization and militancy. The second main strategy was to offer the dockyard workers considerable non-monetary compensations for wages which were low by comparison with the private sector — pensions, security, prospects of promotion, perhaps a higher level of control over the immediate production process than private workers, a slower pace. The Admiralty also offered the prospect of regular work for established men, and created

[28] From one of the follow-up interviews to the main Sheppey Survey. This informant has been given an assumed name.

a division between this group, which was the permanent workforce, and the hired men, whose employment depended on the amount of work — though even this group was in general more regularly employed than private sector workers.

These points may be illustrated by interviews with retired dockers whose memories cover the period from the First World War to the closure of the dockyard in 1960.[29] They emphasize the leisurely pace of work, the indulgency patterns whereby the dockyard authorities kept only modest control over the traditional occupational easement of making 'rabbits' — private jobs done with dockyard tools and materials — and the overwhelmingly Conservative political ideology. Talking to the shop steward who had developed the Sheerness Labour Party in the 1920s, it was clear that the dockyard had little latent radicalism:

You see, the working men's club in the dockyard, it was then, every man practically. Perhaps and in the Conservative Club too. . . . The dockyard came first. Well you see the feelings in the dockyard are this — that the Tories are the people for war, they support that kind of thing and they were the people for a big navy, big army, you see, so you'd have a job to get the people in the dockyard to vote Labour, because they'd close the dockyard.[30]

In the event, of course, it was, ironically, the Conservatives who closed the Sheerness dockyard in 1960 and then twenty years later made the same decision for Chatham. Throughout the 1920s and 1930s, workers had no way of resisting cutbacks in employment and there were regular discharges. 'You stood there and you listened and you waited and you heard. It was last in and first out.'[31] Because the dockyard was the dominant source of income and the dominant employer in the town since its establishment as a community in the early nineteenth century, it dominated many other aspects of life. It promoted attitudes that stressed individual mobility and instrumental collectivism, which may not seem to some to be the basis for the ideal-typical traditional working-class community.

The Rise and Fall of Casual Work

Parallel with this formal, hierarchical, relatively well-documented world of the dockyard, there was another, rougher and less well-documented working-class culture more typical of Samuel's quarry roughs or White's Campbell Bunk. Even the pious and deferential Augustus Daly, who

---

[29] The argument is also very thorough documented for Chatham (Waters, 'Social history of the Chatham dockyard').

[30] From an interview I conducted as part of the pilot work for the main project.

[31] Ibid.

generally paints Sheppey in a very rosy hue, acknowledged that in the early nineteenth century 'the morals of the Sheppey islanders of this period were apparently, somewhat lax, for smuggling was not only exceedingly rife but was accounted an honourable vocation to pursue. The whole populace, it was said, were more or less addicted to this profitable pursuit.'[32] In common with other parts of East Kent, smugglers saw themselves as 'free traders'. This swashbuckling free-trader spirit flourished again in the 1970s, when large quantities of the goods imported into the docks found their way all round the Island. The peak of this activity was in the mid-1970s, before fieldwork on the Island began and a fierce crackdown by the police led, so it is consistently claimed, to piles of transistors appearing at the bottom of Minster Cliffs.[33]

Obviously, many Islanders go fishing and shoot and trap duck and rabbits on the marshes. Much of the Island gives a remote and desolate impression and, until recently, wildlife was abundant. For nearly a century, holiday-makers have doubled the population of the Island in the summer, bringing money and the opportunity for quick-witted entrepreneurs to make small fortunes out of food, drink and 'amusements'. Leysdown-on-Sea attracted hustlers and cowboys and provided apprenticeships in mild crookery for generations of school leavers who, in the 1950s, 1960s and early 1970s, went 'down Leysdown' to work as cheap labour, cleaning the chalets in the holiday camps, serving in cafes and bars and minding stalls and (later) machines in the fairgrounds and amusement arcades. The holiday trade provided a myriad opportunities for small business enterprises to start with little capital, and the regular flow of new clientele prevented the build-up of bad reputations: fiddles could be perpetrated all summer; prices could be exhorbitant; and high labour turnover prevented possible protest but spread bad practices. Some parents refused to let their sons and daughters go off in the summer to pick up bad ways. However, such seasonal employment also had the useful function of providing independence, some pocket money and the experience of a number of bosses, without any opprobrium resulting from having 'changed jobs too frequently'! Being unemployed for a spell in the winter, 'helping your dad' or 'looking after your sister's baby' is perhaps more acceptable when there is a very strong likelihood of finding temporary employment at the beginning of May.

[32] Daly, *History of the Isle of Sheppey*, p. 264.
[33] On my very first visit to the Island in the winter of 1977-8 one of my early informants was recovering in a pub after claiming much of a jettisoned cargo of timber, which had been washed up on the beach in the heavy seas. Getting it on to an inadequate truck in the dark was not easy work. On another occasion, during the same winter, driving down a remote track in the marshes opposite the Island late one very dark, wet night, I came across two heavy lorries loading by an isolated cottage. The tone with which I was told I had taken the wrong road convinced me that some fieldwork situations are best left unexplored.

Unfortunately, by the late 1970s there had been a drastic reduction in the number of summer visitors. Debate raged on the Island about whether it was the lack of facilities or cheaper package holidays abroad.

For many years, Sheppey has been the haven for the poorer section of the south-east London communities. They have relied on the Island to provide them with holidays. Many have bought caravans, some older and more rundown than others, or chalets, on the many sites in and around the Leysdown area. The huge number of vans, chalets and villas has meant a constant flow of people to that end of the island and a constant flow of income to the arcade, shops, stall and entertainment owners.

Thus, an editorial in the local newspaper justified the development of underdevelopment and attacked a report of the South East England Tourist Board and the Department of Environment regulations that demanded hard standings, electricity and main drainage.[34] Few facilities and little surveillance were seen as positive attractions. More organization would reduce the desirability of Leysdown to 'the less affluent holiday maker from this side of London'. In the heyday of Leysdown's prosperity in the 1950s, there was a regular bus service from there to Leytonstone in East London.[35] While to officials in Maidstone and Sittingbourne, Leysdown was seen as 'a real planning disaster based on too-local decision-making',[36] it at least had the merit of attracting regular spare money which could circulate in the local economy.

The holiday trade was blamed by the school for generating an ideology of dishonesty and rule-bending, and in 1978 the truancy rate for the fifth year at the comprehensive school was said to be 20 per cent. Bobby Wilson, the Rolls-Royce-driving owner of the amusement arcade at Leysdown, was a regular recruiter of school leavers.[37] However, the possibility of leaving school early to get regular money was rapidly declining in the late 1970s.

---

[34] *Sheerness Times Guardian*, 24 April 1981.
[35] This service ceased in the early 1970s.
[36] It would be indelicate to reveal the precise source of this remark.
[37] Bobby Wilson was killed in a car accident in October 1983. His death provoked many warm tributes and it was reported that 600 people came to his funeral at Minster Abbey. Wilson came to Sheppey in 1961 and was often referred to as 'Mr Leysdown' since at one time he owned most of the place. It is interesting that this rather swashbuckling entrepreneur should appeal so strongly to the Islanders.

Employment on Sheppey 1960-1980

There is no question that the closure of the Admiralty dockyard in 1960 was, in the words of the Chief Planning Officer for the District, 'a hammer blow to the economy of the Island' (even though, a few weeks later, the *Sheerness Times-Guardian* was describing 'Sheppey's most important occasion of the century ... when momentous history was made' when the new Kingsferry Bridge was opened by the Duchess of Kent). More than 700 dockyard workers were put out of work. Although many left the Island, and the Admiralty paid the fares for some to work in the Chatham yard for a short period, in 1960-61 local unemployment reached 11 per cent when the national rate was just over 2 per cent. The dockyard was bought by Building Developments Ltd for £750,000 as an industrial site. The industrial structure of Sheerness has developed entirely since 1960. The Navy playing fields provided the location for one industrial estate, and the Army playing fields provided the site for the steel mill in the early 1970s.

The development of Sheerness docks happened almost casually. In the early 1960s the odd vessel was being unloaded there and while other ports were moving into new technology, containerization and so forth, Sheerness was not in a position to do so. At a time, therefore, when few ports wanted conventional ships and the London docks were clogged up, Sheerness could unload faster and could get fruit and vegetables up to Covent Garden in two hours. A Stevedores Union was formed in the early 1960s and a distinctive element in the local labour market soon became firmly established. There was no tradition of labour militancy, and since dockers soon became among the highest paid workers on the Island, there was little reason for the situation to change. Furthermore, the dockers could easily get home for lunch: if there was no work they could simply go home and, in the words of the chief executive, 'upset the local decorating market'. In the late 1970s it might cost the owners of a ship £2,500 a day to keep a ship in the docks: in the desire to get ships away owners would pay almost anything, and therefore, in practice, the extra costs of overtime were paid without question and fiddles to extend the amount of permissible overtime were accepted with little argument. From the early 1960s to the late 1970s, registered dockworkers in Sheerness increased to between 360 and 380. The 'official' reason why Sheerness developed rapidly and effectively as a port was its 'good labour relations'.

However, there is another, darker side to the post-1960 development. Most workers on the Island in the early 1960s were largely unskilled and had no tradition of collective organization, shift work or hard industrial discipline. Somewhat unkindly, one official claimed that the workers in the dockyard had been provided with a legalized form of national assistance. More radically, another official claimed that the workers had been dispossessed from their own labour market as new, skilled workers had to be imported from outside to work in the new factories. There was no established union pressure to ensure that incoming employers hired local labour.[38] In the case of the steel mill, 90 per cent of the most skilled workers came from outside the area. However, some of the new firms that were attracted to the Island recognized that its isolation and tradition of low wages were substantial resources. Factories in the clothing industry in particular were attracted by the availability of women workers, whom they could train and expect to keep. Some firms exploited the local labour force by paying low wages, while others paid more, knowing that the differential would ensure that their workers would not leave. The steel mill, which was established in 1972, employed more than 800 workers eight years later. Young, tough, stable, married men were needed who could stand hard, hot work, including shift work, and recruitment never posed a problem.

A detailed study of the industrial structure of the Island was undertaken in 1981,[39] demonstrating how top-heavy it was: of the 39 manufacturing enterprises, 15 employ more than 50 workers, a further 10 employ between 21 and 50 workers and a mere 14 firms employ up to 20 workers. Even if these 14 each had 10 workers, which it is known they do not, that would mean only between 100 and 200 jobs in the small-firm sector on the Island. Inevitably, this makes the Island extremely vulnerable, should the giants of the labour market get into difficulty. Typically, in a healthy labour market, a seedbed of infant industries produces growth, providing, as it were, an inflatable cushion should the main employers be obliged to shed labour. Also, the service sector is very poorly developed. There is a striking lack of any office employment of any scale whatsoever: the largest employers are simply the local branches of banks or building societies.

---

[38] The General and Municipal Workers' Union (now the General, Municipal and Boilermakers' Union) is the largest union on the Island, being at least twice the size of its nearest rival. Office holders change only on the death of incumbents and hence there have been only three branch secretaries at Queenborough since the Union was founded in the 1920s. The GMWU offers a whole range of facilities to its members and was at one time jokingly referred to as 'the funeral union' because of the generous funeral benefits it offered. Most of its members treat it as a convenient private club. Union officials have a secure, highly respected lifetime job, which can be combined with chairmanship of the local Conservative Party with no sense of incongruity. Members regard the Union as a source of service provision and social security more than as a political and campaigning organization. As one union official remarked, 'In Queenborough you feel a sort of loyalty to the firm anyway because it's only a small firm. It's not so much a factory as a way of life after twenty years. The hours suit me and the money is good. It's a way of life, a local job and a very secure job.' Since he said that, the firm has twice been taken over by international corporations.

[39] Pahl with Dennett, *Industry and Employment*.

This dramatic skew in the structure of employment on the Island implies that the twenty-seven employers with more than fifty workers are more important than might be the case elsewhere. For good or ill, the future of the Island's employment is overwhelmingly dependent on them. This small group of the largest employers had about half of the workforce between them, and a representative of each of the main employers was interviewed at length between February and June 1981. As Table 6.3 shows, women comprise 20 per cent of the workforce of the twenty-five largest companies, and their relative proportion of the workforce of individual firms is, by and large, inversely related to their size. Most of these firms have come to the Island since 1960 and half of them are ultimately owned by organizations based outside the United Kingdom. Four of the six largest employers are owned by multi-national firms. At the time of the survey, it was estimated that these twenty-five companies generated an annual turnover of about £100 million and those with the highest turnover are foreign-owned. The rolling mill at Queenborough and the steel mill at Sheerness were partly encouraged to come to Sheppey by the established shipbreaking yards on the Island. The post-war government granted a licence not only to break up ships but also to smelt them into raw material for the UK steel industry. The scrap from a de-industrializing Britain has helped to bring some new investment to Sheppey. The Queenborough rolling mill has moved from ships to old track and wagons from British Rail. It owns the old line which ran to Queenborough jetty in the days when it was a packet post. Owned and managed by an Italian, using an Italian rolling process and employing between twenty and fifty skilled Italian workers at different times, the mill employed about ninety workers in 1981. The rapid expansion was possible through finance from Swiss banks and the chance to buy 6 acres of industrial land adjoining the railway line for a mere £25,000.

Table 6.3   Isle of Sheppey firms, by size of workforce and proportion of women workers

No. of workers in firm*	No. of firms	Average no. of workers per firm	% of women in workforce
Over 750	3	800	11
300–749	3	325 ⎫	17 ⎫
100–299	2	150 ⎬ 255	43 ⎬ 23
Under 100	17	56 ⎭	39
Total	25	185	20

* Total number of workers = 4,635

Many employers mentioned the advantage of Sheppey's 'green labour' — people who could be trained and also had the 'right attitudes'. Wages were not high, and many managers who took part in the survey recognized that it would be very hard to bring up a family on £100 a week in 1981. They would prefer to employ fewer, more highly paid and more skilled workers.

Perhaps the most striking finding from an analysis of the wage rates of Sheppey workers was the glaring discrepancy between what women were paid for semi-skilled work and what men earn for the same category of work. In one company, the lowest paid semi-skilled worker was the maintenance fitter's mate: he earned £2.25 an hour in 1981, which is £90 for a 40-hour week. If this was his minimum wage, it was substantially above the rate that most women on the Island were paid. Women's rates varied from around £1.50 to £1.89 an hour and they generally worked a 37-hour week. In one firm no overtime was possible, so almost the complete female workforce earned a maximum of £55.50 a week. In other firms there was a range from £55 to £75 or £80. When asked about the rates for semi-skilled men and women in the same firm, the discrepancy would be explained by the fact that all the women were on piecework but that such work was not available to men. The fastest women on piecework in a number of factories could earn up to £80 or £90, and in two, exceptional, cases, women were earning over £100 for piecework. In one case that involved very long hours (54) and in the other, where women could rise above the basic rate of £80 to over £100 'easily' on piecework, 70 per cent of them were in their appropriate union.

Ten companies employed at least thirty women as semi-skilled workers, but the opportunities for women to become trained further so as to earn skilled workers' wages seemed very small. One employer claimed that, while there were opportunities for women to become skilled workers, they did not choose to do so. Another said that one woman was following the formal training procedures to become a skilled worker, but because of age considerations she was unlikely ever to become skilled.

Despite their low rewards, the women workers of Sheppey were highly valued and in many ways appeared to be better workers, from the employers' point of view, than the men. Many of the companies who employ a high proportion of women came to the Island specifically because unemployment was high and the women, perhaps more than the men, were trapped on the Island. Those who employed both men and women and who were prepared to make disparaging remarks about the men (about which more later) frequently made it clear that they exempted the women from these remarks. Typically, women workers are loyal, reliable and do not make trouble. Those employers who were seen to be fair and reasonable (and that does not seem to involve paying high wages) got a very loyal response. In one case, a rush of work led management to ask for extra work in the evenings and weekends, and half the staff volunteered to do this. In another instance, a firm found itself short of work and the managing director explained that if the workers insisted on keeping their existing hours of work, he would have to make some redundant. However, he was prepared to devise a work-sharing scheme to keep everyone on, but with reduced hours and earnings. This was accepted, even though this meant a low ceiling for the highest earners and a mere £40 a week for the lowest earners, with two-thirds of the workforce getting less than £50 per week. It seemed clear that the extra effort and complications that these arrangements created could not be justified on strict profit and loss criteria. 'It's a case of making a profit or coming out of it maintaining your staff. I always think that we must look forward to the time when we can employ all the staff full-time.' The idea was to keep the business going as a collective enterprise, partly because that was a decent thing to do. 'If I was ruled by a board of directors, I couldn't do it.'

The Island being a small community and with relatively few alternative wage-earning possibilities for women, some employers saw their future involving a few men to keep the machinery going, with women to do the packaging and boxing. Such work is always classified as semi-skilled, but, of course, it does not have to be done by females. Nevertheless, the wage rates ensure that it is. Employers have been flexible by, for example, allowing women to leave early on Friday to do the shopping and, in general, have been willing to take a woman back after she has left to have a family. As one manager remarked, 'often the wildest ones when they're young become the most reliable ones when they come back.' Since many of the factories are close to the council housing areas of Sheerness and Queenborough, women can even get home at lunch-time if they want to. This must be relatively unusual.

According to one employer, women have become relatively stoical about their marginal position in the labour market and see themselves as something of a reserve army of labour to be taken on in good times and the first to be discarded when times get difficult.

It certainly suits employers to imagine that redundancy causes less distress to women. As one manager remarked, 'we have got people here who are the breadwinners, who are single-parent families who'd obviously take any smashing of their income very hard. But the one who's been working in a family, even though their husband has been unemployed, doesn't regard herself as the breadwinner. You know, it's sort of "oh well, it was fun while it lasted".'

It would be extremely surprising if these two conflicting views of Sheppey women workers were equally true. Some employers see them as *more* loyal and committed than the men, whereas others see them as *less* committed. Some who take the former view are prepared to reciprocate with a similar commitment to their workforce. But one company, which employs 600 workers to assemble parts in their own homes, has been criticized for the low wages paid to these outworkers; according to the rate set by a time and motion study, the homeworkers might be expected to earn 60p an hour, although, of course, many manage to earn much more. This particular company can readily silence its critics by pointing out that it has a turnover of one in six of its outworkers a year and never has a problem of recruitment. The waiting list of those wanting to become homeworkers is as long as those actually on it. This must be clear evidence of the demand of the women of Sheppey to earn money. When wage rates are low, the need for a second wage earner may become a necessity.

All employers were asked how long it would take to replace a skilled manual worker (implying, of course, a man), assuming that they had to do so. The answer was always measured in days or, at most, a few weeks. Thus, in one small manufacturing company which employed no tradesmen, 'two weeks on the job' was said to be adequate to get enough skill to do the work. In another larger company, it was claimed that many of the workers could be trained in a day, although, exceptionally, some workers doing a particularly skilled operation would need three months' training. More typical, perhaps, was the reply that the time for training for both skilled and semi-skilled workers was 'about a fortnight for anything'.

Given these modest demands on male workers' capacities, it was difficult to know precisely what a good worker was. Most employers very generously spent time showing me round their works, and my subjective impression was that those exercising the most complex manual skills were more likely to be women. Indeed, women doing what is defined as semi-skilled work, say as machinists, would require up to six months' training — which is substantially more than the men doing what is called skilled work. Thus, despite the protestations of employers, it does seem that men do not necessarily have great demands put upon them. It is, of course, paradoxical that women who are expected to do relatively demanding and meticulous work are paid by piecework and get lower wages than the men.

When employers are talking about good workers, they do not really mean good workers: they mean good *employees*. That is to say, they want disciplined and reliable workers who accept their pay and conditions without protest or who respond in a very direct way to the stimulus of more income. There is an interesting contrast here in the way employers approach women: generally there is a strict limit on the amount of money they are prepared to pay, but there is more emphasis on their being decent, understanding and reasonable in order to bind the women with ties of loyalty. For the men, the pecuniary nexus was frequently held to be sufficient.

When managers were asked about the distinctiveness of the Sheppey workforce, they mentioned the isolation and 'rural' nature of the Island, the ready availability of seasonal or casual employment until very recently, the family nature of social relationships on the Island, and a value system that expects bosses to be bosses and is suspicious of attempts to share responsibility. It is evident that these factors are interrelated, and it is also clear that previous experiences help to colour contemporary consciousness and understanding. The best bosses are not necessarily those that pay most or believe in power-sharing — rather, the best bosses are those who provide certainty, security and stability, are not too demanding, allow a degree of absenteeism and do not expect the work to be an all-enveloping life interest for the worker.

One manager, in attempting to put his finger on what was most distinctive, thought that the dockyard had created a particular style of worker: 'it gave employment with dignity.' The new employment that came onto the Island in the 1960s and 1970s demanded different qualities from the Sheppey workers. It demanded regular hours; it introduced all kinds of controls and disciplines. There was little concern for the workers' dignity, and, very frequently, firms closed or workers were made redundant as a result of takeovers, mergers or the rationalizations of larger companies which decided that they could dispense with their Sheppey plant. No longer was there a clear and obvious boss — whether of the dockyard, the bottle works, the potteries or the glass factory. As the manager of one of the older companies, which has a long association with the Island, commented: 'they're good workers but suspicious — and rightly so when they've been taken over three times in ten years.' Now, he admits, despite attempts to explain to the shopfloor about the takeovers, there is still confusion: 'they don't even know who owns them!'

There was nothing, it seemed, that many workers could do to avoid being made redundant from some of the companies that came and went in the 1960s. It was not lack of workers' efforts that led to closures and redundancies in the late 1960s; it was under-capitalization, changing markets or some other factor over which they had no control whatsoever. Given this utter powerlessness in the face of forces based largely outside the Island, it is perhaps not surprising that their time-scale should be foreshortened and their attitude to work should be ambivalent. Without exception, employers agreed that on occasions workers would rally round and give of their best when there was a clearly perceived need to do so. They *could* work hard, but did not always *want* to. An unusual comment, made by one of the most thoughtful managers on the Island, was that Sheppey had a 'very middle-class workforce'. By this he meant that there was a distinctive kind of individualism on the Island. Unlike the workers in the North of England from where he came, Sheppey workers show 'a variety of different forms of individualism' and he referred to their opinions, their leisure, pursuits and so on. Certainly, there is an unusually high proportion of home owners on the Island: overall, 69 per cent of the Islanders own their own homes and 61 per cent of manual workers do so. This compares with 45 per cent of manual workers in Britain as a whole who own their own homes.[40]

It seems likely that some of the larger and firmly established employers on the Island have managed to build up a committed workforce. By paying higher wages, they have encouraged their employees to raise their style of consumption so that they become more dependent on higher wages. In time, it is possible to buy in labour as long as working conditions are not too bad. One of the largest employers on the Island was able to claim that there is 'no such thing as bad troops, only bad management': few others were able or could afford to agree with such a sentiment. Most managers felt slightly baffled and beaten by 'the Island's mentality', the Island pace of work and the problem of motivating men to do noisy, repetitive, dirty and sometimes dangerous work for a wage that, as some managers admitted, was little better than the dole for many married men. I suspect that most managers would prefer not to have to employ people at all under these conditions, and many had plans to introduce more machines and to get rid of the worst jobs. A future pattern of factories in which machines are maintained by a few men and most other tasks are done by women seems likely in Sheppey.

A casualized secondary labour market could also be readily observed on the Island: youngsters in the amusement arcades, women behind the bars and pensioners filling in for everything from cleaning to skilled craft work, provide a very varied and fluctuating workforce. Wages for by-employment are always low: either the supply is short or the demand is great or both. By-employment can be hard, exhausting and demoralizing, especially perhaps for those with skills and experience. To see this kind of shadow wage labour as some kind of solution to the problems of a de-industrializing society is dangerous romanticism.

Before leaving this discussion of employment, two examples of other styles of waged work may be mentioned, which illustrate aspects of employment not obtainable from the formal survey. One 'employer' did not appear in the survey because he 'did not employ anyone'. However, he manufactures a product that requires substantial labour, and he has a milkman and several pensioners working for him. The milkman comes to the factory for three hours, four times a week for which he gets 80p an hour, paid monthly. He uses this as a compulsory form of savings to pay his electricity bill. In the afternoon he does voluntary work, caring for the lawn of a bowling green. Another worker is a pensioner whose first job of the day is to open a newspaper shop and mark the papers. After he has been home for breakfast and walked the dog, he does three hours at the factory for £1.50 a day. Then, after a nap in the afternoon, our pensioner does his third job between 5 p.m. and 7 p.m. as a sort of night watchman at £3 a day. His total weekly income in 1979, on top of his pension, was

[40] *Social Trends*, HMSO, London, 1981.

about another £50. According to the owner of this factory, there was a network of spry old age pensioners ready to do these regular, relatively undemanding jobs at low salaries. For them it provides a distraction and a little extra money. Younger people, he claimed, would not accept the low rewards and the discipline of keeping regular hours. Somewhat fancifully, perhaps, I was told that these pensioners living centrally in Sheerness all had telephones and could be called up as an instant reserve army to deal with rush orders, a job of cleaning on the boats or whatever. With their pensions as a long-stop, a tradition of self- help and early rising, they were following the pattern of by-employment that has been described in previous chapters as part of the traditional pattern of getting the work done.

In April 1978 I talked to women on the Warden Bay estate at the east end of the Island, where the time and cost of commuting and the heavy burden of a mortgage put severe strains on married life. In one small close, five husbands out of thirty were unemployed. Opportunities for casual work were limited and competition was intense. Women who had skilled jobs before marriage, working for computer companies and the like, were obliged to accept 50p an hour serving in greengrocers or in the pubs. One woman, in desperation, worked at a day job seven days a week for which she got £21 and then served behind a bar from 7 p.m. till midnight. She worked days and nights for two months, earning less than £40 a week. She had two children aged 5 and 6 and simply never saw them. Some women will have a third weekend job but still not earn much more money. Buses to Sheerness run once every two hours in winter and in 1978 it cost £1 return. Prescriptions of Valium to the wives on the estate doubled during the year before fieldwork began.

The Political Economy of Housing in Perspective

We have seen that members of households engage in different forms of work to get by. Paid employment is generally necessary to buy the hens, but feeding them, shutting them up and letting them out and all the other work necessary before eggs or chicken can be eaten is generally unpaid work by household members. The provision and maintenance of housing is on an altogether different scale. Ordinary working people were, perhaps, more effectively dispossessed by the enclosure movement and their forced migration to the towns, where they were obliged to rent whatever industrialists and speculative builders provided for them.[41]

[41] The miseries and problems associated with housing the workers in nineteenth-century towns have been well documented and discussed (for example, J. N. Tarn, *Five Per Cent Philanthropy*, Cambridge University Press, 1973; A. S. Wohl, *The Eternal Slum*, Edward Arnold, London, 1977). The 1901 Census showed that 45.2 per cent of Finsbury's population lived in one- or two-roomed flats, and Stepney, Shoreditch, St Marylebone and

Middle-class entrepreneurs and philanthropists were much concerned about housing the urban workers, and the more respectable and aspiring tradesmen and white-collar workers recognized that their position in society was centrally linked to where and how they 'built their home'. The idea of working collectively for the family home implies, of course, more than just the physical dwelling and its location: it includes also the way it is furnished and used — the whole style of life of domestic respectability. One strand in this ideology had direct implications for the development of Sheppey — and certain distinctive household work strategies — namely, the development of plotlanding in the early years of this century.

Following the severe agricultural depression in the 1870s, agricultural land prices declined steeply after 1878, so that in certain coastal areas, where land was not in great demand for farming, there was some potentiality for speculative housing development. Entrepreneurs bought land very cheaply in parts of South Essex, Kent and Sussex, divided it into plots 20 ft by 150 ft and sold them for as little as £5 a plot at the turn of the century. Purchasers could construct their own dwellings or simply keep the land as an investment. C. Ward and D. Hardy have documented this process in their research on plotlands: they concentrate on the larger development of such places as Jaywick Sands and Canvey Island in Essex and Peacehaven in Sussex. In areas where the holiday trade was also expanding in Edwardian times, speculators would seem to be in a lucrative enterprise. Opening up land ownership to new social categories appeared to fit in with strong social and economic tendencies. Very little initial capital was required — perhaps a 10 per cent deposit followed by sixteen quarterly payments. Given the Isle of Sheppey's aspirations to develop as a holiday resort, its poorer quality agricultural land and its overall marginal social and economic situation, it was clear that it seemed to be a good candidate for such development.

Before 1890, as I mentioned above, most of the land on the Island was owned by absentee landlords, and the very low returns on grain encouraged them to put their land back into grazing. Its exposed and windswept position made it unsuitable for the traditional Kentish crops, fruit and hops. Larger and more substantial and particularly shrewder investors were less likely to find the Island attractive. The cliffs at Minster and Warden were slipping into the sea and, as Macdougal suggests, 'marsh fever', or malaria, had been a problem in long, hot summers. Indeed, as late as 1917 136 cases of malaria were recorded in the

---

Holborn all had over a third of their inhabitants packed into one- or two-roomed flats (Wohl, *The Eternal Slum*, p. 310). The housing problem was, inextricably and inevitably, a problem of poverty and, as the Chairman of the LCC's housing committee, Sir J. P. Dickson-Poynder, recognized in 1907, the housing problem 'provokes the vexed question of the relations between rent and wages, which easily slides into that of capital and labour' (quoted in Wohl, *The Eternal Slum*, p. 312).

Sheppey/Grain areas.[42] Whether or not this was widely known, it did not deter a number of entrepreneurs from buying land on the Island from about 1900. The Shellness and Leysdown Estate Company was placing advertisements in the local newspapers and was based at Mussel House in Leysdown. In 1904 another advertisement advertised freehold land at £12 a plot 'within 300 yards of Halfway Houses. High, Dry and Healthy. Reduced prices to builders taking a number of plots. The Land Company, 68 Cheapside, London EC.'[43]

Detailed evidence from title deeds suggests that speculators sold land more to each other than to individual plotholders. The Land Company was founded by Frederick Francis Ramuz, JP, who had been Mayor of Southend and had made a fortune from property speculation in south Essex, where plotlanding was more successful. Advertisements were placed in *The Evening News* and brochures were produced and circulated in London. Handbills were distributed in certain streets and posted in selected railway stations, claiming that Sheppey was the 'nearest ocean frontage to London on the Kent coast'.[44]

Ramuz gave his son George 2,000 acres of land at Minster in Sheppey, together with the responsibility for paying off an £11,000 mortgage. George Ramuz never became very wealthy, spending most of his life paying off the debt, but he became an influential local figure, donating playing fields and open space to the community. He set up six little estates on the Island and marked off the estates with kerbstones, still to be seen today. One of these estates stretches from Minster Abbey to the sea cliffs, and 441 plots are set out in the Estate Plan, along Kings Road, Princes Avenue and Imperial Avenue.

In 1961, when interviewed by the local newspaper, George Ramuz described his marketing strategy: 'If we hadn't induced London shopkeepers, tradesmen and publicans, and a few builders who had got some money to invest, I don't think development would have taken place at all. . . . I was working in the City at the time, I had been for some years. I had that connection with them. I had been in the City from 1891 when I was 14.'[45] Very shrewdly, he had focused on the rising class of skilled artisans, clerks and bookkeepers, the people George and Weedon Grossmith describe in *The Diary of a Nobody*. The Land Company brochure was spattered with little couplets designed to appeal to and to foster petit bourgeois values of independence and property ownership:

[42] Macdougal, 'Malaria'.
[43] *Sheerness Guardian and East Kent Advertiser*, 2 January 1904.
[44] Ramuz had his friends among London journalists; an article entitled 'An Unknown Paradise' described Minster as 'sitting on the memorial sea. One could live here, one could see the children grow straight and strong and healthy here. Unlike London, it is a place to make one's home. And next best to that, it is a place to take one's summer rest. Here on the nearer coast of Kent is the ideal holiday home' (*The Morning Leader*, 20 June 1903).
[45] *Sheerness Times-Guardian*, 16 June 1961.

> Clerks and mechanics, commence now to save
> Remember the landless man is a slave
>
> With all investors let maxim stand:
> He ventures safely who invests in land
>
> Parliamentarians, philosophers agree
> The Great Towns' workers ought to be free

Everything was done to encourage would-be purchasers. Ramuz offered free return rail tickets from Holborn and Herne Hill with lunch and champagne before the plot auction in a marquee.[46] There were even specially chartered trains. Any kind of building was encouraged in the handbills:

> Cheap iron or wooden bungalows allowed
> No arbitrary building restrictions

The Land Company built specimen wooden bungalows to encourage potential buyers. In these six-monthly auctions, Ramuz claimed to have sold 3,000 plots to over 1,000 Londoners. In his word, he was 'distributing' the land.[47] So effective was he in this 'distribution' that many plotholders never claimed or developed their land, and there was confusion over title until very recently. In some cases this held up development and in other cases it encouraged squatting or just plain annexation. The chaotic pattern of land ownership defeated the planners. Ramuz probably did more to hinder than to encourage development by scattering the land in this way. Nevertheless, Minster did grow steadily from 1901, particularly in the first decade of the century, when it grew by 146 per cent. This soon posed problems in the provision of infrastructure. Ramuz began by selling water at a halfpenny a bucket from a horse and cart before establishing an inadequate Water Company in 1902. Frequently water had to be rationed; the roads were unmade and there was no sewerage.[48]

However, it was not until the 1960s that the local council took action and 380 plots on Minster Cliffs Estate were acquired by compulsory purchase order on 5 August 1965.[49] In 1980 the council still owned just

---

[46] *The Observer*, 29 October 1967.

[47] When Ramuz died in 1966 his estate was valued at only £16,587.

[48] As one exasperated visitor put it in a letter to the local paper in 1925; 'What can I say bad enough about the mud and the water? . . . Roads there are none, drainage none, lamps none, shops none, and post office — such a palatial building! — a mile or so away. Why do people live here?' (*Sheerness Times Guardian*, 1 January 1925).

[49] Despite the Council's efforts, many plots remained unclaimed. The intention was to amalgamate and resell the plots, with the council providing better infrastructure and facilities out of profits. Plots that were bought for £600 in 1965 were sold in the first council auction of forty plots in 1973 for between £3,000 and £6,500 mainly to private individuals or

over 8 acres, and, inevitably, as time goes on, sales have gone increasingly up-market. The council has, therefore, encouraged a shift to more affluent home owners, since, under the now more stringent planning regulations, architects and builders must submit professional plans. However, they still favour the individual, and plots are sold through 'informal tender', which, officials claim, helps to ensure that most buyers are still local people. Certainly, this method of land allocation would not appeal to any but the very smallest builder, and the larger developer, responsible for most of the private house building in Kent, went elsewhere.

Housing on Sheppey, 1960-1980

Four main developments in the housing of the Islanders have taken place: the expansion of Sheerness for the dockyard workers; a similar development at Queenborough for the early industrial development there, often built by the factory owners themselves; the plotlands of Minster; and the chalet development at Leysdown. All these types of development offer considerable scope for individual domestic refurbishing and improvement, positively encouraged by the council. In the mid-1970s, for example, the council focused on a cluster of streets in Marine Town, Sheerness, built between 1857 and 1865 — Alma Street, James Street, Richmond Street, Clyde Street and Unity Street. This small area, typical of working-class Sheerness, had within it two general stores, a newsagent, a fish and chip shop, two hairdressers and a second-hand furniture shop. There were also three pubs. Most of the 296 dwellings (77 per cent) were owner-occupied, but 12 per cent were unfurnished, privately rented.

Overall, the council found considerable poverty, environmental dereliction and a striking lack of amenities in the houses examined. In just over half the houses, of which many were occupied by elderly people often living alone, the head of the household had no earned income. It was decided to designate the area as a Housing Action Area in January 1977. This allowed substantial funds to be made available, which had the inevitable effect of encouraging the younger occupants to benefit from the grants, often by doing much of the work for themselves. At the time of the council survey in 1976, it was found that the average length of occupation of houses in this area was seventeen years, and thirty-two houses had had the same occupiers for more than forty years. Clearly, an

---

small builders. Since then the Swale Borough Council has been releasing plots in a steady flow: thirty were sold in 1979-80 and at that time the price was between £9,000 and £10,000 for a site on an unmade road. Plots are sold with a 40 ft frontage, twice as wide as those Ramuz sold, but the pattern of piecemeal individual development remains.

area such as this can change very quickly in its social composition as a high proportion of the population die or move to residential homes in the space of a few years.

Such an intensive survey of a few streets was not attempted in the programme of research reported here. As is shown in Chapters 8 and 9, the sample survey provided a detailed snapshot of the whole Island in 1981 but could not pick up the contours of small, relatively self-contained social worlds. Nevertheless, it is most important to emphasize that these distinctive residential areas very often have different cultural styles and traditions which affect fundamentally the level of informal communal work that can be supported.

In 1981 there were 13,250 dwellings on the Island, of which 2,870 or 22 per cent had been built by the local authority. These are mainly in the Rushenden Road area of Queenborough and on the West Minster side of Sheerness. Smaller clusters of local authority housing are at Minster and Halfway. These two main clusters adjoin the two main industrial areas of the Island, providing an opportunity for women living there to get to and from work easily and for all workers to get home for a midday meal if necessary. But this is offset by the disadvantages of pollution and a bad environment. Thus, in July 1981 the dust and fumes from Sheppy Fertilizers were stripping paint from cars and causing sore throats, coughs and watery eyes. Residents claimed then that the dust had been falling on and off for three years but that the last few months had been particularly bad. Complaints led to more thorough tests and the plant was shut for a time. Although the firm was registered with the alkali inspectorate, this occasion was said to be the first they had heard of a problem.[50] Later in the month the firm pleaded guilty to using a wrong chemical mix and was fined £75 in the Magistrates' Court. Similar complaints were regularly made against the steel works and a chemical plant in Sheerness, which is now closed. Certainly, it was the common experience of the researchers coming from the clean air of Canterbury that collars and cars soon got very dirty in the industrial areas. More washing and cleaning would be necessary in working-class Sheppey. The compensation of being able to walk to shops and most facilities relatively easily, which may encourage neighbourly meetings, applies more in Sheerness than Rushenden, but, as will be shown later, these two areas do typify in many respects urban working-class industrial communities. Most local authority housing was built before 1968 with only 14 per cent of the stock built since that date. Perhaps the most striking element in the housing development on the Island in the 1970s was the new private development at Minster and Warden Bay. Between 1965 and 1979 some 2,000 private houses were

[50] Reported in *Sheerness Times-Guardian*, 17 July 1981.

1 (Above, left) Digging for lug worms can provide a substantial part of an eleven-year-old's income. *2 (Above, right)* Alleys, behind the nineteenth-century houses of Sheerness built for workers in the Admiralty dockyard, provide continuity with the past. *3 (Below)* By contrast, it can be seen from the front that many of the houses have been modernized. Often the skilful use of a reinforced steel joist (RSJ) has made the living area more spacious.

4 The collapse of the apprenticeship system means that some young people learn their trade in the street.

5 A transporter train returns to shift another load of Japanese cars from the depot in the Sheppey marshes.

6 *(Above, left)* Trade in secondhand goods of little or no value is largely for the poor and the old. 7 *(Above, right)* Relics of the old Admiralty dockyard coexist with a variety of modern uses. 8 *(Below)* Informal trade can take many forms – the black economy on wheels?

9 Canadian capital finances the steel mill which recycles the scrap metal from Britain's industrial past.

10 Many Sheppey people value living on an island. The Isle of Grain oil refinery dominates less obviously on a hazy summer's day.

built there. Such properties are between 20 and 40 per cent cheaper than on the mainland.[51]

However, it would be wrong to assume that newcomers in privately built houses contrast with established Islanders in the local authority estates. It is a common aspiration on the Island for a self-improving family with upwardly mobile aspirations to move to Minster, or at very least to Halfway, when money for the down payment and mortgage charges has been saved. Just over half the survey respondents had lived in three or more houses on the Island and 15 per cent had lived in five or more houses.

This high level of intra-Island dwelling mobility reflects a particular kind of household work strategy, which depends on home renovation and improvement as a means of raising the value of the property, selling with a capital gain and gradually moving up the housing market and acquiring capital at the same time. The very varied housing stock, the peculiar structure of the land market at Minster and the policy of Swale District Council to sell local authority houses provides a diverse opportunity structure. Older, three-storey houses in Sheerness, once the basis of the boarding house trade, can be converted into flats; the smaller terrace houses can have bathrooms added at the back and the two downstairs rooms made into one with a reinforced steel joist; and the early plotland bungalows can be extended over the years from very modest dwellings to substantial detached houses if adjoining plots are later acquired. At the bottom end of the market there are some 4,900 caravans and 2,000 chalets, which can always serve as temporary accommodation if there is no relative willing to put up a family moving between a house already sold and another in the process of conversion.

Housing is, therefore, a crucial element in the Island's political economy. While the unemployed man in a council house who owned his 'second home' round the corner which he was refurbishing with the income from his wife's employment and his own labour was exceptional, he illustrated nicely a household work strategy involving both housing and employment.

---

[51] This figure was derived from comparing prices of equivalent housing in Faversham and Sheppey advertised by the same estate agent on the same day (18 July 1981) in a local newspaper. The cheapest home in the paper for Sheerness was £9,500 for a three-bedroomed terrace in the town centre in need of 'modernization'. In Faversham, the cheapest was £16,500 for a two-bedroomed equivalent house, some distance outside the town. Similar houses with full modernization and central heating cost £15,500 in Queenborough and depending on facilities and construction, whereas in Faversham the lowest price was £26,000, and the highest £65,000. The prices for virgin land are just as disparate, since in Minster it costs just £9,000-£10,000 for a plot on an unmade road with a 40 ft frontage, whereas in Sittingbourne, an equivalent plot costs £20,000-£25,000. Faversham is about fifteen miles from Sheerness, and Sittingbourne about eight miles from Sheerness, and they fall under the same local authority area.

The different areas of the Island are to a degree polarized politically, with Conservative members of the local council more likely to represent Minster and Warden Bay, and Labour councillors representing Queenborough and Sheerness. Before the local Island council was formed in 1968 there were three separate councils, each with its distinctive political style. Local action groups are typically community-based rather than focused on wider issues. The separate identities of the different areas of the Island have deep roots. The trade unions are also locality- rather than industry-based, even though members could be working in any part of the Island or even on the mainland.

7

Myth and Reality in Sheppey
in the 1980s

When I started research on the Isle of Sheppey I assumed that people's consciousness must have deep roots. They must surely pick up taken-for-granted ways of behaving and responses to their current situation from their early experiences in their childhood homes. The actual work practices of their parents would surely colour their perceptions of the nature and meaning of work and much else besides. I doubted that the material conditions of existence that faced those who lived on the Isle of Sheppey in 1981 would be the overwhelming determinants of how they thought and behaved. Such a simple and direct link between material base and social consciousness seemed offensive to me, implying an unacceptable degree of pliancy which appeared dehumanizing for the people involved. While given existential circumstances are clearly important in determining work practices — unless, for example, there are employment opportunities for women in the local labour market, there is not much that they can individually do about it — people can nevertheless hold sets of latent beliefs and values that have emerged out of their own and their parents', and perhaps grandparents', experiences.

It was on the basis of this line of thought that I was encouraged to dig deeper into aspects of the social and economic history of the Island reported in Chapter 6. I confidently believed that, the more I understood about the Island's past, the more I would be able to share the experiences of those whose families had been on Sheppey for a number of generations. At that time I had been led to believe that most Islanders were long-term residents, a notion the sample survey of 1981 demonstrated to be quite false. However, not then knowing the facts, I spent many evenings simply talking generally to people about the Island, as I met them in their homes or in the cafes or pubs.

Theories from Below:
Islanders' Ways of Making Sense of their World

In the early days, when I was getting the feel of the place, I was presented with three contrasting theories by ordinary people I chatted to as I spent time exploring, in a relatively unfocused way, the Island's character. Since I cannot now recall whether it was Dave, Colin, Steve, Helen or anyone else who most clearly first articulated these theories to me, I will assign my own labels to them.

The Durkheimian Theory

The problem with the Island, according to those who propounded this theory, was that it never recovered from the sudden closure of the dockyard in April 1960. A strong sense of social cohesion existed, built up over the centuries, based on the pride of craftsmanship, the patriotism associated with working for the Army and Navy, and the solidarity based on working men's clubs and the co-operative movement. In the old world, so tradition had it, there was meaning in people's lives, provided by the ritualized Admiralty hierarchy and reflected in a status hierarchy outside the dockyard, with the skilled men living in more respectable areas, supporting church and chapel and having total occupational security.

The shock of suddenly finding the *raison d'être* of a way of life taken away so quickly knocked the self-esteem of the community with a force it could not handle. The decay and dereliction that set in as soon as the announcement was made in 1958 blighted the Island and undermined its *conscience collectif*. Without a clear focus for the community's identity, it fell apart. Youngsters no longer went to the technical school or competed for the much-prized dockyard apprenticeships. (This was the beginning of the end for apprenticeships generally. A hundred years ago there were well over 100 craft apprenticeships on the Island; now there are less than ten.) The Island lost its tradition of skill: new factories were less demanding; an anomic and privatized war of all-against-all in the labour market developed. Unemployment rates began to rise: the Island would never be the same again.

The Marxist Theory

According to this theory, the Islanders have always been an isolated, trapped labour force valued for its docility. Different waves of capital have washed across the Island at different periods, exploiting, extracting and polluting. In the late 1950s and early 1960s the Island had Development Area status, and firms were attracted to it with local and central government assistance, turning underdevelopment into a resource.

This wave of investment was largely dissipated in a decade as many of the firms collapsed or were taken over in the merger boom of the late 1960s and early 1970s and then closed by the new parent companies. Islanders were rudely ejected from employment with little redress. Then, in the early 1970s, international capital invested heavily. In particular, a large, new, Canadian-based steel plant was erected, but by the early 1980s it, too, started to shed labour.[1] By then, competition from the cheaper labour in the Third World countries made it impossible for some companies to hold their markets. Finally, the penetration of foreign products, consequent upon and encouraging the de-industrialization of Britain, led to acres of land changing from sheep pasture to enormous car parks for foreign-made (mostly Japanese) cars. It was estimated that, of the total of 800,000 cars a year imported into Britain in the early 1980s, 100,000 came through Sheerness, encouraging the local MP to say that this was putting Sheerness 'at the centre of world trade'.[2]

Proponents of this theory see a captive reserve army, deskilled and demoralized, buffeted and bruised by world processes of capital accumulation eddying round a backwater.

The Weberian Theory

Those who adopt this stance point to the continued rationalization and bureaucratization of all aspects of the Island's life. In 1968 the three Island local authorities were merged and the system of education became comprehensive, despite much local opposition.[3] The technical school was closed and one large comprehensive school was built in the middle of the Island for just under 2,000 pupils. Then, in 1974, local government was reorganized once again; the District Offices were established on the mainland at Sittingbourne and councillors were more likely to be mainland farmers and businessmen.[4] The growth of the welfare state organized everyday life, generating a resentment against pervasive surveillance and control. People came on to the Island during the day to check, to organize and to inquire. Planners, school attendance officers and careers advisers sorted, sifted, chased and advised.

---

[1] A total of 172 men were made redundant on 2 June 1982.

[2] *Sheerness Times-Guardian*, 23 September 1983.

[3] A research project to monitor this change was funded by the Kent County Council Education Committee at the University of Kent at Canterbury. This was directed by Professor Paul Stirling and carried out by Cyril Rodd. Substantial disagreement about the 'usefulness' of this work led the Education Committee to abandon the project. An interim report, reflecting the bitter resentment of local teachers, was deposited at the Library of the University.

[4] A suggestion put forward by the Boundary Commission in 1983 to put Sheppey into *West* Kent for the purposes of the next election to the European Parliament in June 1984 led the *Sheerness Times-Guardian* to complain, with some justification, 'If you confuse people often enough, as the Boundary Commission seems intent on doing, they will become apathetic and that is bad for democracy' (29 July 1983).

A resentment against the apparently ever-expanding state was a common topic of pub conversation in working-class areas, fuelling those who supported this theory. The development of new, modern estates and the sale of council houses developed or encouraged sharp status distinctions among manual workers, based less on mutual respect and understanding and more on the outward signs of a given style of life. Family members drew apart from each other as the ambitious, hard-working and overtime-seeking moved out to owner-occupied houses in Minster and emphasized their distinctive patterns of consumption. It was the new value system, developed by an aspiring consumer-oriented stratum, that divided and weakened the established community.

These three theories, sketched out by ordinary people trying to make sense of the context in which they live, are all founded to some degree on fact. The dockyard did indeed close, abruptly changing the nature of the town of Sheerness. But Sheerness housed only a third of the Island's population, and it is unlikely that that one event could have had such an effect, although the *Sheerness Times-Guardian*, widely read on the Island, did (and still does) much to spread the myth. Features on various aspects of local history appear frequently in its pages and those with personal memories of the 'good old days' are given generous space in the correspondence columns. Elderly people living in other parts of Britain or in other countries — particularly Canada or New Zealand — write regularly with anecdotes. The Island in the past is frequently equated with the Admiralty dockyard.

The theory about the effect of the ruthlessness of capitalist exploitation is also based on some facts, but the imputed consequences are questionable: in terms of the effects on people's consciousness, employers are more likely to be perceived as benefactors — providing employment is seen to be the most useful way to help the Island. Agencies of the state, on the other hand, are viewed with greater resentment and hostility.

Finally, the organization and management of the Island has, indeed, become more remote. Companies are controlled by distant corporations based overseas and the local government is based on the mainland at Sittingbourne. However, in practice, multi-national corporations are more likely to provide *better* conditions of service for their employees, and the new Swale District Council claims that it is providing proportionately more resources for the Island to make up for its previous neglect. A new swimming pool costing £1 million opened during the period of our research, and a further £1 million was spent on a covered sports centre that was completed in 1984. It is likely that the council's claim is valid.

These three theories are therefore inadequate in different ways, and it would be hard to say more than that there is something in all of them.

And that, of course, is where the discussion in the pub generally ends. Social scientific rigour should do better than that.

There is, however, a fourth, which might be called the psychogenetic, theory often held by those living off the Island and visiting it as an employer or member of a local government or welfare state organization. It was claimed that Sheppey was distinct because its population was stable and self-contained (even in-bred), and had been so for generations. Accounts of the origins of the population varied: some claimed that many were escaped convicts from the prison hulks that were moored on the Medway in the eighteenth century; others suggested that there was substantial inbreeding among a small number of landless quasi-gypsy families or that more recently cockneys had migrated to the Island early in the twentieth century and had created a distinctive cultural style. The IQ of Sheppey schoolchildren was said to be lower than the county average, there was a greater problem in dealing with ESN pupils, and there was a higher proportion of mentally handicapped people on the Island. All this was due to the isolation and the peculiar genetic make-up of the Islanders.

Needless to say, this pernicious myth is completely false, but Islanders are aware of it and adopt a mocking, self-deprecating tone often hiding a fierce pride. I was shown on a number of occasions how a crude drawing of East Anglia and the Thames Estuary could demonstrate that 'Sheppey was a piece of shit in the arse 'ole of England.' But then the conversation would quickly shift and many would emphasize that it was curious how often people came back to the Island after leaving it for a time. It was frequently said that the rest of the world was unfriendly: people felt at home on Sheppey. As one woman unselfconsciously remarked, 'I like it here because it's so central: you've got London and city life in one direction and Canterbury and rural life in the other.'

The Historical Structuring of Land, Labour and Capital

How well do these local home-spun theories fit the account of Sheppey given in the last chapter? Certainly there are distinctive elements about the Island that can be adduced in support of each theory. No one theory can be shown to be the correct one, but each has some element of truth in it. Evidently, the historical geography of the Island illuminates its contemporary material conditions. The siting of the Admiralty dockyard, the docks and the cross-Channel traffic to Holland are all related to location in the Thames Estuary with deep harbour facilities. Many of its industries depended initially on its accessibility or the potential to discharge noxious waste. The glue works was based on the bones from the knackers' yards of London, brought down by barges in the 1890s.

What is commonly called the bottle works, the Canning Town Glass Works, was established in 1908 using Belgian silver sand which came directly to the Queenborough jetty. The iron foundry came to make moulds for the glass works; the reasons for the location of the pottery have already been mentioned. In the two decades after the dockyard closed, Sheppey was attractive to industrialists because of its lack of planning controls and surveillance, the availability of grants in the immediate post-closure period and a low-waged, trapped workforce.

For example, Abbotts Laboratories, one of the largest, most prestigious and highest paying employers on the Island, is part of a Chicago-based pharmaceutical corporation owning sixty companies throughout the world. Outgrowing its original site in Jarrow, it moved to Sheppey in 1961 because it was seeking a site on which it could foment anti-biotic material and it wanted to be able to get rid of the effluent easily. In the event, the company decided not to go ahead with that particular process, but it has a prime coastal site, on which to set out its chemical plant, between Queenborough and Sheerness. Abbotts has a well-deserved reputation as being one of the very best employers on the Island. It is one of the few companies likely to get stronger in the current recession — since people are more likely to be ill under adverse economic conditions, the sale of drugs increases. However, typically, the growth of the plant to perhaps double its size in the 1980s will be more capital-intensive, and only about 100 new workers are likely to be added to its present workforce of some 700.

Another obvious consequence of Sheppey's location and port development is the growth of car importing. Few other places could have provided so much cheap and undeveloped land so very close to the docks. Toyota moved up to Sheppey from near Dover in 1975, attracted by the 'good' tradition of industrial relations and the availability of land on the Queenborough Industrial Estate, and later on Neats Court Marsh behind the Rushenden Road housing estate. Examples could be multiplied. Sheppey was a low-cost location in terms of land, and labour and capital support came from the local authority or, in the case of most of the largest investment, from overseas. Dutch, Canadian, American, German, Swiss, Italian, French and Japanese capital has been put into the Island in the last twenty years in very substantial quantities, and all the indications in the early 1980s suggested that such foreign investment would increase. For example, in October 1983 Twinlocks, which has a factory at Sheerness, was taken over by Acco World Corporation from Illinois. A spokesman for Twinlocks was quoted as saying: 'The takeover is not because we are in difficulties — quite the reverse, because the company last year doubled its profits on the previous year.'

The peculiar housing history stimulated by the dockyard and the holiday industry has encouraged home ownership and home improvement. The injection of petit-bourgeois capital in the early twentieth century did not create much new development, but it fostered a particular *style* of small plot housing development which continued up to the present. These distinctive waves of capital investment have created *a distinctive local political economy*. By emphasizing housing as much as employment, the narrow conception of a local labour market has been broadened to include the role of the state and the rules and regulations that structure social relations in different contexts. The Admiralty controlled its workforce in one way; Sheerness Steel attempt to do it in another by encouraging easy home ownership for its workers by using EEC mortgage subsidies available to workers in the steel industry.

Of course, the main weapon of control is now the threat of redundancy or closure. Managers in multi-national corporations know the risk that they, too, would lose their jobs if the plant were shifted to an even lower-wage area such as Portugal. The Island has always been a victim of circumstances over which it has had no control. Slumps and lay-offs in the dockyard related to the bellicosity of the government have been paralleled, in the quarter-century since the dockyard closed, by more closures and redundancies as firms have collapsed, been taken over or struggled to survive.

This, then, is the complex material context in which households struggle to get by. In 1984, as in 1784 or 1284, ordinary people know (in T.S. Eliot's words)

> Birth, and copulation, and death.
> That's all the facts when you come to brass tacks:
> Birth, and copulation, and death.
>
> (*Sweeney Agonistes*)

The way in which households form and organize their work practices is a complex process: following through the domestic cycle and getting by is constrained fundamentally by material circumstances. The historical development of the material circumstances that make the Isle of Sheppey today is not simply an account of the growth of capitalism. Throughout the nineteenth century, capitalist enterprise hardly penetrated the Island. Such capitalist activity as did exist up to the 1890s was small-scale petit-bourgeois trade and service activity. While Queenborough was industrialized with relatively heavy industry in the early twentieth century, the Island as a whole escaped until the 1960s and 1970s. Hence, since having a number of employers is a relatively new phenomenon on the Island, this may be a reason for them to be viewed as supporters of the Island rather than class enemies. Over and over again during the six years of fieldwork, employers in general were described in favourable terms, despite the very low wages many paid and the dangerous, dirty and boring work many of them required.

A good example of workers' attitudes on the Island was provided at the time of the national steel strike in February 1980; when Sheerness steelworkers defied their union executive and continued to work, pickets came on to the Island in some strength. It was reported in the *Sheerness Times-Guardian*[5] that wives could not afford to have their husbands on strike because of the cost of their mortgages and the expense of their children. Shops and pubs displayed notices refusing to serve pickets, and wives mounted a counter-picket picket. The support for the Sheerness strike breakers was overwhelming in the town, and notices of support were posted everywhere.

It is significant that, at the time of the picketing, history was invoked to justify support for the Sheerness Steel management. It was frequently asserted that the rest of the country did not come to the aid of Sheerness when the dockyard closed. One correspondent to the local newspaper asked:

> Where then were the unions? Where then were the pickets? Led by the late Percy Wells, MP, and our own local civic heads we fought to preserve our way of life — and we fought alone. We lost. Who knew? Who cared? Slowly and painfully over the next decade (aye and more), we hauled ourselves up by our own bootlaces. In that recovery Sheerness Steel played, and continues to play, no small part. Now, through no fault of our own, all we have achieved is, once again, at risk. . . .
>
> Now it would appear that we are to be invaded by 1,000 or 2,000 pickets from various places. . . .
>
> Don't they realize that they are not opposing 500 men of a steel plant but a whole township of 16,000 people? Go home, brothers, please, for this is no Hadfields but a tight community intent upon preserving its way of life.[6]

This was without question the view of the majority of workers on the Island.

The local newspaper in an unusually incoherent editorial likened the steel strike to the closure of the Sheppey Light Railway and said that it was just another issue that would come and go.[7] The branch secretary of the Sheerness Steelworkers Union attacked the local Labour Party for providing accommodation for the pickets: 'I suggest we all vote Conservative and have done with it, if this is the sort of representation from the Labour Party.'[8] A correspondent to the *Sheerness Times-Guardian* suggested, amazingly in the light of the facts, that 'since 1667 the working men's movements and awareness in this town have been second to none. Artisans built the forerunner to this town in their own time. . . . We in this town know about working men. . . . To the men of Sheerness Steel this town says, fight on, stand alone if you must, you follow a fine tradition of courage and initiative that many will admire in

[5] *Sheerness Times-Guardian*, 7 February 1980.
[6] *Sheerness Times-Guardian*, 22 February 1980.
[7] *Sheerness Times-Guardian*, 8 February 1980.
[8] *Sheppey Gazette*, 7 February 1980.

years to come.'[9] This letter, occupying ten column inches in all, was printed in bold type. The newspaper carried pages of letters referring, inevitably, to the Battle of Britain, Dunkirk and the possibility of a '"Passport to Pimlico" type of UDI'. Exiled Islanders wrote from all over England, from New Zealand and elsewhere. The outburst of militant parochialism was quite staggering, and the past was used in a wildly exaggerated and inaccurate way to bolster the myth of the proud Islanders. People living elsewhere wrote to say how proud they were to have been born on the Island — despite being forced to leave through chronic unemployment.

This flood of Churchillian pastiche emphasized that *definitions* of what happened in the past are every bit as important in determining present attitudes and beliefs as what actually happened. The local newspaper, with a circulation of around 8,000, peaked at 9,000 at the time of the picketing and continues to foster the dominance of an imagined past over the present. Its use of history is cavalier and bizarre, but it is clearly enjoyed by its readers — both long-time residents and the newcomers. It must have almost complete coverage of the Island. Hence, in August 1983, an editorial pontificating against burning stubble, crowded roads and dangerous boulders on the beaches began by claiming: 'We've always been a holiday Island, ever since the Vikings summered here centuries ago.'[10] The Admiralty may have gone, but the people of Sheerness needed no encouragement to mount a torchlit procession to celebrate the Falklands War victory.

Working-class Islanders do have a strong commitment to their locality, a deep patriotism and a kind of anarchic individualism. While two-fifths of all households came to the Island since the dockyard closed, the *traditions* of the Island to which they perforce subscribe are those myths based on the pre-closure world. Household work practices, while constrained by the historical development of the material conditions of existence, are also influenced by ideological wrappings linked very loosely to historical experience.

Towards the Year 2000 with a Labour Market in Decline

During the period 1978-83, when the Island was the focus for the research reported here, unemployment was rising steadily. In some desperation the Medway Ports Authority made an unsuccessful application for Free Port status to be granted to the reclaimed Lappel Bank and the Neats Courts Area. In many respects the Island is well-placed for an experiment in removing state controls: as has been shown, aspects of its local

[9] 29 February 1980.
[10] *Sheerness Times-Guardian*, 19 August 1983.

government history have provided it with substantial experience in the consequences of neglect by public authorities. Perhaps institutionalized neglect would provide some economic impetus.

De-industrialization and jobless growth are not ideas that have to be introduced to the Islanders. The development of Sheerness as a port for importing Japanese cars makes the contrast transparently clear. On the same site where Pilkingtons once employed over 400 people, there are probably three times that number of Toyota cars driven there by a handful of workers. Certainly, the car-importing firms are expanding and firms may take on a few extra workers, but this is rarely likely to reach double figures in a year. As the managing director of one successful firm explained, 'We don't just take people on and lay them off. I would rather work my existing staff a little harder than take on more people to let them go after a few weeks.'[11]

Even if Free Port status had been granted, or if controls such as the quota restrictions on imported cars were relaxed substantially, it is unlikely that very many new jobs will be created. The investment of £1.4 million in the new Klippon factory to create twelve new jobs was widely noticed and discussed. Indeed, so sceptical are the Islanders that some resistance to the designation of more land for industrial development at Queenborough was reported. A local councillor argued at a public meeting that, since new industrial development would be unlikely to provide a significant number of jobs for local people, it would be better if it did not come. One speaker at the meeting was reported as saying, 'The council continues to push industry down on us but the time has got to come when we say enough is enough. It's about time other areas had their fair share.'[12] This response from an area with one of the very highest levels of unemployment in southern England may appear surprising. However, it may be a sign that, if there are few realistic hopes for new, decent jobs, people at least want to live in a pleasant environment. This certainly may account for the correspondence addressed to the local (Conservative) MP deploring his willingness to support the expansion of Japanese car imports for the sake of a handful of jobs.

There are certainly very clear signs that Kent County Council believes that it has to make efforts 'to create more wealth' on its own account, without relying on much central government support; and, in common with other local authorities, it is energetically pursuing contacts overseas. A delegation went to Japan in the autumn of 1983 in order to attract Japanese manufacturing industry or assembly plants to Kent. With increasing protectionism in the European Economic Community, the county can claim to be well-placed to distribute products owing to its geographical advantages. Perhaps more significantly, Kent is attempting

[11] Quoted in the *Sheerness Times-Guardian*, 22 July 1983.
[12] *Sheerness Times-Guardian*, 22 July 1983.

to sell a particular kind of labour to international capital. The leader of the county council reported that when in Japan Kent's 'stable workforce' was one of the advantages that was particularly stessed.[13] The county has also established its own Kent Economic Development Board, chaired by a former director general of the National Economic Development Council, Sir Ronald McIntosh. He, too, emphasized the 'good industrial relations record' of Kent workers as one of the county's main assets in an attempt to attract overseas investors to Kent.[14]

It was clearly accepted without question by the management that 'wealth-creating' investment in the county would be universally welcomed by the workers. But in Sheppey, one of the main sites for such investment, attitudes are likely to be ambivalent. Public subsidies for private profits are seen by some as a sensible way of getting more wealth, which can then be redistributed through the taxation and social security systems. But if relatively few new jobs are to be created and the unemployed are still unemployed, it is understandable that Sheppey people should feel it adds insult to injury if the new investment simply spoils their view. It may be that in the later 1980s the county management will be hurt by what they perceive as the mulish and ungrateful opposition of the apparently deprived to the introduction of foreign investment.

As an alternative pattern of development, women may more readily accept employment at relatively modest rates and, more likely, on a part-time basis. The most docile of all labour, and with, as has been shown, a developing tradition on the Isle of Sheppey, it seems likely that women's position in the labour market may be moderately good, at least until the end of the century. The implications of this pattern of employment which may produce part, but not all, of a household's income will be considered in the final chapter. Here it is simply worth noting that in some respects the Isle of Sheppey can be seen to have some of the characteristic problems of a de-industrializing Britain in a particularly extreme form. People, goods and capital are likely to flow through the Island, adding little to the quality of life of those living there. The people come straight off the ferry and do not wish to stay overnight; the goods, mainly imported cars, cover much of the Island in an unsightly way or are moved out in heavy container lorries jamming the Island's roads; and the capital, from plants employing few, but relatively highly rewarded workers, goes to Chicago, Osaka or Rotterdam. Various clever financial arrangements ensure that little of the value added by the people and locality accrues to the National Accounts. The county gets some benefit from initial investment and the increase in rateable value, but the level of unemployment remains high. International corporations are not noted for employing school leavers.

[13] *Sheerness Times-Guardian*, 11 November 1983.
[14] Reported in the *Sheerness Times-Guardian*, 4 November 1983.

Such seems to be the most plausible scenario for the formal economic development of the Isle of Sheppey towards the year 2000. One of the Island's well-known 'characters', long-serving councillor Charles Nevill, wrote an ironic letter to the *Sheerness Times-Guardian* which was published on 7 October 1983. It expresses many of the views and resentments that regularly appear in the correspondence pages, and since the Island appears to be at another turning point as it suffers the impact of de-industrialization, the letter is quoted in full:

Queue here for Falklands tickets ...

Sir,

Applications are being accepted for emigration to the Falklands Islands. It is advised that those interested should not delay in applying as a large response is expected.

It is felt that Sheppey's residents are well suited for such emigration as they have experience of an isolated life-style. But, of course, there is a vast difference between the Falklands Islands and the Isle of Sheppey.

For example, on Sheppey the cost of a child's bus fare to attend school is either unobtainable or under review; the cost of £1.50 per year per pupil for sports-clothes cleaning equipment cannot be afforded; the repair of roads and pavements is almost a thing of the past; and employment (sic) is maintained to equal the blackspots of the United Kingdom unemployment figures.

Although equal in rate contribution to those on the mainland, it is a fact that they fail to receive the equal proportion in return, whereas, on the Falkland Islands, each resident is maintained at well over a million pounds a year.

In order to encourage visitors, a contract has just been given to a British firm (an umpteen million-pound contract!) for a floating pontoon accommodation for visitors.

Of course, there are disadvantages; there are no cinemas, dance halls or amenities, but, as stated previously, this is why Sheppey residents are considered to be ideal immigrants.

They should take full advantage of the current situation. If the money does not come to them, then it would be best if they go to where the money is.

Apply now! Don't wait until Sheppey is threatened by foreign invaders before money is ploughed back in.

All applications are expected to be processed in time to fly direct and land on the new Falklands Islands airstrip in the course of construction.

Go Falklands! Be a millionaire; and you will not be as lonely as there are even some of our sheep there to make you feel at home.

And remember, there you have the Government's ear far more than you have where you live now. Enrol today! — Regional Enrolment Officer for the Falklands, c/o Charles Neville.

This and the previous chapter have provided some account of the arena in which the people of our case study live out their lives. Not every local context will have such a sharp contrast between myth and reality, for, as I have suggested, being an island probably helps. However, it is important to recognize that most people read their local newspapers with greater care than the national ones. There is a sharp disjunction between the national and the local that strongly persists and will no doubt continue to do so. Those who have commented on the changes in British society from 1959 to 1984 have tended to aggregate the local into a national — or perhaps metropolitan — perspective. Thus, for example, discussions about de-industrialization, the decline in manufacturing and shifts in employment have been largely national in orientation. Yet it is clear that these larger processes of change have very distinctive local impacts.

It is possible that variations in life chances between different localities will become much more marked in the next quarter of a century. Some areas will develop rapidly with new jobs and capital investment; other areas will continue to decline. Patterns of geographical polarization, already in evidence, may well become more acute. In the same way that households may retreat within themselves as a way of coping with a turbulent and apparently uncontrollable environment, so too may localities come to look more within themselves. It is not unlikely that there will be greater vigour and determination to cope with social and economic problems at a local level than at the national level.

And it is at the more local level that all forms of work outside employment have their greatest salience. Local initiatives to organize various forms of informal and communal work are developing very vigorously.[15] It is not, perhaps, too fanciful to expect the rediscovery of local products, local crafts and ways of marketing local identity and historical associations. The stubborn concern of many people on Sheppey not to forget what they see as their 'past' should, perhaps, be considered seriously. The interest in old photographs, old postcards and old people's memories seems to be growing. A local publishing company has been established to supply this new market. Meresborough Books, in Rainham, Kent has published over forty books about places in Kent and other county-related topics, and has published a monthly journal, *Bygone Kent*, since 1979.

This nascent localism is a form of social consciousness that cannot be ignored. If, as I argue, the nature and meaning of work can be understood only in a specific social context, then perhaps the general understanding of the way all work is done in our society will inevitably have to be rooted in a deeper understanding of local contexts, such as the Isle of Sheppey.

---

[15] See the Report *Whose Business is Business?* Community Business Ventures Unit, London, 1982 and other studies sponsored by the Calouste Gulbenkian Foundation.

8

Class, the Domestic Cycle and Sources of Labour

My time doing fieldwork of a more unstructured and anthropological nature on the Island in 1978 and 1979 provided a mass of information which threw much light on the forms of work in which certain Island households engaged. However, I could not be certain how universally valid my data might be: in order to acquire a more complete understanding of the social composition of households and their divisions of labour, I was able to commission a large-scale survey to take place in the spring of 1981.[1] Given the constraints of survey methodology, open-ended questions had to be reduced to a minimum, and I soon realized that devising questions that probed who did what work, when, for whom and for how much (if it was paid) posed considerable problems. I required information on both the *forms* of labour in which household members were engaged and the *sources* of labour that the household drew on to get certain tasks done. As I have mentioned, work done in a variety of spheres by household members comprise the household's forms of labour; work that is received by a household is called its sources of labour.

Gathering information on forms of labour is fairly straightforward: collecting employment characteristics presents relatively little difficulty. Questions on the nature of the present occupation of respondent and partner elicited data that could be readily classified into the Registrar General's socio-economic groups, which were later collapsed into class

[1] This survey was undertaken in exemplary manner by Social and Community Planning Research of London (SCPR) under the direction of Gill Courtenay. The construction of the interview schedule and the analysis of the pilot survey was a joint effort by Gill Courtenay, Claire Wallace and myself. SCPR organized the fieldwork of the main survey and coded the data. The team at the University of Kent were provided with straight hole counts of the data in the autumn of 1981 together with the tapes. The problems of transferring these data to the University of London computer so that it could be analysed using SPSS (Statistical Package for the Social Sciences) took longer than expected owing to a number of minor misunderstandings and difficulties. I am very grateful to Spyros Missiakoulis and Joan Dobby for helping with these problems.

categories. Information was also gathered about other earners in the household and about household income. All these data enabled households to be precisely categorized in relation to their involvement in formal labour. Other questions were designed to draw on all the other work respondents did for employers or for any other person or institution outside the household, whether or not they were paid. Inevitably, such questions had to be phrased more and more generally in order to encompass all the possible tasks and activities that respondents could do. Unfortunately, respondents did not always remember or did not always think certain tasks worth mentioning. However, these questions did provide excellent data on occupation, income and a range of informal work.

A further set of questions explored the sources of labour that households used to get forty-one distinctive tasks done. These tasks were chosen in the light of the knowledge derived from my earlier work in Sheppey and I discuss them in detail below. Broadly, sources of labour were provided either formally, through the market (for example, garages), state services (for example, the home help service) or members of the household themselves, or through informal sources (friends, neighbours, relatives or others 'working off the books'), which might have been paid or unpaid. There was substantial variation among households in the divisions of labour between different sources, and this chapter explores the connections between *forms* of labour (focusing specifically on class and income as indicators of a household's position in relation to employment) and the balance of *sources* of labour for the Island's households as a whole.

At the start of the research I confidently assumed that there would be a connection between forms and sources of labour so that, for example, employed people earning high incomes would be less likely to use informal sources of labour for service provisioning than would unemployed people or those on low incomes, or that women who were full-time housewives would do more self-provisioning work for themselves. Put more precisely, what I wanted to know was: 'How do household work practices and divisions of labour relate to the sources of labour used for the provision of services?'

I have since been forced to discard the hypotheses that I had when I began the large-scale research project. In 1980 I thought that the central objective was to explore the trade-off between time and money. I was over-influenced by the frequently heard statement that 'it paid me to take a week off work to paint the house', so that in earlier publications I had assumed that informal work, whether for oneself or for others, was in some sense an *alternative* to full-time employment. The notion that levels of productivity were higher in the so-called domestic economy had persuaded Scott Burns, Gershuny and, indeed, myself that, in some senses, people had a choice to be better off working for themselves than by engaging in formal employment.[2] I embarked on this research project to see whether, indeed, those that did more 'work for themselves' had a different rationality, a modification of the work ethic that, as it were, distracted them from a complete commitment to formal employment. The practical and political implications of such considerations seemed to be of outstanding importance and significance. If the way people do their work is changing in some fundamental way — a kind of re-negotiation of the social division of labour, as some have described it — then detailed documentation of this would clearly be an essential research task. If people were valuing *time* more than *money*, and if, indeed, higher levels of productivity could be achieved with one's own tools in one's own time, then fears about the consequences of high levels of unemployment might be unfounded.

Furthermore, important differences in attitudes to employment and work might exist between men and women, and these distinctive rationalities should also be explored. A quiet revolution in everyday life might be undermining the central importance of employment as a means of livelihood, a form of social control and a fundamental support for personal identity. It cannot be denied that these are important questions and that too much debate has been conducted on hearsay, anecdote and unacceptably feeble empirical data bases. This was the context and challenge for the Sheppey survey, and these considerations very considerably determined the way in which we designed the research instrument.

The fact that most of my initial assumptions have proved to be mistaken in the light of the evidence that was gathered is an extremely heartening and gratifying justification of the power and validity of empirical sociology. I am happy to show that the facts do not fit, that hard, obdurate reality can still correct armchair theorizing or accounts based on inadequate data.[3] I am as delighted that I have been proved wrong as I would have been if I had been proved right. Perhaps more so: if I had simply confirmed my early assumptions, I might have been inclined to wonder whether the time and money devoted to the study had truly been necessary.

It is quite clear that we initially underestimated the importance of household composition and the domestic cycle. Evidently, the household

---

[2] R. E. Pahl, 'Employment, work and the domestic division of labour', *International Journal of Urban and Regional Research*, 4(1), 1980, pp. 1-20; J. I. Gershuny and R. E. Pahl, 'Work outside employment: Some preliminary speculations', *New Universities Quarterly*, 34(1), 1979, pp. 120-35; J. I. Gershuny and R. E. Pahl, 'Britain in the decade of the three economies', *New Society*, 3 January 1980, pp. 7-9.
[3] The accounts in this and the following two chapters stay as close to the data as possible and my more parsimonious presentation marks a clear shift in style. I become more speculative in Chapter 12.

is a constantly changing social unit as members age and other members come and go. Hence, the connection between the work that is provided and the work that is supplied is mediated by the intervening variable of the stage in the domestic cycle of the household. This I now see is a crucial issue, which I must address in as much detail as the expected connection between employment and other forms and sources of labour.

Before I proceed to the discussion of the evidence, I need to describe in more detail the nature of the survey and the research instrument on which I base my arguments.

All empirical investigations, including the government's own census, have limitations imposed by time and cost. Compromises and pragmatic judgements have to be taken in the light of resource limitations, which are generally more significant in the social sciences than in other scientific fields. The overwhelming problem in the Sheppey study was that, with very strict resource limitations, we required both a large enough sample to allow the numbers in the cells to be adequate for analysing distinctive household work practices and divisions, and information on all house- hold members. In practice, that generally meant both partners in households based on couples.

We also wanted to avoid gathering this information on the work done by different members of the household disproportionately from either men or women. Since, at the time of planning the survey, we had only very generalized hypotheses about the determinants of distinctive household work practices, we did not know the bases on which we could draw up a cluster sample. After considering several alternative sample designs, including a proposal to conduct interviews with more than one individual in each sampled household, an unclustered random sample was selected from the electoral register for each of the eighteen polling districts on the Island. Had we decided to interview more than one household member, the total number of households interviewed would have been very substantially reduced. In the event, out of 923 households in scope, 730 were interviewed, a response rate of 79 per cent.[4] A special effort was made to interview alternately the head of household or the housewife in all households where that was appropriate. These terms were not gender-linked: the 'head of the household' was the person who owned or rented the property and the 'housewife' was the person — usually though not necessarily a woman, — who was mainly responsible for the catering and domestic arrangements of the household. A household could have only one head of household and one housewife, though they

---

[4] Full details of the survey design, including a statement of response, some preliminary tables, a copy of the questionnaire and all accompanying cards and code sheets, are available in *Isle of Sheppey Study*, Technical Report by Gill Courtenay, SCPR, 35 Northampton Square, London EC1V 0AX. Those interested in having this information should write to SCPR and not to the author.

could be the same person, and, of course, a person living on his or her own would be both.[5]

An inevitable consequence of having a completely random sample was that a high proportion — 28 per cent — were single-person households, most of whom were retired. However, since many of the questions related to how a range of tasks was done, these households provided an important demonstration of the sources of labour of households who were unable to do much work for themselves and therefore needed other households to help them. A brief outline of the main questions asked in the sample survey is given in Figure 8.1.

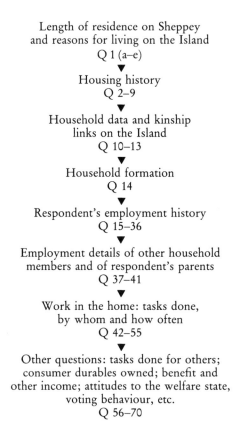

Length of residence on Sheppey
and reasons for living on the Island
Q 1 (a–e)
▼
Housing history
Q 2–9
▼
Household data and kinship
links on the Island
Q 10–13
▼
Household formation
Q 14
▼
Respondent's employment history
Q 15–36
▼
Employment details of other household
members and of respondent's parents
Q 37–41
▼
Work in the home: tasks done,
by whom and how often
Q 42–55
▼
Other questions: tasks done for others;
consumer durables owned; benefit and
other income; attitudes to the welfare state,
voting behaviour, etc.
Q 56–70

Figure 8.1   Outline of the main questions asked in the Sheppey survey

[5] See the *Isle of Sheppey Study* Technical Report for a more detailed explanation of these terms.

The Formal Labour Provided by Households

The main source of income for most people is their formal occupation, and on the basis of this all respondents and their spouses in the Sheppey survey were coded according to the Registrar General's seventeen socio-economic groups (SEGs); these, in turn, were collapsed into three classes with a further, fourth, category for full-time housewives and occupations inadequately described. The classes were made up as follows:

Class 1   SEGs 1, 2, 3, 4 and 13
Class 2   SEGs 5, 6, 8, 12, 14 and 16
Class 3   SEGs 7, 9, 10, 11 and 15
Category 4   SEGs 0 and 17

Broadly speaking, Class 1 is composed of professional and managerial workers, Class 3 is composed of manual workers and Class 2 are those in between. Knowledge of the Sheppey local labour market helped in the allocation of marginal or ambiguous categories. Thus, personal service workers were put in Class 3 and foremen in Class 2, reflecting the way these categories were perceived on the Island. Perhaps more debatably, intermediate non-manual workers were left in Class 2, even though this category might be more appropriately classified as Class 1. This very pragmatic classification has its distinctive problems.

Using these categories, and focusing in this case only on the male's occupation in couple households, it is clear from Table 8.1 that Sheppey has a similar class structure to the country as a whole. Given the

Table 8.1   Social class of Sheppey households compared with the UK (percentages*)

Social class†	Social class of:		
	Male in couple households in Sheppey	Respondent in single-person households in Sheppey	Social class breakdown of United Kingdom†
Class 1	17	6	16
Class 2	35	44	39
Class 3	48	50	45
Total (*N*)	512	185	2,769,102

* Throughout this chapter, percentages in tables do not always sum to 100 because of rounding.
† Excludes full-time housewives and those who have never had employment
Source: 1981 Census, 10% sample tables, OPCS.

particular characteristics of the Sheppey sample, a distinction is made here, which will be used throughout the analysis that follows, between the 204 households with only one, generally elderly, person and the 526 households in which there is a couple of a male and female partner. This latter category will, of course, also include elderly couples who are both retired. Evidently, only those households with more than one person can have a domestic division of labour.

If therefore, for present purposes, we disregard the single-person households (many of whom are lower-status people who have moved into cheaper housing on the Island on retirement), and focus attention on the 526 households in which both partners were classified by socio-economic status, some important intra-class variations can be highlighted. To anticipate later analysis, I may emphasize now that the pattern of household sources of labour is related closely to total household income and also to household tenure. The first substantially influences whether work is done by household members or whether other labour is engaged to do it, and the second influences the kind of work that is necessary to be done.

Tables 8.2(a) and (b) bring together information on households' class, income and tenure, and hence provide a composite guide to their material circumstances. Fully 69 per cent of Class 3 households based on a man and woman couple own their own homes, which is, of course, a reflection of the very high levels of home ownership on the Island as a whole; the proportion of Sheppey working-class 'couple-based' home owners is some 15 percentage points above the average for all households in Britain. Households are classified in this table not simply by the male's occupation but by the occupation of both partners to produce a household class with the male's class given first so that, for example, a Class 2 male married to a Class 3 female would produce a household class of 2.3. By having the class of both partners, it is possible to show the wide variation within categories defined by the occupation of the male chief earner alone. Thus, home-owning couples of Class 3 males married to Class 1 or Class 2 females have very much higher proportions earning 'high' incomes: the difference of 60 and 40 per cent for household classes 3.1 and 3.2 and 18 and 14 per cent for 3.3 and 3.4 is very striking. It will be seen that the high-earning, working-class households in household classes 3.1 and 3.2 who own their own homes have a higher proportion earning 'high' household incomes than household classes that would appear conventionally higher in the household hierarchy; household classes 1.3 and 1.4 and 2.3 and 2.4 have lower proportions in the high household income category than 3.1 or 3.2.

This table, showing the material circumstances of Sheppey households, illustrates clearly that class, based solely on the socio-economic group of the chief (male) earner is, by itself, a misleading indicator. Household class gives a more accurate picture, especially if combined with housing tenure.

Table 8.2(a)   Social class of household by household income:
home-owners (couples only)

Social class of male partner	Social class of female partner	Household income (%):*			Total sample	
		High	Medium	Low	N	%
1	1	50	50	0	4	1
	2	48	42	10	31	9
	3	29	41	29	17	5
	4	11	56	33	9	3
2	1	50	50	0	4	1
	2	43	42	15	74	21
	3	36	39	25	28	8
	4	26	63	11	19	5
3	1	60	20	20	5	1
	2	40	52	9	58	17
	3	18	63	19	62	18
	4	14	43	43	28	8
4	2	0	0	100	3	1
	3	33	33	33	3	1
	4	100	0	0	1	0
Total (*N*)		115	166	65	346	
Total (%)		33	48	19		100

* In this and subsequent tables households were divided into three household income bands based on *net* income. The way this was done is set out as follows:

	Annual net income	Weekly net income	Proportion of households	
			%	N
'Low' income	Less than £3,499	Less than £70	33.4	244
'Medium' income	£3,500–£7,499	£70–£149	36.5	267
'High' income	Over £7,500	£150 or more	18.9	138
Don't know, refused to answer, couldn't remember			11.1	81
			100.0	730

No information was provided by 17% of Class 1, 13% of Class 2, and 10% of Class 3.

Evidently, Class 1 males earn higher salaries, in general, than Class 3 males. However, the particular circumstances of the Sheppey labour market means that working-class women — or, more precisely, women who are prepared to do working-class jobs — are better placed. That is to say, it is easier for women to find 'working-class' employment than 'middle-class' employment. There is little doubt that Abbotts Research Laboratory would just as readily employ a female as a male research

Table 8.2(b)   Social class of household by household income:
non-home-owners (couples only)

Social class of male partner	Social class of female partner	Household income (%):*			Total sample	
		High	Medium	Low	N	%
1	1	0	0	0	0	0
	2	67	0	33	3	3
	3	33	67	0	3	3
	4	0	25	75	4	4
2	1	0	0	0	0	0
	2	29	43	29	14	13
	3	33	50	17	12	11
	4	20	60	20	5	4
3	1	0	100	0	3	3
	2	0	75	25	12	11
	3	19	53	28	43	38
	4	0	50	50	10	9
4	2	0	100	0	2	2
	3	0	100	0	1	1
	4	0	0	0	0	0
Total (N)		20	61	31	112	
Total (%)		18	54	28	100	

* See note to Table 8.2 (a).

chemist with a doctorate; the difficulty is that the men who are in Class 1 on the Island are not married to women with PhDs in chemistry. The opportunities open to the women they are married to are more limited. As a result, the incomes of middle-class women in employment may not be much higher than those of working-class women. Furthermore, working-class women employed as routine factory workers may have greater security than their husbands. In addition, the expenditure patterns of working-class households may, for a variety of reasons, be less demanding than for middle-class households. For example, certain manual tasks connected with maintaining the house or car may be done by members of working-class households themselves whereas, as will be shown later, middle-class households may have to purchase such services formally. Thus, paradoxically, working-class households, given the possibility of multiple earners, may be in a better position to accumulate savings. The fact that they may use these savings to buy their own dwelling, perhaps from the local authority, is another matter. The point I want to make here is simply that working-class households may, in certain labour market contexts, be in a better position to raise their household income through having multiple earners.

From Table 8.3 it can be calculated that 7 per cent of Class 1 males live with partners of the same occupational class as compared with 55 per cent of Class 2 and 49 per cent of Class 3. Also, of 203 women in employment whose partners are also in employment, 20 per cent are in Class 1, 34 per cent in Class 2 and 46 per cent in Class 3. Where both partners are employed there is a very strong likelihood that the couples will own their own homes: only 18 per cent of households where both partners were in employment did not own their own dwellings (see Table 8.4).

Household income is directly related to the number of earners in the household. From Table 8.5 it can be seen that the proportion of households earning 'high' income increases from 16 per cent with one earner through 39 per cent with two to 58 per cent with three.[6] These extra earners are more likely to be grown-up children in working-class households.

Considering now the full sample of 730 households — that is, including the single-person households, which were excluded from the foregoing discussion — our research revealed that 33 per cent were in the 'low'-income category, of which 45 per cent were single-person households, 28 per cent were couples without children living alone, and 12 per cent were single-parent families. The 'medium'-income category comprised 37 per cent of all households in the sample and 58 per cent of these consisted of two adults with their children. Couples with children also comprised the majority of the 19 per cent of the sample in the 'high'-income category. It is interesting to note that, while 17 per cent of households comprising two adults and one child were in the 'high'-income category, the proportion rose to 32 per cent in households comprising two adults and two children. This may be explained partly by the likelihood that fathers of two children may be better established in employment and hence have a higher earning potential and partly by the greater likelihood of older mothers to be in employment. As would be expected, of the 48 households including four or more adults, the overwhelming majority were in the 'high'-income category.

The Domestic Life Cycle of Households

Presenting information on the material circumstances of households by occupation, economic activity, number of earners and housing tenure is relatively straightforward. However, it is clear that economic circumstances vary between different stages in the domestic life cycle. Table 8.6 summarizes the household types on the Isle of Sheppey, distinguishing

[6] See note to Table 8.2(a) for an explanation of income categories.

Table 8.3 Household class by economic activity of both partners

Household class		Both partners are employed full time		Male is employed full-time or part-time				Male is unemployed or retired and woman is employed full-time or part-time		Neither employed		Total sample	
				Woman employed part-time		Woman not employed							
Male	Female	N	%	N	%	N	%	N	%	N	%	N	%
1	1	5	83	1	17	—	33	—	—	—	—	6	1
	2	14	33	9	21	14	33	1	2	5	12	43	8
	3	2	9	9	39	5	22	—	—	7	30	23	4
	4	—	—	—	—	8	57	—	—	6	43	14	3
2	1	2	40	—	—	3	60	—	—	—	—	5	1
	2	29	29	18	18	28	28	8	8	17	17	100	19
	3	3	6	16	34	16	34	3	6	9	19	47	9
	4	1	4	—	—	21	75	—	—	6	21	28	5
3	1	4	50	—	—	2	25	—	—	2	25	8	2
	2	20	27	16	21	24	32	3	4	12	16	75	14
	3	21	18	32	27	40	33	3	3	24	20	120	23
	4	—	—	—	—	23	53	—	—	20	47	43	8
4	1–4	1	—	—	—	3	—	1	—	9	—	14	3
Total	(N)	102		101		187		19		117		526	
Total	(%)	19		19		36		4		22		100	

Total sample group totals (braced): class 1 — N = 86, % = 16; class 2 — N = 180, % = 34; class 3 — N = 246, % = 47.

Table 8.4 Economic activity and tenure of couple households by social class

Household class*	Both partners employed		All other couples %	Total sample	
	Home-owners %	Non-home-owners %		N	%
1	42	6	52	86	17
2	33	4	63	180	36
3	28	8	64	246	48
Total (N)	165	37	310	512	
Total (%)	32	7	61	100	

* In this case, female partner's class is not given for clarity of presentation.

Table 8.5 Number of earners by household income

Number of earners	Household income (%)		Declined to give income details %	Total sample	
	High	Low or Medium		N	%
None	1	86	13	107	20
One (one full-time or two part-time)	16	73	10	184	35
Two (or one full-time and one or two other part-time)	39	49	12	173	33
More than two	58	19	23	62	12
Total (N)	135	323	68	526	
Total (%)	26	61	13	100	

* Couple households only.

between the 526 households based on a couple and the remaining non-couple households. Single-person and couple households in which no other person is present made up 45 per cent of the full sample of 730 households; the remaining 55 per cent of households had other persons in them. Of these other persons, 81 per cent were children, 8 per cent were the respondent's parents or parents-in-law and 7 per cent were other relatives. Only 4 per cent of household members in the sample were non-relatives.

In the context of the present discussion, I am focusing primarily on the position of women in relation to their family-building cycle, as this is the main factor affecting their economic activity rates (see Chapter 3).[7] In

[7] The point about the social acceptability of female entrepreneurship has been well made by R. Scase and R. Goffee, *The Entrepreneurial Middle Class*, Croom Helm, London, 1982.

Table 8.6 Household types of the Sheppey sample

	Non-couple households			Couple households			
	%	N	% of total sample	% of total sample		%	N
Single persons alone	63	129	18	Couples alone	27	37	195
With their child(ren)	24	49	7	With their child(ren)	43	60	317
With other children	1	3	—	With no children but with other adults	1	1	5
With others not children under 16 or partner	11	23	3	With both children and other adults	1	2	9
Totals	100	204	28		72	100	526

some ways, stage in the life cycle is the greatest leveller here, although the dependence on one earner when children are young is inevitably a greater burden for those in households where the single earner has a lower income. Those 384 households in which the male partner was in full-time employment are selected in Table 8.7 in order to show the relationship between domestic cycle and female activity rates.

Table 8.7   *Life-cycle characteristics of female partners of males in full-time employment, by economic activity*

Female partner:	Full-time employed		Part-time employed		Housewife		Other		Total	
	N	%	N	%	N	%	N	%	N	%
Has youngest child under 5	4	5	9	10	73	83	2	3	88	23
Has youngest child aged 5–15	31	23	51	38	47	35	4	3	133	35
Has no children in household; aged:										
35 or under	29	80	2	6	4	11	1	3	36	9
36 or over	37	29	37	29	43	34	10	8	127	33
Totals	101	26	99	26	167	43	17	4	384	100

It can be seen that women aged 35 or under without children are likely to be in full-time employment and those with children under 5 are likely to be full-time housewives. However, by the time the youngest child is aged 5, most women on Sheppey will be back in full or part-time employment. If those households where the youngest child is aged 5-15 are divided according to whether there is or is not another person aged 16 or over in the household, no difference appears in the overall proportion that are in paid employment. Where there is an older person over 16 in the household, however, 29 per cent of women are employed full-time and 32 per cent part-time, whereas without the additional older person only 20 per cent are employed full-time and 42 per cent part-time. It is significant that, for women without dependent children and aged 36 and over, the proportion employed full-time and the proportion employed part-time is the same — 29 per cent. This may reflect problems of re-entry into the labour market for older women, or perhaps women of that generation prefer part-time employment.[8]

It is very clear, then, that the household's composition and stage in the domestic cycle is of crucial importance in influencing the involvement of household members in different forms of labour. Before turning to consider how households with these different characteristics relate to

[8] J. Chaney, *Social Networks and Job Information: The Situation of Women Who Return to Work*, Equal Opportunities Commission, SSRC/EOC, Manchester, 1981.

different sources of labour, it is important to examine a further intervening variable, namely the local area in the Island where the household lives.

As I described in Chapter 6, different areas of the Island developed distinctively at different periods following the concentration of employment at Sheerness and Queenborough and of new housing at Minster and, to a lesser extent, Warden Bay. Contrary to popular belief, most respondents were not born on the Island, and most immigrants arrived between 1960 and 1981: of the 61 per cent of respondents not born on the Island, 65 have come since 1960 and 44 per cent, or 199 households, since 1970. Many of these newcomers were attracted as much by the cheaper accommodation as by the possibility of finding employment. Some came because they had relatives already living on the Island. For whatever reason, it is clear that for very many households moving to the Island was a conscious choice, made only after weighing up a number of alternatives elsewhere and after discussion and debate among family members.

Where the household lives, therefore, is for many the result of a household strategy that has taken many years to effect. Only a quarter of all households had lived in just one house on the Island; a further 40 per cent had lived in two or three houses, but fully a third of all households had lived in four or more houses on Sheppey. These frequent movers were motivated partly by the exigencies of the domestic cycle and partly by the financial advantages that frequent moving provided, particularly if each house was improved largely by the labour of household members. Opportunities for such improvements vary from one part of the Island to another: in Halfway 92 per cent of the houses are owner-occupied, as against 56 per cent in Sheerness or Queenborough with their large council estates.

So, distinctive areas of the Island have distinctive characteristics. For example, Minster, with 13 per cent of sample households, has 28 per cent of Class 1 households whereas Queenborough, with 10 per cent of the sample households, had 26 per cent of Class 3 households. Detailed analysis on the basis of these sub-areas of the Island revealed a similar range of differences. Thus, again, in Queenborough 31 per cent of the sample had more than four relatives living on the Island, whereas in Warden Bay no household had that number. Local areas on the Island have different social styles and different work practices, and use different sources of labour. Long-established areas with high levels of owner-occupation are more likely to develop patterns of communal reciprocity.[9]

---

[9] A very detailed ethnographic study was made of two contrasting areas in Rushenden and Warden Bay, respectively. This work was largely done by Claire Wallace as a result of the SSRC Project being extended three months from September 1983. See End of Grant Report to the ESRC, March 1984, Appendix II.

Unfortunately, while the survey can provide significant results for the Island as a whole, the numbers in the cells for the sub-areas often became too small to bear the same weight of analysis. The nature and style of local interaction cannot be well described using the instrument of a social survey; hence the need for substantial participant observation and more anthropological styles of reporting and analysis, which did, in fact, complement the larger-scale analysis reported here.

While the patterns on the Island as a whole may stay broadly the same, local areas may change as dwellings age or are refurbished, as residents move and age and as job opportunities change. There is a constant dynamic which presents a changing range of local opportunities, particularly for households that are ready and able to take advantage of opportunities in very local housing markets.

Households' Sources of Labour

In the Introduction to Part II, I mentioned that, at the time of the formulation of the research project, the notion of three spheres of work — formal, informal and communal/household — was a central concern, but I found that it was extremely difficult to get systematic information over time about all the work that individuals do for others, whether they get paid or not. Diaries and time budget analysis are, of course, very valuable, and the work by Gershuny and his colleagues, based on Mass Observation data for Britain in the 1930s and BBC Audience Research data at different periods in the post-war period, throws considerable light on general trends of certain broad categories of work.

However, these sources were not designed to deal with the complexities and subtleties of informal work. Formal work in employment can be measured fairly precisely, although difficulties arise with some occupations such as university teaching or with those doing creative work. Housework is hard to measure precisely: polishing a floor seems to be self-evidently housework, but if a neighbour comes in with his tool for sanding the floor, is he doing the 'housework'? Given that non-precise definitions such as 'housework is the work women do in the home' carry with them conventional assumptions and norms that may well be changing, and that, indeed, are part of the focus of this study, ideologically charged terms were consciously avoided.

The alternative approach is to focus on the labour that is done *for* households, including whether or not they do it themselves. The practical and pragmatic notion that work is any task that it is possible to pay someone else to do for one evidently embraces almost all activity. However, with the decline in servants, members of households have to do much of their everyday work for themselves. Friends, relatives, neighbours and the official home help service may do anything from making the bed to washing up for those who are elderly or incapacitated. Not all of these may define doing such a task as work: clearly the woman in the home help service will do so, but the dutiful son or daughter may be 'helping mum'. Certainly, it gets out of a lot of difficulties to focus, in a non-evaluative way, on the characteristics of those doing specific tasks — whether they are paid and whether they are a friend, relative or representatives of a formal firm or agency. This also enables analysis to be made on the basis of whether work is done by household members or non-household members and hence permits exploration of distinctive divisions of labour: divisions between household members, between some households and other households and between households and the money economy, including the distinction between whether the money is paid formally or informally.

With these considerations in mind, we selected a list of tasks to cover a wide range of activities. Such a list could be almost endless, but, since I had already done substantial fieldwork of a pilot nature on the Island, it was not so difficult to get a list which fitted local circumstances and expectations. In October 1978 Claire Wallace began a research project on the transition from school to work on Sheppey which involved living on the Island for the first half of 1979. A second period of fieldwork took her back to the Island in the summer of 1980 before the project that is reported here began. During that summer I bought a house in the centre of Sheerness, to serve as a base and to provide a way of forming social relationships with one section of the Island's population. Getting endless tasks done in the course of that operation taught me many lessons researchers do not normally get. When overwhelmed with problems of damp, cracking plaster and marauding drunkards, it was perhaps some comfort to know that this was truly participant observation.

It was from this kind of experience that Claire Wallace and I drew up the list of forty-one tasks. 'Putting in a reinforced steel joist', for example, was a relatively common task on the Island (14 per cent of the full sample of 730 households had put one into their own house at some time). This may seem odd until it is remembered that many of the nineteenth-century terraced houses in Sheerness can be much improved by knocking the two downstairs rooms into one larger one and adding on a new kitchen at the rear.

Sheppey Survey Work Tasks

1 *House maintenance* (3)
    1 Indoor painting
    2 Plastering
    3 Mending a broken window

2 *Home improvement and decoration* (7)
    4 Double glazing
    5 Putting in a bathroom
    6 Building a garage
    7 Building an extension
    8 Converting an attic to living space
    9 Putting in a reinforced steel joist (RSJ)
  10 Putting in central heating

3 *Routine housework* (12)
  11 Washing up
  12 Tidying house or flat
  13 Hoovering or brushing carpets
  14 Cleaning outside windows
  15 Cooking family meals
  16 Making a packed lunch
  17 Getting a take-away meal
  18 Shopping
  19 Washing clothes
  20 Washing sheets
  21 Ironing clothes
  22 Ironing sheets

4 *Domestic production* (8)
  23 Baking a cake
  24 Making clothes
  25 Knitting
  26 Repairing clothes
  27 Growing vegetables
  28 Making jam
  29 Making bread
  30 Making beer or wine

5 *Car maintenance* (4)
  31 Washing the car
  32 Checking the oil
  33 Tuning the engine
  34 Repairing or checking the brakes

6 *Child care* (7)
  35 Bathing child
  36 Changing nappies
  37 Looking after a sick child
  38 Collecting child from school
  39 Seeing schoolteacher about child
  40 Taking child to doctor
  41 Getting child's hair cut

All respondents were asked if they had ever done each task on the list and then, in the case of house maintenance and similar tasks, they were asked, 'Who did all or most of the work?' In the case of more common domestic tasks, respondents were simply asked who usually does them. Respondents were also asked to name who actually did the task inside the household; outside the household they were asked to say whether it was done by a relative, friend or official firm and whether or not it was paid for. We assumed that paying a friend was informal and paying a firm was formal, although, of course, there was no way of checking whether the firm in question actually declared all its income to the tax authorities. With the answers to these questions, it was possible to group those tasks that were done by distinctive sources of labour — household members, friends and relatives, paid or unpaid (informal sources), firms, garages, landlords or whatever (formal sources of labour).

The remarkable result to emerge from the analysis of these tasks was just *how much work* of various sorts was being done. Thus, of the full sample of 730 households, 80 per cent had done indoor painting themselves and a further 17 per cent had had it done for them at some time, 84 per cent had made a cake themselves, 25 per cent had mended the brakes on the car themselves, 32 per cent had made jam themselves and 8 per cent had put in a reinforced steel joist (RSJ) themselves (with a further 6 per cent getting the job done for them). Most of the labour involved in the work was unpaid: the overwhelming amount was being done *inside the household*. This is expressed diagrammatically in Figure 8.2: both sides of the diagram add up to the total proportion of the sample doing the task, with those not doing the task at all bringing the total up to 100 per cent. Thus, taking the example of tuning the car, half the sample got this task done and it was split remarkably evenly between unpaid and paid work.

Finally, and in striking confirmation of earlier remarks on the relative insignificance of the so-called 'informal economy', the main tasks on which informally paid labour was used were painting, plastering and domestic cleaning (mainly windows). People were more likely to be paid in cash for home decorating, cleaning the windows and general domestic cleaning.

Analysis at the level of the 730 households in the full sample gives some general understanding of broad divisions of labour. In this chapter the analysis is at the aggregated level; in the next chapter the focus shifts to the patterns of household divisions of labour. I now mention briefly a number of obvious points. Those who own their own homes, own cars and have children have a potential demand for more tasks than, say, couples without children living in a local authority rented dwelling. Yet again, older people may have a demand for fewer tasks and yet have to have more of them done for them. So income and life-cycle stage are self-evidently important, remembering that income needs to be seen in its cultural context. That households spend their money in different ways is an obvious truism: an affluent manual worker may engage in more tasks when refurbishing his older house than a professional worker with a high mortgage on a new house. At this stage in the argument we are looking entirely at the demand side, at the differential use of services or demands for labour.

I should make it clear that, for present purposes, certain tasks are more significant than others: those tasks that are overwhelmingly done by household members will be the focus of analysis in Chapter 11. By and large, the tasks fall into the following general pattern:

(i) *tasks that are done by almost all households by household members*: these include the familiar cooking and cleaning, but also painting;

(ii) *tasks that are done by some households and generally done by household members*: these include child care, vegetable growing, car washing and beer or wine making;

(iii) *tasks done by fewer households and generally paid for in the formal market sector*: these include most of the house improvement and extension tasks;

(iv) *tasks that are done with a variety of forms of labour*: these are overwhelmingly painting, plastering, making cloths, knitting, tuning the car engine and fixing brakes.

Evidently, life-cycle and income effects are likely to operate in each category. Figure 8.3 shows the effect of household income on divisions of labour. Low-income and, as we shall see, elderly households are more likely to pay for home maintenance and routine housework; high income households are also more likely to pay for home maintenance and car maintenance.

In Table 8.8 households' social class is related to the sources of labour for those doing two tasks — repairing a broken window and doing work on the brakes of a car. First, it is clear that the tasks are much more likely to be done by households in Class 1 or with 'high' annual household incomes. However, it is interesting that a much higher proportion of Class 3 has the task of seeing to the car's brakes than households with low incomes — 48 per cent as against 23 per cent. This is a reflection of the high household incomes of some working-class households. Second, it is significant that the highest proportion of households using their own members as a source of labour to repair a window are those in the 'high'-income category — presumably also those most able to pay others to do the task for them. Low-income households, including many pensioners, are more likely than Class 3 to pay for the two tasks to be

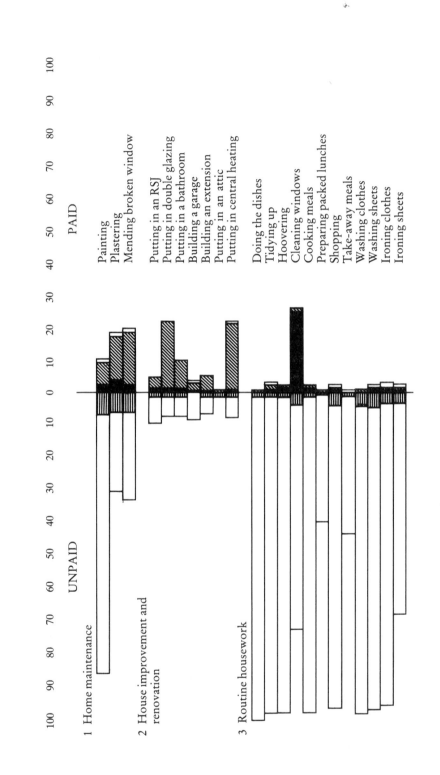

PAID

UNPAID

100 90 80 70 60 50 40 30 20 10 0 10 20 30 40 50 60 70 80 90 100

1 Home maintenance

Painting
Plastering
Mending broken window

2 House improvement and renovation

Putting in an RSJ
Putting in double glazing
Putting in a bathroom
Building a garage
Building an extension
Putting in an attic
Putting in central heating

3 Routine housework

Doing the dishes
Tidying up
Hoovering
Cleaning windows
Cooking meals
Preparing packed lunches
Shopping
Take-away meals
Washing clothes
Washing sheets
Ironing clothes
Ironing sheets

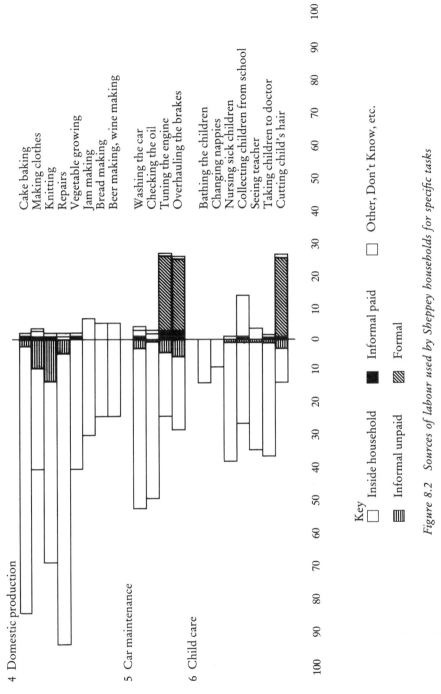

4 Domestic production

Cake baking
Making clothes
Knitting
Repairs
Vegetable growing
Jam making
Bread making
Beer making, wine making

5 Car maintenance

Washing the car
Checking the oil
Tuning the engine
Overhauling the brakes

6 Child care

Bathing the children
Changing nappies
Nursing sick children
Collecting children from school
Seeing teacher
Taking children to doctor
Cutting child's hair

Key

☐ Inside household   ■ Informal paid   ☐ Other, Don't Know, etc.

▥ Informal unpaid   ▨ Formal

Figure 8.2 *Sources of labour used by Sheppey households for specific tasks*

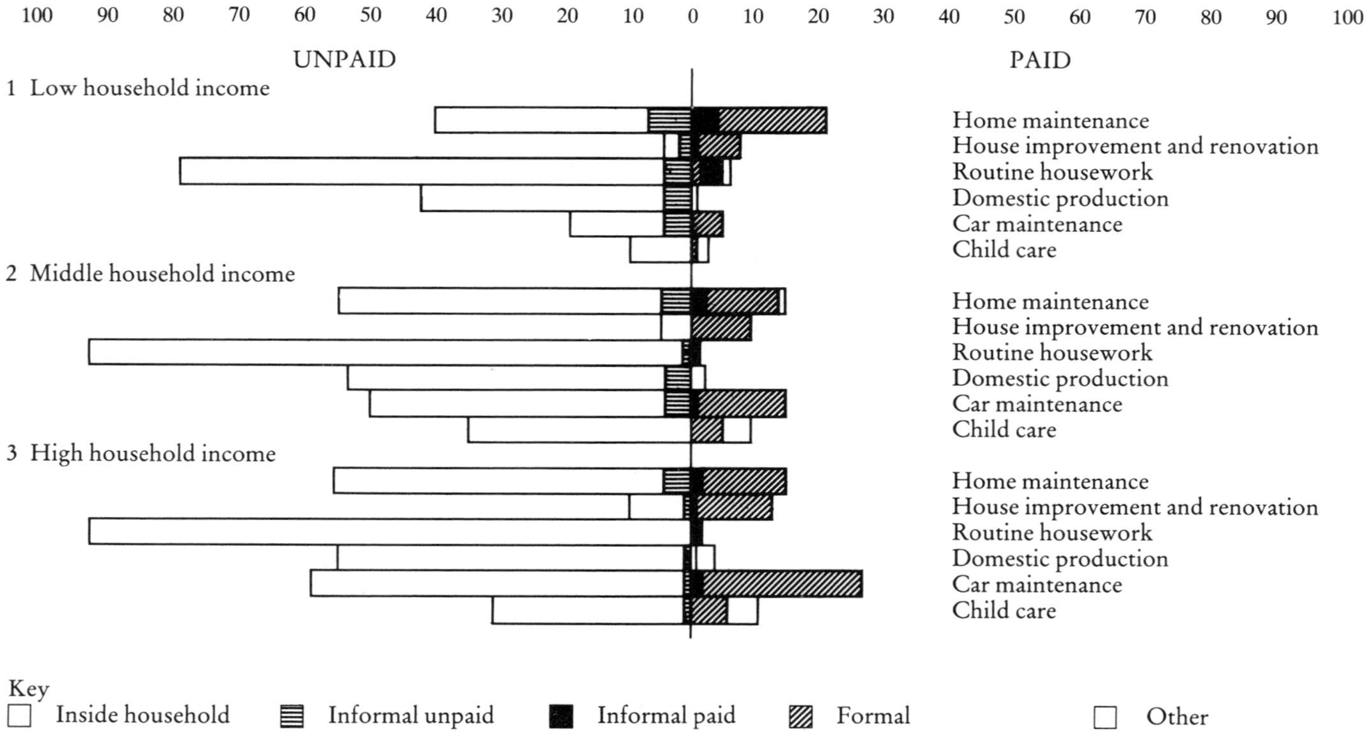

100 90 80 70 60 50 40 30 20 10 0 10 20 30 40 50 60 70 80 90 100
UNPAID
PAID
1 Low household income
Home maintenance
House improvement and renovation
Routine housework
Domestic production
Car maintenance
Child care
2 Middle household income
Home maintenance
House improvement and renovation
Routine housework
Domestic production
Car maintenance
Child care
3 High household income
Home maintenance
House improvement and renovation
Routine housework
Domestic production
Car maintenance
Child care
Key
Inside household
Informal unpaid
Informal paid
Formal
Other

Figure 8.3 Sources of labour for 41 tasks by household income categories

done informally, but it is also interesting that the same proportion of Class 1 households as low-income households (13 per cent) get the task of repairing a broken window done by paying someone informally. Not surprisingly, the lowest proportion of any of the four categories using a household member to work on the car's brakes is in Class 1 households; they would be most likely to take their car to a garage. However, 12 per cent of Class 3 car owners and 20 per cent of car owners in 'low'-income households would pay someone informally to do the work. These distinctions between class and household income are particularly important, showing how a household's capacity to gain income through multiple earners may offset its class position to some extent.

Table 8.8   Getting two tasks done

(a) Class by source of labour

Class	Task	Those in class doing task		Of those doing task: source of labour (%)			
					Informal		
		%	N	Household	Paid	Unpaid	Formal
1	Repairing a broken window	62	61	46	13	5	34
	Doing work on the car's brakes	75	74	28	4	4	62
3	Repairing a broken window	51	174	58	8	1	32
	Doing work on the car's brakes	48	161	58	12	4	26

(b) Household income by source of labour

Income Range*	Task	Those in group doing task		Of those doing task: source of labour (%)			
					Informal		
		%	N	Household	Paid	Unpaid	Formal
'High' income	Repairing a broken window	62	85	63	4	—	33
	Doing work on the car's brakes	83	115	45	1	5	48
'Low' income	Repairing a broken window	46	112	36	13	7	43
	Doing work on the car's brakes	23	56	34	20	4	41

* 'High' income = £7,500 or more p.a. in 1981; 'low' income = £3,500 p.a. in 1981. See also note to Table 8.2.

Table 8.8 was based on two of the forty-one tasks about which information was gathered, and similar analysis could be done for each task and for a range of household characteristics. In order to get a more synoptic view, all the Sheppey Survey work tasks were grouped together in seven clusters (see pp. 214–15). All the activities of all the households were combined — in an admittedly rather unreal way — to give the total number of units of activities that could be done by distinctive sources of labour. Thus, for example, there are 102 households in the sample in which both partners are employed full-time. There are 3 house maintenance tasks that could be done, so the total possible activities for that category in that cluster would be 306. For the sample as a whole, it would obviously be 730 times 41, or 29,930 activities.

We are now in a position to consider at a global level how these activities are divided among different sources of labour. Table 8.9 provides the full data for the complete sample of the sources of labour for all forty-one tasks by three categories of household income. In each cluster of tasks, the high-income households did more activities apart from child care. For present purposes, the most interesting clusters of tasks are house maintenance and home improvement and renovation. In these two areas, the 'high'-income households are most likely to get the work done but *less* likely to use formal sources of labour.

Not only are richer households more likely to do more work, they are more likely to do tasks with their own labour. Thus, 74 per cent of the home maintenance and 39 per cent of the home improvement and renovation are done by members of 'high'-income housholds. The same category is also most likely to use household labour in domestic production and car maintenance. Those with cars, children, their own homes and high-household incomes appear to do a very great amount of work. There is little sign that households with higher incomes are that much more likely overall to use formal service provision — or, indeed, to use more informal sources of labour for which they have the means to pay. In every cluster, the higher-income households have the lowest percentage of informally paid sources of labour. By contrast, the poorest households use informal sources, most particularly *unpaid* informal sources of labour. It is important to bear in mind the degree of unreality produced by this aggregation of tasks, but it does provide some clarity at a high level of generality.

Age makes a difference to the amount of work that is needed, and people do less of all kinds of work as they grow older (see Table 8.10). However, the very busiest age category is aged between 31 and 50 — a time when, for all sources of labour, households in this category have the highest percentage doing various tasks, although child care is the first cluster of tasks to decline from the early forties. A similar pattern is found if one focuses on the forms of labour: the higher proportion of households using their own labour is always one of the two youngest categories.

Table 8.9   Household income by sources of labour for a range of domestic tasks

Household income*	Totals†	Proportion of sample doing job (%)	Within household	Informal unpaid	Informal paid	Formal	Other
			Proportion of those using particular sources of labour for clusters of tasks (%)				
House maintenance							
'High' income	138×3	71	74	5	3	18	0
'Medium' income	267×3	69	73	7	3	16	1
'Low' income	244×3	60	53	12	7	28	0
House improvement and renovation							
'High' income	138×7	22	39	4	3	54	0
'Medium' income	267×7	16	34	2	2	61	1
'Low' income	244×7	10	18	6	7	69	1
Routine housework							
'High' income	138×12	93	98	0	2	0	0
'Medium' income	267×12	90	96	1	3	0	0
'Low' income	244×12	83	90	4	3	2	1
Domestic production							
'High' income	138×8	58	93	2	1	1	3
'Medium' income	267×8	57	88	7	0	0	5
'Low' income	244×8	44	89	7	0	0	3
Car maintenance							
'High' income	138×4	84	70	1	2	27	0
'Medium' income	267×4	66	71	6	2	21	0
'Low' income	244×4	24	67	11	2	19	1
Child care							
'High' income	138×7	40	76	2	0	12	10
'Medium' income	267×7	46	80	1	0	10	9
'Low' income	244×7	14	77	3	0	9	11
All							
'High' income	138×41	63	54	1	1	6	1
'Medium' income	267×41	60	51	2	1	5	1
'Low' income	244×41	44	35	3	1	4	1

* This table excludes the 81 respondents who declined to give income details.
† The totals are based on the number of tasks in each cluster as shown in the list of Sheppey Survey work tasks on pp. 214–15.

Although age is important, however, it should perhaps be considered in the context of the household structure. More detailed analysis focusing on couples with and without children and on single-parent families produced clear and unequivocal results. Couples with children were busy in every sphere of activity, being more likely both to do the activities and

Table 8.10 Proportion of respondents getting work done in sets of aggregated tasks,
by age of respondents

Proportion of households in different age categories doing clusters of
aggregated activities (%)*

Age of respondent	House maintenance	House improvement and renovation	Routine housework	Domestic production	Car maintenance	Child care	Total* N
30 or under	66	10	90	51	59	63	117
31–50	72	19	92	59	77	53	267
51–64	67	19	88	55	53	6	144
65 or over	58	11	82	42	25	2	202
							730

* The totals are based on the number of tasks in each cluster as shown in the list of Sheppey Survey work tasks
on pp. 214–15.

also to use their own household as a source of labour to do them. Single-parent households, by contrast, were much more likely to get work done informally using unpaid sources of labour. Table 8.11 shows these differences very clearly: for single parents, sources of labour follow a distinctive pattern showing that this category is obliged to adopt a distinctive household work strategy. The connection here is not simply that of low income and sources of labour, although that indeed is likely to be a crucial connection, but, particularly, a distinctive household structure. For much of the work that has to be done, partners of different genders provide a convenient work unit. I was initially surprised when I heard someone say that she was going round to a friend to 'borrow her husband for a while'. I later discovered that the phrase was not considered improper, although it was always said with a smile, if not with a wink: it was just a way of tapping a crucial and necessary source of labour.

Single-parent households are obliged to be more dependent on others; couples are more self-contained. The indications are, therefore, that households build up to a peak of activity as they build up their family, establish a comfortable and convenient home and acquire consumer goods such as the motor car, which needs to be repaired and serviced. This, then, raises a paradox. At the very time in the domestic cycle when so many tasks need to be done, the need for money is equally demanding: it is one thing to get the brakes on the car fixed; it is another matter to get the money to buy the car and then tax and insure it. How, then, does the general economic activity of household members relate to all the activities that are being discussed in this chapter? This question is getting close to the heart of the complex issue of household work strategies.

First, what difference does it make if women are employed full-time, part-time or not at all and if their partners are in employment? The results are set out in Tables 8.12a and 8.12b for two spheres of activity. These findings are remarkably consistent: whether or not the female partner is full-time employed, part-time employed or a full-time housewife, the *same amount of work* of the types presented (by and large) seemingly has to be done. One might have expected that in households where both adults are in full-time employment there would be less time for baking a cake or growing vegetables, but that does not seem to be the case. Sheppey full-time housewives do not seem to be living in households where the *overall* divisions of labour are that different from households in which the woman is in full-time employment. However, it is important to remember that nothing has been said so far about *who* does the work in the household: that is discussed in Chapter 10. Here it is simply noted that the employment characteristics of the female partner do not seem to affect the overall pattern of how much work is done in the household. (Child care is not appropriately considered here, since evidently it is largely an obligatory activity in households with children!)

Table 8.11 Selected task clusters by household types and sources of labour

Task cluster	Households with children under 16 headed by:	Proportion doing aggregated activities (%)	Source of labour for those doing aggregated activities (%)				
			Own household	Informally Unpaid	Paid	Formal provision	Other
House maintenance	Single parent	73	61	14	7	19	0
	Two parents	74	76	5	3	15	1
House improvement and renovation	Single parent	9	22	6	6	66	0
	Two parents	19	37	3	4	56	0
Domestic production	Single parent	50	83	14	1	0	2
	Two parents	60	90	5	0	1	3
Car maintenance	Single parent	31	67	22	0	8	3
	Two parents	77	72	3	3	20	1

*Table 8.12   Economic activity by sources of labour for two selected clusters of
tasks, male partner in employment*

	Household members (%)	Informal Unpaid (%)	Paid (%)	Formal provision (%)	Not done (%)	Other (%)
Cluster (a): Sources of labour for aggregated home maintenance tasks						
Female partner						
Employed full-time	48	5	2	13	33	0
Employed part-time	55	3	3	14	26	1
Full-time housewife	56	3	2	11	27	1
Cluster (b): Sources of labour for aggregated domestic provision tasks						
Female partner						
Employed full-time	50	1	0	0	46	2
Employed part-time	53	3	0	0	41	2
Full-time housewife	55	3	0	0	38	3

However, if the economic activity of the female partner apparently makes little difference, the total number of adults employed in the household certainly does. Employment in the formal economy as a factor determining what other sources of labour are used may be more a matter of numbers than of gender: in almost every task the likelihood that it will be done (if it is done) in the household increases with the number of adults in employment. This applies particularly to tasks connected with home renovation or extension. The proportion of households in which painting is done at home, for example, increases from 78 per cent of households with no workers to 100 per cent with three. Couples with unmarried employed offspring living at home and with school-age children old enough not to inhibit the female partner from taking employment *need* more tasks done and are busiest doing them. The position of the household in the domestic cycle is one of the chief determinants of the sources of labour that are used. What needs doing differs throughout the life cycle, and the source of labour varies substantially between youth and old age and between households based on couples and those with only a single adult. The latter, typically, do not have the income to use formal provision of services (although, of course, local authority and welfare provision are important); hence, single-parent households and old people are obliged to use informal sources of labour.

It might, at this point, be useful to digress to consider the question of how frequently tasks are done. Since the intention in this chapter is to present only a very general account of sources of labour, the questions of the *cumulation* of different tasks in the same household or the *repetition* of a few tasks very frequently have so far been ignored. While I return to the former question in the next chapter, some consideration of the frequency with which different sources of labour are used to do certain tasks, given household members' commitments to the formal economy for employment, is given here. The tasks considered are baking a cake and washing and ironing clothes. We felt that these tasks would be most likely to be done by women in the household and that their frequency would be related to the women's employment status. This indeed proved to be the case, as Table 8.13 shows.

While it is astonishing that in nearly two-thirds of households with full-time housewives cakes are baked weekly or more frequently, it is perhaps more impressive that in households where the female partner is employed full-time, a third have cakes made weekly or more frequently by a member of the household, although it would be wrong to assume that this is necessarily the woman. In general, it is clear that these tasks are done more frequently in households where the female partner is not in employment. Since this is likely to be associated with young children, the greater frequency of cooking and cleaning is perhaps less surprising.

Before concluding this chapter, I return to the discussion of class and the sources of labour. Do middle-class households have a markedly different pattern of access to sources of labour than working-class households? Do they consume more services and rely more on the formal economy to supply them? Do middle-class female partners do more or less domestic production than their working-class counterparts? Do Class 2 households — the respectable petit bourgeoisie — exhibit more home-centred values than the classes above and below them? Do Class 3 households use more informal sources of labour than Class 1? For the purpose of this analysis, households were allocated to each of the three classes by the occupation of the male partner in couple households and by the occupation of the respondent in single-person households. The results were remarkably consistent: the divisions of labour were almost exactly similar for each social class. The similarities were so great that there seems little value in any extended illustration. Thus, the proportion of each class engaging in domestic production of one sort or another was 54 per cent for Class 1, 54 per cent for Class 2 and 51 per cent for Class 3. There was some variation in house and car maintenance, since Class 3 households were less likely to own these. And there was some class variation in the sources of labour to do these sets of tasks, as Table 8.14 shows.

This table reflects the greatest difference that can be shown between classes at this aggregated level of analysis. Certainly, Class 1 households are less likely to do these tasks within the home and to buy in formal services from outside. But the differences are not great. However, class differences will be explored in greater detail in the following chapters. It may just be noted here that, when class is combined with economic activity, differences appear greater within the middle class (Class 1) than within the working class (Class 3). For example, taking house maintenance and collapsing some of the sources of labour, since the totals

Table 8.13 *Economic activity of couples and frequency with which selected tasks are done*

Male partner is employed and female partner is:	Daily (%) (a)	(b)	(c)	Several times a week (%) (a)	(b)	(c)	Weekly (%) (a)	(b)	(c)	Fortnightly (%) (a)	(b)	(c)	Less often/ never (%) (a)	(b)	(c)	Total N
Employed full-time	0	14	27	10	35	42	24	47	30	16	3	0	50	1	0	102
Employed part-time	0	14	33	14	47	52	47	36	14	11	1	0	27	1	0	99
Full-time housewife	2	21	46	20	45	47	41	30	6	7	2	0	30	1	0	167

(a) Baking a cake   (b) Ironing clothes   (c) Washing clothes

Table 8.14 *Sources of labour for house and car maintenance, by social class*

Aggregated tasks*	Proportion of class doing tasks (%)	Sources of labour for aggregated tasks* (%) Household members	Informal Unpaid	Paid	Formal provision	Other
House maintenance						
Class 1 (N=98)	73	63	7	4	26	0
Class 2 (N=261)	67	68	7	5	19	1
Class 3 (N=338)	64	68	9	4	18	1
Car maintenance						
Class 1 (N=98)	76	59	3	3	35	1
Class 2 (N=261)	61	69	4	3	24	0
Class 3 (N=338)	47	77	7	2	14	0

* The aggregated tasks comprised three house maintenance and four car maintenance tasks as shown in the list of the Sheppey Survey work tasks as shown on pp. 214–15.

Table 8.15 Social class, economic activity and sources of labour for house maintenance

Social class and economic activity	Total	Those doing tasks		Of those doing tasks:					
				Those who use formally provided labour		Those who do the work themselves		Those who use informal and other labour	
	N	%	N	%	N	%	N	%	N
Middle class (Class 1)									
Both employed	21	67	42	38	16	50	21	12	5
Male employed, female full-time housewife	19	81	46	26	12	72	33	2	1
Working class (Class 3)									
Both employed	41	68	84	12	10	79	66	10	8
Male employed, female full-time housewife	63	70	133	10	13	85	113	6	7

concerned are smaller, Table 8.15 shows that, when Class 1 couples are both employed, there is a much greater likelihood that they will pay for such tasks to be done.

Conclusions

Some important conclusions about sources of labour and divisions of labour have emerged in this chapter, but I have emphasized that the analysis has been at a highly aggregated level. Households in a given category — class, economic activity or income range — have been scrambled together and all the tasks of a given type analysed together. This provides a kind of understanding but, as with all abstraction, does some violence to reality. I have presented enough to show that, in terms of patterns of work and sources of labour, household structure, particularly as that reflects the number of earners and the domestic cycle, appears to be more significant than social class. It is one of the main themes of this book that this has always been so. One recognizes that sociologists will be accused of rediscovering the wheel once again — or at least recognizing the force of history. In the same way that late medieval households, discussed in Chapter 1, needed someone of the opposite sex in order to get by and to help to get the work done, so the exigencies of the domestic cycle and the demands of capitalist consumerism make couple households with multiple earners the best unit for getting by in the late twentieth century, albeit for different reasons.

But if class appears less important than the number and levels of economic activity of household members and the stage of the household in the domestic cycle, it would be rash to jump too readily to the conclusion that, if the domestic cycle is the great leveller, social harmony is attained by the hidden hand of 'birth, copulation, and death'. As the next chapter illustrates, divisions of labour produce new inequalities.

9

The Divisions of Labour
of Households

In the last chapter I was not concerned with the patterns of labour used in getting work done by individual households. Thus, all middle-class households, for example, were grouped together and analysis focused on the combined total of all their sources of labour. However, it is quite possible that, within such a category, some households do substantial work for themselves, whereas others rely entirely on formal or other sources of labour. The emphasis in Chapter 8 was on *clusters* of tasks and the balance between different sources of labour in getting these clusters of tasks done as a whole. Here I emphasize the sources of labour, and how far distinctive types of household use distinctive sources. To explore these divisions the focus of analysis shifts from the *nature of the task* to *the source of the labour*. Which households are more likely consistently to prefer one source of labour to another? What patterns emerge when the cumulative effects of using distinctive sources of labour are considered?

The last chapter showed that a remarkable amount of work is done by members of individual households for themselves.[1] Much of the data were presented in a highly aggregated form and the analysis was inevitably coarse-grained. Now I intend to aim at a finer grain of analysis and to ask whether those households who, say, do their own home decorating also, perhaps, fix their own cars, make jam and also grow their own vegetables. Is there a cumulation of what is termed 'self-provisioning', or do some households specialize in decorating for themselves whereas others specialize in other spheres and use the formal market provision of services for those spheres in which they do not have competence?

Similar questions can be asked in relation to the other sources of labour: do those who use formal services also do more work for themselves or do they get other tasks done informally? What, indeed, are the alternatives? How are the three sources of labour interrelated? Are the

---

[1] Thus, for example, of the 97 per cent of households who had had painting done, 83 per cent of those did it for themselves, and, of the 53 per cent of households who had had a broken window fixed, 53 per cent of those did the work themselves.

formal and informal sources equivalent alternatives for different categories of households? Do all households use a little formal labour or do some use a great deal and others hardly any at all?

Scales of Measurement

These questions require precise answers and we devised three separate scales to indicate how households used the same source of labour over a range of different tasks.

The self-provisioning scale (self-prov) measures the spread of activity that given households do using the labour of members of the households themselves: that is, not simply the *number* of tasks, but rather the *range* of tasks that are done using the labour of household members. Each household gets a score from 0 to 6 depending on the use of its labour over a carefully selected range of possible tasks.

The scale does not show whether a household is able to do its own plastering *and* painting *and* glazing, but whether it has the capacity to do *one* of these activities *as well as* vegetable growing *and* a car maintenance task, and so on. The six-point scale was based on distinct spheres of household or domestic tasks that could be bought in the market. People can buy vegetables, cakes and jerseys; they do not have to dig, bake and knit. Indeed, jerseys bought in shops, in the market or at a bring and buy sale may well be substantially cheaper than those made at home. The tasks for the six-point self-prov scale were then arranged so that households could score one point if they did just one task within each cluster. Tasks of a fairly routine nature were included in the self-prov scale only if they were performed with some frequency, but the larger tasks were included if they were performed at any time at all. The clusters of tasks for the self-provisioning scale are, therefore, as follows:

SPS 1:
Vegetable growing at any time
SPS 2:
Either painting *or* plastering *or* mending a broken window in the last year
SPS 3:
Either checking the oil level *or* tuning the engine *or* doing the work on the brakes of a car at any time
SPS 4:
Either putting in an RSJ *or* double glazing *or* central heating *or* building a bathroom *or* an extension *or* converting an attic at any time
SPS 5:
Either making jam *or* beer *or* wine regularly
SPS 6:
Making *or* knitting clothes at any time

The informal labour scale (inf-lab) was constructed in a similar manner to the self-prov scale, but with the substitution of two other tasks for vegetable growing and the home production of certain items that were, in practice, limited to self-provisioning. Households could score from 0 to 6 on the scale, depending on the range of tasks or clusters of tasks for which they used informal sources of labour, namely friends, neighbours or relatives. Such informal labour might be paid or unpaid and no distinction is made on the scale. Although information was gathered about payment, in practice the distinction was very hard to draw and it seemed to make better sense to put all sources of informal labour in the same category. The tasks making up the scale are as follows:

ILS 1:
Either getting painting *or* plastering *or* a broken window mended in the
last year
ILS 2:
Either getting the car oil level checked *or* the car engine tuned *or* work
done on the brakes at any time
ILS 3:
Either getting an RSJ put in *or* double glazing *or* central heating *or*
building a bathroom *or* an extension *or* converting an attic at any time
ILS 4:
Getting clothes repaired *or* knitted *or* a dress made
ILS 5:
Getting the outside windows cleaned
ILS 6:
Getting a child's hair cut

The formal provision of services scale (form-prov), like the inf-lab, is a six-point scale and was constructed using exactly the same clusters of tasks as the inf-lab. Here, however, the source of labour was a firm or business for domestic maintenance and improvement (form-prov 1 and 3), a garage or firm for work on the car (form-prov 2), a professional dress-maker or knitter for clothes (form-prov 4), a public agency for window cleaning (form-prov 5) and a barber or hairdresser for cutting a child's hair (form-prov 6).

Thus, these three scales measure the range of tasks using each of one distinctive source of labour. I discuss each scale in turn and then, finally, consider the way in which each is related to the others. Using these scales, a relatively precise measure is given of the degree to which specific households use different sources of labour.

The self-provisioning scale (self-prov)

Why do some households do more work for themselves than others? Do they choose to do it as a form of self-expression, or are they almost compelled to do it by the lack of other resources, because they have no money to buy services formally and no other resources to repay informal labour reciprocally? From what has gone before, we may expect that those households based on couples including a number of young children require more tasks to be done and, because of a reduction of income per head owing to the number of dependants in the household, are obliged to do more tasks for themselves. These arguments might apply *a fortiori* to households headed by a manual worker, who is likely to have a lower individual income than a middle-class earner but where both partners are, perhaps, more likely to have skills to do self-provisioning work than are middle-class couples, less well-trained in manual skills. In this way, perhaps, differences in levels of living between the two classes are reduced. Furthermore, it is likely that such high self-provisioners would own their own homes, be inward-looking, privatized and perhaps also more likely to vote Conservative. There might be a secondary peak of self-provisioning at a later stage of the life cycle, in the years before retirement after children have left home, when there is time and energy to devote to domestic tasks as a way of demonstrating a particular style of life.

Certainly, it is quite clear that couple households score more highly on the self-prov scale, as Table 9.1, relating to the sample as a whole, indicates. If the self-prov scale is dichotomized into 'low' (scores 2-4) and 'high' (scores 5-6), then over half the couples score in the 'high' category. This is a better basis for the assertion that substantial domestic work by households takes place, since it avoids the problems posed by certain tasks being appropriate only at certain stages of the life cycle. Particular individual circumstances are thus reduced by using the scale.

For ease of analysis, the dichotomized self-prov scale is used to illustrate some important differences. Selecting only those households where the male is in full-time employment, high self-prov scores are more

Table 9.1 *Household type, by self-provisioning scale (percentages*)*

Self-prov. scale	Couple households	Male-headed non-couple households	Female-headed non-couple households	All
1	—	—	—	—
2	3	13	31	10
3	13	37	31	19
4	28	30	28	28
5	40	17	9	32
6	16	3	1	11
Total (N)	526	40	164	730

* Throughout this chapter, percentages in tables do not always sum to 100 because of rounding.

likely the greater the involvement of his partner in formal employment. Thus, where both partners are in full-time employment, 65 per cent of households score 'high' on the self-prov scale, whereas when the female partner is retired the 'high' proportion falls to 50 per cent. Taking the 65 households with more than two earners, 69 per cent scored 'high' on the self-prov scale. Finally, selecting those households where both partners were in full-time employment but at least one of them was on shift work, the proportion scoring 'high' on the self-prov scale rose to as much as 74 per cent. Yet when male shiftworkers had as a partner a non-employed full-time housewife, the proportion scoring 'high' dropped to 43 per cent.

These findings are unequivocal: employment and self-provisioning go together, rather than one being a substitute for another. Furthermore, in line with the analysis in the previous chapter, class did not make a substantial difference: indeed, counter to the initial hypothesis, the proportion scoring 'high' on the self-prov scale ranged from 64 per cent in Class 1 through 59 per cent in Class 2 to 50 per cent for Class 3. Evidently, this result is partly the consequence of higher car and home ownership in the higher classes, but it still does not follow that households should, apparently, choose to do so many tasks with their own labour.

Some interesting intra-class variations appear when the combined household class classification is used. Thus, when Class 1 males are married to Class 3 females, the proportion scoring 'high' on self-prov scale rises to 70 per cent as against 64 per cent for Class 1 as a whole. Similarly, when Class 3 males are married to higher-status females, their scores are substantially above the rate for the class as a whole. This suggests, perhaps, that status inconsistency between partners is a source of tension or of complex feelings of guilt, which generates a distinct dynamic element into the household work strategy. Lower-status men and women may compensate to their partners by doing more conventionally gender-linked tasks. So lower-status men may do more decorating or car maintenance and lower-status women, more of the female-type tasks. Thus the internal dynamics of the couple modify what would otherwise seem to be a direct linear relationship between higher class and higher rating on the self-prov scale.

Child care work does not appear on the self-prov scale, yet couples with children were overall more likely to score higher than couples with no children (60 per cent compared with 47 per cent). However, the very highest score (79 per cent) is for couples having their youngest child aged between 5 and 15 with the wife or partner over 35 years of age; where there are also older children or other adults in the same household the proportion of 'high' scorers on the self-prov scale is 67 per cent. These latter may, therefore, be contributing not only extra money but also extra working capacity to the household. Analysis showed that level of income *on its own* was less important as a factor affecting levels of self-provisioning, which it must be remembered relate to a range of tasks done by different household members in and around the home. For this reason it is perhaps less surprising that the more adults in the household, the higher the score.

Households, then, do more activities with their own labour if they have a larger gender-divided pool of hands and access to land and capital. Growing their own vegetables requires access to land, whether a garden or an allotment, and owning a house or car requires capital. However, the land and capital by themselves do not necessarily encourage the use of the household's own labour. Ownership of property does not mechanistically determine behaviour: there is not a direct linear correlation between household work practices and household income.

Higher income is a necessary but not a sufficient condition for higher rating on the self-prov scale. A process of polarization has developed on the Island: this produces at one end busy households with many workers, some of whom are in employment, in which a wide range of domestic tasks get done by household members; at the other end are the households with only one or two earners, without a car and probably not owning their own homes or, if they do, having insufficient energy or strength and also insufficient resources to be able to maintain them adequately.

The informal labour scale (inf-lab)

We now move to a division of labour between the producer and the consumer of a service, where the source of labour is outside the household that consumes the service. Informal sources of labour, that is, friends, neighbours and relatives, can be paid or unpaid, and one might initially assume that informal labour is more a resource for the poor than for the rich, for the established than for the newly arrived and for older rather than younger people. One might expect Class 2 and particularly Class 3 to use more such informal sources than Class 1. While informal sources of labour count for quantitatively very little in the overall division of labour, such work can still be highly important for certain specified households. These expectations or hypotheses are now explored.

Informal sources of labour were not so sharply divided by income as we initially expected. The inf-lab scale was dichotomized into 'low' (0 or 1) and 'high' (2 or more). The proportions scoring 'high' on the scale in income categories 'low', 'medium' and 'high' were 17, 16 and 14 per cent respectively. Analysis by social class showed a similar pattern, with the comparable proportions being 17, 16 and 11 per cent, falling from Class 3 to Class 1. Evidently, these are not particularly significant distinctions. Turning then to the number of earners in the household, which were important in the case of the self-prov scale, in the case of the inf-lab scale no significant variation was found, the proportion of households with two or more earners scoring 'high' being much the same as in households with no earners.

Interesting variations did, however, appear when we considered household structure: while, for the sample as a whole, 16 per cent scored 'high' on the inf-lab scale, in the case of single-parent households the proportion rose to 37 per cent. Couples living on their own had only 10 per cent scoring 'high' (see Table 9.2).

Table 9.2   *Informal labour scale rating by household type (percentages)*

Inf-lab scale	Single person	Single person with child	Couple only	Couple with children	All others	All households
Low score						
0	43	22	56	46	60	48
1	40	41	34	37	30	36
High score						
2 or more	17	37	10	18	10	16
Total (N)	129	49	195	317	40	730

A similar pattern is shown for tenure, with those in privately rented accommodation having a markedly greater likelihood of using informal labour. Proportions scoring 2 or more on the inf-lab scale were 15 per cent for owner occupiers, 16 per cent for those renting from the local authority but 26 per cent of the 47 households in the sample renting from a private landlord. Inevitably, in the case of single-parent families, household type and tenure go together. Households living in certain areas of the Island were also more likely to use informal labour, with the older established areas of Sheerness and Queenborough scoring higher on the scale than the more newly developed areas of Halfway and Warden Bay.

Table 9.3 shows that households in which women are in full-time employment use less informal labour those those in which the woman is

Table 9.3   *Inf-lab scale rating by the economic activity of selected households with male partner in full-time employment (percentages)*

Inf-lab scale	Occupational status of female partner			
	F/T empl.	P/T empl.	F/T H'wife	All
0	58	49	46	192
1	31	32	41	140
2+	11	19	13	53
Total (N)	102	99	184	385

employed part-time or is a full-time housewife, suggesting that women may have a more significant role to play than men in reciprocating informal labour. This is an important aspect of informal work that is considered below. Where informal labour is unpaid it has to be repaid with reciprocal services. Those in employment may not have the time to provide such reciprocity and those too old or infirm cannot reciprocate. Hence, it may be that the households who use paid informal labour are those that cannot do the task themselves but, equally, cannot afford the formal market prices.

Perhaps some forms of informal labour, as is the case with formal labour, depend on the capacity to repay — but in a different currency. For the sample as a whole, younger respondents use more informal labour than older ones (Table 9.4), giving some support to the suggestion that they can repay more readily: 22 per cent of those households with respondents aged 30 or under score 'high' (2 or more) on the inf-lab scale as against 15 per cent of those households where the respondent is 65 and over.

Table 9.4   Inf-lab scale rating by the age of respondent (percentages)

Inf-lab scale	Age of respondent				All
	30 or under	31–50	51–64	65 and over	
0	38	51	51	46	48
1	39	35	33	39	36
2+	22	14	16	15	16
Total (*N*)	117	267	144	202	730

However, if we consider the age of respondents in single-person households only, it is clear that older people living on their own are obliged to rely on informal sources of labour, both because of their need for services and because of their lack of material resources.

For those single persons aged 65 and over, 18 per cent scored 2 or more on the inf-lab scale. If we compare the two tasks of painting and plastering, it is striking that among couples only seven out of nine households who pay informally for painting to be done are 65 and over and none are under 40, whereas for plastering, of the twenty-one households who paid for this task informally, thirteen are under 40 and none are 65 and over. This differentiation of task by age is an important distinction: younger people get plastering done for them informally; older people get painting done.

So far we have considered the economic variables of class, income and number of earners and some of the variables associated with household structure. The final factor to which I turn is the stage in the domestic cycle for couple households. The results are set out in Table 9.5.

Table 9.5   Household structure and inf-lab scale ratings

Household characteristics	Inf-lab scale (%)			Total (N)
	0	1	2+	
Couple households with children under 16				
Youngest child under 5	32	49	19	94
Youngest child 5–15	46	38	16	98
Partners living alone with no children under 16				
Female partner aged 35 or younger	67	21	12	42
Female partner aged 36 and over	53	38	8	150
More complex households				
Couples with other people all over 16	54	25	20	83
Couples with other people over 16 and youngest child 5–15	70	23	7	43
				510
Other household types				16
All couple-based households				526
All households	51	35	14	

The pattern is clear: women with young children at the early stages of the domestic cycle need more informal help and are in a position to repay it. By and large couples living alone, especially when they are older, use fewer informal sources of labour. However, households with a more complex structure, including more adults, use more informal labour: these households probably have dependent relatives and, perhaps, are more dependent on informal and communal supports or, with more household members, are better placed to provide reciprocal services.

To conclude, I have shown that there are certain well-defined categories that are most likely to use informal sources of labour. These are:

1 single-parent families with no other adult in the household;
2 married couples with children under 15, particularly those with women under 30;
3 single persons 65 and over living on their own.

These findings run counter to much received opinion, and I discuss them again after the analysis of the informal labour that is done for other households. Finally, I should emphasize that, on the whole, households scored very modestly on this scale. While 55 per cent of households scored 5 or 6 on the self-prov scale, no household scored more than 4 on the inf-lab scale and only 14 per cent of households scored 2 or more. This is an emphatic refutation of the notion that the use of informal labour is very widespread.

The formal provision of services scale (form-prov)

This scale, on the face of it, would seem to be the simplest to analyse. Households will use formal sources of labour when they cannot do the work for themselves, owing to age or ill-health, or when they have enough money to be able to pay for services, thus freeing them for other activities which they prefer to do. The hypothesis is, therefore, that older, more established households with multiple earners would use this source of labour most. These expectations were borne out by the data. The higher the household income and the greater the number of earners in the household, the higher the score on the form-prov scale. Of households in the 'low'-income band, 16 per cent scored 2 or more points on the scale, whereas for those in the 'high'-income band, 46 per cent scored 2 or more. Those in the 'middle'-income category had a similarly intermediate position on the scale — 30 per cent scored 2 or more. The relationship between income and form-prov scale score was direct and unequivocal.

There was a similar direct relationship with number of earners: 14 per cent of households with no earners scored 2 or more against 45 per cent in those households with two or more earners. The correlation was, again, direct and positive, as it was also with the number of adults in the household. With only one adult, 9 per cent of such households scored 2 or more on the form-prov scale. This rose to 31 per cent for households with two adults, 41 per cent for households with three and 36 per cent with four or more. As one might expect, owner-occupiers relied on the formal provision of services more than did tenants, and council tenants more than private tenants. Most of this form of labour is in the new housing areas of Halfway and Warden Bay: precisely the opposite pattern found for the inf-lab scale. Consistent with the foregoing, there is a clear linear relationship between social class and form-prov scale: the higher the social class, the greater the use of formal sources of labour.

From this account there is little in the analysis that refutes expectations. Households in which both partners are in employment (whether or not the woman is full-time or part-time) will score higher than those in which the partners are retired or unemployed. Again, as one would expect, couples between the age of 31 and 50 were the most likely to use formal sources of labour, as Table 9.6 clearly shows. While 28 per cent of the

Table 9.6   Formal provision of services scale rating by the age of respondent (percentages)

Form prov scale	Age of respondent				
	30 or younger	31–50	51–64	65 or over	All
0	30	20	31	53	33
1	45	36	44	36	39
2	21	30	23	11	22
3+	2	13	1	—	6
Total (*N*)	117	267	144	202	730

Table 9.7   Household structure and form-prov scale ratings

Household characteristics	Form-prov scale (%)			Total (N)
	0	1	2+	
Couple households with children under 16				
Youngest child under 5	21	36	42	94
Youngest child 5–15	14	43	43	98
Partners living alone with no children under 16				
Female partner aged 35 or younger	33	47	19	42
Female partner aged 36 and over	36	41	23	150
More complex households				
Couples with other people all over 16	22	51	29	83
Couples with other people over 16 and youngest child 5–15	21	21	58	43
				510
Other household types				16
All couple-based households				526
All households	25	40	34	

sample as a whole scored 2 or more on the form-prov scale, households with respondents aged 31-50 had 43 per cent scoring at this level.

However, as with the inf-lab scale, the more detailed analysis of the domestic cycle of couple households is revealing. Households with children aged over 5 and with one or more other people aged over 16 (apart from the children's parents) in the household score the highest, and older couple without children score the lowest.

The conclusions relating to households' use of formal sources of labour are clear. Households which consume the most labour from formal sources are likely to have the female partner in employment, for her to be over 35 and for there to be other adults in the household adding to the household income. The youngest child is still likely to be under 15, which helps to increase the household's demand for services, but with multiple earners and higher household incomes these demands can be met. The higher the social class, the greater the level of economic activity, and where partners are aged between 35 and 50, the greater the propensity to employ formal labour. The pattern is neat and coherent: it shows by contrast the more complex pattern of the other two sources of labour scales.

Interrelationship of the Scales

It may now be helpful to draw together some of the findings related to these three scales and to explore their interconnections. First, I have shown that there is a direct linear relationship between both the self-prov and form-prov scales and household income and an inverse linear relationship between income and the inf-lab scale. Higher-income households either use their own labour or buy it in the formal sector: more typically they do both. Lower-income households do less informal work for themselves, with certain specific categories of low-income households depending disproportionately on informal labour from outside the household. All three scales are directly related to the number of earners in the household, but again the inf-lab scale runs in the reverse direction to the other two. The more adults in a household, particularly if they are earners, the more self-sufficient it is and the less it has to rely on community resources. The same pattern is reflected in housing tenure: owner-occupiers use more services than tenants but also, in general, have higher incomes. Local authority tenants appear to be more dependent on locality and kin support. We have seen that the scales vary according to area of the Island, but this is more because locality is an intervening variable than because it has a causal influence in its own right.

I have consistently stressed the importance of household structure: couples with children where the woman is over 35 are the most vigorous in consuming services, using their own labour and drawing on the formal

Table 9.8 Household class by proportion of households scoring 'high' on the three scales (percentages)

	Household class												
Male partner	1				2				3				All
Female partner	1	2	3	4	1	2	3	4	1	2	3	4	All
Score													
'High' (5–6) on Self-prov scale	67	65	70	50	60	59	64	54	62	65	43	42	55
'High' (2+) on Inf-lab scale	—	19	8	4	—	14	17	7	—	15	17	9	14
'High' (2+) on Form-prov scale	50	56	47	57	20	38	41	32	13	33	24	25	35
Total number in each household class* (N)	6	43	23	14	5	100	47	28	8	75	120	43	512

* 14 households for which there were inadequate data have been omitted from this table.

Table 9.9 Economic activity of both partners, by proportion of households scoring 'high' on the three scales* (percentages)

Household class	1			2			3			All
Female partner's economic activity	F/T empl.	P/T empl.	F/T b'wife	F/T empl.	P/T empl.	F/T b'wife	F/T empl.	P/T empl.	F/T b'wife	
'High' (5–6) on Self-prov scale	71	74	58	59	64	64	66	60	49	61
'High' (2+) on Inf-lab scale	15	16	16	12	9	16	10	27	13	15
'High' (2+) on Form-prov scale	57	47	63	25	51	46	46	32	21	39
Total (N)	21	19	19	32	33	34	41	47	63	309

* Households selected only where male partner is in full-time employment. In this table the class categories are based solely on the male partner's employment.

provision of services. Where the woman is employed, particularly on a full-time basis, and where there are other earners in the household, the scores on the self-prov and form-prov scales will be greatest and the scores on the inf-lab scale the lowest. These relationships with household structure are stronger than with social class, although, again, the relationship of high self-prov and form-prov scale ratings with higher class and high inf-lab scale rating with lower class was in general found to be the case, but there were important differences *within* classes depending on the social class position of the woman.

Table 9.8 illustrates those households scoring 'high' on each of the three scales by household class. In the self-prov scale there is a distinction among households with males in Class 3 and their wives in different categories, with 20 percentage points between those in 3.1 and 3.2 and those in 3.3 and 3.4. (I mentioned this on p. 236.) In the case of informal sources of labour, higher-status wives in households with males in Class 1 receive more services, whereas where the male is in Class 2 or 3 the position is reversed — except in the case of housewives: all households with full-time housewives receive more informal labour, and a high proportion of these are likely to be elderly. When the woman is in employment less labour is used from informal sources: the proportion of households using no sources of informal labour declines from 58 per cent, when both partners are employed full-time, to 46 per cent where the woman was a full-time housewife. The impact of female employment on the three scales is shown in Table 9.9.

Perhaps surprisingly, in Class 3 households having both partners in employment, more formal services are bought than in Class 1 households where the woman is employed part-time. It is also significant that the Class 1 households where both partners are in employment do more self-provisioning work than any other category, followed by Class 3 households with both partners employed. (I should mention that the highly paid stevedores and steel workers are classified as Class 3. Such men have both high income and more time, owing to shift work and the uneven flow of cargo through the docks, so that they are able to buy services and do more work for themselves.)

It is an important and significant conclusion of this study that household self-provisioning is not a substitute for formal services, as has sometimes been asserted. For example, Richard Rose has argued:

When demand for labour in the Official Economy slackens, individuals will spend less time in work, and marginal workers will be counted out of the labour force. But this gives more time and more incentive for individuals to produce goods and services in the Domestic Economy. . . . When the Official Economy is slack, individuals can use their domestic resources to maintain consumption.[2]

[2] See Richard Rose, *Getting By in Three Economies: The Resources of the Official Unofficial and Domestic Economies*, Centre for the Study of Public Policy, University of Strathclyde,

According to data gathered from the Sheppey survey, Professor Rose is mistaken and has been misled by unreliable sources.

Self-provisioning and the formal provisioning of services go together, with the same households scoring high on each. The informal labour scale is related strongly inversely to the formal provision of services and less strongly inversely to self-provisioning.

Correlation between	Spearman's coefficient
Self-prov and form-prov scales	+0.4061
Inf-lab and self-prov scales	−0.1072
Inf-lab and form-prov scales	−0.767

So much, then, for the way different sources of labour are interrelated in getting the work of the household done. However, I must finally consider the work that members of the household do for other households. The division of household labour is discussed in the next chapter, since this issue is an accepted focus of discussion in the literature. I have already considered the household's participation in the labour market, so that the only work that remains for me to discuss here is the unrecorded work that members of households do for others, whether or not they are paid.

Unrecorded Labour Performed by Household Members for Members of other Households

In response to the question, 'Do you currently do any work on your own account to get extra money?', only 4 per cent of the sample replied in the affirmative; a further 1 per cent of respondents acknowledged that they did other work for an employer or firm for which they got paid (presumably in cash or some other informal way). This is what might be termed 'shadow wage labour': that is to say, payments may or may not be declared to the Inland Revenue. Given that the respondents were alternately male and female, the numbers of each sex who acknowledged that they got some extra money informally were very small. Of the 11 who were men, 10 were also in full-time employment and the other one was unemployed.[3] Of these 10 male full-time workers, 5 were in households in the 'high'-income category. By contrast, of the 16 women,

---

1983, pp. 33–4. I regret that some of my earlier more polemical writing may have misled some commentators, but Professor Rose does not make much of that. Rather, he cites a variety of other sources, some of which have been discussed above in Chapter 4. All the evidence of the present study suggests that Professor Rose has been substantially confused.

[3] No doubt sections of the popular press would want to make much of this one 'honest scrounger' whom we found in our sample. Other labour-for-others by unemployed men will be discussed below.

half were full-time housewives and 10 were in households in the low-income category. The relationship between economic circumstances and paid informal work appears to be differentiated by gender, but even with a sample of 730, the numbers were too small for findings to appear very significant.

The main source of information on the labour of household members for other households was in response to a question that was posed as follows: 'We have talked about a number of tasks that are done in the household. Now I'd like to know if there are any jobs that you do *outside* your home, for other people?' One in four of respondents answered in the affirmative, and they were asked to name these tasks and were prompted to say if there were any others. These replies were separately coded from the verbatim answers into appropriate categories. It is these data that form the basis of the analysis that follows.

Which households were those most likely to provide informal labour for others? Were they the older established Islanders well committed to local social networks? Were they younger or older, with children or without? Do working-class households provide more informal labour than middle-class households? Does income make a difference? Are those in formal employment who are also busily engaged in self-provisioning too occupied to do more? What divisions are there between men and women in doing informal labour for others?

These were the questions that the analysis set out to answer: many of them could be answered briefly and precisely. If households are divided according to whether they arrived on the Island before 1970 or in 1970 and thereafter and whether the respondent was aged 40 and under or 41 and over, the proportions are exactly the same in both cases. Similarly, if weekly household income is cross-tabulated by the number of earners in the household, there is very little difference between households in the categories so devised, although there are interesting indications of variations between men and women. The numbers in the cells are rather

Table 9.10 Number of respondent's relatives on Island by whether informal work is done (percentages)

Respondent's relatives on Island	Informal work is:		
	Not done	Done	All
2 or less	60	48	57
3 or more	40	52	43
Total (N) = 100%	550	180	730

*The question on which this table is based is as follows: 'We have talked about a number of tasks that are done in the household. Now I'd like to know if there are any jobs that you do *outside* your home, for other people. [if yes] What are they? Are there any others? [list below].'

Table 9.11 Tasks performed informally for other households*

Task	For relatives (N)		For non-relatives (N)		Totals (N)	
	M	F	M	F	M	F
1 Shopping	5	6	4	25	9	31
2 Babysitting	3	12	—	8	3	20
3 Housework	2	10	—	2	2	12
4 Washing clothes	—	4	—	2	—	6
5 Visit, 'stay with', keep company	—	—	2	4	2	4
6 Hairdressing	1	4	—	1	1	5
7 Pet care	—	—	1	4	1	4
8 Gardening	7	4	13	2	20	6
9 Dressmaking	—	3	—	3	—	6
10 Decorating	9	1	7	2	16	3
11 Provision of transport	1	1	3	4	4	5
12 Repairs, carpentry, etc.	14	—	22	2	36	2
13 Help with local activities	1	1	6	7	7	8
14 Help with voluntary work	1	—	3	12	4	12
15 Other help	10	5	9	16	19	21
Totals	54	51	70	97	124	145

Summary:

Type of work	Men		Women		Totals	
	N	%	N	%	N	%
Routine domestic work (1, 3, 4)	11	18	49	82	60	22
Social support (2, 5, 7)	6	18	28	82	34	13
Personal services (6, 9)	1	8	11	92	12	4
Home improvement (8, 10, 12)	72	87	11	13	83	31
Formal community work (13, 14)	11	35	20	65	31	12
Transport (11)	4	44	5	56	9	3
Other help (15)	19	48	21	53	40	15
Totals	124	46	145	54	269	100

* See note to table 9.10.

small but there are very strong indications that women in the households with lowest incomes provide more informal labour and men in the more affluent households do more. This differentiation between men and women by income of household is one of the most interesting conclusions to come out of the analysis of this question. Analysis by class and by area of the Island showed no significant variations. Even the occupational status of the respondent made very little difference to the amount of labour provided by the household overall. Perhaps the most striking finding is the importance of having a number of relatives on the Island, as Table 9.10 shows.

The divisions between informal labour done for relatives and for non-relatives were also explored. Of a total of 269 separate tasks mentioned by respondents, 39 per cent were done for relatives and 61 per cent for non-relatives. Table 9.11 shows that for the sample as a whole approximately equal proportions of men and women do informal labour but they engage in different tasks. Men overwhelmingly do home improvement and women do routine domestic work, mainly shopping, for others. Women also do more voluntary work.

Both the main survey and the in-depth interviews, which were held with selected repondents a year later, suggested that people typically claimed that they did more informal work for others than they received themselves, indicating, perhaps, the general concern of people not to appear dependent on others. The most surprising conclusion, despite all our considerable efforts to document the so-called 'informal' or 'black' economy of popular misconception, was how little labour for other households was given in comparison with the efforts of self-provisioning within the household. By far the most common tasks done for other households with informal labour were simply extensions of work done within the household — home improvement and maintenance and routine domestic assistance. There was little indication from the survey data that unemployed men did more or less informal labour than the average. This is a very important point. We analysed in some detail the use unemployed men made of informal *sources* of labour and discovered that unemployed people simply did not use such labour. This was partly because they could not afford to run a car and hence had no need of someone to fix it, or were not living in dwellings that they owned. The one task where unemployed men did use informal labour was in plastering, but even with this task those men in employment were more likely than unemployed men to use informal sources of labour.

In general, men are likely to do more informal work if they are in full-time employment, whereas women are more likely to do more if they are full-time housewives. This is because the informal labour that men do involves tools and materials and the informal labour that women do requires time (shopping for elderly neighbours and the like).

Finally, informal labour for other households is analysed in relation to the sources of labour scales that we discussed above. Those using formal sources of labour to do various tasks were also more likely to provide informal labour for others. Thus, only 19 per cent of those using no formal provision of services do informal labour for others against 32 per cent of those scoring 2 on the form-prov scale. The inf-lab scale shows no variation at all between different points on the scale. Relating work done inside the household with work done outside for others, there was a variation by gender, as Table 9.12 shows. More informal work is done for others in households that do more work for themselves.

Furthermore, it is likely that informal work for other households is

Table 9.12 *Household's self-prov rating by respondent's informal work for others**

Self-prov scale score	Informal work by respondents for other households			
		Done (%)		
	Not done (%)	M	F	All (N)
Low (2–4)	78	7	14	415
High (5–6)	71	17	12	315
Total	75	25		730

* Informal work is defined in the note to table 9.10.

given by men with skills who also do much self-provisioning work for themselves. As we have previously noted, the busy people do more: households scoring high on the self-prov scale do more for others, and there is a clear division by gender between high-scoring households and low-scoring households on this scale. This conclusion was borne out by more detailed analysis of a small category of manual workers individually earning high incomes[4] and most owning their own homes. These 'affluent' manual workers were also doing high levels of informal labour for others. The polarization of households in terms of all forms of work was strikingly confirmed.

Those who do informal work for others are, therefore, more likely to be choosing to do so. Doing informal work is not so much a coping strategy of the poor as a reflection of a particular kind of life style based on the skills and reciprocities of the work of everyday life. On the other hand, those who, as it were, consume informal labour are more likely to be the less well-off elderly people, single-parent families and households with children under 5.

[4] More than £125 a week net in 1981.

An Excursus on Do-It-Yourself

In all the scales we have considered so far, the emphasis was entirely on *range* and not on *depth* of sources of labour for clusters of tasks. In order to compensate for this bias we devised a new DIY scale, where we put together all the ten domestic repair and maintenance tasks into one scale and households scored if they had done one or more of these tasks by using the labour of a member of the household:

1 Painting

2 Plastering

3 Mending a broken window

4 Putting in a reinforced steel joist

5 Putting in double glazing

6 Putting in a new bathroom

7 Building a garage

8 Building an extension to the home

9 Converting an attic

10 Putting in central heating.

We limited analysis to couple households. Table 9.13 shows the DIY scale by age of respondent. The dominance of those in middle life is clear: again, it is households in this age range with children that dominate. Among those who did *not* score, 69 per cent were couples without children as against 31 per cent with children. By point 4 on the scale these

Table 9.13 *Age of respondents in couple households, by DIY scale*

DIY scale	Age of respondents (%)				Total	
	30 or under	*31–50*	*51–64*	*65+*	*N*	*%*
0	17	31	9	43	42	8
1	19	42	20	18	187	35
2	21	43	23	13	150	28
3	13	63	18	5	84	16
4	—	75	25	—	38	7
5	20	50	20	10	8	2
6	—	—	—	—	10	2
7	—	—	—	—	6	1
8	—	—	—	—	2	—
					527*	100

* The total is aberrant since one household could not be classified in all the other couple tables for lack of information but the age of the respondent is known.

positions were reversed — 29 per cent of childless couples reached this score against 66 per cent of couples with children.

More DIY is done in working-class households with multiple earners. The relationship between the employment status of the couple and the DIY scale is set out in Table 9.14. The remarkable conclusion illustrated by this table is that the employment status of the female partner makes little different to involvement in DIY activities: if anything, those couples where both partners are employed do *more* of such activity than other households! The DIY scale underlines in a most emphatic fashion the conclusions derived from analysis of the self-prov scale. Economic activity and high levels of the use of household labour for self-provisioning go together. Those most committed to the labour market are also the most committed to using their own labour in their own time for their own purposes. I return to discuss some of the wider social and political implications of this finding in the final chapter.

Table 9.14   Economic activity of females in selected couple households where the male partner is in full-time employment, by DIY scale (percentages)

	Female partner is:		
DIY scale	*F/T empl.*	*P/T empl.*	*F/T h'wife*
0	9	6	2
1	33	30	23
2	30	28	14
3	17	17	11
4	6	9	5
5+	3	4	4
Total (*N*)	102	99	167

10

The Domestic Division of Labour between Partners in Households

Up to now I have considered the work done in the household in a disaggregated form and have not discussed which of the partners does those tasks carried out within the household. The Sheppey survey was designed to explore this issue with greater precision than has been possible in much other empirical research devoted to this question.[1] The sample size of over five hundred couples enabled us to document the division of labour between partners for all stages of the domestic cycle at different socio-economic levels and with different combinations of economic activity for household members.

This depth of detailed information enables us to give precise answers to questions that relate to the effects both of new domestic technology and of women's economic activity, on the way work is or is not shared within the home. Do men, for example, do more domestic work connected with the maintenance of the dwelling, the maintenance of the car and the production of vegetables and of beer or wine, so that, over some length of time — thirty or forty years — they contribute equal effort to the household fund of labour? Is there a more equal division of labour earlier or later in the domestic cycle? Are women with young children, which have been the focus of many studies, at a very atypical phase in the life cycle of the domestic division of labour? Perhaps for a period of some ten years women may have a greater burden of domestic labour, but over the life cycle that burden is substantially reduced. Men may enjoy doing tasks when they are retired that they have not done with any great regularity

This chapter was written jointly with Spyros Missiakoulis.

[1] Examples of the more rigorous approach to measuring the domestic division of labour are R. Stafford, E. Backman and P. Dibona, 'The division of labour among cohabiting and married couples', *Journal of Marriage and the Family*, 39, 1977, pp. 43-57; R. A. Berk and S. F. Berk, *Labor and Leisure at Home*, Sage Publications, London, 1979; and J. Huber and G. Spitze, *Sex Stratification: Children, Housework and Jobs*, Academic Press, New York and London, 1983 (especially Chapter 4, 'The Division of Labour').

for forty years. The way households divide their labours clearly must be dependent on a longitudinal analysis of the same people, and this, unhappily, cannot be achieved with the research strategy that was adopted here or with other recent studies. While it will be possible to describe what different age cohorts did in 1981, there is no certainty that those now aged, say, 25-35 will behave in the same way as the present cohort aged 55-65 when they in turn reach that age.

In the various discussions of the domestic division of labour or sometimes, simply, of housework, a number of matters have been of overriding significance. First, there is the theme that sought to clarify who benefited from the labour that women devoted to household tasks. One possible candidate was the capitalist system — higher profits could be gained if men had their clothes washed and food cooked by a woman who was maintained by the wages paid to the man. The woman's work was deemed to be productive in that increased surplus value could thereby accrue to capitalism. This line of thinking refuted the suggestion that women who were out of employment were also out of the dominating relations of capitalist production.

Another possible candidate who might be systematically benefiting from the unpaid labour of women in the home would be, somewhat obviously, their male partners. The assumption is that such men are better off, as it is sometimes colloquially expressed, 'giving half their goose to get the other half cooked'. Such an assumption is singularly economistic and does not give consideration to the pleasures and satisfactions of love and companionship, particularly in the context of parenthood. However, if one wants to pursue the logic of this position, it is hard to deny that housekeepers employed full-time command higher wages than most men can afford; furthermore a servant, even if such could be afforded, cannot always be as satisfying as an emotionally committed partner. Nevertheless, in many cases the launderette and take-away might be less of a burden than a cantankerous and lazy partner, and this approach, which sees men universally benefiting, is more persuasive at a general level.

Again, in logic, if the male partner does the cooking and cleaning and there are no children, then, presumably, those emphasizing gender would see such men as being exploited. The notion that one gender systematically and universally benefits from the way housework is divided is unsatisfactory, since it depends on a conception of a rather rigid gender-defined division of labour that may not exist in such a rigid way in practice, and it also has to assume a kind of emotional neutrality between the partners. However, it is clear that in a given labour market, if one gender has systematically and consistently greater earning potential, the other gender automatically becomes the cheaper housekeeper and has thereby less choice in life activities. Unquestionably, the labour market position of men and women has been consistently skewed towards the former and this has direct consequences for the domestic division of labour.[2] However, this position is not always seen as labour-market-determined.

Some researchers have based their study of the domestic division of labour on detailed analyses of household members' use of time over a typical 24-hour day or sometimes longer periods. Such data were not available to us and, indeed, there are some valid criticisms of this method that should, perhaps, be mentioned. As R. A. Berk and S. F. Berk point out, there are considerable difficulties and ambiguities associated with such data. More than one task may be done 'at the same time', and it is by no means clear that the intervals used by the researchers are significant for household members. Berk and Berk say:

our field notes indicated repeatedly that consideration and discussion of the division of household labour was undertaken using specific *tasks* and not time as meaningful units. *Never* did we hear statements like . . . 'I spend an hour and a half on child care while he spends five minutes taking out the garbage.' The following example is far more typical:
Q: You mentioned that Frank helps by shovelling snow on the drive-way. Does he help with the housework on a regular or occasional basis?
A: Each of us has jobs in the house. He does the wiring, plumbing, carpentry, puts the kids to bed and gives them baths.[3]

It is certainly arguable that task analysis is the most efficient and effective way of getting precise answers to the question 'Who does the work of the household?'

What is 'necessary' household work is highly problematic and, to a large degree, culturally determined. It may, in some absolute sense, be more necessary to mend the roof if the rain is coming in than to, say, iron the sheets or polish the furniture. However, the cultural conditioning that supports the latter, reinforced by the normative expectations of other women, effectively constrains women to do certain apparently less necessary tasks. Men are less likely to be constrained by the normative expectations of other men to do 'necessary' tasks connected with domestic refurbishing and maintenance. What constitutes a necessary task is determined pragmatically: if households do the task then they must deem such tasks to be important. If they do the task more frequently, this reflects *their* assessment of its importance or value. If a man does not polish the household car but the woman does polish the domestic furniture, this is no guide to the functional importance of either task: rather it is a reflection of the relative weight of normative and cultural constraints.[4]

---

[2] The subordinate position of women in the sphere of employment was discussed above in Chapter 3. For an unexceptional and formal statement of this position, see J. A. Pleck, 'The work-family role system', *Social Problems*, 24, 1977, pp. 417-27.

[3] R. A. Berk and S. F. Berk, 'A simultaneous equation model for the division of household labour', *Sociological Methods and Research*, 6(4), 1978, p. 439.

[4] For the purposes of this chapter we have made no attempt to judge the degree to which

Certainly, it would be wrong to assume that one gender necessarily dominates the other gender in ensuring that certain tasks are done. Rather, it is likely that in some tasks the pressures are more intra-gender and in others they are inter-gender. The 'good housewife' role is perceived differently in different social categories and the best judges of how such roles are performed are more likely to be other women. Somewhat cynically, women could be seen as the unpaid domestic factory inspectors working on behalf of men, but since the latter would be unclear as to what constituted appropriate performance in certain areas, such a view cannot be seriously sustained.

The Construction of the DOMDIV Index

In order to provide a more precise measure of the gender-linkedness of each of a range of 41 tasks and also a precise index of the overall pattern of the domestic division of labour within households in the sample, we have devised a new index.[5] This enables comparisons between the division of labour of domestic tasks (DLDT) in households with different social and economic characteristics. For example, are households that have, say, one or more cars and are owner-occupiers more or less 'balanced' in their domestic division of labour? Does the addition of new forms of domestic work produce a different DLDT from households with a more limited range of potential tasks?

The range of tasks in the Sheppey Survey covered not only the conventional 'female' tasks of cooking, cleaning and child care, but also the conventional 'male' tasks of house repair, maintenance and extension, vegetable growing and car care. Respondents were asked whether the task was done and, if so, whether it was done inside or outside the home and, if the former, who did it. In the case of tasks where frequency was important, this was also documented. In some cases, of course, tasks were shared.[6]

---

individuals are more or less constrained to do certain tasks. Such matters are ultimately more philosophical than empirical. We have simply documented *who* does the task: we did not ask *why* tasks were done.

[5] We recognize that at different stages of the life cycle some tasks will be more important than others. Clearly, in household with very young children there is a greater necessity to do certain tasks whereas in households without dependants such obligations are substantially reduced. The number of tasks about which information could be gathered could be almost limitless. For practical and pragmatic reasons the number had to be limited. Our interest here is not *whether* given tasks are done but, *if* the task is done, who does it? The actual tasks done vary over the life cycle as a dynamic process, and at each stage of the life cycle some tasks are important and some are not. As will be explained below, we weighted the tasks by measures to reflect the conventionality of the tasks and the frequency with which they were done.

[6] For the precise wording of the questions relating to all the 41 tasks analysed in this chapter see the full questionnaire which is available as explained in note 4 on p. 201.

Quite evidently, we had to devise a system of weighting to take into account the characteristics of both the task and the household. Clearly, the crude equation of, say, 'cleaning the car' with 'cooking' would bias the results. Some way of giving weight to necessary, regular tasks had to be devised. Similarly, households differ in their capacity to generate conventionally male tasks. Ways of offsetting the 'male' advantage of home and car ownership had to be devised. The 41 tasks were carefully selected to reflect a broad range of domestic activity in order to avoid a situation where the nature of the tasks selected could bias the results. Thus, to make the point in an extreme way, if 30 tasks connected with child care and 11 tasks connected with car care were selected and no attempt was made to compensate, the results would be predictably biased. We hope that the list of tasks is sensibly determined, but inevitably there is no final way of selecting the 40, 100 or even 1,000 most significant tasks to measure the DLDT. The best that can be done is to select a manageable number of tasks and to weight the scores appropriately.

Our attempt at a more precise measurement of the DLDT enables us to compare households with different characteristics and to isolate those factors and their corresponding weights which determine the DLDT. Such measurement enables us to determine the fairness of the DLDT. This measure of the DLDT is what we are now going to call the DOMDIV index. Precise measures of the domestic division of labour that have been adopted in the literature inevitably vary in the way their indices are constructed.[7] Inevitably, all researchers must begin with the question 'Who does the task?' in some form or other, but there is substantial variation in scoring systems and in the different weightings adopted to reflect a specific task's characteristics. Our method for computing the value of the index for each household took into account three factors for each of the total number of domestic tasks performed in that household. These factors correspond to who actually performs the task in the household, who usually performs the task in question in the community we studied, and the frequency with which the task is carried out in the particular household. Thus the scale enables us to aggregate overall the separate domestic tasks and the extent to which the practice of each household departed from what was usual in the community. The DOMDIV index is a real number defined as follows for the *i*th household:

---

[7] The final measures of the domestic division of labour vary from relatively crude proportions (Berk and Berk, 'A simultaneous equation model') to scores adjusted for each task's 'traditionality' and the frequency of its performance (Stafford, Backman and Dibona, 'Division of labour'). In the most recent research report (Huber and Spitze, *Sex Stratification*) the DDL is measured by the husband's mean score. For five tasks, which are standardized to take account of the possibility that they might be performed by someone other than the couple, the following scoring system is applied: 1 = wife always, 2 = wife usually, 3 = both share equally, 4 = husband usually, 5 = husband always. Hence a high score would indicate more work done by the husband.

$$DOMDIV_i = \sum_{t=1}^{T} S_{it} \, N_t \, F_t$$

Where T = total number of tasks (41 in the case of our sample)

S = score assigned to each tasks according to who performs it

N = adjustment to S for the nature of the task or its 'conventionality factor'

F = adjustment to S for the frequency with which the task is done

S and F are empirically observable and data were provided from the survey mentioned above. N, however, has to be constructed since it is not necessarily observable — whether, say, cooking or washing-up is more conventionally 'female'.

The Scoring System

We classified each task carried out in each household as 'male' or 'female', according to common assumptions, irrespective of the household's individual characteristics. While it might be expected that there would be considerable ambiguity on this point, when gender typing was tested on a small group of people, considerable unanimity was found. As a result of this exercise, seventeen tasks were classified as 'male' and the rest as 'female'. We considered a number of possible ways of allocating scores for each task, and the final scoring system we adopted is shown in Table 10.1.[8] We felt that it was inappropriate to allocate the same scoring weight to households where the task is shared as to those households that do not do the task at all or, if they do do it, pay someone outside the household, and this distinction is reflected in the scoring system we adopted. To make our scoring system quite explicit: scores are only gained if the task is done — whether it is done separately or shared. If the task is not done

Table 10.1 Scheme for allocating scores according to who does the task

| Task is conventionally seen to be | Task is actually | | | |
	Done by Male	Female	Shared	Not done
Male	−1	2	½	0
Female	−2	1	−½	0

[8] Since the 41 tasks were not exactly divided between 'male' and 'female' tasks, the scoring skews the results towards the female. But since the 41 tasks were directly related to the pattern of work actually done by household members, a skewed result towards the female simply reflects the actual circumstances.

there is no score, and therefore the index is not affected one way or another. As a result, there is no need to adjust the final index according to how many tasks are performed in the household. Our scoring system had to be somewhat rudimentary, but any other scoring system would be open to similar criticisms.

The Weighting for Conventionality

Given that we have defined each task as being conventionally 'male' or 'female', we now have the problem of determining the *degree* to which each task is more or less 'male' or more or less 'female'. Thus, we want to know, for example, how much 'more or less female' the task of changing the baby's nappies might be compared with, say, the task of shopping. Devising a system of weighting to reflect the *degree* of conventionality enables us to avoid a crude dichotomy based on defining tasks as simply 'male' or simply 'female'. Our method enables us to provide a more subtle gradation of what we may clumsily term 'femaleness' or 'maleness'. Clearly, we cannot directly determine this conventionality index from the data reporting the behaviour of specific partners: we are obliged, therefore, to derive the weighting for our conventionality index from the sample as a whole. Our initial assumption was that certain household characteristics determine who performs a specific task — for example, the extent to which women's employment may affect the amount of shopping they do, or the age of a couple may affect who does home-improvement work.[9]

Now, therefore, let x_{ij} *be a variable which is 1 if the i*th household has the *j* characteristic and 0 if it has not. Then let *b* be the weight of the *j*th characteristic in determining who does the tth task, assuming that the task was done by one or both of the partners. We finally assume that the sum of all *b*, corresponding to the households' characteristics, would indicate whether the task was performed by the male, the female, or was shared. Thus we are able to sum up the contribution of each particular characteristic in a given household for each household as follows:

$$D_{it} = \sum_j b_{tj} x_{ij}$$

If	$D_{it} < A_t$	the task is done by a male.
And if	$A_t < D_{it} < C_t$	the task is done by a female.
And if	$C_t < D_{it}$	the task is shared.

[9] Readers who do not want to follow the formal presentation of the method of constructing the DOMDIV index are encouraged to move on to p. 270 where the results are discussed.

The limits A and C will be different for each task. The greater the interval from A to C, the greater will be the likelihood that the female does the task. This may be expressed diagrammatically as in Figure 10.1. If all b and the limits A and C that correspond to each task are known, the task performer can be predicted in the following way. First we compute D and then we observe whether D is less than A (male), or between A and C (female), or greater than C (shared). Evidently, in order to compare two or more tasks we must know both A and C, or rather the length of the interval AC (i.e. $C - A$). To make things easier we set A equal to zero for *all* tasks. Clearly, now C itself is the length of AC and it can be used as an index. This is now termed the conventionality index. It should now be clear that the higher the C, the more likely the task is done by the female and, conversely, the lower the C, the more likely that the task is done by the male. We are now in a position to make detailed comparisons between tasks.

Male does the task	Female does the task	Task is shared
$-\infty$		$+\infty$
A_t	C_t	

Figure 10.1

We now have to estimate the relative weight of household characteristics in affecting who does the task and also the conventionality index of the task. In order to do this the polychotomous ordered probit model was used. We may thus express D_{it} as

$$D_{it} = \sum_j b_{tj} x_{ij} + u_{it}$$

The difference between this expression of the formula and the one described previously is the addition of u_{it}, which is a disturbance term following the standard normal distribution and accounts for possible errors in the modelling process.[10] Table 10.2 provides a matrix of the 27

[10] It should be clear that D_{it} values are not observed: we can ascertain whether, if the task in question is done within the household, it is done by the male, the female or shared between the two, providing, as it were, a trichotomous observation. Given these categorical values, we were obliged to use the polychotomous probit model, and in terms of both theory and practice we followed the method set out in R. D. McKelvey and W. Zavoina, 'A statistical model for the analysis of ordinal level dependent variables', *Journal of Mathematical Sociology*, 4, 1975, pp. 103-20. Those who wish to understand the statistical procedures in more detail should consult that paper. We do not repeat their exposition here but simply state that in order to estimate b and C we required observations on D and X. For the former we simply have the trichotomous observation already mentioned; for the latter we have the information from the survey.

Table 10.2 Results of the probit model to predict who performs each task

Variable [a]	Task no. [a]								
	1	2	11	12	13	14	15	16	17
Constant	1.640†	-1.900†	-0.771	-1.111	-0.762	-0.228	0.289	-0.632	-1.796
HC 11	—	—	0.483	1.395*	0.953	0.408	—	—	—
HC 12	-1.143†	0.567	0.639	0.851	0.510	0.858*	0.291	-0.100	0.388
HC 13	-1.221†	0.677	0.969†	0.780	0.426	0.698	-0.279	0.287	0.950
HC 14	-1.738‡	—	1.132‡	0.714	-0.012	0.040	-0.234	0.252	-0.529
HC 21	-1.515*	—	1.040	1.281	1.218	-0.137	—	-0.952	0.288
HC 22	-0.732*	0.307	1.091‡	1.002†	0.112	0.491	0.156	-0.324	0.552
HC 23	-1.076†	0.248	0.821*	1.022*	0.195	0.197	-0.771	0.001	0.294
HC 24	-1.131†	0.501	0.888*	1.355†	0.219	0.219	-0.105	0.100	0.339
HC 31	-1.148*	—	1.131†	0.870	-0.383	0.048	1.107*	-0.060	-0.211
HC 32	-1.026†	0.770	1.070†	1.092†	0.588	0.114	0.213	-0.137	0.312
HC 33	-1.094‡	0.305	1.272‡	0.996†	0.255	0.256	-0.083	-0.142	0.423
HC 34	-1.288‡	0.465	0.995†	1.370	0.457	0.514	-0.056	0.096	0.219
URBAN	-0.565‡	0.259	0.243*	-0.036	-0.002	0.176	0.106	0.176	-0.284
MINST	-0.146	0.131	0.297*	-0.056	-0.209	-0.181	0.216	0.182	-0.496†
INCLO	-0.300*	-0.052	0.331†	-0.247	0.027	-0.002	0.272	0.107	0.167
INCHI	-0.173	-0.269	0.080	-0.046	0.210	-0.019	-0.076	0.058	0.160
FFT	0.088	0.401	-0.143	0.670‡	0.392†	0.004	0.481†	0.373	0.461†
FPT	-0.093	0.009	0.143	0.193	-0.017	-0.099	-0.074	0.085	-0.266
FUN	-0.064	1.478*	0.002	0.079	-0.382	-0.731*	-0.169	0.536	-0.108
FRE	-0.472	—	-0.474*	0.173	-0.272	-0.257	0.147	0.069	0.001
MFT	-0.377	—	0.421	1.382†	1.347†	0.172	1.938‡	1.065	0.426
MPT	-0.382	—	-0.038	-0.392	0.432	0.722	—	—	—
MUN	-0.699	—	0.691	1.583‡	1.111*	0.212	1.875‡	1.119	0.298
MRE	-0.214	—	0.836	1.610‡	1.292†	-0.007	1.852‡	0.743	-0.025
MAGE	-0.002	-0.012	0.005	0.002	-0.005	0.004	0.014	-0.037	-0.009
FAGE	-0.002	0.003	-0.005	0.007	0.007	-0.013	-0.022	0.033*	0.021
ADULTS	0.029	0.167	0.194*	0.142	0.191*	0.212*	0.08	0.322†	0.173
C	0.448‡	0.173*	1.684‡	2.864‡	2.244‡	1.226‡	3.556‡	2.147‡	0.507‡

* 0.10; † 0.05; ‡ 0.01
[a] See Table 10.3 and Figure 8.2 for the description of the variables and the task numbers.

Table 10.2 continued

					Task no.[a]					
18	19	20	21	22	23	25	26	27	28	29
1.552†	0.049	0.676	0.146	0.991	-0.665	0.030	1.479†	1.295		-1.622
-0.972	—	—	—	—	—	—	—	—		—
-1.213†	0.225	0.032	-0.655	-1.066	0.774	0.322	-0.053	0.187		0.010
-0.923	-0.147	-0.112	-0.094	-1.223	0.858	1.376	-0.688	-1.156		-0.439
-1.290*	0.314	0.360	0.466	0.608	0.770	-0.078	-0.874	-0.064		—
-1.254	—	—	—	—	—	—	—	-0.216		—
-1.105*	0.168	0.267	-0.085	-0.315	0.802	0.329	-0.294	-0.175		-1.027
-1.600‡	0.167	0.224	-0.222	-0.714	0.737	0.172	0.016	0.406		-0.626
-1.792‡	-0.173	0.303	0.059	-1.188	1.108†	0.290	-0.418	-0.238		-0.726
-0.956	0.386	0.398	-0.765	-0.876	1.069	—	0.107	-0.973		—
-0.992*	-0.336	-0.429	-0.181	-1.562†	0.978†	0.069	-0.392	-0.059	-0.683	0.208
-1.235†	0.150	0.100	-0.418	-0.828	0.833*	0.432	-0.221	-0.234	-1.275*	0.846
-1.384†	0.066	0.095	-0.253	-1.228	0.824*	0.305	0.089	-0.030	-0.667	—
-0.307‡	-0.415†	-0.253	-0.220	-0.629†	-0.098	0.021	0.078	-0.657‡	0.191	0.280
-0.200	-0.123	-0.098	-0.422	-0.520	0.169	0.524	0.048	-0.483*	0.120	-0.438
0.047	0.039	0.141	0.111	0.157	-0.034	-0.314	-0.111	-0.469†	-0.622	-0.706
-0.132	-0.209	-0.135	0.142	0.100	0.094	1.182†	0.034	-0.232	-0.292‡	-0.023
-0.177	0.323	0.383	0.284	0.121	0.515†	-0.439	0.376	0.096	-0.095*	0.961*
-0.386†	-0.150	-0.164	0.088	0.150	0.381	-0.715	0.085	0.400	0.240†	0.317
-0.132	-0.240	-0.202	0.240	-1.964‡	0.608	—	0.500	-0.027	—	0.822
0.189	-0.102	0.179	0.011	-0.152	0.321	1.184	-0.120	0.170	-0.876	-0.609
1.688‡	2.006‡	1.781‡	2.023‡	2.136‡	1.507‡	2.361‡	0.032	-0.732	1.584*	2.726†
1.187	—	—	—	—	—	—	—	-1.082	—	—
1.355†	1.883‡	1.971‡	1.690‡	23.00‡	1.792‡	2.782†	-0.175	-0.873	0.896	1.913
1.845‡	1.974‡	2.326‡	1.878‡	1.717‡	1.760‡	0.778	-0.195	-0.911	2.154‡	1.917
0.002	0.008	-0.005	0.005	0.029	0.005	-0.031	-0.017	-0.003	0.005	0.049
-0.012	0.005	0.0004	-0.008	-0.020	-0.016	0.011	0.016	0.001	-0.005	0.004
0.166*	-0.058	0.002	0.289†	0.218	0.260*	0.402	0.151	-0.032	0.163	-0.316
1.660‡	3.952‡	4.099‡	3.877‡	4.859‡	3.591‡	5.542‡	3.237‡	0.583‡	4.037‡	4.301‡

*: 0.10; †: 0.05; ‡: 0.01

[a] See Table 10.3 and Figure 8.2 for the description of the variables and the task numbers.

Table 10.2 continued

			Task no. [a]					
30	31	32	35	37	38	39	40	41
-5.658‡	1.930*	-1.303	0.755	5.397‡	1.637	2.007*	3.461‡	4.119†
—	0.907	—	—	—	—	—	—	—
—	-0.547	—	-0.981	-0.827	-1.090	-0.274	0.107	-0.211
1.887*	-0.638	—	0.423	-0.385	-1.315	-0.001	-0.407	0.469
—	-0.333	1.088	-2.194†	0.071	-1.297*	-0.344	0.464	—
—	0.524	—	—	—	—	—	—	—
2.456‡	-0.593	0.549	-1.416	-0.868*	-0.565	-0.566	0.113	-1.324
0.104	-0.230	0.830†	-0.948	-0.815	-0.862	-0.425	-0.535	1.129
0.005	-1.054	—	-0.461	-0.559	-0.401	-0.377	-0.308	-2.316
—	0.276	—	—	—	-1.236	-1.341	0.533	—
1.180	-0.462	0.005	-1.261	-0.169	-0.669	0.118	-0.362	-1.120
0.412	-0.616	0.296	-0.906	-0.444	-0.568	-0.197	-0.070	0.276
0.104	-0.164	—	-1.818†	-0.795	-0.534	-0.334	-0.712	-0.398
1.098†	-0.348*	-0.244	-0.407	-0.317	-0.064	-0.437*	-0.193	-0.870
0.642	0.104	0.406	0.094	-0.083	0.089	0.143	0.400	-0.299
-0.705	-0.214	-0.314	-0.404	0.022	-0.116	0.004	-0.083	0.762
-0.175	-0.041	0.108	—	0.046	0.140	-0.221	-0.204	0.706
-0.894	-0.237	0.290	0.799	0.377	0.192	0.046	0.363	-0.424
-0.009	-0.037	0.424	-0.560	0.137	0.527*	0.085	0.026	-1.426*
—	0.178	—	0.984	-1.629†	0.069	-0.401	-1.440†	-2.059*
-0.464	-0.085	—	—	—	—	—	—	—
—	-1.511†	-0.898	—	-1.284*	0.354	0.513	-0.443	-0.858
—	-0.735	—	—	—	—	—	—	—
—	-1.301*	-1.054	—	-1.374*	0.135	0.071	-1.094	—
—	-1.053	-0.980	—	—	—	—	—	—
-0.147‡	-0.033	0.006	0.081	-0.024	-0.009	0.025	-0.027	-0.070
0.167‡	0.017	-0.026	-0.074†	-0.002	-0.002	-0.013	0.007	0.124
0.927‡	0.005	0.440†	1.345	-0.060	0.291	-0.236	0.007	-1.127
0.807‡	0.547‡	0.598‡	2.665‡	3.294‡	2.496‡	1.773‡	2.915‡	5.063‡

* 0.10; † 0.05; ‡ 0.01
[a] See Table 10.3 and Figure 8.2 for the description of the variables and the task numbers.

Table 10.3   List of variables used in the probit estimation

Variable name	Description
HCij	Household class dummy variable: 1 = male belongs to the ith class and the female to the jth class; 0 = otherwise
URBAN	1 = area of residence in Sheerness, Queenborough, Rushenden and Halfway; 0 = otherwise
MINST	1 = area of residence in Minster; 0 = otherwise
INCHI	1 = households income is more than £150/week; 0 = otherwise
INCLO	1 = households income is less than £70/week; 0 = otherwise
FFT	1 = female is full-time employed; 0 = otherwise
FPT	1 = female is part-time employed; 0 = otherwise
FUN	1 = female is unemployed; 0 = otherwise
FRE	1 = female is retired; 0 = otherwise
MFT	1 = male is full-time employed; 0 = otherwise
MPT	1 = male is part-time employed; 0 = otherwise
MUN	1 = male is unemployed, 0 = otherwise
MRE	1 = male is retired; 0 = otherwise
FAGE	Female's age in years
MAGE	Male's age in years
ADULTS	The number of adults living together

household variables by 29 tasks with the computed b values.[11] The main variables chosen were the socio-economic status of both partners, their economic activity, the household income, the ages of the partners, the number of adults in the household and the geographical location of the household on the Isle of Sheppey. The variables are defined more precisely in Table 10.3.

Two examples may help to clarify Table 10.2. Let us assume that we wish to calculate the C for a given household for a given task — first, that of cleaning the outside windows. For the sample as a whole, in 131 households the man does the task, in 142 households the female does the task and in 66 households the task is shared. Let us now, solely for the sake of illustration, select a household with the following characteristics and list the appropriate estimated coefficients for each, reading down the appropriate column in Table 10.2:

[11] For 12 out of the 41 tasks, the variation in who did the task was very small so that the amount of variance was negligible. We therefore excluded those tasks from probit estimation. The ten male tasks that were excluded were mending a broken window, double glazing, putting in a bathroom, building a garage, building an extension, converting an attic to living space, putting in a reinforced steel joist, putting in central heating, tuning the engine of a car and repairing or checking the brakes. The two female tasks excluded were making clothes and changing nappies. We then allocated the minimum estimated C from the 29 tasks to the 10 male tasks and the maximum C to the 2 female tasks. These values are 0.173 and 5.542 for plastering and knitting, respectively.

Characteristics	b coefficient
Socio-economic status of partner = 2.2	0.491
Living in urban Sheppey	0.176
Household income is over £150 p.w. or over £300 with only 1 earner	−0.002
The female partner is in full-time employment	0.004
The male partner is in full-time employment	0.172
The female is aged 44 (−0.013×44)	−0.572
The male is aged 49 (0.004×49)	0.196
There are three adults in the household	0.636
Constant	−0.228
	———
	0.773

It will be noted that the *C* for the task of cleaning the outside windows is 1.226. If the final outcome had been higher than this, then, in that particular household, one would predict that the task is more likely to be shared. As it is, the final result, 0.773, is less than the *C* but more than 0, so in that case the task is most likely to be done by the female. Our second hypothetical example, taking the task of vegetable gardening, follows the same procedure as above:

Characteristics	b coefficient
Partners in socio-economic category 3.3	−0.234
Household income less then £70 p.w.	−0.232
Female partner is unemployed	−0.027
Male partner is unemployed	−0.873
Female is aged 23 (×0.001)	0.023
Male is aged 26 (× −0.003)	−0.078
There are two adults in the household	−0.064
Constant	1.295
	———
	−0.190

This particular household scores less than zero (−0.190), so there is a strong likelihood that the man would do the vegetable gardening in a household with these characteristics.

This conventionality index, computed for each household, is then used in the equation to calculate the DOMDIV index for each household. When the task is done by the female partner the conventionality factor, *N* in the equation on page 259, = C, but when the task is done by the male partner $N = 1/C$. This adjustment is necessary to make the scoring system fairer. Were it not for this adjustment, female partners would score 3 for cooking but only 0.17 for painting.

The Weighting for Frequency

The second element used to adjust the score is a factor to represent the *frequency* with which the task is done. Here tasks are classified according to their expected frequency (cooking meals daily, making beer or wine less often than once a month and so on). However, it is recognized that some households would perform tasks more or less frequently than expected. Table 10.4 was, therefore, constructed to give the values of F_t for all possible circumstances. Of course, in practice many of these cells, although logically possible, were not filled. The assumption was that those tasks performed daily were more important or 'necessary' than those performed less frequently. This clearly puts a bias towards conventionally female tasks such as cooking, cleaning and child care activities, giving them greater weight than the less frequently, but perhaps no less necessary, tasks connected with the repair and maintenance of the domestic dwelling. However, as stated earlier, this probably reflects a household's own order of priorities more faithfully than any alternative method.

Table 10.4   Scheme for weighting the scores according to the frequency with which the task is done

Conventional expectation of the frequency with which tasks are done	Tasks are actually done:				
	Daily	Weekly	Fortnightly	Monthly	Less often
Daily	1	½	⅓	¼	⅕
Weekly	1	½	¼	⅙	⅛
Fortnightly	1	⅔	⅓	⅙	1/9
Monthly	1	¾	½	¼	⅛
Less often	1	⅘	⅗	⅖	⅕

We recognize that there must be an element of arbitrariness in adjusting for frequency in this way, but we consider that it would be inadmissable to ignore the frequency with which a given task is done. All weighting systems have their distinctive difficulties.

We have now described the construction of the DOMDIV index. For each household we assigned a score to each of a total of T tasks, depending in each case on who empirically performed the task. We then adjusted these scores to take account of the frequency with which a task was done and its conventionality index. In this way, a higher score was given to men who performed 'female' tasks and vice versa. We must emphasize that both frequency and conventionality were estimated from our data with the assumptions that we have mentioned.

Before proceeding further, we should consider the important question of the possibility of bias, depending on whether the informant was male or female. It is possible, for example, that males might over-emphasize the amount of work they contributed to a certain task and, perhaps, that women might understate their own contribution. However, if men reporting what they did coincided closely with what women reported on behalf of their partners, then we may be reassured that bias on the part of the respondent is unlikely. Table 10.5 shows the results of such a test. There may be a slight tendency for men to claim that they share more, whereas women feel that they more often usually do the task themselves, but the differences are minor and, overall, the results are extremely reassuring. There was no bias dependent on the sex of the respondent. A further question attempted to elicit whether respondents felt that they did more or less of their fair share of such tasks, and the responses to this question are set out in Table 10.6.

The results here are remarkable, remembering that male and female partners were interviewed alternately and each had to report on the other partner as well as for himself or herself. While it is clear that 24 per cent of the female partners feel they are doing *more* than their fair share, 21 per

Table 10.5　*Variations in responses, by sex of respondent (percentages)*

| | Respondent claims that the task is: | | | | |
| | Done by: | | | | |
	Male	Female	Shared	Other	Total (N)
(a) Washing-up					
Respondent is:					
Male	8	48	43	1	263
Female	8	52	37	2	263
					526
(b) Tidying the dwelling					
Respondent is:					
Male	2	68	29	—	263
Female	2	74	22	2	263
					526
(c) Brushing/hoovering carpets					
Respondent is:					
Male	8	64	26	2	263
Female	6	71	21	2	263
					526

Table 10.6   Respondents' conception of the fairness of the way tasks are shared

Respondent is	Respondent feels that s/he does:				Total (N)
	Fair share	More than fair share	Less than fair share	Other	
Male	74	4	21	1	263
Female	74	24	2	—	263

cent of male partners think that they are doing *less* than their fair share (for whatever reason). Hence, there is agreement on the discrepancy between the genders, an astonishing finding, confirming the honesty of respondents.

The computation of the C index enables us to get some indication of the relative importance of certain variables in affecting who does the task in the sample as a whole. The most important variable, most likely to affect significantly who does a specific task, is the employment status of the partners. As might be expected, our evidence suggests that the conventional female tasks of cooking, cleaning and washing are more likely to be done by the woman if one or both partners are employed full-time than in households where the woman partner is in employment part-time. This is because women employed part-time are most likely to have young children. Even more strikingly, it is clearly demonstrated that, when the male partner is unemployed, there is *more* likelihood that domestic tasks are done by the female; even in the case of washing up, there was a greater likelihood that the task would be done by the woman.

The general effect of employment status on the domestic division of labour is considered below. Here it is sufficient to note that more tasks were affected by that variable than any other. The combined socio-economic status of the partners, or what may be conveniently, if not very precisely, termed the household's class, was the second most important variable. This affected painting — a very 'masculine' task (C = 0.448) — and washing up — a more 'feminine' task (C = 1.684). It also affected tidying the dwelling, doing the main weekly shopping, making wine or beer and bathing the child. The variable reflecting geographical location affected vegetable growing (more likely to be the woman in urban areas), painting, making wine or beer, washing clothes and ironing sheets, doing the main shopping and the use of take-away foods. Income affected who did vegetable growing and who did the washing up. The number of adults did not seem to lead to more tasks being done by men: on the contrary, in nearly every case the effect was to increase the likelihood that women did the task. This was striking, for example, in the case of packed lunches, where, the more adults in the household, the more likely the woman did the task.

Clearly, considering merely one variable for one task has only limited value, and it is necessary both to combine variables and to consider the complete domestic division of labour over all tasks. It should be emphasized that, while employment status affects who does the task more than any other single variable, nevertheless, women being employed full-time or men being unemployed do not, as single variables, produce any significant shift away from a likelihood that the woman would do the task.

The Domestic Division of Labour

Each couple household, then, has a DOMDIV score, derived as described above, and it is evidently now possible to provide mean scores for households with given characteristics in common. This enables a very precise answer to such questions as whether households in different social classes have overall different patterns in the domestic division of labour. Are middle-class households, in general, more likely to share tasks (DOMDIV closer to 0)? Do younger couples share tasks more than older ones? Do couples where both are in full-time employment share tasks that much more than those where both are retired? What difference does it make if the male is unemployed — does he do more domestic work around the home? Finally, how does the DOMDIV score relate to the scores on the sources of labour scales? Do households scoring higher on the formal provision of services (form-prov) scale share more or less in the divisions of domestic tasks? What difference is made by the number of tasks a given household does? Do men do more domestic labour when there is more to be done? Is one of the consequences of distinctive household work strategies in access to sources of labour a distinctive pattern in the domestic division of labour? These and other questions can now be answered.[12]

The overall distribution for given intervals in the DOMDIV index for the Sheppey sample is shown in Figure 10.2. Clearly, it is overwhelmingly obvious that women do most of the work in the household, given that positive scores indicate that the domestic division of labour is more unequally shared by women. Furthermore, in the majority of households, not only do women take a larger *share* of domestic work as a whole, they also do substantial *amounts* — as the skew to higher positive scores indicates. The mean DOMDIV value is 15.6 and the full range is from −52.2 to +42.7. There were just a very few exceptional 'male housewives', caring for a physically handicapped or seriously ill spouse.

---

[12] A more comprehensive account showing the results of modelling using regression analysis is in preparation and will be published by Missiakoulis and Pahl in a specialized journal. Further details are available from the authors.

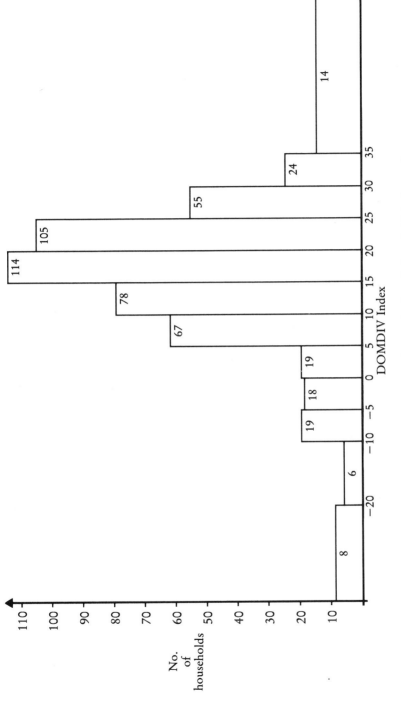

Figure 10.2 DOMDIV distribution of indexes for households in the sample

It will be seen, however, that only 8 men scored −20 or less against 198 women who scored +20 or more. We now turn to discuss in more detail the association of the DOMDIV index with more detailed characteristics of the households in the sample.

Beginning the analysis with social class, the DOMDIV scores are given in full in Table 10.7. It will be seen that there is very little variation between classes, and the social status of the female partner appears to be as important as that of the male. If homologous status is held to be the norm for each class, then the scores are almost exactly the same for each

Table 10.7　Variation in DOMDIV score, by household class

Household class		DOMDIV score	N
Male class	Female class		
1	1	14	6
	2	18	43
	3	17	23
	Housewife	17	14
2	1	10	5
	2	14	100
	3	16	47
	Housewife	17	28
3	1	13	8
	2	13	75
	3	15	120
	Housewife	16	43

of the classes — DOMDIV scores 14, 14 and 15 respectively. However, it is clear that in households where males have partners who are categorized as of lower status or who are full-time housewives, DOMDIV scores tend to be high.

If one takes the category with the largest number in each household class category (determined by the class of the male partner), namely 1.2, 2.2 and 3.3, then the scores fall from 18 in 1.2 through 14 in 2.2 to 15 in 3.3. The lower middle-class socially homologous couples are, however, matched by the 3.2s which have the lower score still of 13. Sharing of domestic labour increases, in general, the lower down the social scale.

Turning now to household economic activity, a most striking and significant finding emerges in Table 10.8. The employment of the female partner has a dramatic effect on the DOMDIV score. Even when the male partner is unemployed, the DOMDIV score remains related to the female partner's employment activity. Hence, the mean score of the five part-time female workers living with unemployed men is 21. If the economic activity of individuals is considered on its own, the mean score for households when the woman is employment in full-time work is as low as 8; whereas the mean score in all households where the man is full-time employed is 16. In households where the male earner is unemployed the score actually rises to 17. No other variable produced

Table 10.8   *Variation in DOMDIV score, by economic activity*

	DOMDIV score	N
Male is in full-time employment and:		
Female partner also F/T employed	10	102
Female partner employed part-time	16	99
Female partner is F/T housewife	22	167

such contrasting results, although the composition and structure of the household is certainly important. Thus, while the score for couples only is 12, that for couples and children is 18. Where the youngest child is under 5 and the female partner is aged 35 or younger, the DOMDIV score rises to 23.

It is important to recognize that the domestic division of labour is related directly to age and stage in the domestic cycle. Some writers on this subject make the entirely unwarranted assumption that the domestic division of labour is somehow fixed and immutable. In the early 1970s there was a tendency for some authors, themselves aged in their late 20s or early 30s, to do research on their peers and then to make generalizations about who did the housework or how the domestic division of labour was inequitably distributed for all ages and all stages of the domestic life cycle. More careful research would surely demonstrate that this is manifestly not so; while the Sheppey Survey shows that the mean DOMDIV score is 19 for households with female partners aged between 26 and 35, this drops to as low as 10 when the female partner is 65 or over. This difference is due partly to the fact that the number of tasks that households carry out reduces markedly over the domestic cycle. By and large, the more tasks done in a household, the higher the DOMDIV score. Households doing 19 tasks had a mean DOMDIV score of 11; those doing 23 tasks had a mean DOMDIV score of 20, and the mean DOMDIV score remained around that mark as the number of tasks increased. The main reason for this is the increased number of entirely 'female' tasks that are associated with child care. Women with young children are almost invariably in households with high DOMDIV scores.

One of the main hypotheses of the original research design was that the way households manipulated and had access to different sources of labour would relate directly to the division of labour by gender within the household and political behaviour outside. However, when the mean DOMDIV score is related to scores on the sources of work scales there are no significant variations whatsoever. Thus, score 2 on the self-prov scale has a mean score of DOMDIV 13 and score 5 on the self-prov scale has a mean score of 14. Similar lack of variation is found on both the formal provision of services (form-prov) scale and the informal labour (inf-lab) scale. The domestic division of labour is related directly to the economic activity of the female partner, the ages of the partners and their stage in the domestic cycle, and to not much else.

Perhaps it might be helpful if the ideal characteristics for a lower (more equal) DOMDIV score were set out. Ideally, the female partner should be over 45, in full-time employment in a Class 2 or Class 1 occupation, living with a Class 3 male partner on her own. To get peak domestic division of labour conditions (to the woman's advantage) the man should be in part-time employment. If the woman is in a Class 1 occupation she would be better off living with a Class 2 or Class 3 male. Her situation could be improved a little more by having another adult person in the household. The woman will probably get the best domestic division of labour situation when she and her partner are retired.

To complete the analysis of DOMDIV scores, it can be reported that there is no significant correlation between DOMDIV scores and voting behaviour. There is some slight indication that men in households where tasks are more equally distributed will be more likely to vote Labour, but the distinction is marginal.

This analysis of the domestic division of labour, based on the 526 Isle of Sheppey couples, points without question to the overwhelming importance of the age and economic activity of the female partner in affecting the household's domestic division of labour. Those who have emphasized the importance of class analysis have underestimated, in this context, the crucial importance of the domestic cycle.

In order to check the foregoing analysis, household DOMDIV scores were put into bands, with scores less than 0 being classed as 'low', 0-7 as 'medium' and scores of 8 or above as 'high'. It is then possible to analyse what kinds of households were most likely to fall within each band. This analysis is complementary to that which was based on mean DOMDIV scores. For the sample as a whole (that is the 526 couples), 10 per cent were in the 'low' category (more likely for men to take a greater share in

Table 10.9   Various household characteristics, by DOMDIV bands (percentages)

DOMDIV band	All	Female partner 35 or younger with youngest child under 5	Couple with no children, female partner over 35	Both partners in full-time employment	Owns dwelling	Dwelling rented from council
Low	10	—	15	18	9	15
Medium	9	8	11	22	11	3
High	81	92	75	61	80	82
Total (N)	526	92	150	102	399	94

Table 10.10   Household social class, by DOMDIV bands (percentages)

DOMDIV band	All	Male class:	1				2				3			
		Female class:	1	2	3	4	1	2	3	4	1	2	3	4
Low	10		—	2	4	14	40	10	8	7	12	11	12	9
Medium	9		33	12	4	—	—	13	2	7	12	15	8	5
High	81		66	86	91	86	60	77	89	86	75	75	80	86
Total (*N*)	526		6	43	23	14	5	100	47	28	8	75	121	43

domestic tasks), 9 per cent were in the 'medium' band and 81 per cent were in the 'high' band — the conventional households where the female partner did most of the domestic labour. These results are presented in Tables 10.9 and 10.10.

Clearly, when both partners are in full-time employment there is the least likelihood of the conventional pattern of the domestic division of labour. However, 61 per cent are in the 'high' category compared with 96 per cent when the male is in full-time employment and the female partner is a full-time housewife. Evidently, when the children are young and the female partner is not in employment there is much greater likelihood of an asymmetrical domestic division of labour. However, it is most important to recognize that this is a transitional and relatively short-lived period. For much larger periods in the life cycle domestic tasks will be shared more equitably. It is interesting that class is a less significant variable relating to the domestic division of labour than is employment activity. Household classes 2.2 and 3.2 appear to share tasks the most. Of greater interest is the direct relationship between the number of hours the female is engaged in employment and the proportion of households in the three DOMDIV bands, as shown in Table 10.11.

The more hours the female partner is in employment, the less conventional is the domestic division of labour. Conversely, the *fewer* the hours that male partners are in employment the less conventional is the

Table 10.11   Hours of work spent in employment, by respondent by DOMDIV bands

DOMDIV bands	All		Hours in employment per week							
			30 or less		31–40		41–50		51 or more	
	M	F	M	F	M	F	M	F	M	F
Low	10	9	17	6	8	11	9	33	6	33
Medium	9	9	7	5	12	16	3	56	12	17
High	81	82	76	88	80	73	88	11	82	50
Total (*N*)			71	202	95	44	57	9	34	6

domestic division of labour (given that males are, in fact, in employment). Unemployed male partners with female partners as full-time housewives have 89 per cent of households in the 'high', most conventional, band. In the very few households where female respondents were employed on shift work (11 cases), 45 per cent were in the 'low' band and 45 per cent in the 'high' band.

Conclusion

The conclusions from this analysis of the domestic division of labour in the Sheppey households are very clear. Women who are in employment or who are physically incapacitated have, as it were, three choices in relation to a range of conventional domestic tasks: they can leave many of the tasks undone, they can pay someone else to do them, or the male partner can do a greater share. Hence a fairly precise prediction of the domestic division of labour can be made using indicators relating to female activity and stage in the domestic cycle. The fact that the most conventional pattern of the domestic division of labour arises when there are small children under 5 in the household is clearly demonstrated in Table 10.12. But so, equally, is the considerably greater sharing present at later stages of the life cycle when the female partner returns to part-time and, even more, full-time employment.

Table 10.12   Characteristics of selected households and DOMDIV scores

	DOMDIV	N
Couple households where woman is aged 35 or younger and		
Has no children	14	42
Has youngest child under 5	23	92
Has youngest child aged 5–15	18	61
Woman is 36 or over and has		
Youngest child aged 5–15	17	37
Youngest child 5–15 and other person(s) in household (probably older children)	15	43
Has no children under 15 but has other person(s) in the household (possibly other children or other relatives)	15	83
Only partner in household	12	150

11

Polarization of Workers' Lives:
Jim and Linda; Beryl and George

On the Problems of Description

I do not imagine that my descriptions of the division of labour in the last three chapters have been consistently easy reading. Given the size of the Sheppey survey, I felt that the overwhelming priority was to be precise, and, in presenting cross-tabulations, scales and complex statistical procedures, I have deliberately eschewed quotation and anecdote that might have brought them alive.

There are well-known devices for the codification and identification of selected quotations. Many studies, based on relatively few intensive interviews, have to report, as far as possible, what people said, since that is the main source of information available to the reader: presenting the data in tables with very small numbers in each cell can be very misleading. Larger surveys, such as the Sheppey survey, generally give respondents the opportunity to comment in their own words in answer to certain questions, and these are the comments that are typically categorized, filed in a card index system and, as it were, brought out on demand to illustrate a point. In the case of the present study, a number of extensive interviews were held with thirty-two selected households, often at considerable length, sometimes involving two or more visits.[1] All these interviews were recorded on tape and many of them were transcribed. In addition, a number of further interviews were held in two carefully selected areas of the Island in order to explore the interactions between respondents, providing a cross-check on their responses. Gathering this information was very time-consuming and so, too, was its analysis. Files of data on distinctive categories of households were assembled. Appropriate quotations were laboriously coded and filed in the accepted way, ready to be slipped into the text at the appropriate place to provide stylistic support for the author — and some relief for the reader. So, putting in the *vox*

---

[1] These interviews were carried out by Claire Wallace and myself and they formed an essential part of the overall investigation, only aspects of which are reported in this present study. I interviewed those who are the subjects of this chapter and I have changed their names to make it less easy for them to be identified.

populi would have been easy, since all the preparatory work had been done.

It seems unreasonably perverse and over-scrupulous to deny the reader these expected aids to empathetic understanding. The essence of the argument of the last three chapters is the complexity of, and inter-connections between, household work practices and sources of labour. If I had attempted to demonstrate the divisions of labour by using single quotations from the many different and diverse households that were studied, it would have done violence to the complexity that the interviews revealed. There would, I felt, have been a danger that such quotations would have both simplified and insulted the humanity that the figures, on inspection, soon reveal. I decided instead to give some perspective to the themes and arguments of the preceding chapters by two case studies.

The first of the two households chosen is presented at considerable length. Again, careful consideration was given to how such cases should be described. One possibility was to present little vignettes of different households — those who receive much informal labour, such as the elderly; those who share the domestic division of labour almost completely equally, such as a fireman married to a nurse; those who are very heavily involved in informal work for others; the unemployed, the self-employed and those who had built their own dwellings;[2] the affluent workers of Sheppey; the 'male housewives' and so on. However, the inevitable result of such a presentation would be confusing and idiosyncratic. It was clear, for example, that there were almost as many distinctive styles and circumstances of households in which there was considerable symmetry in the way couples shared the labours of the household, as there were households in that category. To pick on one would be to over-emphasize firemen or whatever. There would be little point in providing a quantitative analysis, specifically designed to get a measure of the patterns of the divisions of labour, and then to undermine it by cases that seemed to fit a stereotype or even by the intuitive construction of 'ideal types'. This may appear to be labouring a point, but it is extremely important: the intention is to communicate as clearly as possible, with a diversity of approaches and research styles, who does what work, when, for whom and for how much (if it is paid). The survey provided a snapshot: that is what people reported about their formal employment, their sources of labour and their domestic divisions of labour in the spring and early summer of 1981. Change could be inferred

[2] We referred to these as homesteaders. A surprisingly large number of Sheppey households had done this (7 per cent of the sample). This particular household work strategy cannot be held to be of very general significance for Britain as a whole, but it does illustrate superbly the way all members of a household can work together for a common goal. This category has been the object of a special study by Claire Wallace as part of the SSRC-funded project. A preliminary account of this strategy was presented to the World Congress of Sociology at Mexico City in 1982: R. E. Pahl and C. D. Wallace, 'The restructuring of capital, the local political economy and household work strategies: All forms of work in context.'

only by internal analysis of the characteristics and behaviour of distinctive cohorts in the sample. This is a weakness that can be partially overcome with more intensive analysis of a small number of households.

As I mentioned in the Introduction, I started on this work with the aid of a small grant from the Nuffield Foundation for which I am very grateful. I spent the academic year 1977-8 interviewing intensively a few households that were referred to me by a clergyman in Rochester and doctors on the Isle of Sheppey. I asked them to direct me to households that were in a variety of different circumstances, since at that stage I was not clear what I was looking for, or what a household work strategy actually was. Using this rather arbitrary method was evidently a hit-or-miss approach, but had the merit of giving me a complete and willing entrée. The doctors simply said, 'There's a professor who would like to talk to you at length about how you and your family are managing with the high inflation and so on. Would you be prepared to chat with him? It will all be completely confidential.' (This was said in 1978.) Hence when I arrived at people's doors saying, 'Dr — said you'd be ready to have a chat with me', I was welcomed in at once (on one memorable occasion with the words, 'Come in, I hear you want to know about my fiddles').[3]

The first case reported in this chapter began, therefore, in 1978 and was continued with the support of an SSRC grant. Other cases were also followed through but not in the same depth. I had no knowledge of what the household was like or, of course, what would happen to it. I have tried to present the first case of Linda and Jim more or less chronologically so that the reader moves through five years of the household's life. I have also allowed the respondents to say as much as possible in their own words. My main editing was simply in reorganizing the sequence of what they said. All the interviews were tape-recorded, and I both read the transcription and listened to the tape in preparing the account that follows. Towards the end, when readers are more familiar with the way Linda and Jim speak, I put in more commentary and summarize events, largely to speed up the story. The way Linda expresses herself is as important as the content of what she says. My hope is that the reader will get some understanding of process from this account.

While I have re-ordered material within the context of one interview, I have not moved material between interviews. I was learning more about the household each time I went. These formal interviews — six in all — lasted for at least two hours and sometimes longer. However, I visited the house on many occasions between interviews. This clearly led Linda and Jim to think about what I wanted to find out and perhaps, to that extent, the later interviews are less 'pure' than the earlier ones. On the other

[3] Much of this work was reported in R. E. Pahl, 'Employment, work and the domestic division of labour', *International Journal of Urban and Regional Research*, 4(1), 1980, pp. 1–20. The case studies of that article appear in the Appendix.

hand, Linda and Jim can claim that they have given more consistent opinions and that is what they would prefer to have recorded. This is a position that must be respected. They knew I was writing a book and they knew they would figure in it. Linda and Jim have read what I have written and they will think about that as the interviews continue over the years ahead. My intention is to provide a document of life where the divisions and sources of labour can be seen as much as a process as a pattern.

The choice of Linda and Jim for the first case made it clear that the second case had to be an affluent manual worker in order to illustrate the theme of polarization, which is emerging as one of the main conclusions of the Sheppey study.[4] This second household will be introduced later.

LINDA AND JIM

Linda and Jim live in a council house in what is held to be one of the rougher parts of Sheerness. The front room is comfortable and well furnished and Jim has now built a bar in the corner. The room behind is warm, friendly, with piles of newly-washed clothes and other signs of an orderly domestic routine. The kitchen leads off this, jutting into the garden. Jim parks his car in the front garden. The house is cluttered with a superfluity of stuff of one sort or another — but this gives a friendly and welcoming impression. A cup of tea appears at any time of the day or evening. Linda is a jolly, rather stout woman with a ready grin and a rather husky laugh. When things are treating her well her hair is blonde and she is forever laughing, chatting and cracking jokes. She loves to talk and is very quick to pick up a line of questioning and to add her interpretation of events and circumstances. She likes to explain current differences among her brothers and sisters in terms of their individual relationships with her parents in their early years. It pleases her to draw on the past as a way of explaining the present and she can easily move back and forwards in time as a way of making sense of what she is describing.

Her husband Jim is much less articulate. He does not really like talking about himself and is much more ill at ease. Stocky, well built and with dark hair beginning to turn grey, it is clear that he has spent much of his life in the open air. Gentle, quiet and good natured, he tends to sit quietly while Linda gives forth. However, there always seems to be a close and understanding relationship between them and, as opposites, they appear to complement each other.

---

[4] See R. E. Pahl and C. D. Wallace, 'Household work strategies in economic recession', in N. Redclift and E. Mingione (eds), *Beyond Employment: Household, Gender and Subsistence*, Basil Blackwell, Oxford, 1984.

Linda's Story: 1978

Linda was born in 1944; she was one of twelve children. By 1960, at the age of 16, she had married. Her family had always struggled to get by — even in years of so-called affluence in the 1950s. She described her mother's side of the family: 'well she always says they were true Romanies but they weren't, they were what you call didicoys, you know, a form of gypsies but lower down the scale, because even in that kind of life there's class. You know, you're either up there with the Romanies or you're a gypsy or you're a didicoy, which is the bottom end. And her father was a rag and bone merchant; they used to travel round in an old trailer and they used to work, go from farm to farm, they used to travel round all the season. I suppose they used to get their — I don't know if there was dole money then, or what it was, but they used to get that and still travel round and do the work through the season and then sell flowers and things — you know, pegs in winter.' Linda's mother had always done that kind of casual wage labour and self-employment. Her father, on the other hand, 'never had a job because he had something wrong with his chest, I think it was bronchial asthma — that's what he died of in the end. He was never strong enough to take a proper job.'

So Linda's parents adopted role reversal: 'He used mostly to keep the house while Mum went in the fields. Now and again he would go off and get a bit extra for himself but mainly he was the woman of the house.' He used to breed rabbits to sell them and the children found him a more gentle and approachable person than their mother. 'He was softer than, like, me Mum was, 'cos although we used to get a belt now and again, if you yelled before the belt hit you, you know, you never got it. But it never worked with me Mum.'

Before Linda started school she went with her mother into the fields and, when she was old enough to earn money, she was made to make her contribution to the household income. Linda's mother 'used to keep us home from school in turn to go you know. You'd think you was doing all right until it came to pay-day and you'd see what you earnt — and she'd give you a couple of bob back, you know, you'd think you were going to get a pound note for once in your life. And you never did get it.'

Linda's early life provides a good insight into the socialization of women into casual work and by-employment: until she was 13 in 1957 the whole family used to go off hop picking near Faversham. 'We used to move everything out and go and live in the tin huts that they had. We used to go in the beginning of September and come back at the end of October. We all look back and say, you know, they were the best days of our lives really, they were lovely. Until the machines came in' (and hand-picking of hops was finished). But the whole experience was remembered like a holiday. 'There were so many of us we had to have three huts and Dad knocked them all into one and just put curtains to partition if off. And they used to stuff the mattresses with straw. So we were all there, you know, as kids. We used to go out at five in the morning and you had to pick, you had to work all day and then you could play at night afterwards you know.

'You didn't get paid weekly; they used to pay you — well the parents — off at the end of the season, so you never got nothing all the time. You used to get your groceries in a little tin place. I think the Co-op ran it then, and they'd mark it down and that was all stopped out of your money at the end of the season. But Dad used to get rabbits. We used to live on rabbit pie, rabbit stew and mashed potato and swede because that was all in the fields around us. So they just used to help themselves, you know. Really, I suppose we lived a lot cheaper than we do now; you just used to go and take it and go and snare a rabbit with the dogs. We used to cook outside you know, on the open fires, and Sundays Dad used to get us all outside in a great big tin bath and we was all bathed outside on a Sunday.

'I often say, you know, I wish they'd go back to picking by hand, then I'd take my kids to see what fun they could have and they'd really enjoy it.

'And then we came back to school, like, for the winter term and that was the only time of the year we'd go in new clothes, because she used to rig us all out, out of the hop-picking. That was your reward for working through the season. You had new clothes for the winter season for school.'

At weekends, as soon as she was 14, Linda took casual employment at the holiday camps in Leysdown on Saturdays and Sundays. Then in 1959, when she was 15, she left school and went to work full-time at the holiday camp. 'We was always conditioned with doing domestic, like cleaning or washing up and working in cafes and things like that, you know. When I worked in the Station Cafe — it was then — I was assistant cook and we used to get £2 19s 0d. And all the girls were all going for these canvas white shoes then, with little stiletto heels and they were all buying them. And they said "Well buy yourself a pair and then make it up to your Mum next week. She won't mind." Well, I got them and got them home and she beat them round me head because I hadn't got her money.'

Linda was then just 15, hardly out of school, and she met Jim, who was in the Merchant Navy and was some eight years older. 'You know, when we went to see the vicar in the beginning he thought my husband was marrying me out of pity, you know. He thought I was, sort of, in a bad place: he wanted to get me out of it and, you know, he tried to talk us out of it. You know, the first thing my Mum said? "Well I don't know about that: I'm going to lose her two pound a week house-keeping money." Because we used to have to give her two pound a week. Even if you only earnt two pound and a couple of pennies over, you still have to owe her two pound.

'We got married when I was 16 and I went with him — he just caught the last call up for the National Service and worked for the Colonel and you know he was a batman then. And I worked as a nanny or general help with him and we did that two years and then came back.' It was 1962 and Linda was 18. After his years in the Merchant Navy and the Army, Linda's husband thought he would start up his own little business in Sheppey. There was not much employment in the Island at the time, which had not recovered from the blow of the dockyard closure. So he started up a window-cleaning business. Unfortunately the enterprise failed. 'He got behind with his stamps and tax and things, you know, he got in a bit of trouble with that, so we had to sell the insurance things, give all them up to get us out of that. And we did that twice you know — until you were bashing your head against a brick wall. 'Cos if it wasn't the tax man it was the insurance people that were after him. And I was expecting the last one then and it got a bit, you know, nerve-wracking in the end. You never knew what was going to happen next. So he sold the window-cleaning round to get us out of debt.'

That was in 1972 and the steel mill was just starting up, so Linda's husband got a job on an overhead crane but he could only stand it for a week. 'I think it was a bit nerve-wracking being up there with all that hot metal and everything . . . and the noise. He didn't like the noise.' The higher pay did not provide a strong enough incentive. 'As he said, a man's got to work all his life so, you know, it's better to have regular money, even if it's not a lot. If you get a lot of overtime you get used to it and you live — well, you only live to what money you've got coming in, don't you? I mean, if you've got an extra £20 come in one week it goes, you know, either on extra food or clothes and things.'

In the mid-1960s Linda had started her family and she joined the casualized wage-labour force of East Kent, used by the local farmers to harvest their produce in the way they have done for centuries. 'Well, we all go in the summer, we go in the fields. We used to go in the winter when we all had babies and we used to take them with us. But when they start school you are tied 'cos you've got to take them and bring them back. We usually start off with cherries — perhaps in July — and then we go to peas, beans, strawberries and then apples, pears. And then we go potatoes and greens-cutting and you can carry right through if you've no little ones to worry about — picking brussels and things.' Linda leaves Sheppey for some of this work. 'We travel, we have to travel — the furthest we go is Swanley, you know, on the way to London, or over to the Isle of Grain, which is about one hour's travelling. We all go as a group. Most of the other women are women that are me Mum's age — or they've lived round us all for years. Most of them we grew up with. About eight of us go in an old minibus. It used to be Land Army in the war years but it's called the Kent Land Corps now and they find you work to do. You don't have to pay transport or anything. I always like to go in October 'cos it gets the kids Christmas money — you know, extra for the kids. It's all piece-work. You get so much a box — or on potatoes we did get £7 a day last year [that was in 1975] — but that only lasts about five weeks so you get all you can in those five weeks.' Linda got paid in cash: 'No tax or anything.' This is the general pattern on East Kent farms: casualized shadow wage-labour.

The account so far was given to me in the spring of 1978 when Linda and her husband and their three children (Kim born in 1965, Marilyn in 1971 and Trevor in 1972) were managing reasonably well. 'Well, just, we manage just, you know. We live day to day really and with the kids getting a bit bigger each time, you know, it's just getting more and more difficult to pay out.' The way the money was spent followed custom rather than discussion. 'It's all put in my purse — but if he needs money — I mean, that's up till Saturday because after Saturday there's just enough for the kids' dinner money for school Monday, until I get the family allowance Tuesday. Well, I get my shopping, like groceries, and I've got a freezer so I spend about £25 usually on a Thursday for the things I can keep for the week, you know. I don't buy so much meat now as we did.'

Luckily, Linda's husband is good with his hands and can make or fix anything, and he sometimes earnt extra money using his informal labour. However, he is by nature a shy and retiring man and he did not go out of his way to find such work, although Linda is, as she said, much more pushy. 'A lot of the time it's through me telling people. Well, mostly it's through people saying that they're going to have, perhaps, wardrobes fitted upstairs and then, you know, I'd say, "Well, he's very good at anything like that, you know". But I won't make arrangements for him 'cos I wouldn't like him, you know, to say he'd do it and then he doesn't want to do it, and then, you know, I'll ask him and he'll say, "Well, all right, I'll get on with it".' When it came to charging for his informal labour Jim was vague and just mentioned a figure, completely unrelated to the amount of work he had put into the job. 'He does a lot of work for old people and he doesn't like to charge them too much because they're old. I always say to him, "Well, some of these old people, they've got a lot more money than we have, you know, because they've no kids to feed and clothe." But he is like that with the older people. He likes to help them more than take anything off them.' Money from such informal work was quickly spent. 'If he's got a job and he's got £20 extra we go to Cartiers at Sittingbourne and we go and buy £20 worth of food just for the freezer. When we do get extra money that's where it goes really; into Cartiers freezer shop. But when I'm in the fields, if I'm doing beans or anything or brussels — which we haven't done for a couple of years —

then I would be in pocket because I could do it and do it all in the freezer.'

Linda's informal wages went, traditionally, towards kitting out the children for the new term. 'I don't know why, but it's just a thing we've been brought up that way, after September all the kids have to be rigged out from shoes and coats to everything, you know, for the winter season. I do them one at a time, you know, one week at a time and then, after that, then everything goes into Christmas money for the kids and for the food.' The family has never had a holiday.

Linda and her husband also got extra food from the occupational easements of friends and relatives. Thus, she got bread from her sister-in-law. 'She shouldn't give it away like she does but, you know, if I go up the bakery of a morning she'll give me two nice, hot loaves — or something like that.' That happened most mornings. However, like so much else in Linda's life, that little perk is now finished. 'That's closing down. It's the local bakery — she'll lose her job eventually — I shall find it hard again because it's 28p a loaf now.' Then there's the meat: despite many of her friends and relatives housing deep-freezes stocked with 'free meat' in the early 1970s, Linda did not believe in stealing anything and it was known that the so-called 'free' meat had come out of the docks. 'The only time we have free meat is when my husband cuts the meat up for the farmer, because he sometimes has pigs, you know, and does them for his freezer. Well, if he goes up and joints them all up for him, he gives us a couple of bits of pork out of that.'

Linda felt almost self-righteous about her lack of involvement with the other free meat. When her sister had fourteen legs of lamb in her freezer, Linda had none of it. Although it wasn't offered, she didn't ask for it. However, she had less scruples about other things. 'We've luck, sometimes a farmer we know — he gives us a box of oranges, perhaps once in three months.' I couldn't resist asking with a straight face how the farmer had managed to grow oranges. 'Well, he don't *grow* them, he *transports* them from the docks. They're supposed to be broken boxes, but I don't ask him where they come from. He brings them for the kids. And I had a friend, well my husband's friend really, he works in Mars sweet factory. Often we'll get a few boxes of assorted, different sweets and things. He'll come for the kids. But they don't have pocket money. They used to. When I'm working in the fields, if I'm working through the summer, then they have pocket money. But they've got to know now. If I'm working they have pocket money, but if I'm not they don't get it.'

Coming from a large family, Linda has many relatives on the Island and some of them benefited from the greater prosperity in the 1970s. Some, indeed, were stevedores or steel mill workers. Some had wives in full-time employment and live in luxury in their own homes in Minster or Halfway. Others had grown-up children living at home and collectively acquired substantial household incomes. Linda was conscious of being the poor, rather struggling one and she was reluctant to own up to her difficulties. 'If I needed money, I was in trouble with a debt or something, I could go to any of my brothers then but, you know, I've been near enough that situation at times but I wouldn't go and ask them, although I know I could, but we've always managed to get out of it, you know.' One of her sisters was married to someone who got good money on shifts at the steel mill, but Linda did not appear to be envious: 'It's nice to see her get it now because she had it rough in the beginning.' Her brother, next door but one, was a stevedore: 'He never held down a job until he got into the stevedores and that was only because his wife's uncle was a foreman or something in there that he got in . . .' There was really a remarkable range in wealth among Linda's siblings: one had just come back from a holiday in Spain, but Linda, who has never had a holiday, showed no envy. 'I mean some of us have, you know, got more than others. But they've all had their . . . but I think when you're brought up like we were you can face hard times more than somebody that's been brought up with having everything because you can adapt yourself just as much to go down as you can up, you know.'

For six years Linda's husband had been working for a firm based on Sheppey, which contracted to moor the oil tankers taking raw material to the BP oil refinery on the Isle of Grain. They also transported the crew of the tankers back and forth while they were in docks. He worked a shift system: 24 hours on and 48 hours off. This was convenient, since he then had time to use his informal labour to make some extra money.

In my talks with Linda, I was impressed by the clarity with which she could perceive her situation in its context and the objective way in which she gave me an account of all the members of her very wide-ranging family on the Island. She told me about their marriages, how they managed their money and their various problems. I was then encouraged to go and talk with them, which I did, gradually building up a picture of a large and complex working-class family. Some were doing better, some less well, but, by and large, in 1978 and 1979, the family was getting by. There was a gap between my year's pilot study and the main SSRC-funded project, which was due to begin in October 1980, so I did not get back to have another long talk with Linda for some months.

The pendulum swings: 1980

Between 1978 and 1980 Linda and her family flourished. At the time of my previous visit, Linda had been to her doctor who diagnosed that she had an arthritic hip and would not be able to work in the fields anymore. As she put it: 'I'd always had it in the spine, but then they found out the hip and he said "no more spud-bashing for you, you know, that's your lot".' But that was only a short-term setback and Linda was extremely fortunate in getting a job with the home help service cleaning in old people's houses, for which, working in the mornings only, she got 'about £32 after stoppages. Well, the most I had was about £54. That's going till about 3 o'clock in the afternoon or starting off early in the morning. That makes a lot of difference.'

As a result of having two regular incomes in the household, there was, for the first time since the household was formed, a degree of financial security. As Jim, her husband, was now getting about £85 a week net, their combined income enabled them to get by quite well. As Linda said with some pride, 'last year we got on our feet, you know, paid all our bills and things and bought all the kids clothes and things for school, that type of thing, then you don't have to worry. And then when a big bill comes in, like after Christmas last year, I could help him pay the bills off and we still had a few quid.' Things were so good for the household that they decided to have a holiday — for the first time ever — and they went to a Butlins holiday camp for a week, which was a great success. 'We really worked hard and saved up for it and the kids loved it and we both enjoyed it, you know, we enjoyed ourselves and we were sort of looking forward to going again next year 'cos the kids wanted me to book up when we were there, 'cos you get £20 off and at that time we couldn't afford it and we said we'd see after Christmas, you know, and if everything goes well we'll come back again. That was the first time, you know, and I thought it was lovely. We all carried on talking about it for weeks afterwards because we had such a good time. You know, we was all right for money and, you know, we sort of had our holiday and come back and we still weren't short of money. Didn't come back to any bills and we weren't broke when we came back. But that's the end of that. We won't be going this year.'

Two weeks before Linda told me this her husband learned that, at the age of 43, he had been made redundant. This catastrophe hit the household most cruelly just when everything seemed to be working out well and they had reached some degree of modest prosperity on between £120 and £140 a week. They had a few weeks to think through the implications. Their eldest daughter was leaving school in the spring and the hope was that she would find employment, and Jim was at that stage hopeful of finding something else soon. But the first issue they considered was the question of Linda's employment.

'I've been talking to different people and they said, "Well, you know, you want to give up your job" and I said, "Why?" and they said, "Well, you're only allowed to earn so much and what you earn over that they take off of him when he puts his claim in, so you're no better off for going to work, you know, you're going to get just as much money for staying at home." But I don't want to do that because I like the job. It's all with old people and I get on well with them. I like the job and it just gives you an extra bit of money so that you don't have to look in your purse and think "Oh, I can't spend that, that's for something." At least you've got a couple of quid in your purse market day — if I want to treat the kids I've got a couple of pounds to do it. [Also] I think it gets you out of the house, you know. And then you've got something else to talk about. The old people have always got something to tell you. I'm out for five hours and then I come in and busy myself until the kids come in and then I have to sit and listen to them, you know, what they've had going on all day. Otherwise, you're stuck in from 9 o'clock when they go to school and when he's been away you just — well, you feel you've wasted really. You think "What am I doing sitting here not doing myself or anybody else any good?".'

How the household gets the work done

Linda's eldest daughter, Kim, does her share of the domestic work. 'She washes up every night and then, as I do the washing, she'll start the ironing. Sometimes she gets a bit fed up with it, you can't blame her, can you? 'Cos there's five of us. Sometimes I do a weekend for an old lady over the road and then she'll hoover all through, and a couple of Sundays ago, I wasn't feeling at all great and she cooked the Sunday dinner. Yes, she's pretty good.' During the school holidays the two younger children presented a problem when both parents were in employment. 'Usually my Mum takes my youngest one with her to the pub where she cleans for my brother and then there's Marilyn, my middle one, and Kim — she'll keep everything clean and keep it all down for me and I'm normally only over the road, you know, so it's handy, I can pop in and out and if anything's wrong they know where I am. Normally, when they're on holiday I make a list and pin it up in the kitchen, sort of, where I'm going to be, the address and everything, so that if my eldest wanted me she'd know where.'

Linda is fortunate in that Jim too does substantial cooking and cleaning and child care. 'He doesn't think that there's any jobs that he won't do because it's woman's work. If it needs doing and I'm out at work, he'll do it anyway. It's like the oven — I hate cleaning the oven but he'll do the oven because he knows I detest doing it . . . But you know, that's one of the jobs I detest doing and he'll do them.' Jim is a good cook, he learnt this in the Merchant Navy, and he also spends a lot of time with the children. 'Oh yes, he's very good to the kids. Well, you know, where he'll sit down and do all that. Things they make, he'll give them, tell them "Why don't you do this, I'll make you, knock you up something in wood. You can do it. I'll get you some paint." And he'll go out and buy paint and things for them to do. And he'll sit and do things with them where I don't, 'cos I don't sit still long enough to do things like that. . . .

'He takes them to school and he collects them when he's home. Always. I think they're close to him. I think, in fact they are, really. Like he wasn't here yesterday. He was away for 24 hours and I was locking up, you know. Doing the things he normally does. And we'll go upstairs and even the youngest one will say, "Cor, isn't it funny without Dad here", sort of thing. And then he'll say this morning, when he went off to school, "Daddy be picking us up tonight? My Dad'll be home tomorrow?"

'Like, he'll get their tea tonight and I'll get our tea later, his and mine, because we have ours later. He'll do that and he'll probably have washed up.

'Oh yes, we've always shared jobs. He's always been like that, good. He's not changed at all over the years.' No matter how hard I questioned Linda it seemed there was nothing that Jim could not or would not do around the house. I suggested that when he became unemployed he might do even more but she doubted that it was possible. He couldn't do more, 'Not to what he does now. I don't think. I mean sometimes I come home and he has done something. He put a cabinet up he'd made — he had some odd pine wood left over from something he'd made — so he made a bathroom cabinet. And he'll come in and he's bought a toothbrush stand thing for a cup and he'll put that up and he won't say anything till someone goes up there and sees it something different. You know, he's always doing different things for other people.'

The looming redundancy cast a cloud over the whole family. Whenever Jim came back from work Linda asked him, 'Anything else happened? Anything else come up? Have you heard about any jobs? And then we start from there.' Linda was sensitive about pushing him into the first alternative job that came along. ''Cos you can't say to a man that's just been made redundant; you've got to put the ideas his way and let him think they're his anyway. You know, it's not for me to say you've got to take that job because, you know, because I want you to take that job, so I haven't got to worry about money. But what he decides I'll go along with and I know it'll be for the best anyway.'

The transition from school to . . .

Linda admitted that she was worried about the future. The few short months of security were over. She was more worried about whether her elder daughter, Kim, about to leave school in the spring of 1981, would find employment. 'If I could see a way of Kim getting a job and being settled, I'd be all right; I'd concentrate more on what we're going to do, but I want to get her sorted out first. She thought she had a job lined up but I phoned up again last night and he said no, he couldn't take her on after all. She wanted to stay on in the beginning and then they said there wasn't much . . . she'd come out with some CSEs but not good grades, you know, in the biology, because that's the only thing she likes. And they told her, it's not worth staying on for that . . . She wants to do farm work, or anything to do with animals, outdoors. I suppose that stems from being with me in the fields, from babies, see. And she just can't bear the thought of going and being shut in again. Somebody told me that a farmer up at Elmley up at the other end of the Island . . . And I got in touch with the farmer and apparently he'd only take students from the agricultural college, you know. She has to be in that line. She wants to go in and learn from the bottom and see what she could do after that. But he didn't want to know.'

Finding a job when her father had just been made redundant added a burden on a young girl's shoulders when she was only just 16. Linda reported how she felt. 'She said, "Oh, you know, they can't do that to you, Dad, can they?" And he said, "Yes, they can" and she said, "But that's not fair. You've been there a long time. Why is it you? Why don't they . . ." And he said, "Well, it's not only me, there's ten . . .". She said, "Yes, but why have you got to be one of them? You always go to work. You don't take time off." You know. Why should her Dad get it because he always goes, he never mucks them about. And then she says, "Well, what are we going to do then?" Then she'll say, "Well, don't worry, I'll be leaving school soon." And she's not sort of looking that she hasn't got a job. She's not looking at that. She's thinking, you know, we haven't got to keep her once she leaves school, and she thinks that makes a lot of difference, but really it won't make any difference at all.'

Kim is a willing girl, who doesn't mind hard work, and so, as Linda says, 'You'd think it wouldn't be too hard to get a job — but on the Island it's going to be. And I wouldn't like to think she'd have to go off the Island 'cos I think I've never gone off the Island much. I think I'd worry what was happening to her.'

Linda knows pretty well what will happen when poverty strikes, but her daughter finds it hard. She has got used to getting new shoes and clothes. 'But you know,' says Linda, 'if it came to the worst I'd go back to going to the jumble sales on Saturday and looking in the Spastic Shop. I don't think you ever get out of that, 'cos even before we went on holiday, instead of buying swimming costumes I was going into the Spastic Shop and looking for them in there and then saying to them, "If you get one in, hold onto it for me". 'Cos when I looked at the price of a swimsuit, I thought "Cor blimey, you don't think I'm going to pay that!".'

Then, talking with her daughter about the redundancy, Linda remarked, 'She doesn't seem to sort of worry about it. She says, "Oh well, we'll manage, Mum, won't we?" And I said to her, "Probably you'll have to go back to jumble sales", and she hates jumble sales. She says, "Oh no, I'm not going back to that".'

But Linda recognized that they would have to get back to that. Very reluctantly she decided to cut back and not do more than twenty-one hours a week in her job, but to hang on to that amount even if she then had to lose some of her earnings in taxation. She and Jim spent many hours talking over the future. 'We decided like whereas before we weren't that well off — before I went out to work regularly — we only, sort of, we had his money, and it wasn't all that great, but it was enough to keep going. But you know what we were saying is, it's easier for us to come down to not having much again than it is for somebody who's had big money all the time.'

Nevertheless, in contrast to our talks in 1978, Linda was, in 1980, rather more resentful of the labour aristocracy on the Island. 'I don't think it's right, 'cos even now in this dock if there's not many ships in you see the dockers go down to work and you see them come home just after 9 but then they're on pay all that time. They're home and then you've got other men that've got to work solid eight hours, you know, do a really hard day's work, and don't get as much money as they do for it. Well, I think, you know, people like me around the Island are getting a bit bitter about it, 'cos, you know, well, they think they're the untouchables, they are.'

In addition to the money Linda and Jim earned formally and informally, there were two other sources of money in the household. Kim was looking after three children on Saturdays and got £7 for working nine and a half hours from 8.30 a.m. to 6 p.m. 'But the woman has started to put on her. She went yesterday instead of Saturday and she didn't come in until half past eight and she still only paid her the £7. She started to bath the kids and do a bit of cleaning. I'm saying to her, "Don't do it, 'cos once you start it, that's your job from then on".'

The other source of income came from Kim's friend who had a deformed lip and whose mother had seemingly rejected her. Kim had felt sorry for her and brought her home, and the girl's mother was apparently glad to be freed from the responsibility of looking after her and paid for her board at intervals. 'We treat her in the same way as we treat our own kids but she's remedial. She's very backward. She still goes to Sheppey School, 'cos they have special classes for very backward children, though I've noticed a lot of difference in her since she's been with us. She used to sit and keep her face covered up when she was eating and she doesn't do that. She's even started to help around the house, which is a big help to my eldest girl. She can do the ironing . . . Like she was here yesterday because my daughter was doing her job up looking after these kiddies and she said, "Anything you want me to do?", and I said, "You can peel the spuds if you like while I go and do one of the old girls, sort of thing." And she did that.'

Despite the ups and downs of the struggle to get by, under reasonably stable circumstances Linda could keep the house together: the work got done and they could achieve some modest comfort and happiness. The members of the household were not afraid of hard work, they liked to help others and they were generous with their time and emotions. Their standards of honesty and decency shone through and there was a considerable concern for the troubles of others. They liked being together. Linda says, 'I like it in the winter more than anything 'cos when they're all in and it's dark at 6, I know everyone's in and I feel sort of locked in and secure and safe. You know, we're all right, nothing can happen to us, we're all in together.'

Then Jim was made redundant. In October 1980 he was still in employment, but his days were numbered: I talked to him about how he felt and how he'd managed his life so far.

Jim's Story: Autumn 1980

Jim's father was in the Admiralty and his family had moved into Kent from Surrey, where the climate was not good for his sister's health, coming to the Island in about 1950. His father took early retirement when the Customs shed closed in Sheerness and he now lives with his wife in Leysdown. Jim visited his parents regularly — at least two or three times a week. They own their home and have never lived in a council house. They did not approve of Linda when Jim first got married, but there are no problems now. Jim does lots of jobs around the house for them.

Jim was 43 when he became redundant and had been with that employer for eight years. Before that he had done a variety of jobs, in addition to the period of self-employment described by Linda. He had worked on the dredgers at Greenwich, and had had a number of tasks in the building trade — including work on constructing the M2 motorway. During his six years of self-employment in the 1960s, he did general repairs, window cleaning and so forth. For a time he worked for Sheppy Fertilizers, popularly known as the glue factory: 'That wasn't very nice, you know. First job they gave me when I went there was cutting up dead carcasses with an axe and I wasn't very keen, but I saved it until I got another job — which is the way things went, from one job to another.' For Jim a good job is an interesting job. 'I don't like doing the same thing all the time — well, the same as everyone. I don't think anyone likes doing repetitous work — assembly line or something like this. I don't think anyone likes this very much. But I'd say I like to be outside — I like to work on the water. I'd go on the water anywhere — even in winter. I'd sooner go there than in a factory all the time.' But would he go back to the glue factory rather than go on the dole? He remembers how hard it was: 'I've been humping for 12-hour shifts and you had to sling about 90-ton bags over a period of twelve hours. You come home and sit down and go to sleep. I think it would be better to be on the dole than that. The plant was making fertilizer and we was at the other end of the plant. There was, like, a big hopper that fills up with granular fertilizer and there's an old chap at the top filling bags up and they go through a sewing machine and then we had a trolley and we had to catch the bags as they came off the end of the shute and stack them on the trolley — a ton on the trolley and we had to stack them 20 ft high, so we had to keep throwing them up and it would go up again. This doesn't happen today, does it? It's all forklifts — it just isn't the same. As I say, I think it would be better to be on the dole than to do that kind of job again. I don't think I could do it now anyway. But there's no job on the Island that I wouldn't do. Nothing really. I'd even go back to the glue works.'

As we spoke, Jim knew there was no escape from the inevitable: 'If nothing changes I should be redundant by Friday and then we get two months' pay in lieu of notice.' Now, whose fault was that?[5] How had he lost his employment? Bad management? Declining profits? World recession? Greedy workers? Very slowly, Jim and I pieced the story together — the events, the arguments and his feelings about it all.

One man's redundancy:
Renegotiating the division of labour in Jim's company

'It was only about two weeks ago, they told us. Work has been falling off. There's so much oil — it's gone up so much: it's so expensive, it's not selling and the bulk of our work being with oil tankers, it's just not coming in. The ships just aren't coming in. The refinery over at the Isle of Grain is full up. They're more or less using it as a storage depot. They're not refining much.

'Well, they just told us, they told us that they wanted ten redundancies, that's what they said, the management. There's been redundancies before — a few years ago. You get in a peculiar position sometimes: the shop steward wants to go. He wants redundancy money because I think he's going self-employed, so the redundancy money will help him. They came down and wanted eight in the end, and then we got some older chaps, they decided to retire early and others wanted to go for other jobs, so really it brought it down to just two: me and another chap.

'Well, I'm a bit angry. I'm not bitter but I am a bit angry — not so much with my employer, although I am a bit angry about it — but with the chaps at work, you know, at the moment. That'll probably wear off, you know, but it's when you've more or less lived with somebody for eight years, you know, you expect them to give you a bit of support when something comes along, you know. Not to consider themselves, as they are doing. I know a few of them are more concerned with keeping a shift system rather than a day-work system because they want to carry on with their part-time work as well. You see, we work 24 hours on at the moment and we're 48 hours off — and all of them do part-time work — I think they earn more at that than they do at work. Mostly in the building trade. I know a few are more concerned at losing that than changing the

[5] For a very similar account and similar responses, see C. Wadel, 'Now whose fault is that? The struggle for self-esteem in the face of chronic unemployment', *Newfoundland Social and Economic Studies*, no. 11, Memorial University of Newfoundland, 1973.

system to try and help alleviate the redundancies. Well, this is my feeling, anyway. This is what it appears. When the question of redundancies first came up, the first thing I heard people talking about at work were — not redundancies — but what they were going to do if they were going to go on the day-work system. How are they going to do their other jobs. And it surprised me, you know.

'Out of the sixteen that's left, there'd be about six or seven out of them that have got other jobs. I don't really know because there's three separate shifts and the only time you see the other men is when you're changing over, so it's a job to say. I know some of them have, some of them have just got little ones like I have. The others are earning more in their part-time jobs . . . there are a couple of lads like that, you know, out delivering milk three or four times a week and I know it's a job to give it up when you're used to it. It's awkward really — but they're not all like that — there's just a few and these few seem to be able to sway the rest.'

Paradoxically, the union was being used to protect the interests of the men with second jobs rather than those like Jim who just happened to be one of the two last in who were being forced into redundancy. Worst of all, the shop steward seemed to be almost a willing accomplice to the management's plans. 'They don't like him very much but the trouble is when you're in a situation like we are, you're in a minority. When it comes to voting for anything, like, see we're in a difficult situation. Our job can't be worked without overtime, you know, the way the job's worked it can't be done any other way. To keep us on, where you might get three or four hours' overtime in a week, they'd have to pay a man a full week's pay, to retain him to do that four hours a week. It's a service industry; we're not producing anything, you see. They asked the men if they could think of a system themselves, and there's all kinds of things being bandied about, but nothing has really come of it and, well, in my opinion, it's a bit of a mess.

'Surprisingly, you don't know people until something comes up, do you? It was suggested that they took a cut in pay to help things along, you know, but the majority of them did not want to know. We've discussed it. I don't want to argue about it. We'd be out-voted anyway, so it's a bit pointless arguing about it. I mean, they know our feelings of course. It's surprising really — you've been with men — we've practically lived together. We're with each other all the time for 24 hours a day. Oh yes, I think they've let us down. Even if they had to go, I'd like to see a bit more of a fight about it, you know.

'I've always been in the union and I shall still carry on being in the union because the union's the men, isn't it? It's not a thing, is it? It's the men you're working with. I mean, you could have a completely different crew of men in another job. It would be completely different.'

Another serious problem that Jim raised was that the employees did not trust the employer: they felt that the latter had too strong an incentive to be deceitful. And the men had long memories of incidents which influenced their contemporary attitudes.

'If they could believe what their employers tell them, I think you'd find it would be a completely different story. If the employer comes in and says, "right, boys, we're having it rough, we're hard up", the employees don't always believe him. We know what happens — the money is drawn from the company that's making the money and goes into the other holding companies and they can show their books are empty. If you knew the truth of it, I'd work for nothing — or for example to eat — if I knew it might be all right later on and I knew he was telling me the truth. Oh aye, you'd find the men would work harder, even if they was getting less money, if they knew the company or firm they was working for was in trouble. They're quite willing to take a cut in wages, I believe, to help them out, if they could believe what they was told. The few that have got jobs are swaying the others. The others would most probably change their minds if they could believe what they were being told. It's a question of believing, 'cos you've seen some funny things happen on the job, they was crying out that the company was hard up and they wanted to get rid of some men and one thing and another.' The owner of the business and his son, now the manager since the death of his father, had a meeting with the union, and in the midst of the discussion the more inexperienced son spoke out of turn. As Jim put it, 'The son piped up and said "well, we only made £30,000 the last two months" and the chap that was there at the meeting said, "If looks could have killed he'd have dropped dead." But there was no work at all and that's where we got the idea that they had a retainer from BP to keep the men there — for emergencies and the like, without doing any more — and this is where the disbelief comes in. You know, they say they're hard up — they might be, but you can't really believe them. It's just a matter of having trust with them, in what they're telling you — which I think it the big downfall of the way things go in the country, you know: men just don't trust them.'

Jim and I got into a lengthy discussion about how things seemed to have gone so wrong. His stance was fundamentally fatalistic. There was no chance of doing anything in the union, the government was mishandling the situation in his view, the politicians were just in it for what they could get, and the working people were basically greedy. Gradually, as the discussion developed, Jim came round to two main themes: the fundamental nature of work and the inequitable distribution of the world's resources. Overall he felt confused, puzzled and helpless.

'I suppose it all boils down to money, doesn't it? Money is the only thing that can change things, and where does money come from? It comes from people working. The Third World countries — they haven't got very much: they're going to expect a reasonable standard of living — which you can't blame them, can you? It always annoys me — when you see all these great stacks of corn all rotting and there's all those people hungry. Just 'cos someone won't pay to take it out there. I don't think it's right at all. I think it's bloody wrong: it seems to work on "I've got it and I'm going to keep it." I think there ought to be a fairer system in the world. Perhaps I'm too much of an idealist, I don't know. I'd like to see everything shared out more equally all over the world. As we've got surpluses of this and that, why should we have them when we don't need them?

'Why can't a man go to work if he wants to go to work? You can't see the reason. You think, well surely the way things are going, the country's in trouble, you think to yourself, well surely it's better to go to work, than stay at home with the government paying you money. Economically, to me it seems stupid. Surely it would be better the money they give me to be given to my employer, so that I would keep working? I just can't see the reason for it. How can it help a country by putting people out of work, when they're telling you on the other hand you've got to produce more? Will someone come and tell me? I really can't say much about it; it's confusing to me actually. You just can't see any way out of it, you know.'

Facing life on the dole:
The crucial division — in or out of employment

I asked Jim how he would feel if Linda became the main earner; if he failed to find a job and she went full-time in hers. He was quite cheerful about that prospect. 'Oh well, I wouldn't mind changing roles — I do some of the housework now, you know. We work together and all this and I don't think I'd really mind if *she* didn't mind. I'd have to do the washing, which I don't do at the moment. I help clean up and I cook the meals, but I suppose I'd have to take over the whole lot. I don't mind doing housework. I've done the washing but I never seem to get it the same as my wife does — I seem to associate that more with women, I don't know why but I do.

'I'd look at it this way: if my wife was able to earn more money than me by going out to work, I'd say, well, you go out to work and I'll stay at home! I'd end up a male housewife! It wouldn't affect me at all really. Mind you, I think I'd be a lot more clockwork than a woman. Because I've been to sea, in the services. I'd have days for things, where my wife doesn't seem to. You know, she'll do things when she feels like it, but I'd be more inclined to work to a timetable. I think it is easier in some ways. We both cook (my wife does cook sometimes), but I think it would be easier somehow — if you were in sole charge you'd know what you were doing, and what you'd got, and things like that.'

However, it was important for Jim that this role reversal depended on the *household* as a unit earning its keep. It was important that Linda should *earn* her money, and then he would play his part in a natural (though reversed) division of labour. 'To me that would still be a job — still *someone* earning money. *If it's my wife or me, it would be the same as having a job really* [my emphasis]. I wouldn't be living off the state, in other words.'

Similarly, Jim thought that he would be more content if he could continue in his informal work. 'I suppose it helps mentally if you're producing some little thing or other. But I haven't done it yet so I don't know.' I pushed Jim at this point and asked him if he would prefer to be employed humping heavy sacks: 'The only way I could look at it, I suppose, was if I had this job which is not very satisfying, but it's satisfying in as much as it keeps my family better by going in that job. I suppose that's the only bit of pride you could get out of it — you are keeping your family.

'You get a stigma, especially the children at school when their parents — or their father — is unemployed, you know, they get free meal tickets. Partly because of that I try to keep it away from them — I give them a packed lunch.'

That's what Jim was dreading most: 'Just not being able to provide the things my family have now. If the children come up and want something, they want to buy a book, then I've got to say "no", 'cos I won't have the money. I think these are the things that hurt me more than anything else. You can't provide what they really want, you know. Like the odd 10p or 20p when they go to the shop or something like that, which I don't really know I'd be able to give them. I think that this is the worst. Things *you've* got to go without, you can accept it. It's explaining it to the children why *they've* got to go without. They don't understand. I said to my boy the other day, "you won't have too much of this anymore if I go out of work" and he said, "well, why don't you get another job?" I said, "well, there isn't any" and he says "well, there is jobs: Uncle Steve's got a job." But, as I say, you can't explain it to them can you?'

So in a few days Jim was going to be made redundant. He was more puzzled than angry and not really bitter. The men who would not fight for him had all worked in the Sheerness Dockyard in the past. The curse of the Admiralty employees' docility was there in 1980, twenty years after the closure. Jim was a thoughtful man with considerable talents. But at 43 he was out. 'I'll miss going to work: I enjoy my job. I think I'll miss this more than anything else really. It's the first job I've ever had that I could say "I like going to work".'

And he lost it. At the end of October 1980 he was made redundant. Three years later he was still unemployed. During that period I kept in touch with Jim and Linda and had many formal and informal chats with them. How they coped in those three years is the focus of the next section.

After Redundancy — The Shaping of a New Pattern

Halfway through January 1981, I talked again with Jim and Linda. They had had a good Christmas. They had been using the redundancy money and morale was quite high. 'We bought new furniture for here, something we've never had in the twenty years we've been married. We could really only afford to do this room out of it. And we gave the kids a good Christmas, and he paid his car up and we paid a couple of bills and things up.' But, Linda ruefully remarked, 'I honestly thought ours would go further or last longer than it did.'

After two and a half months of being unemployed, Jim was still hopeful of finding another job and went regularly to the pub to pick up gossip. That was a bit frustrating, as the Island was rife with gossip about new jobs and, as Linda put it, 'You get a lead and you can't find any more about it, so you're everlasting chasing the man who you don't really know to see if you can find out any more information.' As Jim described his frustrations, Linda demonstrated her natural capacity as a sociologist by remarking aphoristically, 'It's true what they say: it's not what you know now but who you know.'

Jim's day had not changed that much. He had always been at home a lot and he had always done work around the house. He had always collected the children from school but now he was getting up earlier — at 7.30 a.m. — and took them in the morning as well. He was also cooking more: 'more often than not he cooks the dinner', and Linda continued: 'I like him being at home rather than at work, you know — if we could afford it'.

Jim was watching more TV documentaries: the experience he has been through was raising his consciousness: 'I've been much more aware of politics in the last eighteen months than I ever have been'. And Linda, ever more articulate, elaborated: 'If something like this happens, and it affects you personally, then you start taking more interest of why that's happened to you. And you're looking for something to blame, anyway, so that opens your eyes up and you start thinking about it and taking more notice.' Other people in their family were also feeling the squeeze and Steve, the stevedore, was only getting his basic wage, substantially reducing his household's income since their high earnings were based on generous overtime. Jim explained, forgetting for the moment that he was unemployed, 'my basic rate is higher than theirs.'

There seemed no chance that Jim's old firm would have him back. The men that remained changed the system so that they got more money than they had received before the redundancies. Those in work, therefore, were better off than before. Jim and Linda were bringing in £81 — £30 from Linda's work, £37.50 from 'the dole' and the rest from child benefit. They had been thinking hard about their bills — £14 a week on rent, £7 a week on milk, another £7 on gas and electricity, and 'then there's the insurance man.' Jim remarked, 'I've always had money in my pocket and I haven't got any at the moment.' All the money that was left after the bills were paid went into the purse. Very reluctantly they faced the possibility, or perhaps inevitability, of 'going on social security'. 'We might be better off with Linda being out of work', which was probably true, but 'that's the last thing I want', she said.

Linda was still more worried about her daughter, still with no prospects and then due to leave school at Easter. Kim had lost her Saturday job, since the woman whose children she had been looking after no longer had her own employment. Linda went to the careers officer at the school 'and he told me, "why don't I phone round and find her some work" and I thought "That's what he's there for".' But pity the poor careers officer: he had nothing to offer. What could he say? The likelihood was that Kim would enrol on the Youth Opportunities Programme (YOP) and Linda was scathing about that: 'They get them to do the menial tasks, and they're only getting £23.50, and it's slave labour really. They're using the kids to get this work done at cheap rates and, really, I don't want her to go under. I think it's all wrong. I know she should be doing something but I'd sooner she was here and helped me in the home and keep her own dole money, if it come to that, to buy her own clothes. And then I read in the paper that Margaret Thatcher was saying that if they don't take up these opportunities then she wouldn't give them any dole money. I thought, "I don't know, they're going to get the kids all ways".'

'They just use them and they're everybody's dogsbody — it seems they're using kids and when they give out the unemployment figures for the Island, they're not in it because they're under that thing. It's all wrong, isn't it?'

Both Jim and Linda feared and resented the probing and questioning that applying for supplementary benefit support entailed. They feared that they would lose their last vestiges of independence and pride: 'If you're on social security and you're on *x* amount of pounds each week then you're trapped. You can't improve yourself because you haven't got a job and they won't let you do any part-time work, so what are you to do? I think the only thing you can do is steal, I suppose. Then they still give you social security. I'm beginning to wonder if it does pay you to be honest when you declare everything. You talk to someone and they say "oh you stupid cow, what did you want to tell them that for?" They say, "you're not supposed to tell them that" So you wonder if it's worth telling them everything, and that's why we don't want to apply for social security and why we didn't bother to push the rent rebate, because you've got to sit and tell some woman sitting there, and she wants to know everything, your life history more or less. And you may not even get it. So you think it's a waste of time and you try and do without it.'

Curiously, Linda was still in her part-time job and yet was the one who appeared to be most in distress. 'You've got to keep looking: you've got to worry about it before you get there. People say you've got to live from day to day but you don't just live from day to day. You've still got to be next week or next month, all the time. I think if Kim don't get a job when she leaves school, it's not going to be much of a life for her. I always wanted her not to have the sort of life that I had. I wanted her to be able to have money to spend and to get her to save, and, you know, to start her off well. As each week goes by, you can see that it's not going to happen.'

The family was clearly closely bound together, and the household of six — parents, three children and a lodger — were just about surviving on a little over £80 a week in 1981. But it could not last and they knew it: they had been subsidizing income with the meagre capital of the redundancy money. And it was not simply a matter of crude survival. Expenditure is related to cultural practices: as the ever-perceptive Linda observed, 'it's all the working class but it affects people differently 'cos we've all got different ways of life. I mean, I smoke: I'd hate to give that up.'

Father and Daughter Unemployed: 1982

The next formal interview with Jim and Linda was over a year later in March 1982. I had been calling in from time to time, and I had seen Jim quite regularly in the course of my visits to the Island when I was interviewing the employers as part of the main SSRC project.

In March 1982 things were grim. 'I don't remember them ever being worse than they are now', Linda said. 'I suppose when you're younger you can only remember the good things, but I don't. I mean, the shops that have shut, the new ones that have opened and gone down. I mean Tuesday in Sheerness is the only day that you see lots of people about. And that's only 'cos it's market day . . . On Wednesday it's like a ghost town when you go out. It's bad enough for men on the Island, but I think it's worse for women. If there's a cleaning job going, even if it's a pub cleaning job, it's not advertised because someone knows somebody and has told them. Whereas before perhaps they wouldn't do a pub cleaning job, they'll go and do it now, just to get that extra few pounds.

'We're quite lucky really because I've been here all my life and a lot of people know you and I think being a home help made quite a lot of difference — getting well-known. That means you always know people that need help and somebody, say, will ask me. I did for Kim — she's got one she does for a lady. She does Saturday and Sunday and gets £4, well that's her I help out. Mind you, she earns that over there — well, she's blind and she's completely incontinent so it's quite a job.

'Jim's mother's been ill so we've been having them down on Sundays . . . we have them down as much as we can, Sundays for dinner and tea and quite often mum'll bring something for the tea — the pudding, you know.'

Money was very tight in the household in the spring of 1982. Sadly, they had had to go on supplementary benefit and Jim got £65 a week. Ludicrously, Linda had to give up her job. As she said, 'I was bringing home £36 after tax and stamp and everything and Jim was getting £15 and then we were getting £10.50 child benefit so that was £61.' So it paid her to stop work.

Kim was also 'on supplementary'. 'She gets £33 a fortnight. We can't take any more off her, you see; the social security — they set out what they think she should pay us and they take that off of what they're going to give her anyway, regardless of whether you get it or you take it.'

The household was permanently embattled with the State, struggling with rules, regulations and the niceties of the arithmetic necessary to work out how to get by best. The younger two children were growing fast and Linda felt they needed new coats so she made a claim for assistance. 'I wasn't asking for furs or anything. All I wanted was a couple of parkas from the market — just to see if they'd help. They said no. I said, "Well, I know people who do get it." But they said, "Only in exceptional circumstances". I said, "They've grown out of them, that's the matter with them." They said, "We don't do that just because they've grown out of them." He said, "Well, supposing you had a flood or something like that, then we'd give you two new coats." So I thought I've got a lot of chance of getting two new coats.'

It was clear that the household could not survive in its present state without more money. Jim took the children to school by car (they were just within the three mile limit and so were not eligible for free transport or any allowance) and they also had a phone. Their gas and electricity bills tended to be rather high. So ways and means of getting a few extra pounds here and there had to be explored. But whatever they got, it was a pittance and they worked very hard to get it.

A collective strategy to be a household business

A week or so before I arrived for this conversation in March 1982, there had been a great state of excitement. They had got the idea that they could run a private meals-on-wheels service for the elderly. Jim would do the cooking and both Linda and Kim would join the business, helping, delivering and so forth. When I arrived they were both sitting at a table banging away at a calculator working out their costs. Jim had got a van from his father and was working out how to convert it, installing calor gas cookers and so on. They were wildly excited. Jim had been to see his bank manager who had agreed to a loan and he had found a source of secondhand catering equipment. His brother-in-law got him a card to go to the cash-and-carry and he'd been round the morning of the day I came, gathering the prices of food in bulk. He was bursting to talk figures with me — relative cost of meat and vegetables, propane *v.* calor gas, special insurance schemes, how much he would pay Kim as an employee. The basic plan was to provide forty hot meals every day, including Christmas Day and Boxing Day, to elderly people on the Island.

At last there seemed to be real hope of everyone getting to work: they were bursting with eagerness to work hard. They did not care how many hours they might have to work. They would be working together. They were desperate not to make any mistakes, to get their costings right, and they seemed to have a remarkable capacity to grasp the details and complexities of the operation they hoped to start.

There was a very good reason to expect the scheme to work, since all that was required was for Kent County Council to subsidize the service to a modest extent. The old people were typically without any other resources than the old age pension and could not afford the full cost of the meal. All publicly supported meals-on-wheels services recognize this, and no private scheme could possibly provide a full meal for 65p (which is what the old people pay). However, all the signs were that Kent County Council would support the scheme. The divisional director of social services had given it his support and had been impressed by the capacities of Linda and Jim when he had interviewed them. So in March 1982 all that was needed was formal approval. They were desperate to get started.

Each week I phoned up to find out how things were going, as I was hoping to monitor the way the business developed as a case study. But the weeks went by with no news. I tried to keep their spirits up because by now I was strongly committed to the project. But somewhere in the bureaucracy of Kent County Council the scheme floundered. Casting aside the dispassionate observer role, I raised the matter at the highest level in the county. 'Just the sort of thing we should support.' 'Provide employment and provide a service.' 'Most encouraging that the unemployed have such initiative.' 'Could be an example to follow in other areas with other services.' 'Give a lead to other authorities less ready to support the private sector.'

But Linda and Jim didn't get their support. Jim went to see the group organizing activities for young people in the area and some KCC employees thought that the scheme was going ahead under this other organization's auspices. All was muddle and confusion. It was a terrible blow to them both. They were so sure that it was going to work, and had had so much support from the social workers. It was almost as big a blow as being made redundant. They were being hit alternately by the private sector and the public sector. How could they get their household satisfactorily through life when there was no formal employment and they were legally prohibited from doing odd-jobs?

Linda had to borrow money from her brother to pay the electricity bill. Sometimes she did not have to pay it back. Her parents-in-law paid the telephone. The household was dependent on friends and relatives, but there was something undignified and shaming about it all.

Linda as Head of Household?: 1983

A year later, at the end of February 1983, Linda was clearly struggling. 'You lose a lot of your fight. You're inclined to think is it worth it?' And Jim admits he's disappointed and wonders who to blame — 'Is it me? You think, are you doing enough? But there's not much you can do, you know. I mean, years ago I used to go round all the factories, but now you can't get past the gate. Now they've got a man at the gate, which they never used to have years ago. You just walked in the door.'

Linda's latest idea was to become a relief warden at an old people's home. She would have to be there for 48 hours a week and, while the pay would be only £35 a week, it would have two possible benefits. First, it might well lead to the post of full warden later on, and Linda's experience in the home help service led her to think that she would stand a good chance of getting promoted. Second, she would then be the only full-time earner in the household, and since her weekly wage would be low, it could, she thought, be made up by family income supplement (FIS). This would make them better off than on supplementary benefits because the family could also claim rent rebates. Furthermore, under FIS there would be no disincentive to earn extra money as the rate is fixed on an annual basis. Once again, the household was keyed up in anticipation that a way to get by had at last been found. 'We wouldn't be having any money given us. What we got would be what we were earning. So you just reverse roles and I'll be the breadwinner.'

However, this time Linda was cautious. She'd make absolutely certain she understood the rules and regulations. But it was difficult to find out on Sheppey what the rules were, and she was advised to write to the DHSS FIS Section at Blackpool. A duplicated letter had arrived that morning with one sentence carefully underlined twice in red biro: 'Your family does not include a man who is normally in renumerative full-time work.' Gender discrimination was the latest barrier preventing Linda and Jim from getting by through their own efforts. Jim wondered whether the FIS Act was affected by the Sexual Discrimination Bill. Linda, coming from a home where the mother had been the chief earner, was appalled at the discrimination. She could not understand why, yet again, she was being thwarted. 'You can't change it because when you're dealing with them people it's the government again. They'd say that's the rule. It's mean.'

The State defined the divisions of labour.

'It's silly really because if Jim took a low paid job he would be able to get all the benefits and get all the money made up, but if I take a low paid job I don't get it. And you're still doing it for your family, so you're not depending on the social services. So it must be cheaper for them in the long run and yet they stop you doing it.'

There's much more that could be said about Linda and Jim and in some ways they deserve a book to themselves. Their story is continuing.[6] They are living through the worst time of their lives. Linda will have the last word:

'I think it should have been a time when we should have been on our feet, and sort of sitting back a bit. And you can't do that. All the worry. Marilyn's got a trip going to France. Well, I just couldn't do it. Marilyn's school you can pay in bit by bit; they give you time. But Trevor, though he's the youngest one, he's more caring and, well, "It doesn't matter to me she's going to France, it doesn't matter about me, I don't want to go". So I've been paying for her. I paid the last £5 today because I worked last night. The trip's paid for, but if I don't get any more work like that, she's still going to want something to spend when she goes . . . Oh, that does make me bitter. I'm very bitter about that 'cos I feel that we're wasted, that we've got something to offer and nobody wants it.'

BERYL AND GEORGE

The Other End of the Island

George and Beryl live 'up Minster' in a terraced house in a smart new development. The fresh paint and neat impression enables one to see at a glance that the household is not short of money. I join them in the front room and we distribute ourselves around the three-piece suite. I sit with my back to the window. George, looking tanned, healthy and relaxed, sprawls on the sofa and Beryl sits opposite me on the edge of the chair, slightly askew. All the furniture looks fairly new — there is a very bright, extravagantly designed carpet, a huge plant in the corner and various others dotted about. All the ornaments are brass and there is a kind of picture clock on the wall. There is a range of glossy books, including John Seymour's *Self Sufficiency*, the *Oxford Book of Quotations*, various glossy guides to country houses and gardens, and other dictionaries and works of reference. Two hi-fi speakers are fitted on the wall and there is a collection of records, mostly popular classics.

George is one of the Island's affluent workers. He is a stevedore in the docks and his wife, Beryl, has a part-time job as a cook from 8.30 a.m. to

---

[6] In March 1984, as the book goes to press, Jim is starting a small business, providing his own meals-on-wheels service to elderly people on the Island. Linda phoned me in February 1984 to tell me the news that at last Jim had got the support he needed. They are both eager that I follow their story into the better life that they can now see opening up in front of them.

3.45 p.m. Their two children are married and live in their own homes on the Island. In 1981 they were not short of money, earning between £200 and £249 a week between them. George comes from a Sheppey family: born in 1930, he left school when he was 14 and spent some years in the RAF where, he says, he learnt to wash and iron (which he dislikes doing) and to cook, which he enjoys. Both George and Beryl see themselves as true Islanders; they have lived permanently on Sheppey since 1956. Their present house is their fourth and the one, they say, they have been working towards all their lives. They began in a council house and worked and saved to move into the private sector; then, when they were living further down the road, they selected their present house while it was being built. They have reached the peak of their household housing strategy and both feel completely contented and satisfied: they have no wish to move elsewhere. George cycles to work despite having a car, which probably accounts for his tan. It is easy for them to keep closely in touch with their married son, who lives at Halfway, and their married daughter in Sheerness.

Both of their children are doing up their houses and George helps them. Last year, he helped his son to paint the outside of his house. There is a regular, unstructured pattern of visiting. George's own mother and father live a couple of miles away and he sees them a couple of times a week. With all this family visiting, there is not much time left for going out, but George and Beryl do enjoy making excursions together in their car. They belong to the National Trust. When I talked to them in June 1982, they had visited Leeds Castle a couple of weeks previously and these weekend outings are a regular feature of their lives. They prefer not to go out alone; they may go out together to the local working men's club in the evening or take the car to go to the Conservative Club in Sheerness (George voted Labour in 1979, and in 1981 he said he was going to vote for the Alliance candidate at the next election).

Since George and Beryl have more or less achieved what they set out to do in life, I was interested to know more about how they lived with their modest affluence and how they divided the work that had to be done in the home. It emerged that the one was closely related to the other. Beryl said simply, 'We do what we want to do, really.' They go on holiday most years: they have been to Germany and Austria in the past; last year they went to Bournemouth. As Beryl says, 'Of course, we can go more or less anywhere, although we would have to save up to go to the Far East.'

However, not content simply to enjoy their pleasant round of family visits, weekend outings and annual holidays, they were intending to embark on a complete refurbishing of their house. 'We've been in the house eleven years and we decided to re-do it all.' So they decided not to have a summer holiday but to go away for a number of long weekends during the year. They were planning their housework like a military campaign and had obviously devoted a considerable amount of time to thinking through a rational work strategy. They told me their plans like two work colleagues setting up a business. When they said they were planning to 'concentrate on the house', that is exactly what they meant. Their idea was to start at the top of the house and then 'work down and through the back door'. They had devised a plan together so that George would take his five weeks' holiday from the docks to phase in with the correct stage of work. He would also use the time between his shifts to keep up with smaller jobs. They were planning to put in a new front door with new draught-proofing, buy new furniture, fit a new shower, artex the ceiling in the passage and up the stairs and, of course, paint and re-paper throughout the house. This plan of work was due to be completed by Christmas.

George would have done all the artexing himself when he was younger, but now he preferred to get 'specialists' to do the work for him. It was generally held on the Island that artexing was not a job for an amateur, and the informal provision of that service is considered with suspicion. I was often told of ceilings ruined by 'cowboys' and George's hesitancy to use his own skills should be seen in that context. A firm would also be called in to fit the new front door and the double glazing. Otherwise, George and Beryl would do all the work themselves. They were looking forward to it as the culmination of two years' planning. George's desire to hire 'specialists' is a product of his affluence. He had been apprenticed to a plumber before he joined the RAF and had done much more skilled work in home maintenance when he was younger. he helps his son and daughter in their homes, but now, I suspect, he rather enjoys being able to choose which aspects of domestic self-provisioning he does himself and which aspects he obtains through the formal provision of services.

George and Beryl don't like going into debt and they would modify the timing of their plan if overtime in the docks was cut. In June 1982, George was working an average of fifty hours a week in the docks. They were most keen to start in the bedrooms (which I did not see), where, they said, things were wearing out and nothing had been refurbished since the children had left home. They wanted to cast out all the old carpets and furniture and start afresh. Choosing the paint, wallpaper, curtains and everything else was part of the overall enterprise that satisfied them and brought them together as a team.

How George and Beryl Divide their Work

Beryl said, 'When we're both working, we both share the work, don't we? Of course, if George is off earlier, he'll probably start doing whatever has to be done.' George does much of the cooking. Since Beryl is a skilled cook and does that all day, she is understandably reluctant to carry over her employment into her work. George says he does the Sunday roast easily and when I asked him whether he sticks to a few regular menus, he was ready to boast in front of Beryl how he likes to try new recipes: he even makes his own curry powder. Beryl remarked that 'He reckons his gravy is better than mine' and she said how much she enjoyed 'coming home to a chicken curry or a chicken casserole all ready to eat'. When I persistently questioned them about whether there was a division between them in the work they did in the home, they had difficulty in thinking of anything that George couldn't do, although they agreed he didn't like ironing. Beryl characteristically remarked, 'If he decides he wants to do something like cooking, I go and leave him to it; it's as simple as that.' However hard I tried, I could not get them to acknowledge any disputes or difficulties in getting the domestic work done. In the case of shopping, either George or Beryl puts items on a pad. If they happened to buy more than they needed, they simply put it in the freezer.

Of the 41 tasks in the formal interview schedule (see pp. 214–15), George and Beryl did only 24, since none of the child care tasks applied. Of these 24 tasks, 6 were shared, 8 were done mainly by Beryl and 10 tasks were done by George. Four of George's tasks were connected with car maintenance, but he also provided the vegetables, made beer and made his own packed lunches, as well as doing other home maintenance work.

Beryl said that, when they were younger, there was a more rigid division of labour: when there were children in the house 'My place was in the home and I saw to everything. But now we're both working we do things fifty-fifty and try to keep things running smoothly.' For instance, in the morning 'whoever gets up there first does the bed — straightens the continental quilt. There's no set "you do this and I'll do that." Whatever we see needs doing at a time, we do it.' I asked Beryl who actually had final responsibility for the housework and suggested that perhaps George was really helping her in her work. That question caused Beryl some difficulty: she started to reply with conventional clichés but then recognized that what she was saying in terms of normative statements did not fit her behaviour. 'I don't think my husband *should* help me but I'm very grateful that he does. A woman is naturally — a woman's place is in the home — but it's not like that, is it?' I then asked her whether, if she mowed the lawn, she would think that she was helping George and in that case she admitted she would probably think she was helping him. However, she wasn't happy in making a distinction between 'her work' and 'his work' and preferred to say, 'I think at the moment it is a fifty-fifty affair.'

I wondered whether this symmetrical division of labour was a function in their stage in the life cycle. Surprisingly, they would not accept this. Beryl said that George used to get up in the night for the children more times than she did and they told me that both their son and son-in-law were helping their wives more now than when they first got married.

Indeed, George says he now does *less* than he used to — this is partly because he now prefers and is able to buy in more services and partly because he does not have the same incentive to brew beer or grow vegetables on his allotment. Try as I might, I could not get them to budge from their basic position: both Beryl and George said in almost similar words, 'The first one that sees it does it; it's as easy as that.' I wondered whether there was perhaps a confusion about meals sometimes, as the arrangements were vague and the first one home took responsibility. There was a chance both would bring home steak on the same day. They were quite unruffled. 'If it is something that'll keep, it goes in the fridge or we freeze it.' Clearly, the fact that they could each pay out for steak on the same day simply did not strike them as a problem.

Money doesn't buy happiness ... but it certainly helps

Beryl and George give every indication of being happy and contented. They have no worries, they never have any difficulties with bills, and 'every penny that comes in doesn't automatically go out.' The crucial clue to their strategy was, as they put it, they 'cut their coat according to their cloth'. What they want and what they get are broadly in harmony. They admit that they were short at times in the past but now they live happily within their means and their approach to the domestic refurbishing reflects very well their personal beliefs. 'We never buy anything that we cannot afford and we don't believe in taking on an extra commitment.' Hence, they will not do all the work irrespective of their current circumstances. 'We are very concerned to balance the work we do with the resources coming in.' Once the house is spick and span, they are looking ahead to planning more joint holidays together. It is an easy and relaxed life. George simply pays the bills as they come in.

All the evidence suggests that this couple have a level of contentment that is not easily undermined. George, being a stevedore, could not be sacked and he knew that he had security until he retired. Their children were off their hands and were no financial burden, although they did take up much of their time out of employment. Because so much spare time was spent with parents, children and grandchildren, there was little time left to spend with other friends and neighbours. But George is always ready to lend a tool or give a neighbour a lift in his car, and he regularly does so. If a neighbour asks him to collect a son or daughter who is out late at night, he is always glad to help. There are now unemployed people living in the area and George and Beryl have tried to be tactful, offering help in a roundabout way, recognizing the social burden and complexity of giving.[7]

[7] M. Mauss, *The Gift*, Cohen and West, 1954.

Beryl and George epitomized the respectable affluent working class households on the Island, and, while they were in a minority, there were many like them. Their affluence spread out to other members of their family whom they could help with skill, labour and hospitality. Beryl goes to her part-time job in a catering firm 'partly for the money and partly to get out of the home'. Now, at the age of 50, she has thirty-four years' experience, and, as long as the firm is in business, she is unlikely to lose her job. They are like Jim and Linda might have been if Jim had been in the docks instead of on the water. The contrast between the contented, relaxed style of Beryl and George and the tense, anxious and struggling life of Linda and Jim could hardly be greater. In many ways, the latter couple had more enterprise, initiative and determination to achieve, yet they were oppressed by circumstances they could not control.

Conclusions

Clearly, not all affluent manual workers share the domestic work as closely as Beryl and George; nor, for that matter, do all unemployed husbands generally do as much as Jim. Nevertheless, there were many more like Beryl and George than I originally expected when I started this fieldwork. The more solidly based empirical material in the last three chapters provides the necessary context for these two examples. I do not want to discuss the implications of these cases at length, since this is already an over-long chapter. Readers will be able to draw their own conclusions readily enough, simply through the stark contrast between the two households. To conclude that ordinary working people need money is banal but overwhelmingly important. Jim and George have broadly the same range of skills and abilities. Both have spent time away from a conventional job, in the Merchant Navy and the RAF respectively; both do substantial work in and around the dwelling, and both take considerable pride in their personal craft skills. If anything, Jim and Linda have a broader range of qualities and aptitudes and appear to be more entrepreneurial and energetic. Yet British society in the early 1980s does not, apparently, want these skills and aptitudes. Linda and Jim are, understandably, puzzled people. The two households do not live next door to each other, but they quite easily could do so. The distribution of work on the Island is producing a pattern of polarization that may affect next-door neighbours in the way these case studies illustrate. One household has multiple earners and has a surplus of income which poses the pleasant problem of how to spend it in new ways; next door may be a household with growing children under 5, who cannot go out because their parents cannot afford to buy them shoes. The ruling at the local social security office is that there is no case for discretionary payments for children's shoes if they are not yet at school.

I said in the Introduction to this book that I would not argue by anecdote. The example of the children without shoes comes from another case study, and there are many more cases from which I could draw more material. However, the unequivocal conclusion of Chapter 9 is given a new dimension by the material in this chapter: there is a complex process of polarization developing among ordinary working people, the consequences of which have not yet had much impact on contemporary social theory and practice. I provide some general consideration of the issues raised in this book in Part III.

Part III

Work in a
Wider Context

12

Households, Work and Society

The main aim of this book has been to explore the interrelations between forms of work and sources of labour. In the first part I showed how these have changed, and in the second part I focused on the local political economy of the Isle of Sheppey as the context for detailed empirical analyses of household work strategies. The account in Part I demonstrated that the claim that there is something unprecedented about the nature of work in the 1980s is misplaced: the *unprecedented* period, in terms of the patterns of the last 250 years, was the boom period of full employment for men in the 1950s and 1960s. That period of rising real wages, of demand for teenage and immigrant labour and of expanding state expenditure in health, social services and education has formed the base level, the conception of what is normal, for politicians, media commentators and many academics.

A consideration of all forms of work suggests that, while the total amount of work done is more likely to be increasing than declining for most households, new divisions of labour are emerging. It seems clear that the distribution of all forms of work is becoming increasingly unbalanced. A process of polarization is developing, with households busily engaged in all forms of work at one pole and households unable to do a wide range of work at the other.[1] Furthermore, the divisions of labour within and between households are changing, as, too, are the divisions of labour between households and other agencies such as the state and, finally, between states themselves.

These new divisions of labour that are emerging or are being

---

[1] This process was foreseen as a possibility by W. W. Daniel in January 1980 when, in his evidence to the House of Lords Select Committee on Unemployment, he said that he saw 'the spectre of a new social structure, of a new division arising in our society, and in our economy, where we have an increasing proportion of households where nobody works at the same time as there is an increasing proportion of multiple wage and salary earners. You have a new poor who are very poor, and homes in which children are brought up without anybody at work. You get quite a different picture if you focus upon people as individuals as opposed to focusing on people as members of households' (16 January 1980, para. 119).

renegotiated[2] suggest that much conventional analysis needs to be reconsidered. The assumption that the occupation of the male chief earner is the most important determinant of the social and political consciousness of the household is open to serious doubt. The division between the more affluent home-owning households of ordinary working people and the less advantaged under-class households is coming to be more significant than conventional divisions based on the manual/non-manual distinction. The household with its distinctive value system based on domesticity has a political force that cannot be reduced to the communal employment experience of one of its members.

In this final chapter I turn from the analytical description of actual work practices in Chapters 8-11 to a consideration of the social processes that underlie those patterns of forms of work and sources of labour. Why do households behave in the ways they do? Are households being increasingly liberated or increasingly constrained? If the underlying processes are not directly or indirectly embedded in the basic material conditions, where else should one look? And, if they are so linked, what are the mechanisms that connect the conditions to the behaviour?

Three important lines of thought have been put forward as the basis for a reconsideration of the broad connections between households, work and society. The first emphasizes the benign forces within capitalism that generate social innovation, in particular developments in technology. The second focuses on the uneven development of capitalism and sees the development of other forms of work within the household as regressive and malign. The third approach emphasizes the shift away from the sphere of production to the sphere of consumption as the main source of people's consciousness and social goals. Each of these three lines of thought has contributed in some way to my position and I shall both present them and criticize them before moving on.

Household, Work and Society: Alternative Lines of Thought

1 Social innovation within capitalism

This position is based on the assumption that a combination of technological innovation in manufacturing industry and social innovation in households' behaviour, particularly in the way goods and services are produced inside the household, generates tendencies that result in a

---

[2] 'What is clear is that the informal economy is an integral part of the renegotiation of the division of labour which I have sketched, and that all discussion of the politics of welfare and the social distribution of effort and reward must be imprecise until an accurate description of economic exchanges, unconstrained by conventional economic measures, is produced by social scientists' (A. H. Halsey, 'A sociologist's viewpoint', in *The Welfare State in Crisis*, OECD, Paris, 1981, p. 26).

qualitatively different kind of society. More work is done in households as members use their own labour and their own capital equipment to produce goods and services for themselves. The logic of economic development, which moves away from primary production through manufacturing to the provision of services, is halted. Accelerating productivity in manufacturing industry, relative to that of the final service industry, means that goods get cheaper relative to final services. Hence, households buy manufactured goods that enable them to produce more services for themselves. Essentially, such a line of thought is based on the efficiency and innovative capacity of capitalism and on a value system that supports and approves innovative patterns of household consumption. The way people spend their time and money itself generates an economic response in the balance and content of goods and services.

Such a line of thought has been developed over the years by Jonathan Gershuny, and I will use his work to elaborate on it more fully.[3] Gershuny does not discuss either capitalism or class in his account of the development of a kind of self-service economy; he assumes that it is a net social benefit for the labour and some of the capital costs of the provision of services to be shifted to the household. Goods and services become cheaper, better and more convenient. Such factors implicitly offset costs in time and any redistribution of work within the household.[4] Social innovation, for Gershuny, involves both technological development of process innovation at the workplace and a similar process centred on the household. He foresees a matching of a new wave of technological innovation — microprocessors, information storage devices and new information-transmission infrastructure — with a new demand for home-centred services:

In *domestic services* we can construct systems for automatic centralized monitoring and control of a range of household functions (heating, lighting, safety), and these household systems can themselves be linked to local security or safety services. In addition, we might imagine information packages giving advice on household operations.[5]

Unfortunately, as I have already argued in Chapter 5 (pp. 117–21), the distributional consequences of this line of thought are not considered by

---

[3] See J. Gershuny's recent book, *Social Innovation and the Division of Labour*, Oxford University Press, 1983, for the most fully worked out statement of his position.

[4] The farmers of East Kent have shifted much of the costs of distribution of fruit to the consumer. Not only are we encouraged to pick our own soft fruit in season, but out of season we serve ourselves to apples in 'farm shops'. The farmer leaves a supply of apples, scales and a tin with money in it in a farm building. The customer serves himself with fruit, leaves the money (taking change if necessary) and drives himself away in his own car. The farmer replenishes the stock of apples from his cold store and takes out money at intervals. Even if all the available takings are stolen — in practice unlikely on a regular basis — the farmer is still better off then he would be hiring even the cheapest labour.

[5] Gershuny, *Social Innovations*, p. 166.

Gershuny. He simply asserts that in the past 'the poor got richer over time',[6] and claims that in the future the process he describes as 'social innovation' will do two things:

It increases the demand for labour, in the formal economy, by establishing new markets for the new products used in the 'innovative modes of production', and also in the informal sector. And it reduces the supply of labour to the money economy.[7]

He goes on to say that

We must recognize that trends of events are in part determined by a logic that is internal to our social institutions and material environment, and quite out of our control, [although the future course of development] is to some extent malleable.[8]

Yet, even in his most optimistic view of future economic and political developments, Gershuny admits that any new demand for labour will be for the skilled and not for the unskilled, and that the growth of informal production is more likely to reduce women's paid work disproportionately.[9] In the face of such apparently inherent inequalities, he seems helpless to effect any change. For example, he remarks that the absence of 'sexual equity' is the result of unprogressive social attitudes:

Despite recent and quite substantial changes in publicly expressible attitudes, domestic work is still regarded as chiefly women's work. The fact of their perceived responsibility for domestic work reduces the amount of time women have available for paid work, *which places them at a disadvantage in the wage labour market.* And here is the inequality: precisely *because* similar sorts of men and women, *because* husbands and wives may be expected to want to work similar lengths of time, while women maintain their special responsibility for housework, women are more likely to take on part-time jobs (which are generally of inferior status), they have less energy to concentrate on their jobs, less flexibility to work longer hours when they are needed, so they cannot compete on equal terms with men.[10]

Evidently Gershuny does not condone such attitudes, but he describes them in such a way as to imply that they are inevitable. So, these two interactive processes of innovation in technology and household behaviour produce new mixes of work for different social categories. Manual workers decline relative to 'knowledge' workers and new work is done by household members.

Gershuny mentions in passing a point that I consider to be

[6] Ibid., p. 14.
[7] Ibid., p. 177.
[8] Ibid., p. 177.
[9] Ibid., p. 183.
[10] Ibid., p. 153 (Gershuny's emphasis).

outstandingly important and that I have already documented in detail in Chapters 8 and 9, namely that

households increasingly acquire their services by a *combination* of unpaid work with capital goods and materials purchased with money earned in paid employment. Households without formal employment may therefore find that their abilities to engage in informal production activities are also impaired. And the more that a particular society provides its final services on an informal rather than a formal basis, the more expensive are its formal services. So, the process of 'informalization' of production does not necessarily alleviate the burden of unemployment.[11]

Gershuny recognizes such inequalities and patterns of polarization, but he does not address them as a central part of his argument. His analysis of the way time and money interact in the development of a self-service society to produce a diminishing marginal utility of income is important, as long as it is not forgotten that households still need substantial amounts of money in order to engage in self-service activity.

However imaginative Gershuny's work is,[12] one must read between the lines of his book to discover the new patterns of inequality that are being generated and indeed emphasized by the processes of social innovation he describes. By under-emphasizing the distributional consequences, and by inferring that what people do is what they actually want to do, those who adopt this line of thinking may be unwittingly closing options and ignoring potential political reactions of a conventional or unconventional kind. Nevertheless, this line of thinking is valuable and provides a distinct and rigorous approach to the connections between household, work and society.

2 Informal and domestic work as survival strategies of the poor

Followers of this line of thought seem to be in opposition to those in the previous category. Distributional consequences are central to their approach, and it is the malign effects of capital accumulation, rather than the benefits of technological innovation, that are stressed. The demand for increasing profits rather than the benefits of increased productivity is seen as the main motor of change, and the inequitable burden falling on the working class is of greater concern than the benefits that may accrue to the more advantaged. The capitalist crisis produces increasing unemployment so that wage labourers can no longer support themselves and their dependants. The only way such disadvantaged workers can survive is by engaging in illegal work or reverting to proto-industrial

[11] Ibid., p. 48.
[12] I readily acknowledge that I have been continuously stimulated and helped by his work for the last seven years.

patterns of domestic labour. Thus, the new patterns of household work arise out of a disjunction in the relations between capital accumulation and the reproductive patterns for a growing section of the population.

The distributional effects in class terms of structural changes in the economy are well illustrated in Italy, and Mingione's work is a good example of a Marxist analysis that develops this line of thought.[13] He points to sections of the Italian population 'adapting' themselves to these more global processes of capital accumulation by combining various forms of domestic and informal work.[14] For Mingione, capitalism has, as it were, sucked in wage labourers, turning them into a commodity — labour — and then, with the growth of unemployment (for whatever reason), has discarded them. Unable to meet their consumption needs, the discarded workers are forced to reduce their demand for goods and services and instead to 'work for self-consumption and informal consumption'.[15] Such workers and their families, 'progressively abandoned by the formal economic cycle',[16] are forced into black and illegal employment and unpaid work, and the state is forced to increase public subsidies. These structural changes are seen by Mingione to be largely irreversible, given the logic of capitalist development: 'decentralization, informalization of certain economic sectors and the growth of domestic work are, in general, defensive measures in the context of the capitalist management of a very difficult and prolonged crisis.'[17]

The situation in Italy described by Mingione is not of totally unrelieved gloom. He claims that

a greater independence and reproductive solidarity is now possible in modern urban environments. . . . [N]ew forms of local solidarity . . . need not lead to the development of groups in competition with each other (to obtain a share of scanty public resources) but, instead to the promotion of radical changes in systems of reproduction, against mass consumerism and in favour of a greater co-operation and independence of the local collectivity.[18]

If this last unsubstantiated utopianism is left aside, it is clear that the Italian experience leads Mingione to view the growth of more informal work in the household as an unprogressive coping response of the poor and marginalized. This is not so far from the position adopted by Rose,[19] who also sees the 'domestic economy' as means for getting by in the

---

[13] E. Mingione, 'Informalization, restructuring and the survival strategies of the working class', *International Journal of Urban and Regional Research*, 7(3), 1983, pp. 311-39. See also 'Informalization and survival strategies in Southern Italy', in E. Mingione and N. Redclift (eds), *Beyond Employment*, Basil Blackwell, Oxford, 1984, for more detailed empirical justification for his arguments to which I refer.

[14] Ibid., p. 311.

[15] Ibid., p. 317.

[16] Ibid., p. 319.

[17] Ibid., p. 328.

[18] Ibid., p. 330.

[19] Cf. Chapter 9, p. 246.

turbulent economic conditions of the time. Rose, too, sees benefits accruing to the household from what he calls 'the altruistic and affectionate exchange of services outside the money economy'.[20]

The forced growth of informal work that Mingione describes for Italy can be appropriately described in a Marxist perspective, but there is, in fact, a remarkable congruence between such an approach and the views of some right-wing economists in Britain. They, too, see informal work as a survival strategy of the poor, although they adopt quite different policy perspectives. Patrick Minford has argued that unemployed people 'can do useful things at home and even earn some small amounts legally while claiming benefits',[21] and he proposes that unemployment benefits be reduced in order to encourage workers to take low-paid employment. Even though Minford's assumption is empirically invalid, there is a congruence between Mingione's and Minford's views that the poor and disadvantaged do other forms of work in the household and that the way to reduce this is to stimulate more employment (albeit by very different methods and with very different assumptions).

Evidently, it is somewhat bizarre to bring together an analysis of illegal domestic outwork and uncontrolled sweatshop manufacturing in Italy with a discussion of what unemployed people in Liverpool, who do not own their homes, do with their time. These are different forms of informal work. Coping strategies of the poor will clearly vary enormously between different industrial societies, whether capitalist or socialist. In the Soviet Union it has been shown that the poorest families in cities are the most likely to grow extra vegetables in private gardens.[22] Opportunistic ways of getting by provided an essential element in the history of all forms of work (see Chapter 2). In so far as there is now structural unemployment, a distinctive form of poverty is being created by the process of capitalist development. Furthermore, opportunities for informal work among the unemployed are probably declining, and those in employment are better placed to engage in all other forms of work as well (see Chapter 4).

3 The shift from production to consumption in determining consciousness

This approach emphasizes the convergence in goals and aspirations of a large section of society, which in recent years has become the majority in most Western societies. The resulting households, more privatized,

---

[20] R. Rose, *Getting By in Three Economies: The Resources of Official, Unofficial and Domestic Economies*, Centre for the Study of Public Policies, University of Strathclyde, 1983, p. 25.
[21] P. Minford, *Journal of Economic Affairs*, 3(2), 1983, p. 97.
[22] See the fascinating discussion in L. Gordon and E. Klopov, *Man After Work*, Progress Publishers, Moscow, 1975, pp. 44, 91-4.

inward-looking, home-centred and autonomous, are consumption-oriented and consider that they can achieve their individual goals more readily through private plans than through collective action. This large 'middle mass' comprises between 55 and 65 per cent of all households in Britain, with a deprived underclass of between 20 and 25 per cent in poverty beneath them and a well salaried or capital-owning bourgeoisie of about 12-15 per cent above them. Most of these households in the middle mass own their own homes and, judging from the Sheppey Survey, gain substantial satisfaction from creating a style of life based on small-scale domesticity.

Perhaps the most widely noticed exponent of this line of thought is André Gorz, who sees continuing technological development leading to the elimination of the social producer. The reason for the declining significance of production for workers — both manual and non-manual — is simply that it is unnecessary for them to be involved in employment for very many hours in a day, week or lifetime. In his book, *Farewell to the Working Class*, Gorz refers to the 'non-class of post-industrial proletarians' who no longer have to free themselves within work but rather have to free themselves *from* work (by which he means employment) by rejecting its nature, content and necessity. This is a confusing notion, since, while neither capitalism nor 'the workers' want the employment, there is still just as strong a need for *money* — by workers to buy the means to enjoy their 'free' time and by the capitalist system, which needs an expanding home market for goods and services.

Gorz seeks to describe a new sphere of freedom outside the realm of necessity of employment, and argues that

Essentially, the 'freedom' which the majority of the population of the overdeveloped nations seeks to protect from 'collectivism' and the 'totalitarian' threat, is the freedom to create a private niche protecting one's personal life against all pressures and external social obligations. This niche may be represented by family life, a home of one's own, a back garden, a do-it-yourself workshop, a boat, a country cottage, a collection of antiques, music, gastronomy, sport, love, etc. Its importance varies inversely with the degree of job satisfaction and in direct proportion with the intensity of social pressures. . . . 'Real life' begins out of work, and work itself has become a means towards the extension of the sphere of non-work, a temporary occupation by which individuals acquire the possibility of pursuing their main activities.[23]

According to Gorz, this development of private spheres and styles of consumption subverts the social relations established by capitalism and may in the end, in his words, 'eliminate capitalism'. He goes on to claim that parallel to the sphere of commodity production is the sphere of household production, which 'has in practice always been as important as

[23] A. Gorz, *Farewell to the Working Class*, Pluto Press, London, 1982, pp. 80-8.

the sphere of economic production, providing it with a concealed material base through the unremunerated and unmeasured housework of women and, to a lesser extent, of children and grandparents'.[24]

Gorz's argument is highly simplified, idealistic and in some respects sexist, incorporating a polarized view of work that throughout this book I have argued is mistaken. Nevertheless, he does touch on a theme that has been developed rigorously by Patrick Dunleavy and Peter Saunders, namely that domestic property ownership and styles of consumption behaviour may have broader political implications.[25] Dunleavy argues against a division in consumption patterns based solely on occupational differences between the 'middle' and the 'working' class. Manual workers are highly fragmented in terms of what he calls their 'consumption locations', owing in large measure to the role of the state in the sphere of housing. Saunders has come more recently to the conclusion that 'class is not the be all and end all of social cleavages and conflicts.'[26] He emphasizes housing tenure as neither the basis nor the expression of class formation, but as the most important element in 'consumption sector cleavages'.

It would be ludicrous to assert that tenure of the domestic dwelling is taking the place of paid work as the main determinant of most people's life chances and sense of social identity in the middle mass. But it would be equally ludicrous to deny the potency of home ownership, both as a source of capital accumulation and as a focus for self-provisioning.[27] However, just as it would be wrong to assert a simple direct relationship between the occupation of the chief male earner and all members of the household's social and political behaviour, so, too, must one avoid a crude dwelling-determinism. As I argued in Chapter 4, weaknesses in Marx's theory of action have been consistently overlooked. A degree of working-class solidarity has been imputed that has been hard to substantiate empirically.[28] The 'traditional' working class is arguably the privatized, home-centred domestic unit based on the nuclear family, and,

[24] Ibid., p. 82.

[25] See P. Dunleavy, 'The urban bases of political alignment', *British Journal of Political Science*, 9, 1979, pp. 409-43; and P. Saunders, *Beyond Housing Classes: The Sociological Significance of Private Property Rights in Means of Consumption*, Working Paper 33, Urban and Regional Studies, University of Sussex, 1983. Also of relevance in this context is C. Offe, 'Alternative strategies in consumer policy', Chapter 10 of his collection of essays: *Contradictions of the Welfare State*, Hutchinson, London, 1984.

[26] Saunders, *Beyond Housing Classes*, p. 11.

[27] R. E. Pahl, *Whose City?* Penguin, Harmondsworth, 1974, Chapter 12 and at p. 298.

[28] K. Kumar, 'Class and political action in nineteenth-century England', *European Journal of Sociology*, 24, 1983, pp. 3-43; and 'Can the workers be revolutionary?' *European Journal of Political Research*, 6, 1978, pp. 357-79. For an alternative approach to these problems see G. Stedman-Jones, *Language of Class*, Cambridge University Press, 1984. For an interesting account of nineteenth-century working-class traditionalism 'including a substantial amount of fatalism', see P. N. Stearns, 'The effort at continuity in working-class culture', *Journal of Modern History*, 52, 1980, pp. 626-55.

as the historical demographers have demonstrated, such households have a long history in pre-industrial England.[29]

In any discussion of 'working-class' consciousness and collective action, it is useful to remember the distinction between instrumental and affective collectivism. When the economic and political situation was heavily stacked against those with nothing but their capacity to sell their labour power to keep them from penury, the extension of the voting franchise and the development of trades union rights were the necessary first goals to be attained. Private strategies might work for members of a labour aristocracy, but for the majority of workers an instrumental collective response was the only realistic alternative. But this collective power, which aimed at the extension of equal rights of citizenship, produced results that were either short-lived or less satisfactory than expected. Trades unions have power in expanding industries, but they are less able to protect their members against de-industrialization. When plants close or move to new sites outside the country, militancy is more likely to encourage rather than hinder the process. The shift in manufacturing industry towards 'jobless growth' based on capital-intensive development has undermined the power of collective labour. Trades unions cannot guarantee employment for their members who are made redundant. Furthermore, in the political arena, the municipal socialism that produced large tower blocks and council estates seemed more likely to suggest a second-class citizenry than a victory for the campaign to get better housing for ordinary people. The Council and the Corporation came to epitomize 'them', perhaps more potently than employers as a category, except in certain industries such as mining and car manufacturing. (However frequently nurses or social workers might go out on strike, it is hard for them to be able to symbolize the typical British worker in the way miners or car workers seemingly can, whether this be due to sexism or lack of solidarity.[30]) Certainly, employers on Sheppey are seen by many as better-paid workers, whose job it is to provide the means of getting money for other workers.[31]

[29] One of the best accounts of working-class life is R. Roberts, *The Classic Slum*, Penguin, Harmondsworth, 1973. See also the lively and not unsympathetic account in Chapters 10 and 11 of F. Mount, *The Subversive Family*, Jonathan Cape, London, 1982. This domesticity does not please everyone. 'Beware of Domesticity' say the authors of *The Anti-Social Family*. 'For many people, work is so unrewarding that they centre their lives around the home.' (But when was it otherwise? one asks.) 'Decorating the home, furnishing it, equipping it with gadgetry become major activities. Family leisure and child-centred life style become the sources of their deepest satisfaction.... As every socialist knows, it becomes almost impossible to attract a decent crowd to a public meeting.' (M. Barrett and M. McIntosh, *The Anti-Social Family*, Verso Editions, London, 1983, p. 146).
[30] Certainly it is odd and unconvincing that the collective solidarity of service workers should be referred to as 'industrial action'.
[31] See also R. E. Pahl, 'The restructuring of capital, the local political economy and house-hold work strategies: All forms of work in context', in D. Gregory and J. Urry (eds), *Social Relations and Spatial Structures*, Macmillan, London, 1984.

If, then, 'working-class solidarity' has been largely an instrumental form of collectivism, when it fails to deliver — or delivers council estates and comprehensive schools which do not seem self-evidently good things — it should not be surprising if the same instrumentalism becomes more individualistic.[32] For many ordinary people, very little can be done at the workplace to improve their personal life chances. They may be able to get a certain amount of extra money by plant-bargaining, overtime or putting more effort into piece-work; but such activity is relatively marginal compared with moving out of a local authority rented house to a house they own and on which and in which they can work as they like. They can express themselves more creatively in their own homes than they can in their employment.

The more affective solidarity of working-class life has been held by some as an essential element in class identity, with the implication that there are political consequences in the form of support for the party that epitomizes collective goals. Much is made of brass bands, works outings and support for football clubs; less emphasis is given to more individual interests such as fishing or gardening. Similarly, bourgeois forms of affective collectivism, such as fox-hunting, making mayhem after various rowing events or organizations such as the Rotary Club, the Lions, charity coffee mornings, and so on, are perhaps under-emphasized. It seems pointless and rather silly to attempt to limit affective collective action to any one level in the social structure. The glassy-eyed solidarity of a bumps supper night, or the fervour expressed collectively at the annual conference of the Institute of Directors, should make one very cautious about relating that kind of collectivism to a lower-class position. Similarly, even in terms of instrumental collectivism, the National Farmers' Union may well be making a better job of it than the parallel organization for agricultural workers. The argument that a certain section of the social structure has some special, privileged access to affective solidarity, which determines its consciousness in a distinctive way, has as much validity as dividing up the population into classes based on those who sing choral works and those who do not.

Changes in technology, the shift in emphasis from the worker as producer to the worker as consumer, the growth of new forms of work associated with consumption and a switch by ordinary working people to more individual forms of instrumental action are among the elements that are undermining the centrality of one form of work — employment — as a mainspring for class consciousness and cohesion (in so far as this has ever been the case). These are certainly complex matters, and the evidence from Sheppey suggests that Gorz is bidding farewell to the working class somewhat prematurely. Nevertheless, the polarization thesis and a

[32] For an analysis of different forms of instrumental action in a different context, see R. E. Pahl, 'Instrumentality and community in the process of urbanization', *Sociological Inquiry*, 43(3-4), 1973, pp. 241-60.

growing concern with forms of work outside employment suggest not embourgeoisement, but a growing middle mass. The new line of class cleavage is now between the middle mass and the underclass beneath it.

These three lines of thought are to some extent complementary: it is hard to divorce the impact of technology from the development of capitalism, and the increasing salience of consumption cannot be separated from differences in the growth of productivity of goods and of final services. Elements of each of these approaches to the underlying processes affecting all forms of work are exemplified by the Sheppey study.

Processes in Household Work Strategies

There are four sometimes contradictory processes that collectively produce the self-provisioning of the kind I discussed in Chapters 8 and 9. First, there is the process of privatization of the public sector, exemplified by the encouragement of private transport at the expense of public, the sale of council houses and the transfer back to 'the community' of the care of the elderly and the physically and mentally handicapped. Second, there is the growth in the provision by households of services that were once provided by formal service agencies such as laundries and cinemas and are now provided by privately owned goods such as washing machines and video recorders. In both cases households may accept the process either voluntarily or involuntarily. Households that would prefer the mainte- nance of rural bus services, cinemas and residential homes for the elderly have to accept their reduction along with those who enjoy using their own cars and caring for their own elderly relatives.

Third, there is the growth of self-provisioning, which does not necessarily depend on the ownership of capital goods but can be a consequence of the pleasure and satisfaction derived from doing the work for oneself. Making jam, home decorating, special cooking, growing vegetables and a host of other activities are done not simply because of cheapness or the greater productivity of labour — the real cost of home-made jam or home-grown vegetables can be far greater than the commercial alterna- tives — but for the satisfaction of doing the work in one's own time, with one's own tools, in one's own way, to one's own standards, to produce personal and distinction satisfactions. This personal satisfaction from work done for oneself or one's family should not be underestimated.

Fourth, there is the overall set of values concerned with homeliness, cosiness, domesticity and a belief that, if one can control just a small part of this large and threatening world, then one has achieved something worthwhile. When Linda said (in Chapter 11) that she liked the winter when everyone was in at 6 and she felt locked in, secure and safe, she was referring to these values: 'You know, we're all right, nothing can happen to us, we're all in together.'[33] A previous generation put little reminders on the wall, asserting that there was no place like home. The word 'home' is impossible to define precisely, because it epitomizes a set of personal experiences: even the most footloose and liberated person, determined to cast off the shackles of an enslaving social structure, is still likely to have important memories of home and is also likely to arrange her or his possessions, however few, in a distinctive and personal way. The labour movement, which prides itself on its historical roots, appeared curiously blind to ordinary people's determination to control a small part of their environment and to fashion it in their own way. The planners, bureaucrats and managers in the offices of the local authority[34] devised rules, standards and entitlements: the ends, they claimed, justified the means.

Yet for many people the means are more important than the ends: the pile of 'useful things' — old doors, planks, bricks, iron bars and the like — that accumulate in the gardens and yards of rural owner-occupied houses 'in case they come in handy one day' symbolizes the importance of private, personal plans over municipal tidiness. Perhaps the municipal socialism of twentieth-century Britain has not come to terms with the essence of individualism in ordinary English people. Indeed, not only have those with a collectivist ideology imposed this as the so-called natural or 'instinctive' political response of ordinary workers,[35] but they have managed to imply that those who object to the tyrannies of the town hall have been de-radicalized. Only one form of radical behaviour is permissible, according to this perspective, and that must involve solidaristic collectivism.

English Individualism and Self-provisioning

In the previous discussion of technology, capitalism and the so-called 'post-industrial non-worker', little consideration was given to the distinctiveness of national cultural values. As Macfarlane has shown, there is a long history of English individualism,[36] and it would be surprising if this did not have contemporary significance. I mentioned in the Introduction that there has been a tendency in much sociological analysis to indulge in wishful rather than critical thinking: the notion that

[33] Cf. Chapter 11, p. 292.
[34] I am surprised that this widespread use of the word 'Authority' in England to describe the smallest unit of local government is not more often questioned. See, in this context, J. G. Davies, *The Evangelistic Bureaucrat: A Study of a Planning Exercise in Newcastle-upon-Tyne*, Tavistock, London, 1972.
[35] See J. H. Goldthorpe, D. Lockwood, F. Bechhofer and J. Platt, *The Affluent Worker: Political Attitudes and Behaviour*, Cambridge University Press, 1968, p. 75.
[36] A. Macfarlane, *The Origins of English Individualism*, Basil Blackwell, Oxford, 1978.

socialism necessarily implies collectivism has only recently been questioned. People have been puzzled to discover that what they most wanted — a home of their own — was in some way a betrayal of some greater goal. 'Privatization' was scorned by the municipal socialists, who thus alienated themselves from their natural supporters. Nevertheless, there is an alternative tradition of radical individualism which is more easily expressed through the practices of everyday life and in the struggles against the bumbledom of official bureaucracies. This tradition did not develop simply as a reaction to industrial capitalism, nor does it reside in the proprieties of petty bourgeois respectability.

In 1646, John Lilburne published his 'Remonstrance of Many Thousand Citizens, and Other Free Born People of England to their Owne House of Commons' in which he complained: 'Truly it is a sad thing but too true, a plaine quiet-minded man in any place in *England*, is just like a harmless sheep in a Thicket, can hardly move or stirre, but hee shall be stretch'd, and loose his wooll: such *Committees* have ye made in all Cities and Counties, and none are so ill used as honest Godly men.'[37] Such a cry, which I perceive as being truly radical and not reactionary, has been voiced at intervals over the last four centuries but has not found adequate political expression. It has been swamped by municipal socialism and the teleological planners.[38] For a time, ordinary people were prepared to go along with solidaristic collectivism as perhaps the only way to get major advances into citizenship. Now, it seems, the citizens of the middle mass are asserting themselves in their private lives.

Questions were asked in the Sheppey survey about past and future voting behaviour and attitudes to the welfare state. Responses were ambiguous: party political activity is moribund on the Island and people felt that local government was remote and seemingly unconcerned about local problems. It was difficult to raise any interest in broader political questions with most people, and turn-out at local and national elections was characteristically low. The vigour with which people renovated or improved their houses or planned a move was in striking contrast. I see this organization of everyday practices as an essentially political activity. The people of Sheppey rank each other easily and readily. Every street has a tone or style, and it is well understood whether it is rising or falling in status. Even the roughest roads have their smart ends. These micro-residential status areas have existed on the Island for 150 years and have considerable salience for people's sense of worth and self- esteem. A visible sign of where one lives is of greater significance than where one is

[37] Don M. Wolfe (ed.), *Leveller Manifestos of the Puritan Revolution*, Humanities Press, New York, 1944, pp. 127-8.
[38] For a masterly account of teleological planners in another context, see G. Konrad and I. Szelenyi, *The Intellectuals on the Road to Class Power*, Harcourt Brace Javonovich, New York, 1979.

employed. Talk in the pubs is much more likely to be about work outside employment — if, indeed, it is about work at all.

People who want a better way of life for themselves and their families perceive that they can most readily achieve this through a distinctive mix of all forms of work by all members of the household. Money is absolutely essential, of course, but this is better provided by employers, factory owners and managers through employment than by the government with stigmatizing benefits and allowances. And jobs in the factories are most likely to be found through a friend or relative, not through any institution or organization based off the Island.

The renegotiation of the divisions of labour is a political process in the broadest sense. There seems little that the people of Sheppey can do about the new international division of labour and its effect on the local job market.[39] However, the way that households get work done does provide some scope for choice and innovation.

Is the Household Capitalism's Tamest Worker?

If the work in and around the home is becoming more productive and more rewarding, some might argue that the household will become a more effective instrument to serve the interests of capitalism than well unionized workers ever were. Households with mortgages, hire purchase commitments and a number of members in employment are in one sense more vulnerable to the loss of employment, but in another sense they are less dependent on one chief earner and the effectiveness of, typically, *his* union. Furthermore, it could be argued that the household may also serve as an effective instrument for the perpetuation of what some describe as patriarchal patterns of domination and oppression. Certainly, the Sheppey data show that women do most of the work in and around the household, even if they are also in employment. While there may be signs of some shift towards a greater sharing of tasks in households where both members are in employment, when the male is unemployed there is no sign of such a shift. Patterns of work in the households are undeniably heavily structured by age and sex.

This book has been about all that work which lies outside the formal productive system, and I have described the historical processes that have produced distinctive styles of household practices. These practices have been moulded in part by the relatively autonomous values associated with English individualism. Evidently, households have to reproduce labour power — whether or not there is employment for the workers to go to — and they have to reproduce a society's population. The reproduction of labour may be seen as cultural reproduction and the reproduction of the

[39] Cf. Pahl, 'The restructuring of capital'.

complete social formation as social reproduction. The household is important as the arena in which the different goals and criteria for organizing work are clarified. In one sense, capitalism is not, as it were, interested in who engages in wage labour but in a given amount of wage labour getting done. A household organizes the earning potential of its members in terms of its internal age and gender relations and operates in a distinctive cultural milieu. Labour power has to be maintained on a day-to-day basis, as well as between generations, and this process of reproduction is now done almost entirely by women. The unemployed man needs to be maintained and reproduced as much as the worker in the steel works. While the state may supply the resources in the former case, the woman still provides the labour. This linking of women to cultural and social reproduction could not be done so easily in the past, when the divisions of labour were based on different criteria. One important difference now is the lack of servants — both male and female.

Cultural reproduction requires a set of social relations that themselves have to be reproduced — the life cycle of the domestic unit and the environment in which it exists.[40] Thus, maintaining the house and its furnishings is part of this overall process of reproduction and is largely done by men. Clearly, the state now plays a large part in helping households through these various forms of reproduction, and there is a host of rules, procedures and entitlements to do with birth, contraception and death, although much health and welfare provision is left to members of households to manage for themselves. The notion of 'reproduction' in the abstract has little or no explanatory power: it cannot account for cultural differences — why certain social forms and norms are needed in one context and not in another — nor can it account for the fact that certain households and categories can, as it were, reproduce themselves better than others.

Nevertheless, focusing on this very soggy notion of reproduction has some value if it at least makes clear that households have some wider purpose or function in society, and it is important to ask whose interest they serve. Mingione rather gloomily observes,

Social reproduction is a very vague and undefined concept; it includes directly or indirectly every social event so that it becomes impossible to analyse it separately from the accumulation/development process. . . . This topic and approach have been largely ignored in the long history of Marxist studies and it requires almost complete reconstruction to achieve essential intellectual rigour.[41]

I am not persuaded that such a reconstruction would serve any useful intellectual purpose. It seems to me to be self-evident that social, cultural and biological reproduction are the central social processes of society and

[40] For the most clear-headed discussion of such distinctions, see the admirably succinct statement by F. Edholm, O. Harris and K. Young, 'Conceptualizing women', *Critique of Anthropology*, 3(9-10), 1977, pp. 101-30.
[41] Mingione, 'Informalization', p. 312.

that the household has been the basic instrument for achieving such reproduction at least since the thirteenth century (as discussed in Chapter 1) and probably well before that. However, since women do most of the work in the household, then, logically, they do society's basic work; but this does not imply that they should necessarily do so. Further questions have to be posed about the social costs and consequences of such an asymmetrical burden of work. If each household under present circumstances is an apparent mini-unit of oppression, it is reasonable to ask whether the work could be done in a more equitable way: in a broader renegotiation of the divisions of labour, the cultural expectations and material constraints that limit certain forms of work to certain members of domestic units need to be questioned.

I recognize that I have not considered *independent*, as opposed to household, strategies, and I have not explored the particular problems of single-parent families: largely for ease of presentation, much of the analysis has focused on couples. It is surely wrong to assume that all young unmarried mothers are in that position by mistake: there is a range of possible strategies. Paradoxically, the state will provide more resources for the mother and child than it will for the woman as an unemployed worker, and in some localities the single mother is also more likely to be given a local authority dwelling.[42] Couple-based households, on the other hand, can get far more work done, and female single-parent households 'borrow' husbands from their friends to do various domestic tasks.[43] However, I must acknowledge that I have not assessed the relative effectiveness of different household forms, since at present I have no way of establishing criteria for judging effectiveness.

Throughout this book I have implicitly assumed that households are the best 'getting-by units'. But there is a legitimate criticism that such units achieve their particular effectiveness as units only on the assumption of the continued subordination of women, who invariably have final responsibility for the basic forms of reproduction, that is for most of the work. Whose interests households serve is a very pertinent question: they seem to serve the interests of men and capital very well. However, such a facile assumption needs to be examined.

The notion that capitalism, patriarchy or some other reified abstraction has 'needs' that determine the nature of households' composition and behaviour is an unsubtle, functionalist notion of only very limited heuristic value. I introduced some discussion of this issue in Chapter 4 (pp. 111–13). Households have always had needs of their own: people want to live in modest comfort, and this goal is generated independently

---

[42] While a number of women may have adopted this strategy, there is clearly need for more research to determine how far it was truly a conscious choice and how far their problems such as social isolation outweigh the advantage of apparently greater state benefits in the short term accruing from motherhood rather than employment.

[43] Cf. p. 225.

of the constraints of any particular social formation. In order to live comfortably, a substantial amount of work must get done, and this is achieved more readily if it is shared between people with different skills and capacities. In pre-industrial England all forms of work were divided among the various members of the household, including servants and children. Today, new tools, such as power drills, enable certain tasks to be done by household members that in the past were done by specialist craftsmen. So, the household does not simply reflect capitalism's needs; nor, for that matter, does capitalism reflect the households' needs, however innovatory such a notion may appear. Rather, there is a symbiotic relationship between the two: I prefer to emphasize the dynamic conservatism of the household, acting in the way it has always done — as a relatively autonomous social unit pursuing its own goals and defending its own interests.

In order to avoid a kind of vulgar ethnocentrism, which attributes the cause of all social forms of which one does not approve to an oppressive capitalism, it is worth considering the example of the Soviet Union. Detailed studies of household work practices based on time-budget analysis demonstrate a growth of self-provisioning in Soviet urban households similar to that found on the Isle of Sheppey.

In their role in securing the normal functioning of the family, such types of housework as repairing furniture, household effects, kitchen utensils and appliances, and living quarters, as well as carpentry, are in practice indistinguish-able from care of clothing or cleaning the apartment. . . . Among the urban industrial workers that we studied, time spent on these activities by men was five to six times more than the time spent by women — from 3 to 4-5 hours a week as opposed to from half an hour to an hour. . . . This is also a feature of activities in the personal subsidiary farming plot, of work in gardens and care for domestic cattle and fowl; in this area the role of men . . . . is also greater in major cities, working men spend 2-3 hours per week in the personal, subsidiary farming plot, women, half an hour a week.[44]

Gordon and Klopov go on to argue that these activities, based on the 'domination of male labour' in certain branches of the household economy, have generated their own independent sociological effects on the men, which 'leave their imprint on their whole tenor of life'. They observe that new material values are created and that these values are more qualitative, since the products of such work are consumed by the household and are not sold. This subsistence work exists in the large Soviet cities, as the authors acknowledge, partly because of the recent peasant background of the workers concerned:

[44] Gordon and Klopov, *Man After Work*, p. 91.

habits, traditions and patterns formed in a semi-subsistence economy — including the concept that domestic labour is an extraordinarily important source for providing for the family, the habit of working with one's hands, etc. — survive for a long time on urban soil.[45]

However, Gordon and Klopov go on to insist that this self-provisioning should not be seen as 'simply rudiments of the village way of life'. They claim that a *new* value system is emerging in the cities based on this work. Such activities as gardening, the repair of household appliances and carpentry help to turn 'the daily routine into a sphere for the development of personality.... One must keep in mind the growing importance of this tendency in urban life.'[46]

Such arguments, supported by detailed empirical evidence from the Soviet Union, suggest that household work practices generate their own values in a variety of social formations as well as under different historical circumstances. Max Weber's dictum that all sociology must be comparative is, sadly, often forgotten. Understanding the divisions of labour is not helped by referring to slogans such as capitalism or patriarchy. The beginnings of comparative analysis of the new divisions of labour may be discerned in recent years, and one of the most fertile sources of new ideas is Hungary.[47] I should also mention a research project carried out in New Zealand at about the same time as the Sheppey study. Quite independently, we produced very similar results and came to very similar conclusions. Such congruence is even more remarkable since this parallel study was organized independently, without collusion, in the one other university in the world bearing the same name as my own university.[48]

A further criticism that may have particular force in the British context is the suggestion that the household is over-capitalized. The 'need' for each household to have its own distinctive range of capital equipment may make it more difficult to establish new domestic units. Perhaps the gap between having no domestic dwelling and having one equipped with refrigerator, washing machine, cooker, television and a host of other seemingly essential furnishings is too great. This putative over-capitalization of the household may result in more and larger households: young people cannot easily leave and set up on their own, the advantages

---

[45] Ibid., p. 93.
[46] Ibid., pp. 93-4.
[47] See, for example, E. Sik, 'The institutional system of labour allocation', paper given to the seminar on 'The Informal Economy, Social Conflicts and the Future of Industrial Societies', Frascati, Italy, November 1982; P. Galasi and E. Sik, 'Allocation du travail et économie socialiste: le cas de la Hongrie', *Economies et Sociétés*, 10, 1982, pp. 1089–1110.
[48] See E. Pawson and G. Cant, 'Redefining "work": The role of informal household activities', in R. Bedford and A. Sturman (eds), *Canterbury at the Cross-roads*, University of Canterbury, Christchurch, New Zealand, 1983, pp. 159-72; and E. Pawson, 'Recession, work and the family in New Zealand', paper first presented to the Conference of the Institute of British Geographers, Edinburgh, 1983.

of central heating and washing machines add to the social pressures to accommodate elderly relatives. Clearly, capitalist manufacturing industry might prefer each household to have the full range of domestic equipment, but it would be wrong to assume without question that this is necessarily an unequivocal social and individual benefit. The repair and maintenance of this equipment, and of cars in particular, add to the work and worry of household members.

The domestic values of cosiness and nest-building do not necessarily involve turning the dwelling into a mini semi-automated factory and garage: households may be better units to get by in, and the male/female partnership may be the most effective work group, only because dwellings are generally allocated to households (not individuals) in the public sector, or because they require substantial capital to purchase. Once responsible for a dwelling, an individual is hard-pressed to care for others and run all the equipment on his or her own. This is to turn the Gershuny argument on its head: manufacturing industry produces the goods that encourage a particular kind of domestic unit with its highly constrained pattern of work. It would be quite wrong of me to give the impression that households, in general, lack internal conflicts and contradictions and have clearly defined goals in which they seek to maximize their resources. Reality is much more complex and ambiguous.

Certainly, some households do work as units geared up to a specific goal. The best examples on Sheppey were those that adopted the conscious strategy of building their own homes. The resources of all members of the household could be mobilized to such a clear and easily recognized goal. However, this strategy could collapse once the goal was achieved, and there might well be retrospective redistribution of costs by some members of the household, undermining the satisfactions of success.

Larger households seem to serve capitalism best, not simply as units to purchase capital equipment and consumer goods, but as more flexible income-earning units. Chapters 8 and 9 showed unequivocally that employment status is the key to participation in all forms of work and that there is not a trade-off between time and money, yet in couple households the female partner will typically be in employment only if another member of the household is also in employment. A total household income is likely to be composed of a number of components, which may be set out as follows:

1 *The family wage*: this is paid to a 'chief earner', typically a male, and is assumed to be sufficient to support a number of dependants, often with further state assistance and allowances.
2 *Full-time individual wage*: this is paid to certain categories of workers who are assumed to be living with other members of a domestic unit, in order to help them with the costs of running a home. Many

individual wages are seen in effect as modest living expenses. By sharing accommodation, unrelated individuals can sometimes manage on such wages.

3 *Sub-individual wage*: this is paid to certain highly specific categories, for example young people on government training schemes. Such wages are substantially below individual wages and make the recipients completely dependent on household units.

4 *Wages for part-time work*: these can vary substantially depending on the nature of the work and the hours employed. Recipients are typically women who contribute their wage to a larger household income, or single parents unable to work longer hours and frequently dependent on further state support.

This system of family and component wages[49] illustrates how the household, first, may serve as an instrument supporting individuals with less money than would be necessary if they were each separate households; second, appears to be stratified by gender to support, in general terms, a pattern of male dominance; and finally, by working in this way, may reduce labour costs for employers paying component wages. I discussed the importance and growth of part-time work for women in Chapter 3; this form of work will probably continue to grow, or at least will decline less rapidly than other forms of employment.

There appears, then, to be a relationship between household size and capitalist profits: multiple earners contributing component wages to the household income may, collectively, provide a relatively high standard of living for the household at a lower cost to the employer or the state. Furthermore, with a conventional domestic division of labour, one 'housewife' can serve or support several wage earners. Economies of scale in the purchase and use of capital equipment allow such households to be more efficient work units. It is no accident that high levels of self-provisioning were associated with multiple-earner households.

People are most likely to find employment informally through advice and information provided by friends and relatives.[50] This pattern has been consistent over many years, and all the indications are that it is likely to continue. Households with members in employment are in the best position to find employment for other household members, particularly among ordinary working people.

Thus, the polarization that I described in Chapter 9 involves a process

---

[49] I am indebted to A. Stewart of the University of Cambridge for this felicitous phrase.
[50] R. Whipp and M. Grieco, 'Family and the workplace: The social organization of work', *Warwick University Research Papers*, no. 239, Department of Economics, University of Warwick, July 1983. Informal methods of recruitment are increasing in importance for manual workers. In 1973 43 per cent of manual workers were recruited by informal methods, in 1977 this proportion had increased to 52 per cent and this declined a little to 49 per cent in 1982 (*Labour Market Quarterly Report*, MSC, February 1984, Table B, p. 6).

of positive and negative feedback; households with members in employment are most likely to engage in all other forms of work, and the reverse is the case in households where no one is in employment. There is a kind of ratchet effect, so that once households get into a benign spiral upwards their collective efforts keep them there. This can apply, of course, only at certain stages of the domestic cycle. There is a clear relationship between the needs of capital for labour and certain stages in the domestic cycle: some stages are more productive than others, in terms of the range and the forms of work undertaken.

All Forms of Work towards the Year 2000

So far in this chapter, I have shown how a new focus on all forms of work in the household tends to blur the distinction between the conventionally separate middle and working classes. Examination of home ownership, multiple earners and stage in the life cycle has shown how households are the essential units of production and reproduction, as they always have been. Some domestic units at certain stages of the domestic cycle can neatly intermesh with employers' labour requirements. Inevitably, however, certain households do not fit in so well; as a result, they suffer.

One new element for the future may be the growth in ownership of domestic property among a wider section of the population. The majority of people born after 1970 are likely to inherit a house, or a portion of one, from their parents or grandparents. This seems to be a situation without precedent. Those not owning their dwellings in the year 2000 are likely to be a small, poor and politically ineffective minority.

Of all the forms of work, the one that has the most political significance for the middle mass is self-provisioning. This political fact has been slow to find expression in party terms. Strikingly little creative political thinking took place in Britain between 1964 and 1984; these were twenty years of uncertain drifting after the British colonial empire was dispersed and the process of de-industrialization began to accelerate. The fact that most people during this period were extremely busy expanding and developing all forms of work was barely noticed. But there are signs that some intellectuals are rediscovering the practical politics of ordinary people. The rediscovery of Gramsci, and (for example) the work of Rudolph Bahro in Germany and Sebastiano Timpanaro in Italy, are helping to put the individual back into socialism. The reaction against oppressive bureaucracies can be found throughout the political spectrum: it simply had further to go on the Left.

Centralization and nationalization have been undermined by micro-technology and automation as much as by the recognition of the evils and dangers of bureaucratization. More now can be produced by fewer people, and this leads not just to the renegotiation of the social division of labour but also to the declining centrality of employment, one form of work, as the basis for social and political consciousness. New forms of consciousness have only very recently been recognized and articulated. Raymond Williams points to such a new change of mind:

when we have replaced the concept of 'society as production' with the broader concept of a form of human relationships within a physical world: in the full sense a way of life.... It can then make a difference that this alternative is being classified theoretically. The central element is the shift from 'production' to 'livelihood': from an alienated generality to direct and practical ways of life. These are the real bases from which co-operative relationships can grow, and the rooted forms which are wholly compatible with, rather than contradictory to, other major energies and interests. They are also at this historical stage, in the very development of the means of production, the shifts that most people will in any case have to make.[51]

Williams has consistently refused to be bemused by the self-images of the age and has recognized the centrality of what he calls 'the reproduction of a restricted everyday reality', which, he goes on to say, 'we have temporarily bypassed, or ideally superseded but which is there and settled and is what we have really to believe'.[52]

It is this reproduction of a restricted everyday reality that I have been documenting and analysing on the Isle of Sheppey over the past six years. My understanding from that experience is that the ideas of Gershuny, Mingione and Gorz, with which I began this chapter, are all partially correct. Social innovation, survival strategies and personal political liberation are all part of what is involved in creating a contemporary sociology to understand work and society towards the year 2000. The nature and pattern of employment is evidently changing very fast. In 1983, for the first time in two hundred years, Britain recorded a deficit in trade with the rest of the world in manufactured goods. The nation that pioneered the Industrial Revolution came to the point when it had to import more manufactured goods than it exported. The international division of labour is also clearly changing. Between 1960 and 1980, the number of part-time workers doubled to about 4.4 million, whereas the number of full-time workers fell by over 2 million. Of the 4.4 million part-time workers, 3.8 million were female. This, again, is a substantial shift in the division of labour in employment. Most of the increase in part-time work is in the service sector; most of the decline in full-time work is in manufacturing. All this is well-known, and serves to demonstrate the impossibility of clinging to old concepts associated with an earlier stage in the development of capitalism.

I conclude with a warning. However much I have stressed the

[51] R. Williams, *Towards 2000*, Chatto and Windus, London, 1983, pp. 266-7.
[52] Ibid., p. 268.

importance of all forms of work in this book, it is clear that only the work of employment or self-employment generates income. And money is necessary to do all the other forms of work. In general, I can report that the work ethic is alive and well: people enjoy working and there is plenty to do. Often they may not particularly enjoy their employment, but they do enjoy and need the money that it brings. If there were a national minimum wage instead of the present system of benefits and allowances, the total amount of work done would almost certainly increase. With more money, people could do more work — whether or not it was paid. The contrast between the households with money being productive and busy and the households without money being unproductive and idle is the overwhelming conclusion of the empirical part of this book. This may be paradoxical, but it is true.

There is no doubt that the divisions of labour will continue to change. The old established order of whatever golden age people prefer to believe in has gone. The ways in which ordinary people struggle to organize all the work they do to get by — very often despite, not because of, well-meaning yet insensitive interventions — seem not to have been understood, even though they are going on all around us. Perhaps if the importance of all forms of work is seen, and if what ordinary women and men say about their lives is listened to and understood, we could begin to hope that out of that restricted everyday reality a more humane society will emerge.

Appendix

Getting By in Everyday Life: Two Case Studies

1 The Parsons

Mr Parsons was made redundant five and a half years ago when the company for which he worked closed down the plant as part of its rationalization programme. He was lucky to be young and fit enough to be taken on as a postman, a job which he much enjoys. Now that his children are older he can afford to accept a much lower wage, particularly as his wife works full-time in a wallpaper shop. He was trained in the army as an electrician and he can do most jobs around the house himself. As he finishes his work as a postman at 1 p.m. he has the rest of the day to work for himself and this he does very vigorously: as he says, 'I'm a gardening fanatic.' Mrs Parsons works in an annual cycle using her deep freeze to store the vegetables which come in, from the January brussels sprouts to the October runner beans. 'He used to bring in a terrific amount and it was too much for me to stand there and do. Now he'll bring me perhaps five or six pounds and then I put them into half-pound bags. I'm working some nights here until 10 o'clock freezing them down.' When I interviewed her she was just finishing the rhubarb and starting on the gooseberries. A slacker period in June is followed by a hectic period from July to September. They both enjoy the pressure of their work and see it as fun. When the last vegetables are frozen they turn, in November, to decorating. Mrs Parsons gets a 40 per cent discount through working in the wallpaper shop and the couple agree on an annual work programme for keeping their house, rented from the council, immaculate. She has wallpaper put aside for every room in the house. The only way that they can manage their full and energetic life is to have the capital equipment to support them. Machines to help cut and wash the vegetables and a pressure cooker to reduce cooking time are much prized. Since Mrs Parsons works until 5.30 it is her husband who often cooks the meals. She

This study was first published in R. E. Pahl, 'Employment, work and the domestic division of labour', *International Journal of Urban and Regional Research*, 4 (1), 1980, 1–20.

happily complimented him on the fruit cake he had recently made and told me, 'We had spaghetti bolognese tonight.' 'Not out of a tin', Mr Parsons quickly added. 'I can come home to a meal that's already waiting for me when I come home. It's a great help really.' The Parsons household is a mini vegetable factory: 'I think I could supply this whole road', says Mrs Parsons, and Mr Parsons admitted that he sold vegetables, 'It's nothing for me to go and pick twelve cucumbers in one day, well obviously I can't eat twelve cucumbers a day.' Unfortunately pressure on space in the deep-freeze had left Mrs Parsons without potatoes and she was obliged to fall back on the formal economy. 'It's heart-breaking. I've got to go out and buy them now.' Generally Mr Parsons uses his position as postman to buy things like potatoes; he travels and compares prices, but Mrs Parsons never does that:

For me to go out and buy vegetables, I wouldn't know where to start because I'm so used to going to my freezer and getting it. It's a lot of hard work but I benefit by it in the end. When people are out dashing from shop to shop looking for the best buy, all I've got to do is walk out to that shed and I've got the best buy in the freezer.

The domestic economy ties Mr and Mrs Parsons to their home for most of the year. Even Sunday mornings are fully occupied as Mr Parsons is chairman of the local Allotment Society and sells horticultural supplies at discount rates from a shed. As Mr Parsons said, 'We try to arrange it to have every other Sunday off but it doesn't always work.' Mrs Parsons explained, 'Then he's on his allotment and he's there if they want him. The phone has been ringing quite busily lately for chrysanthemum plants which he sells as well. They've just had a spring market and took four hundred pounds.' All the goods and tools for the Allotment Society are delivered to the Parsons' house. He uses his carport as a store. Nothing ever gets stolen, 'Never a thing is touched. Nobody will touch that. We have a neighbour keep an eye on it, or his dad — "Oh, Peter's had a delivery, I'll just go over and see what's what".'

Mr and Mrs Parsons live in a familiar world of friends and relations. Mr Parsons' mother was the twenty-second one of her family so he was not short of aunts and uncles and his wife's mother was one of twelve. Neighbours, too, link in to a tightly-knit social world. The woman a couple of doors away works in the same shop as Mrs Parsons and their husbands were at school together, 'You're frightened to speak to people sometimes, in case you might say something that you shouldn't.'

Mr Parsons' work in the formal economy is poorly paid but it provides him with a social position. 'I poke letters in the same letter-boxes every day but I enjoy it. Because I'm out in the air, I've got nobody to govern me. I leave the governor back in the office and you meet a lot of people. I say "good morning" to the same people practically every morning.' The money he gets pays for gas and electricity and rent. His wife's pay helps towards the extras: they go away for a holiday each year and they are both keen on buying machinery to support their domestic economy. Mrs Parsons has decided to switch from an electric cooker to a gas cooker to save fuel but her husband will use it as much as she does. Their daughter, who is just about to leave school, earns money by babysitting for her married sister or cutting someone's hair (she is hoping to be a hairdresser). The local coalman keeps horses and she helps him and gets more money delivering dung in a barrel to the allotment. But sometimes the dung is paid for in vegetables.

2 The Simpsons

Mrs Simpson's husband is unemployed: aged 33 he is unlikely to get a job again. He is an unskilled worker and finds it difficult to get more money than he presently receives through various forms of social security payments. His wife works informally in the hidden economy doing various kinds of home selling and home manufacturing, putting together electrical components in an outwork system. She makes her children help her and the whole family has to sit round for hours on end. As she correctly remarked, 'It's slave labour.' Mrs Simpson organizes her work force. 'The little girl (five next month) sticks the labels on the boxes and the two boys (nine and ten) have to do two hundred each, each lot that we do.' Their speed 'depends on whether they want to get out to play quick'. As she explains, 'There's a lot of people do it, we're not the only ones that are out of work and do it. I can tell you what it's paying for — washing machine, it pays my gas, my electric, it helps to buy things for the kids.' She also sells Avon cosmetics. 'I sometimes manage to buy Christmas presents out of it and my own talcs and what have you. That's mainly what I started doing it for.'

While Mrs Simpson is doing work for money (she also runs a small newspaper and sweet shop once a week) her husband is doing other unpaid work. His uncle has a large garden from which he produces the families' vegetables. He also decorates various relatives' homes for which he sometimes receives money. 'Actually he's been over helping an uncle today, painting. I'm waiting for my bathroom to be done but he won't do that.'

Q: 'Perhaps you could get your brother-in-law to do that for you?'
A: 'Yes I said perhaps if I get a neighbour or something to do it for me, it'll be alright.'
Q: 'Does a lot of that go on, all doing turns for each other like that?'
A: 'I think so.'
Q: 'But mainly in the family?'
A: 'Well, the ones that he's been doing for today, they're good, they lend him money. Like they've given a lovely piece of meat today.'

Q: 'Straight meat?'
A: 'Oh straight meat yes. He bought a bullock. I think it was a bullock. He went over there this afternoon and he was chopping it all up. Bones for the dogs.'
Q: 'Where did he get it?'
A: 'He bought it.'
Q: 'From the market?'
A: 'No. He knows a farmer. It was killed on the farm yesterday. We can keep that till Sunday.'
Q: 'A nice bit of meat?'
A: 'It is. It's a lovely piece. He does favours for them and they do favours back.'

Mr Simpson sometimes gets money, which he likes to spend on beer, for the odd jobs he does. Sometimes he goes out fishing with his friends and brings them fish home. 'I never know what they're called. I just eat them and enjoy them.' At other times he goes out to get meat with his ferret or his gun. As Mrs Simpson remarked laconically, 'Yes, he goes poaching. We get everything illegally.' And she enjoys the fruits of her husband's labours, 'We lived well last winter on ducks.' She really likes duck and is not entirely happy with the reciprocities her husband get bound up in, 'He'll start giving them here, there and everywhere. You know — he's promised sombody one, but I did alright.'

The trouble with Mrs Simpson's domestic economy is that she has nowhere to store the meat, fish and vegetables that come into the house.

I haven't got round to getting myself a freezer. I keep saying I'm going to get one. I will, I will get one . . . very often we could have had things like the fish and the rabbits and the ducks come to that, if we'd had a freezer. It doesn't matter how many you get, they can go in the freezer and you didn't have to give them away. Well, I don't think he does give them away. I think he flogs them. Well, it covers the shots and buys him a pint. I think that's what he does in some ways, although I don't see what he does.

The children's clothes present a problem, but Mrs Simpson prefers to get money herself for these or exchange clothes within the family rather than making special claims on the social security system. She feels very strongly it is *her* responsibility to find the resources to 'keep them well rigged out' and feels confident that she need not be dependent on either the state or her husband for this. Indeed he takes money from her for beer, cigarettes or gun shot. 'He probably has more money for himself than I have. I mean I never have money for me. I never class money as mine personally.'

Q: Whose is it? The family?'
A: 'Yes.'

She borrows money from her mother to whom she is probably permanently in debt. She thinks hard about her Christmas presents and attempts to give her something substantial. She and her sister have just given her a spaniel. 'It's just my way of showing her how much I do think of her . . . without her I think I can honestly say I don't know how I'd manage. She'll lend me money for the gas bill; as long as she's got it she'll lend it to me.'

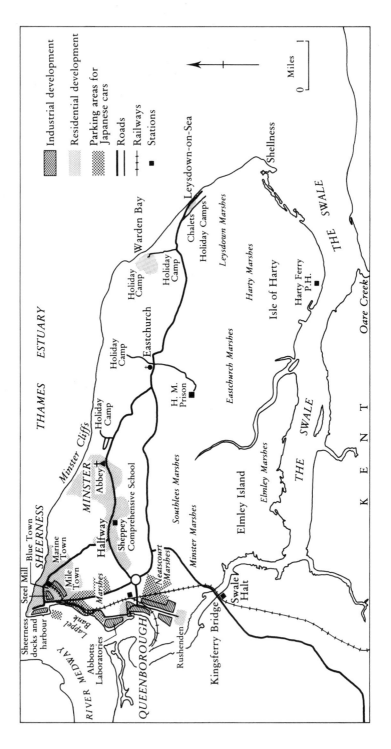

The Isle of Sheppey in Kent

Industrial development

Residential development

Parking areas for Japanese cars

Roads

Railways

Stations

THAMES   ESTUARY

Miles

0

Leysdown-on-Sea

Shellness

THE SWALE

Warden Bay

Chalets

Holiday Camps

Leysdown Marshes

Holiday Camp

Holiday Camp

Harry Marshes

Minster Cliffs

Holiday Camp

Eastchurch

Isle of Harty

Harty Ferry P.H.

Holiday Camp

H. M. Prison

Eastchurch Marshes

MINSTER

Abbey

Oare Creek

SHEERNESS

Blue Town

Southlees Marshes

THE SWALE

Steel Mill

Marine Town

Sheppey Comprehensive School

Elmley Marshes

K   E   N   T

Sheerness docks and harbour

Mile Town

Halfway

Minster Marshes

Elmley Island

Abbotts Laboratories

Marshes

Lappel Bank

Neatscourt Marshes

RIVER MEDWAY

QUEENBOROUGH

Rushenden

Swale Halt

Kingsferry Bridge

References

ALEXANDER, S., Women's work in nineteenth-century London: A study of the years 1820-1850. In J. Mitchell and A. Oakley (eds), *The Rights and Wrongs of Women*, Penguin Books, Harmondsworth, 1976.

ANDERSON, M., *Family Structure in Nineteenth-Century Lancashire*, Cambridge University Press, 1971.

ANGELL, R.C., *The Family Encounters the Depression*, Scrivenor, New York, 1936.

ANTHONY, P.D., *The Ideology of Work*, Tavistock, London, 1977.

ARIES, P., *Centuries of Childhood*, Jonathan Cape, London, 1962.

ARNOLD, E. et al., Microelectronics and women's employment, *Department of Employment Gazette*, September 1982, 377-384.

ASHBY, M.K., *Joseph Ashby of Tysoe*, Cambridge University Press, 1961.

BANKS, J.A., *Property and Parenthood*, Routledge and Kegan Paul, London, 1954.

BARLEY, M.W., Rural housing in England. In J. Thirsk (ed.) *The Agrarian History of England and Wales*, Vol. IV, *1500-1640*, Cambridge University Press, 1967.

BARR, A. et al., The incredible sloane hulk, *Harpers and Queens*, October 1982, 232-239.

BARRETT, M. and McINTOSH, M., *The Anti-Social Family*, Verso Books, London, 1982.

BATSTONE, E., BORASTON, I. and FRANKEL, S., *Shop Stewards in Action*, Basil Blackwell, Oxford, 1977.

BECHHOFER, F. and ELLIOTT, B. (eds), *The Petite Bourgeoisie*, Macmillan, London, 1981.

BELL, C. and NEWBY, H. (eds), *Doing Sociological Research*, Allen and Unwin, London, 1977.

BELL, F.E.E., *At the Works; A Study of a Manufacturing Town by Lady Bell*, Arnold, London, 1907.

BERGER, J. and MOHR, J., *A Seventh Man*, Pelican Books, Harmondsworth, 1975.

BERK, R.A. and BERK, S.F., A simultaneous equation model for the division of household labour, *Sociological Methods and Research*, 6(4), 1978, 431-468.

BERK, R.A. and BERK, S.F., *Labor and Leisure at Home*, Sage Publications, London, 1979.

BEST, G., *Mid-Victorian Britain 1851-1875*, Weidenfeld and Nicolson, London, 1971.

BLACKABY, F. (ed.), *De-industrialization*, Heinemann Educational Books, London, 1979.

BLACKBURN, R.M. and MANN, M., *The Working Class in the Labour Market*, Macmillan, London, 1979.

BLAU, P.M., *Exchange and Power in Social Life*, John Wiley, Chichester, 1964.

BOSANQUET, H. (ed.), *Social Conditions in Provincial Towns*, publisher not known, 1912.

BOTT, E., *Family and Social Network*, Tavistock, London, 1957.

BRANCA, P., A new perspective on women's work: A comparative typology, *Journal of Social History*, 9(2), 1975, 129-153.

BRAVERMAN, H., *Labor and Monopoly Capital*, Monthly Review Press, New York, 1974.

BROMLEY, R. and GERRY, C., *Casual Work and Poverty in Third World Cities*, John Wiley, Chichester and New York, 1979.

BUCK, N., *An Admiralty Dockyard in the Mid-Nineteenth Century: Aspects of the Social and Economic History of Sheerness.* Final Report to the SSRC of a research project funded by grant no. HR6939/1, 1981.

BULMER, M., *Working Class Images of Society*, Routledge and Kegan Paul, London, 1975.

BURMAN, S. (ed.), *Fit Work for Women*, Croom Helm, London, 1979.

BURNETT, J., *Useful Toil*, Allen Lane, London, 1974.

BURNS, S., *The Household Economy*, Beacon Press, Boston, 1977.

CADBURY, E., MATHESON, M.C. and SHANN, G., *Women's Work and Wages*, Fisher and Unwin, London, 1906.

CALHOUN, C., *The Question of Class Struggle*, Basil Blackwell, Oxford, 1982.

CHANEY, J., *Social Networks and Job Information: The Situation of Women Who Return to Work*, Equal Opportunities Commission, SSRC/EOC Manchester, 1981.

CHAYTOR, M., Household and kinship: Ryton in the late sixteenth and early seventeenth centuries, *History Workshop Journal*, 10, 1980, 25-60.

CLARK, A., *The Working Life of Women in the Seventeenth Century*, Frank Cass, London, 1968; reprint, originally published in 1919.

CLAYRE, A., *Work and Play*, Weidenfeld and Nicolson, London, 1974.

COFFIELD, F., BORRILL, C. and MARSHALL, S., How young people try to survive being unemployed, *New Society*, 2 June 1983, 332-334.

CONNOLLY, P., A critique of the 'informal sector' as an applied concept. In N. Redclift and E. Mingione (eds) *Beyond Employment*, Basil Blackwell, Oxford, 1984.

COOKE, P. et al., New technology and regional development in austerity Britain: The case of the semiconductor industry. Paper prepared for the SSRC Conference on Urban Change and Conflict, Department of Town Planning, UWIST, 1983.

CRAIG, C., GARNSEY, E. and RUBERY, J., Women's pay in informal payment systems, *Employment Gazette*, 91(4), 1983, 139-148.

CROSSICK, G.J., *An Artisan Elite in Victorian Society: Kentish London 1840-1880*, Croom Helm, London, 1978.

DALY, A.A., *History of the Isle of Sheppey*, Simpkin, Marshall, Hamilton, Kent and Co., London, 1904.

DAUNTON, M.J., Public place and private sphere: The Victorian city and the working-class household. In D. Fraser and A. Sutcliffe (eds), *The Pursuit of Urban History*, Edward Arnold, London, 1983.

DAVIDOFF, L., The separation of home and work? Landladies and lodgers in nineteenth and twentieth-century England. In S. Burman (ed.) *Fit Work for Women*, Croom Helm, London, 1979.

DAVIDOFF, L. and HALL, C., The architecture of public and private life: English middle-class society in a provincial town 1780-1850. In D. Fraser and A. Sutcliffe (eds), *The Pursuit of Urban History*, Edward Arnold, London, 1983.

DAVIES, C.S., *North Country Bred: A Working Class Family Chronicle*, Routledge and Kegan Paul, London, 1963.

DAVIES, R., Informal sector or subordinate mode of production? A model. In R. Bromley and C. Gerry (eds), *Casual Work and Poverty in Third World Cities*, John Wiley, Chichester and New York, 1979.

DAVIS, J.G., *The Evangelistic Bureaucrat: A Study of a Planning Exercise in Newcastle-upon-Tyne*, Tavistock, London, 1972.

DAVIS, J.H., Gifts and the UK economy, *Man*, 7(3), 1972, 408-429.

DAVIS, J.H., The particular theory of exchange, *European Journal of Sociology*, 1975, 151-168.

DAVIS, J.H., *People of the Mediterranean*, Routledge and Kegan Paul, London, 1977.

DEFOE, D., *The Complete English Tradesman*, London, 1726.

DE GRAZIA, R., Clandestine employment: A problem of our times, *International Labour Review*, 119(5), 1980, 549-563.

DENNIS, N., HENRIQUES, F. and SLAUGHTER, C., *Coal is Our Life*, Eyre and Spottiswoode, London, 1956.

DEPARTMENT OF EMPLOYMENT, Changing composition of the labour force 1976-1991, *Employment Gazette*, 1979, 546-550.

DEPARTMENT OF EMPLOYMENT, Numbers of self-employed people 1971-1979, *Employment Gazette*, 90(1), 1982, 15-18.

DEPARTMENT OF EMPLOYMENT, Trends in working hours, *Employment Gazette*, 90(11), 1982, 477-486.

DEPARTMENT OF EMPLOYMENT, A changing labour force: Constants and variables, *Employment Gazette*, 91(2), 1983, 49-54.

Departmental Committee of Inquiry into Allotments (Thorpe Report), Cmnd 4166, HMSO, London, 1967.

DILNOT, A. and MORRIS, C.N., What do we know about the black economy? *Fiscal Studies*, 2(1), 1981, 58-73.

DITTON, J., *Part-time Crimes: An Ethnography of Fiddling and Pilferage*, Macmillan, London, 1977.

DITTON, J., Perks, pilferage and the fiddle: The historical structure of invisible wages, *Theory and Society*, 4, 1977, 1-38.

DUNLEAVY, P., The urban bases of political alignment, *British Journal of Political Science*, 9, 1979, 409-443.

EARNSHAW, HAYES and SONS, *Report on DIY/Home Improvement*, Eurometer Publications, London, 1980.

EBERY, M. and PRESTON, B., *Domestic Service in Late Victorian and Edwardian England 1871-1914*, Department of Geography Paper no. 42, University of Reading, 1976.

EDHOLM, F., HARRIS, O. and YOUNG, K., Conceptualizing women, *Critique of Anthropology*, 3(9-10), 1977, 101-130.

ELLIOTT, V.B., Mobility and marriage in pre-industrial England. Unpublished PhD thesis, University of Cambridge, 1978.

ELLISTON ALLEN, D., *British Tastes*, Panther Books, London, 1969.

EVANS, F., Historical aspects of the development of housework. Unpublished postgraduate paper, University of Kent at Canterbury, 1983.

EVANS, M. and MORGAN, D., *Work on Women*, Tavistock, London, 1979.

EVERITT, A., Farm labourers. In J. Thirsk (ed.), *The Agrarian History of England*, vol. IV, *1500-1640*, Cambridge University Press, 1967.

Family Expenditure Survey, HMSO, London, 1982.

FEIGE, L., *The Theory and Measurement of the Unobserved Sector of the US Economy*, publisher not known, Leiden, 1981.

FERMAN, L.A., BERNDT, L. and SELO, E., *Analysis of the Irregular Economy: Cash Flow in the Informal Sector*, University of Michigan/Wayne State University, Chicago, 1978.

FRASER, D. and SUTCLIFFE, A. (eds), *The Pursuit of Urban History*, Edward Arnold, London, 1983.

FUSSELL, G.E. and FUSSELL, K.R., *The English Countrywoman: A Farmhouse Social History AD1500-1900*, Andrew Melrose, London, 1953.

GALASI, P. and SIK, E., Allocation du travail et économie socialiste: le cas de la Hongrie, *Economies et sociétés*, 10, 1982, 1089-1110.

GARRATY, J.A., *Unemployment in History*, Harper and Row, New York and London, 1978.

GEORGE, C.H., The making of the English bourgeoisie 1500-1750, *Science and Society*, Winter 1971.

GEORGE, M., From 'Goodwife' to 'Mistress': The transformation of the female in bourgeois culture, *Science and Society*, 37(2), 1973, 152-177.

GERSHUNY, J.I., *After Industrial Society?* Macmillan, London, 1978.

GERSHUNY, J.I., The informal economy: Its role in industrial society, *Futures*, February 1979, 3-15.

GERSHUNY, J.I., *Social Innovation and the Division of Labour*, Oxford University Press, 1983.

GERSHUNY, J.I. and MILES, I.D., *The New Service Economy: The Transformation of Employment in Industrial Societies*, Frances Pinter, London, 1983.

GERSHUNY, J.I. and PAHL, R.E., Work outside employment: Some preliminary speculations, *New Universities Quarterly*, 34(1), 1979, 120-135.

GERSHUNY, J.I. and PAHL, R.E., Britain in the decade of the three economies, *New Society*, 3 January 1983, 7-9.

GERSHUNY, J.I. and THOMAS, G.S., *Changing Patterns of Time Use*, Occasional Paper Series no. 13, Science Policy Research Unit, University of Sussex, 1980.

GITTINS, D., *Fair Sex: Family Size and Structure 1900-1939*, Hutchinson, London, 1982.

GODELIER, M., Work and its representations: A research proposal, *History Workshop Journal*, 10, 1980, 164-174.

GOFF, C., *A Woman of the Tudor Age*, John Murray, London, 1930.

GOLDING, P. and MIDDLETON, S., Why is the press so obsessed with welfare scroungers? *New Society*, 26 October 1978.

GOLDTHORPE, J.H., LOCKWOOD, D., BECHHOFER, F. and PLATT, J., *The Affluent Worker: Political Attitudes and Behaviour*, Cambridge University Press, 1968.

GOLDTHORPE, J.H., *Intellectuals and the Working Class in Modern Britain*, University of Essex, 1979.

GOODE, W.J. and HATT, P.K., *Methods in Social Research*, McGraw Hill, New York, 1952.

GORDON, L. and KLOPOV, E., *Man After Work*, Progress Publishers, Moscow, 1975.

GORER, G., *Exploring English Character*, Cresset Press, London, 1955.

GORZ, A., *Farewell to the Working Class*, Pluto Press, London, 1982.

GRAY, R., *The Labour Aristocracy in Victorian Edinburgh*, Oxford University Press, 1976.

GUTMANN, P.M., The subterranean economy, *Financial Analyst's Journal*, November-December 1977.

GUTMANN, P.M., Statistical illusions, mistaken policies, *Challenge*, November-December 1979, 14-17.

HALL, C., The history of the housewife. In E. Malos (ed.), *The Politics of Housework*, Allison and Busby, London, 1980.

HALSEY, A.H., A sociologist's viewpoint, in *The Welfare State in Crisis*, OECD, Paris, 1981.

HARRIS, O., Households as natural units. In K. Young et al. (eds), *Of Marriage and the Market*, CSE Books, London, 1981.

HARRIS, O., Households and their boundaries, *History Workshop Journal*, 14, 1982, 143-152.

HARRISON, J.F.C., *The Early Victorians 1832-1851*, Weidenfeld and Nicolson, London, 1971.

HART, K., Informal income opportunities and urban employment in Ghana, *Journal of Modern African Studies*, 11, 1973, 61-89.

HARTMAN, H.I., Capitalism and women's work in the home. Unpublished PhD thesis, Yale University, 1974.

HEATH, A., *Rational Choice and Social Exchange*, Cambridge University Press, 1976.

HECHT, J.J., *The Domestic Servant Class in Eighteenth Century England*, Routledge and Kegan Paul, London, 1956.

HENRY, S., *The Hidden Economy*, Martin Robertson, London, 1978.

HEWITT, M., *Wives and Mothers in Victorian Industry*, Rockliff, London, 1958.

HEY, D.G., *An English Rural Community*, Leicester University Press, 1974.

HIGGS, E., Domestic servants and households in Victorian England, *Social History*, 8(2), 1983, 201-210.

HILL, C., Potage for freeborn Englishmen: Attitudes to wage labour in the sixteenth and seventeenth centuries. In C.H. Feinstein (ed.), *Socialism, Capitalism and Economic Growth*, Cambridge University Press, 1967.

HILL, T.P., Do-it-yourself and GDP, *Review of Income and Wealth*, 25(1), 1979, 31-40.

HILTON, R.H., *The English Peasantry in the Later Middle Ages*, Clarendon Press, Oxford, 1975.

HOBSBAWM, E.J., The British standard of living 1790-1850. In E.J. Hobsbawm (ed.), *Labouring Men*, Weidenfeld and Nicolson, London, 1964.

HOLLEY, J.C., The two family economies of industrialism: Factory workers in Victorian Scotland, *Journal of Family History*, 6(1), 1981, 57-69.

HOMANS, G.C., *Social Behaviour: Its Elementary Forms*, 2nd edn, Harcourt Brace Jovanovich, New York, 1974.

HOWARTH, E.G. and WILSON, M., *West Ham: A Study in Social and Industrial Problems*, Dent, London, 1907.

HUBER, J. and SPITZE, G., *Sex Stratification: Children, Housework and Jobs*, Academic Press, New York and London, 1983.

HUMPHRIES, J., Class struggle and the persistence of the working class family, *Cambridge Journal of Economics*, 1, 1977, 241-258.

HUMPHRIES, J., The working class family, women's liberation and class struggle: The case of nineteenth-century British history, *Review of Radical Political Economics*, 9(3), 1977, 25-41.

HUMPHRIES, J., Protective legislation, the capitalist state and working class men: The case of the 1842 Mines Regulation Act, *Feminist Review*, 7, 1981, 1-32.

HURSTFIELD, J., Part-time pittance, *Low Pay Review*, no. 1, 1980.

ILLICH, I., *The Right to Useful Unemployment and its Professional Enemies*, Marion Boyars, London, 1978.

JENKINS, C. and SHERMAN, B., *The Collapse of Work*, Eyre Methuen, London, 1979.

KLEIN, J., *Samples from English Cultures*, vol. 1, Routledge and Kegan Paul, London, 1965.

KLEIN, V., *Britain's Married Women Workers*, Routledge and Kegan Paul, London, 1965.

KOMAROVSKY, M., *The Unemployed Man and his Family*, Institute of Social and Religious Research, 1940; reprinted by Octagon Books, New York, 1971.

KONRAD, G. and SZELENYI, I., *The Intellectuals on the Road to Class Power*, Harcourt Brace Jovanovich, New York, 1979.

KUMAR, K., Can the workers be revolutionary? *European Journal of Political Research*, 6, 1978, 357-379.

KUMAR, K., Unemployment as a problem in the development of industrial societies. Paper prepared for the EEC-FAST programme, Marseilles, 23-26 November 1981.

KUMAR, K., Class and political action in nineteenth-century England, *European Journal of Sociology*, 24, 1983, 3-43.

LATHAM, R. and MATHEWS, W. (eds), *The Diary of Samuel Pepys*, vol. VI, G. Bell and Sons, London, 1972.

LAYARD, R. et al., The causes of poverty. Background paper no. 5 to Report no. 6, *Royal Commission on the Distribution of Income and Wealth*, HMSO, London, 1978.

LEEDS TRADE UNION AND COMMUNITY RESOURCE AND IN-FORMATION CENTRE, *New Technology and Women's Employment*, Equal Opportunities Commission, London, 1982.

LEICESTER, C., Towards a fully part-time Britain, *Personnel Management*, 14(6), June 1982, 28-31.

LEWIS, J., *The Politics of Motherhood*, Croom Helm, London, 1980.

LEWIS, J., The social history of social policy: Infant welfare in Edwardian England, *Journal of Social Policy*, 9(4), 1980, 463-486.

LLOYDS BANK, *Economic Bulletin*, 42, June 1982.

LOANE, M.E., *From Their Point of View*, Edward Arnold, London, 1908.

LOCKWOOD, D., Sources of variation in working class images of society, *Sociological Review*, 14(3), 1966, 249-267.

LOCKWOOD, D., The weakest link in the chain: Some comments on the Marxist theory of action, *Research in the Sociology of Work*, 1, 1981, 435-481.

MACAFEE, K., A glimpse of the hidden economy in the national accounts, *Economic Trends*, February 1980, 81-87.

MACDONALD, K.R., The Isle of Sheppey and the Swale. MA thesis, Kings College, London, 1949.

MACDOUGAL, P., Malaria: Its influence on a North Kent community, *Archaeologia Cantiana*, 95, 1979, 255-264.

MACFARLANE, A., *The Family Life of Ralph Josselin: A Seventeenth Century Clergyman*, Cambridge University Press, 1970.

MACFARLANE, A., *The Origins of English Individualism*, Basil Blackwell, Oxford, 1978.

MACGREGOR, S., *The Politics of Poverty*, Longman, London, 1981.

MACPHERSON, C.B., *The Political Theory of Possessive Individualism*, Oxford University Press, 1962.

MALCOLMSON, R.W., *Life and Labour in England 1700-1780*, Hutchinson, London, 1981.

MANPOWER SERVICES COMMISSION, *MSC Manpower Review*, London, 1982.

MANPOWER SERVICES COMMISSION, *Labour Market Quarterly Report*, February 1983.

MARS, G., *Cheats at Work*, George Allen and Unwin, London, 1983.

MARSDEN, D. and DUFF, E., *Workless: Some Unemployed Men and their Families*, Pelican Books, Harmondsworth, 1975.

MARWICK, A., *British Society since 1945*, Allen Lane, London, 1982.

MARX, K., *Early Writings*, translated and edited by T.B. Bottomore, Penguin Books, Harmondsworth, 1964.

MARX, K., *Capital*, Vol. III, Lawrence and Wishart, London, 1972.

MARX, K. and ENGELS, F., *On Britain*, Lawrence and Wishart, London, 1962.

MATHAEI, J.A., *An Economic History of Women in America: Women's Work, the Sexual Division of Labour, and the Development of Capitalism*, Harvester Press, Brighton, 1982.

MAUSS, M., *The Gift*, Cohen and West, London, 1954.

McBRIDE, T., *The Domestic Revolution*, Croom Helm, London, 1976.

McINTOSH, M., *The Anti-Social Family*, Verso Editions, London, 1983.

McKELVEY, R.D. and ZAVOINA, W., A statistical model for the analysis of ordinal level dependent variables, *Journal of Mathematical Sociology*, 4, 1975, 103-120.

MEISSNER, M., HUMPHREYS, E.M., MEIS, S.M. and SCHEU, W.J., No exit for wives: Sexual division of labour and the cumulation of household demands, *Canadian Review of Sociology and Anthropology*, 12(4), 1977, 424-439.

MIDDLETON, C., Peasants, patriarchy and the feudal mode of production in England: A Marxist appraisal, *Sociological Review*, 29(1), 1981, 105-154.

MINFORD, P., *Journal of Economic Affairs*, 3(2), 1983, pp. 94–98.

MINGIONE, E., Informalization, restructuring and the survival strategies of the working class, *International Journal of Urban and Regional Research*, 7(3), 1983, 311-339.

MINGIONE, E., Informalization and survival strategies in Southern Italy. In N. Redclift and E. Mingione (eds) *Beyond Employment: Household, Gender and Subsistence*, Basil Blackwell, Oxford, 1984.

MINISTRY OF AGRICULTURE, FISHERIES AND FOODS, *Studies in Urban Household Diets 1944-1949*, HMSO, London, 1956.

MITCHELL, J.C., Case and situation analysis, *Sociological Review*, new series, 31(2), 1983, 187-211.

MORRIS, W., *The Collected Works*, Longmans Green, London, 1910-15.

MOUNT, F., *The Subversive Family*, Jonathan Cape, London, 1982.

MOWAT, C.L., *Britain Between the Wars*, Methuen, London, 1963.

NEWBY, H., *The State of Research into Stratification in Britain*, Social Science Research Council, London, 1982.

NEWSON, J. and NEWSON, E., *Patterns of Infant Care in an Urban Community*, Penguin Books, Harmondsworth, 1965.

NEWSON, J. and NEWSON, E., *Four Years Old in an Urban Community*, Allen and Unwin, London, 1968.

OAKLEY, A., *Housewife*, Allen Lane, London, 1974.

OFFE, C., Alternative strategies in consumer policy, in C. Offe (ed.), *Contradictions of the Welfare State*, Chapter 10, Hutchinson, London, 1984.

O'HIGGINS, M., *Measuring the Hidden Economy: A Review of Evidence and Methodologies*, Outer Circle Policy Unit, London, 1980.

OLLMAN, B., *Alienation*, Cambridge University Press, 1971.

OPCS Monitor, MN 82/3, Office of Population Censuses and Surveys, London, 1982.

OPPENHEIM, M., (1) Maritime history and (2) The Royal Dockyards. In W. Page (ed.), *The Victoria County History of Kent*, St Catherine Press, London, 1926.

OUTER CIRCLE POLICY UNIT, *Policing the Hidden Economy*, OCPU, London, 1979.

PAHL, R.E., Instrumentality and community in the process of urbanization, *Sociological Inquiry*, 43(3–4), 1973, pp. 241–60.

PAHL, R.E., Sociology's conflicting tradition, *New Society*, 30 May 1974, 504-507.

PAHL, R.E., *Whose City?* Penguin, Harmondsworth, 1975.

PAHL, R.E., Patterns of urban life in the next fifteen years, *New Universities Quarterly*, 30(4), 1976, 402-419.

PAHL, R.E., Playing the rationality game. In C. Bell and H. Newby (eds), *Doing Sociological Research*, Allen and Unwin, London.

PAHL, R.E., Employment, work and the domestic division of labour, *International Journal of Urban and Regional Research*, 4(1), 1980, 1-20.

PAHL, R.E., The restructuring of capital, the local political economy and household work strategies: All forms of work in context. In D. Gregory and J. ry (eds), *Social Relations and Spatial Structures*, Macmillan, London, 1984.

PAHL, R.E. with DENNETT, J.H., *Industry and Employment on the Isle of Sheppey*, University of Kent at Canterbury, part of the Final Report to the SSRC of project no. G00230036, 1981.

PAHL, R.E. and WALLACE, C.D., Household work strategies in economic recession. In N. Redclift and E. Mingione (eds), *Beyond Employment: Household, Gender and Subsistence*, Basil Blackwell, Oxford, 1984.

PAHL, R.E. and WINKLER, J.T., The coming corporatism, *New Society*, 10 October 1974, 72-76.

PARKER, H., Social security foments the black economy, *Journal of Economic Affairs*, 3(1), 1982, 32-35.

PAWSON, E., Recession, work and the family in New Zealand. Paper first presented to the Conference of the Institute of British Geographers, Edinburgh, 1983.

PAWSON, E. and CANT, G., Redefining 'work': The role of informal household activities. In R. Bedford and A. Sturman (eds), *Canterbury at the Cross-roads*, University of Canterbury, Christchurch, New Zealand, 1983.

PENNEY, N. (ed.), *The Household Account Book of Sarah Fell of Swarthmore*, Cambridge University Press, 1920.

PILGRIM TRUST, *Men Without Work*, Cambridge University Press, 1938.

PLATT, C., *The English Medieval Town*, Secker and Warburg, London, 1976.

PLECK, J.A., The work-family role system, *Social Problems*, 24, 1977, 417-427.

POLLERT, A., *Girls, Wives, Factory Lives*, Macmillan, London, 1981.

POLLOCK, L.A., *Forgotten Children: Parent Child Relations from 1500-1900*, Cambridge University Press, 1983.

POLYCELL, *The Polycell Report on the DIY Market*, Paragon Communications, London, 1981.

POPAY, J., RIMMER, L. and ROSSITER, C., *One Parent Families*, Study Commission on the Family, London, 1983.

PORTER, R.D., *Some Notes on Estimating the Underground Economy*, Federal Reserve Board, Washington DC, 1979.

PORTER, R.D. and THURMAN, S.S., *Currency Ratio and the Subterranean Economy: Additional Comments*, Federal Reserve Board, Washington DC, 1979.

REDCLIFT, N. and MINGIONE, E., *Beyond Employment: Household, Gender and Subsistence*, Basil Blackwell, Oxford, 1984.

REID, D.A., The decline of Saint Monday 1766-1876, *Past and Present*, 71, 1976, 76-101.

Report of the House of Lords Select Committee on Unemployment, HMSO, London, 1982.

RICHARDS, E., Women in the British economy since about 1700: An interpretation, *History*, 59, 1974, 337-357.

RIMMER, L. and POPAY, J., *Employment trends and the family*, Study Commission on the Family, London, 1982.

ROBERTS, E., Working class women in the North West, *Oral History*, 5(2), 1977, 7-30.

ROBERTS, E., Working wives and their families. In T. Barker and M. Drake (eds), *Population and Society in Britain 1850-1980*, Batsford, London, 1982.

ROBERTS, E., *A Woman's Place*, Basil Blackwell, Oxford, 1984.

ROBERTS, R., *The Classic Slum*, Penguin, Harmondsworth, 1973.

ROSE, R., *Getting By in Three Economies: The Resources of Official, Unofficial and Domestic Economies*, Centre for the Study of Public Policy, University of Strathclyde, 1983.

RULE, J., *The Experience of Labour in the Eighteenth Century*, Croom Helm, London, 1981.

RUNCIMAN, W.G., *A Treatise on Sociological Theory*, Vol. 1, *The Methodology of Social Theory*, Cambridge University Press, 1983.

SAHLINS, M., *Stone Age Economics*, Tavistock, London, 1972.

SAMUEL, R., 'Quarry roughs': Life and labour in Headington Quarry 1860-1920. An essay in oral history. In R. Samuel (ed.), *Village Life and Labour*, Routledge and Kegan Paul, London, 1975.

SANDAY, P.R., *Female Power and Male Dominance: On the Origins of Sexual Inequality*, Cambridge University Press, 1981.

SAUNDERS, P., *Beyond Housing Classes: The Sociological Significance of Private Property Rights in Means of Consumption*, Working Paper 33, Urban and Regional Studies, University of Sussex, 1983.

SCASE, R. and GOFFEE, R., *The Real World of the Small Business Owner*, Croom Helm, London, 1980.

SCASE, R. and GOFFEE, R., *The Entrepreneurial Middle Class*, Croom Helm, London, 1982.

SCHOFIELD, R.S., Age specific mobility in an eighteenth century rural parish, *Annales de Demographie Historique*, 1970, 261-274.

SCOTT, J.W. and TILLY, L.A., Women's work and the family in nineteenth-century Europe, *Comparative Studies in Society and History*, 17(1), 1975, 36-64.

SEABROOK, J., *Unemployment*, Quartet Books, London, 1982.

SEGALEN, M., *Love and Power in the Peasant Family*, Basil Blackwell, Oxford, 1983.

SEN, G., The sexual division of labour and the working-class family: Towards a conceptual synthesis of class relations and the subordination of women, *Review of Radical Political Economics*, 12:2, 1980, 76-86.

SHAMMAS, C., The domestic environment in early modern England and America, *Journal of Social History*, 14(1), 1980, 3-24.

SHERWELL, A., *Life in West London*, publisher not known, 1897.

SHORTER, E., *The Making of the Modern Family*, Fontana Books, London, 1977.

SIK, E., The institutional system of labour allocation. Paper given to the seminar on 'The Informal Economy, Social Conflicts and the Future of Industrial Societies', Frascati, Italy, November 1982.

SIMES, D.K., The Soviet parallel market, *Survey*, 21(3)96, 1975, 42-52.

SMITH, A., The informal economy, *Lloyds Bank Review*, 141, 1981, 45-61.

SMITH, R.A.L., *Canterbury Cathedral Priory*, Cambridge University Press, 1943.

SMITH, R.M., Kin and neighbours in a thirteenth-century Suffolk community, *Journal of Family History*, 4(3), 1979, 219-256.

SNELL, K.D.M., Agricultural seasonal unemployment, the standards of living and women's work in the south and east 1690-1860, *Economic History Review*, 1980, 407-437.

SNIDERMAN, P. and BROADY, R., Coping: The ethic of self-reliance, *American Journal of Political Science*, 26(3), 1977, 501–21.

Social Trends, nos 1, 2, 5 and 9, Central Statistical Office, London, 1970, 1971, 1974 and 1978.

SOKOLOFF, N.J., *Between Money and Love*, Praeger, New York, 1980.

SOUTH EAST JOINT PLANNING TEAM, *Strategic Plan for the South East Studies*, vol. 2, *Social and Environmental Aspects*, HMSO, London, 1971.

STAFFORD, F.P., Women's use of time converging with men, *Monthly Labour Review*, 104(2), 1980, 57-59.

STAFFORD, R., BACKMAN, E. and DIBONA, P., The division of labour among cohabiting and married couples, *Journal of Marriage and the Family*, 39, 1977, 43-57.

STEARNS, P.N., Working-class women in Britain. In M. Vicinus (ed.), *Suffer and Be Still*, Bloomington, Indiana University Press, 1972.

STEARNS, P.N., The effort of continuity in working-class culture, *Journal of Modern History*, 52, 1980, 625-655.

STEDMAN–JONES, G., *Outcast London: A Study in the Relationship between Classes in Victorian Society*, Oxford University Press, 1971.

STEDMAN-JONES, G., *Language of Class*, Cambridge University Press, 1984.

STENTON, D.M., *The English Woman in History*, George Allen and Unwin, London, 1957; reprinted by Schocken Books, New York, 1977.

SZELENYI, I., Structural changes of and alternatives to capitalist development in the contemporary urban and regional system, *International Journal of Urban and Regional Research*, 5(1), 1981, 1-14.

TARN, J.N., *Five Per Cent Philanthropy*, Cambridge University Press, 1973.

TAYLOR, R., Marilyn's friends and Rita's customers: A study of party-selling as play and work, *Sociological Review*, 26(3), new series, 1978, 573-594.

THATCHER, A.R., Labour supply and employment trends, in F. Blackaby (ed.), *De-industrialization*, Heinemann Educational Books, London, 1979.

THOMAS, G.S. and SHANNON, C.Z., Technology and household labour: Are the times a-changing? Paper presented at British Sociological Association Conferences, Manchester, 1982.

THOMAS, K., Work and leisure in pre-industrial society, *Past and Present*, 29, 1964, 50-62.

THOMPSON, E.P., Time, work discipline and industrial capitalism, *Past and Present*, 38, 1967, 56-97.

THOMPSON, P., *The Edwardians*, Paladin Books, London, 1977.

THOMPSON, P. with WAILEY, T. and LUMMIS, T. *Living the Fishing*, Routledge and Kegan Paul, London, 1983.

TILLY, L.A., Individual lives and family strategies, *Journal of Family History*, Summer 1979, 137-152.

TILLY, L.A. and SCOTT, J.W., *Women, Work and Family*, Holt, Rinehart and Winston, New York and London, 1978.

TOMALIN, C., *Parents and Children*, Oxford University Press, 1981.

TREBLE, J.H. (ed.), *Urban Poverty in Britain 1830-1914*, Batsford/Academic Press, London, 1979.

UNIVERSITY OF LIVERPOOL DEPARTMENT OF SOCIAL SCIENCE, *The Dock Worker*, University of Liverpool, 1954.

U.S. SELECT COMMITTEE, *Soviet Internal Developments*, US Government Printing Office, Washington DC, 1980.

VANEK, J., Keeping busy: Time spent in housework, United States, 1920-1970. Unpublished PhD thesis, University of Michigan, 1973.

VICINUS, M. (ed.), *Suffer and Be Still*, Bloomington, Indiana University Press, 1972.

VINCENT, D., *Bread, Knowledge and Freedom*, Europa Publications, London, 1981.

WADEL, C., Now whose fault is that? The struggle for self-esteem in the face of chronic unemployment, *Newfoundland Social and Economic Studies*, no. 11, Memorial University of Newfoundland, 1973.

WALL, R., Regional and temporal variations in English household structure from 1650. In J. Hobraft and P. Rees (eds), *Regional Demographic Development*, Croom Helm, London, 1979.

WALLACE, C. with PAHL, R.E. and DENNETT, J.H., *Housing and Residential Areas on the Isle of Sheppey*, University of Kent at Canterbury, part of Final Report to the SSRC on grant no. G00230036, 1981.

WALLMAN, S. (ed.), Introduction. In *A Social Anthropology of Work*, Academic Press, London, 1979.

WALLMAN, S. and associates, *Living in South London*, Gower Press/LSE, London, 1982.

WARD, C. and HARDY, D., *Planning, Property and Freedom: A History of Plotlands in South East England*. Final Report to the SSRC for Grant No. HR6393, September 1981.

WARD, C. and HARDY, D., *Arcadia For All*, forthcoming.

WARWICK, D., *Talk of the Village: Introduction to a Contemporary Study of the Social and Cultural Organization of Featherstone*, University of Leeds, 1984.

WATERS, M., The Social History of the Chatham Dockyard Workforce 1860-1906. Unpublished PhD thesis, University of Essex, 1979.

WHIPP, R. and GRIECO, M., Family and the workplace: The social organization of work, *Warwick Economic Research Papers*, no. 239, Department of Economics, University of Warwick, July 1983.

WHITE, J., Campbell Bunk: A lumpen community in London between the wars, *History Workshop Journal*, 8, 1979, 1-49.

WIBBERLEY, G.P., *Agriculture and Urban Growth*, Michael Joseph, London, 1959.

WILLIAMS, A., *Life in a Railway Factory*, Duckworth, London, 1915.

WILLIAMS, C. and JONES, T., *Royal Commission on the Poor Laws, Report on the Effect of Outdoor Relief on Wages and the Conditions of Employment*, HMSO, London, 1909.

WILLIAMS, G., *Women and Work*, Nicholson and Watson, London, 1945.

WILLIAMS, R., *Towards 2000*, Chatto and Windus, London, 1983.

WOHL, A.S., *The Eternal Slum*, Edward Arnold, London, 1977.

WOLFE, D.M. (ed.), *Leveller Manifestos of the Puritan Revolution*, Humanities Press, New York, 1944.

WOOD, S. (ed.), *The Degradation of Work?* Hutchinson, London, 1982.

WOODWARD, D., Wage rates and living standards in pre-industrial England, *Past and Present*, 91, 1981, pp. 28–46.

WRIGHT, T., *Some Habits and Customs of the Working Classes*, Tinsley Brothers, London, 1867.

WRIGHTSON, K., *English Society 1580-1680*, Hutchinson, London, 1982.

YOUNG, K. et al., *Of Marriage and the Market*, CSE Books, London, 1981.

YOUNG, M. and WILLMOTT, P., *Family and Kinship in East London*, Penguin, Harmondsworth, 1957.

ZNANIECKI, F., *The Method of Sociology*, Rinehart, New York, 1934.

Index